PEER-TO-PEER

Harnessing the Benefits of a Disruptive Technology

Edited by Andy Oram

O'REILLY®

Beijing · Cambridge · Farnham · Köln · Paris · Sebastopol · Taipei · Tokyo

Peer-to-Peer: Harnessing the Power of Disruptive Technologies
Edited by Andy Oram

Copyright © 2001 O'Reilly & Associates, Inc. All rights reserved.
Printed in the United States of America.

Published by O'Reilly & Associates, Inc., 101 Morris Street, Sebastopol, CA 95472.

Editor: Andy Oram

Production Editor: Darren Kelly

Cover Designer: Edie Freedman

Printing History:

> March 2001:   First Edition.

Library of Congress Cataloging-in-Publication Data is available at:
www.oreilly.com/catalog/peer2peer/chapter/copyright.html

ISBN: 0-596-00110-X
[C]   [4/01]

Contents

Part III: Technical Topics

Preface

Andy Oram, O'Reilly & Associates, Inc.

The term *peer-to-peer* rudely shoved its way to front and center stage of the computing field around the middle of the year 2000. Just as the early 20th-century advocates of psychoanalysis saw sex everywhere, industry analysts and marketing managers are starting to call everything they like in computers and telecommunications "peer-to-peer." At the same time, technologists report that fear and mistrust still hang around this concept, sometimes making it hard for them to get a fair hearing from venture capitalists and policy makers.

Yes, a new energy is erupting in the computing field, and a new cuisine is brewing. Leaving sexiness aside, this preface tries to show that the term peer-to-peer is a useful way to understand a number of current trends that are exemplified by projects and research in this book. Seemingly small technological innovations in peer-to-peer can radically alter the day-to-day use of computer systems, as well as the way ordinary people interact using computer systems.

But to really understand what makes peer-to-peer tick, where it is viable, and what it can do for you, you have to proceed to the later chapters of the book. Each is written by technology leaders who are working 'round the clock to create the new technologies that form the subject of this book. By following their thoughts and research, you can learn the state of the field today and where it might go in the future.

Some context and a definition

I mentioned at the beginning of this preface that the idea of peer-to-peer was the new eyebrow-raiser for the summer of 2000. At that point in history, it looked like the Internet had fallen into predictable patterns. Retail outlets had turned the Web into the newest mail order channel, while entertainment firms used it to rally fans of pop culture. Portals and search engines presented a small slice of

Internet offerings in the desperate struggle to win eyes for banner ads. The average user, stuck behind a firewall at work or burdened with usage restrictions on a home connection, settled down to sending email and passive viewing.

In a word, boredom. Nothing much for creative souls to look forward to. An Olympic sports ceremony that would go on forever.

At that moment the computer field was awakened by a number of shocks. The technologies were not precisely new, but people realized for the first time that they were having a wide social impact:

Napster

This famous and immensely popular music exchange system caused quite a ruckus, first over its demands on campus bandwidth, and later for its famous legal problems. The technology is similar to earlier systems that got less attention, and even today is rather limited (since it was designed for pop songs, though similar systems have been developed for other types of data). But Napster had a revolutionary impact because of a basic design choice: after the initial search for material, clients connect to each other and exchange data directly from one system's disk to the other.

SETI@home

This project attracted the fascination of millions of people long before the Napster phenomenon, and it brought to public attention the promising technique of distributing a computation across numerous personal computers. This technique, which exploited the enormous amounts of idle time going to waste on PCs, had been used before in projects to crack encryption challenges, but after SETI@home began, a number of companies started up with the goal of making the technique commercially viable.

Freenet

Several years before the peer-to-peer mania, University of Edinburgh researcher Ian Clarke started to create an elegantly simple and symmetric file exchange system that has proven to be among the purest of current models for peer-to-peer systems. Client and server are the same thing in this system; there is absolutely no centralization.

Gnutella

This experimental system almost disappeared before being discovered and championed by open source developers. It is another file exchange system that, like Freenet, stresses decentralization. Its potential for enhanced searches is currently being explored.

Jabber

This open source project combines instant messaging (supporting many popular systems) with XML. The emergence of Jabber proclaimed that XML was more than a tool for business-to-business (B2B) transaction processing, and in fact could be used to create spontaneous communities of ordinary users by structuring the information of interest to them.

.NET

This is the most far-reaching initiative Microsoft has released for many years, and they've announced that they're betting the house on it. .NET makes Microsoft's earlier component technology easier to use and brings it to more places, so that web servers and even web browsers can divide jobs among themselves. XML and SOAP (a protocol for doing object-oriented programming over the Web) are a part of .NET.

Analysts trying to find the source of inspiration for these developments have also noted a new world of sporadically connected Internet nodes emerging in laptops, handhelds, and cell phones, with more such nodes promised for the future in the form of household devices.

What thread winds itself around all these developments? In various ways they return content, choice, and control to ordinary users. Tiny endpoints on the Internet, sometimes without even knowing each other, exchange information and form communities. There are no more clients and servers—or at least, the servers retract themselves discreetly. Instead, the significant communication takes place between cooperating peers. That is why, diverse as these developments are, it is appropriate to lump them together under the rubric peer-to-peer.

While the technologies just listed are so new we cannot yet tell where their impact will be, peer-to-peer is also the oldest architecture in the world of communications. Telephones are peer-to-peer, as is the original UUCP implementation of Usenet. IP routing, the basis of the Internet, is peer-to-peer, even now when the largest access points raise themselves above the rest. Endpoints have also historically been peers, because until the past decade every Internet-connected system hosted both servers and clients. Aside from dial-up users, the second-class status of today's PC browser crowd didn't exist. Thus, as some of the authors in this book point out, peer-to-peer technologies return the Internet to its original vision, in which everyone creates as well as consumes.

Many early peer-to-peer projects have an overtly political mission: routing around censorship. Peer-to-peer techniques developed in deliberate evasion of mainstream networking turned out to be very useful within mainstream networking. There is nothing surprising about this move from a specialized and somewhat ostracized group of experimenters to the center of commercial activity; similar trends can be found in the history of many technologies. After all, organizations that are used to working within the dominant paradigm don't normally try to change that paradigm; change is more likely to come from those pushing a new cause. Many of the anti-censorship projects and their leaders are featured in this book, because they have worked for a long time on the relevant peer-to-peer issues and have a lot of experience to offer.

Peer-to-peer can be seen as the continuation of a theme that has always characterized Internet evolution: loosening the virtual from the physical. DNS decoupled names from physical systems, while URNs were meant to let users retrieve documents without knowing the domain names of their hosts. Virtual hosting and replicated servers changed the one-to-one relationship of names to systems. Perhaps it is time for another major conceptual leap, where we let go of the notion of location. Welcome to the Heisenberg Principle as applied to the Internet.

The two-way Internet also has a social impact, and while this book is mostly about the technical promise of peer-to-peer, authors also talk about its exciting social promise. Communities have been forming on the Internet for a long time, but they have been limited by the flat interactive qualities of email and network newsgroups. People can exchange recommendations and ideas over these media, but they have great difficulty commenting on each other's postings, structuring information, performing searches, or creating summaries. If tools provided ways to organize information intelligently, and if each person could serve up his or her own data and retrieve others' data, the possibilities for collaboration would take off. Peer-to-peer technologies could enhance almost any group of people who share an interest—technical, cultural, political, medical, you name it.

How this book came into being

The feat of compiling original material from the wide range of experts who contributed to this book is a story all in itself.

Long before the buzz about peer-to-peer erupted in the summer of 2000, several people at O'Reilly & Associates had been talking to leaders of interesting technologies who later found themselves identified as part of the peer-to-peer movement. At that time, for instance, we were finishing a book on SETI@home (*Beyond Contact*, by Brian McConnell) and just starting a book on Jabber. Tim O'Reilly knew Ray Ozzie of Groove Networks (the creator of Lotus Notes), Marc Hedlund and Nelson Minar of Popular Power, and a number of other technologists working on technologies like those in this book.

As for me, I became aware of the technologies through my interest in Internet and computing policy. When the first alarmist news reports were published about Freenet and Gnutella, calling them mechanisms for evading copyright controls and censorship, I figured that anything with enough power to frighten major forces must be based on interesting and useful technologies. My hunch was borne out more readily than I could have imagined; the articles I published in defense of the technologies proved to be very popular, and Tim O'Reilly asked me to edit a book on the topic.

As a result, contributors came from many sources. Some were already known to O'Reilly & Associates, some were found through a grapevine of interested technologists, and some approached us when word got out that we were writing about peer-to-peer. We solicited chapters from several people who could have made valuable contributions but had to decline for lack of time or other reasons. I am fully willing to admit we missed some valuable contributors simply because we did not know about them, but perhaps that can be rectified in a future edition.

In addition to choosing authors, I spent a lot of effort making sure their topics accurately represented the field. I asked each author to find a topic that he or she found compelling, and I weighed each topic to make sure it was general enough to be of interest to a wide range of readers.

I was partial to topics that answered the immediate questions knowledgeable computer people ask when they hear about peer-to-peer, such as "Will performance become terrible as it scales?" or "How can you trust people?" Naturally, I admonished authors to be completely honest and to cover weaknesses as well as strengths.

We did our best, in the short time we had, to cover everything of importance while avoiding overlap. Some valuable topics could not be covered. For instance, no one among the authors we found felt comfortable writing about search techniques, which are clearly important to making peer-to-peer systems useful. I believe the reason we didn't get to search techniques is that it represents a relatively high level of system design and system use—a level the field has not yet achieved. Experiments are being conducted (such as InfraSearch, a system built on Gnutella), but the requisite body of knowledge is not in place for a chapter in this book. All the topics in the following pages—trust, accountability, metadata—have to be in place before searching is viable. Sometime in the future, when the problems in these areas are ironed out, we will be ready to discuss search techniques.

Thanks to Steve Burbeck, Ian Clarke, Scott Miller, and Terry Steichen, whose technical reviews were critical to assuring accurate information and sharpening the arguments in this book. Thanks also to the many authors who generously and gently reviewed each other's work, and to those people whose aid is listed in particular chapters.

Thanks also to the following O'Reilly staff: Darren Kelly, production editor; Leanne Soylemez, who was the copyeditor; Rachel Wheeler, who was the proof-reader; Matthew Hutchinson, Jane Ellin, Sarah Jane Shangraw, and Claire Cloutier, who provided quality control; Judy Hoer, who wrote the index; Lucy Muellner and Linley Dolby, who did interior composition; Edie Freedman, who designed the cover of this book; Emma Colby, who produced the cover layout; Melanie Wang and David Futato, who designed the interior layout; Mike Sierra, who implemented the design; and Robert Romano and Jessamyn Read, who produced the illustrations.

Contents of this book

It's fun to find a common thread in a variety of projects, but simply noting philosophical parallels is not enough to make the term peer-to-peer useful. Rather, it is valuable only if it helps us develop and deploy the various technologies. In other words, if putting two technologies under the peer-to-peer umbrella shows that they share a set of problems, and that the solution found for one technology can perhaps be applied to another, we benefit from the buzzword. This book, then, spends most of its time on general topics rather than the details of particular existing projects.

Part I, *Context and Overview*, contains the observations of several thinkers in the computer industry about the movements that have come to be called peer-to-peer. These authors discuss what can be included in the term, where it is innovative or not so innovative, and where its future may lie.

Chapter 1, *A Network of Peers: Peer-to-Peer Models Through the History of the Internet*, describes where peer-to-peer systems might offer benefits, and the problems of fitting such systems into the current Internet. It includes a history of early antecedents. The chapter is written by Nelson Minar and Marc Hedlund, the chief officers of Popular Power.

Chapter 2, *Listening to Napster*, tries to tie down what peer-to-peer means and what we can learn from the factors that made Napster so popular. The chapter is written by investment advisor and essayist Clay Shirky.

Chapter 3, *Remaking the Peer-to-Peer Meme*, contrasts the way the public often views a buzzword such as peer-to-peer with more constructive approaches. It is written by Tim O'Reilly, founder and CEO of O'Reilly & Associates, Inc.

Chapter 4, *The Cornucopia of the Commons*, reveals the importance of maximizing the value that normal, selfish use adds to a service. It is written by Dan Bricklin, cocreator of Visicalc, the first computer spreadsheet.

Some aspects of peer-to-peer can be understood only by looking at real systems. Part II, *Projects*, contains chapters of varying length about some important systems that are currently in operation or under development.

Chapter 5, *SETI@home*, presents one of the most famous of the early crop of peer-to-peer technologies. Project Director David Anderson explains why the team chose to crunch astronomical data on millions of scattered systems and how they pulled it off.

Chapter 6, *Jabber: Conversational Technologies*, presents the wonderful possibilities inherent in using the Internet to form communities of people as well as automated agents contacting each other freely. It is written by Jeremie Miller, leader of the Jabber project.

Chapter 7, *Mixmaster Remailers*, covers a classic system for allowing anonymous email. Other systems described in this book depend on Mixmaster to protect end-user privacy, and it represents an important and long-standing example of peer-to-peer in itself. It is written by Adam Langley, a Freenet developer.

Chapter 8, *Gnutella*, offers not only an introduction to one of the most important of current projects, but also an entertaining discussion of the value of using peer-to-peer techniques. The chapter is written by Gene Kan, one of the developers most strongly associated with Gnutella.

Chapter 9, *Freenet*, describes an important project that should be examined by anyone interested in peer-to-peer. The chapter explains how the system passes around requests and how various cryptographic keys permit searches and the retrieval of documents. It is written by Adam Langley.

Chapter 10, *Red Rover*, describes a fascinating system for avoiding censorship and recrimination for the distribution of files using electronic mail. It is written by Alan Brown, the developer of Red Rover.

Chapter 11, *Publius*, describes a system that distributes material through a collection of servers in order to prevent censorship. Although Publius is not a pure peer-to-peer system, its design offers insight and unique solutions to many of the problems faced by peer-to-peer designers and users. The chapter is written by Marc Waldman, Lorrie Faith Cranor, and Avi Rubin, the members of the Publius team.

Chapter 12, *Free Haven*, introduces another set of distributed storage services that promotes anonymity with the addition of some new techniques in improving accountability in the face of this anonymity. It is written by Roger Dingledine, Michael Freedman, and David Molnar, leaders of the Free Haven team.

In Part III, *Technical Topics*, project leaders choose various key topics and explore the problems, purposes, and promises of the technology.

Chapter 13, *Metadata*, shows how to turn raw data into useful information and how that information can support information seekers and communities. Metadata can be created through XML, RDF, and other standard formats. The chapter is written by Rael Dornfest, an O'Reilly Network developer, and Dan Brickley, a longstanding RDF advocate and chair of the World Wide Web Consortium's RDF Interest Group.

Chapter 14, *Performance*, covers a topic that has been much in the news recently and comes to mind immediately when people consider peer-to-peer for real-life systems. This chapter examines how well a peer-to-peer project can scale, using simulation to provide projections for Freenet and Gnutella. It is written by Theodore Hong of the Freenet project.

Chapter 15, *Trust*, begins a series of chapters on the intertwined issues of privacy, authentication, anonymity, and reliability. This chapter covers the basic elements of security, some of which will be well known to most readers, but some of which are fairly novel. It is written by the members of the Publius team.

Chapter 16, *Accountability*, covers ways to avoid the "tragedy of the commons" in shared systems—in other words, the temptation for many users to freeload off the resources contributed by a few. This problem is endemic to many peer-to-peer systems, and has led to several suggestions for micropayment systems (like Mojo Nation) and reputation systems. The chapter is written by leaders of the Free Haven team.

Chapter 17, *Reputation*, discusses ways to automate the collection and processing of information from previous transactions to help users decide whether they can trust a server with a new transaction. The chapter is written by Richard Lethin, founder of Reputation Technologies, Inc.

Chapter 18, *Security*, offers the assurance that it is technically possible for people in a peer-to-peer system to authenticate each other and ensure the integrity and secrecy of their communications. The chapter accomplishes this by describing the industrial-strength security system used in Groove, a new commercial groupware system for small collections of people. It is written by Jon Udell, an independent author/consultant, and Nimisha Asthagiri and Walter Tuvell, staff of Groove Networks.

Chapter 19, *Interoperability Through Gateways*, discusses how the best of all worlds could be achieved by connecting one system to another. It includes an encapsulated comparison of several peer-to-peer systems and the advantages each one offers. It is written by Brandon Wiley, a developer of the Freenet project.

The appendix lists some interesting projects, companies, and standards that could reasonably be considered examples of peer-to-peer technology.

Peer-to-peer web site

O'Reilly has created the web site *http://openp2p.com* to cover peer-to-peer (P2P) technology for developers and technical managers. The site covers these technologies from inside the communities producing them and tries to profile the leading technologists, thinkers, and programmers in the P2P space by providing a deep technical perspective.

We'd like to hear from you

Please address comments and questions concerning this book to the publisher:

O'Reilly & Associates, Inc.
101 Morris Street Sebastopol, CA 95472
(800) 998-9938 (in the United States or Canada)
(707) 829-0515 (international or local)
(707) 829-0104 (fax)

We have a web page for this book, where we list errata, examples, or any additional information. You can access this page at:

http://www.oreilly.com/catalog/peertopeer

To comment or ask technical questions about this book, send email to:

bookquestions@oreilly.com

For more information about our books, conferences, software, Resource Centers, and the O'Reilly Network, see our web site at:

http://www.oreilly.com

Context and Overview

This part of the book offers some high-level views, defining the term "peer-to-peer" and placing current projects in a social and technological context.

chapter one

A Network of Peers

Peer-to-Peer Models Through the History of the Internet

Nelson Minar and Marc Hedlund, Popular Power

The Internet is a shared resource, a cooperative network built out of millions of hosts all over the world. Today there are more applications than ever that want to use the network, consume bandwidth, and send packets far and wide. Since 1994, the general public has been racing to join the community of computers on the Internet, placing strain on the most basic of resources: network bandwidth. And the increasing reliance on the Internet for critical applications has brought with it new security requirements, resulting in firewalls that strongly partition the Net into pieces. Through rain and snow and congested Network Access Providers (NAPs), the email goes through, and the system has scaled vastly beyond its original design.

In the year 2000, though, something has changed—or, perhaps, reverted. The network model that survived the enormous growth of the previous five years has been turned on its head. What was down has become up; what was passive is now active. Through the music-sharing application called Napster, and the larger movement dubbed "peer-to-peer," the millions of users connecting to the Internet have started using their ever more powerful home computers for more than just browsing the Web and trading email. Instead, machines in the home and on the desktop are connecting to each other directly, forming groups and collaborating to become user-created search engines, virtual supercomputers, and filesystems.

Not everyone thinks this is such a great idea. Some objections (dealt with elsewhere in this volume) cite legal or moral concerns. Other problems are technical. Many network providers, having set up their systems with the idea that users would spend most of their time downloading data from central servers, have economic objections to peer-to-peer models. Some have begun to cut off access to peer-to-peer services on the basis that they violate user agreements and consume too much bandwidth (for illicit purposes, at that). As reported by the online News.com site, a third of U.S. colleges surveyed have banned Napster because students using it have sometimes saturated campus networks.

In our own company, Popular Power, we have encountered many of these problems as we create a peer-to-peer distributed computing resource out of millions of computers all over the Internet. We have identified many specific problems where the Internet architecture has been strained; we have also found workarounds for many of these problems and have come to understand what true solutions would be like. Surprisingly, we often find ourselves looking back to the Internet of 10 or 15 years ago to consider how best to solve a problem.

The original Internet was fundamentally designed as a peer-to-peer system. Over time it has become increasingly client/server, with millions of consumer clients communicating with a relatively privileged set of servers. The current crop of peer-to-peer applications is using the Internet much as it was originally designed: as a medium for communication for machines that share resources with each other as equals. Because this network model is more revolutionary for its scale and its particular implementations than for its concept, a good number of past Internet applications can provide lessons to architects of new peer-to-peer applications. In some cases, designers of current applications can learn from distributed Internet systems like Usenet and the Domain Name System (DNS); in others, the changes that the Internet has undergone during its commercialization may need to be reversed or modified to accommodate new peer-to-peer applications. In either case, the lessons these systems provide are instructive, and may help us, as application designers, avoid causing the death of the Internet.[*]

A revisionist history of peer-to-peer (1969–1995)

The Internet as originally conceived in the late 1960s was a peer-to-peer system. The goal of the original ARPANET was to share computing resources around the U.S. The challenge for this effort was to integrate different kinds of existing networks as well as future technologies with one common network architecture that would allow every host to be an equal player. The first few hosts on the ARPANET—UCLA, SRI, UCSB, and the University of Utah—were already independent computing sites with equal status. The ARPANET connected them together not in a master/slave or client/server relationship, but rather as equal computing peers.

---

[*] The authors wish to thank Debbie Pfeifer for invaluable help in editing this chapter.

The early Internet was also much more open and free than today's network. Firewalls were unknown until the late 1980s. Generally, any two machines on the Internet could send packets to each other. The Net was the playground of cooperative researchers who generally did not need protection from each other. The protocols and systems were obscure and specialized enough that security break-ins were rare and generally harmless. As we shall see later, the modern Internet is much more partitioned.

The early "killer apps" of the Internet, FTP and Telnet, were themselves client/server applications. A Telnet client logged into a compute server, and an FTP client sent and received files from a file server. But while a single application was client/server, the usage patterns as a whole were symmetric. Every host on the Net could FTP or Telnet to any other host, and in the early days of minicomputers and mainframes, the servers usually acted as clients as well.

This fundamental symmetry is what made the Internet so radical. In turn, it enabled a variety of more complex systems such as Usenet and DNS that used peer-to-peer communication patterns in an interesting fashion. In subsequent years, the Internet has become more and more restricted to client/server-type applications. But as peer-to-peer applications become common again, we believe the Internet must revert to its initial design.

Let's look at two long-established fixtures of computer networking that include important peer-to-peer components: Usenet and DNS.

Usenet

Usenet news implements a decentralized model of control that in some ways is the grandfather of today's new peer-to-peer applications such as Gnutella and Freenet. Fundamentally, Usenet is a system that, using no central control, copies files between computers. Since Usenet has been around since 1979, it offers a number of lessons and is worth considering for contemporary file-sharing applications.

The Usenet system was originally based on a facility called the Unix-to-Unix-copy protocol, or UUCP. UUCP was a mechanism by which one Unix machine would automatically dial another, exchange files with it, and disconnect. This mechanism allowed Unix sites to exchange email, files, system patches, or other messages. The Usenet used UUCP to exchange messages within a set of topics, so that students at the University of North Carolina and Duke University could each "post" messages to a topic, read messages from others on the same topic, and trade messages between the two schools. The Usenet grew from these original two hosts to hundreds of thousands of sites. As the network grew, so did the number and structure of the topics in which a message could be posted. Usenet today uses a TCP/IP-based protocol known as the Network News Transport Protocol (NNTP), which allows two machines on the Usenet network to discover new newsgroups efficiently and exchange new messages in each group.

The basic model of Usenet provides a great deal of local control and relatively simple administration. A Usenet site joins the rest of the world by setting up a news exchange connection with at least one other news server on the Usenet network. Today, exchange is typically provided by a company's ISP. The administrator tells the company's news server to get in touch with the ISP's news server and exchange messages on a regular schedule. Company employees contact the company's local news server, and transact with it to read and post news messages. When a user in the company posts a new message in a newsgroup, the next time the company news server contacts the ISP's server it will notify the ISP's server that it has a new article and then transmit that article. At the same time, the ISP's server sends its new articles to the company's server.

Today, the volume of Usenet traffic is enormous, and not every server will want to carry the full complement of newsgroups or messages. The company administrator can control the size of the news installation by specifying which newsgroups the server will carry. In addition, the administrator can specify an expiration time by group or hierarchy, so that articles in a newsgroup will be retained for that time period but no longer. These controls allow each organization to voluntarily join the network on its own terms. Many organizations decide not to carry newsgroups that transmit sexually oriented or illegal material. This is a distinct difference from, say, Freenet, which (as a design choice) does not let a user know what material he or she has received.

Usenet has evolved some of the best examples of decentralized control structures on the Net. There is no central authority that controls the news system. The addition of new newsgroups to the main topic hierarchy is controlled by a rigorous democratic process, using the Usenet group *news.admin* to propose and discuss the creation of new groups. After a new group is proposed and discussed for a set period of time, anyone with an email address may submit an email vote for or against the proposal. If a newsgroup vote passes, a new group message is sent and propagated through the Usenet network.

There is even an institutionalized form of anarchy, the *alt.** hierarchy, that subverts the *news.admin* process in a codified way. An *alt* newsgroup can be added at any time by anybody, but sites that don't want to deal with the resulting absurdity can avoid the whole hierarchy. The beauty of Usenet is that each of the participating hosts can set their own local policies, but the network as a whole functions through the cooperation and good will of the community. Many of the peer-to-peer systems currently emerging have not yet effectively addressed decentralized control as a goal. Others, such as Freenet, deliberately avoid giving local administrators control over the content of their machines because this control would weaken the political aims of the system. In each case, the interesting question is: how much control can or should the local administrator have?

NNTP as a protocol contains a number of optimizations that modern peer-to-peer systems would do well to copy. For instance, news messages maintain a "Path" header that traces their transmission from one news server to another. If news server A receives a request from server B, and A's copy of a message lists B in the Path header, A will not try to retransmit that message to B. Since the purpose of NNTP transmission is to make sure every news server on Usenet can receive an article (if it wants to), the Path header avoids a flood of repeated messages. Gnutella, as an example, does not use a similar system when transmitting search requests, so as a result a single Gnutella node can receive the same request repeatedly.

The open, decentralized nature of Usenet can be harmful as well as beneficial. Usenet has been enormously successful as a system in the sense that it has survived since 1979 and continues to be home to thriving communities of experts. It has swelled far beyond its modest beginnings. But in many ways the trusting, decentralized nature of the protocol has reduced its utility and made it an extremely noisy communication channel. Particularly, as we will discuss later, Usenet fell victim to spam early in the rise of the commercial Internet. Still, Usenet's systems for decentralized control, its methods of avoiding a network flood, and other characteristics make it an excellent object lesson for designers of peer-to-peer systems.

DNS

The Domain Name System (DNS) is an example of a system that blends peer-to-peer networking with a hierarchical model of information ownership. The remarkable thing about DNS is how well it has scaled, from the few thousand hosts it was originally designed to support in 1983 to the hundreds of millions of hosts currently on the Internet. The lessons from DNS are directly applicable to contemporary peer-to-peer data sharing applications.

DNS was established as a solution to a file-sharing problem. In the early days of the Internet, the way to map a human-friendly name like *bbn* to an IP address like *4.2.49.2* was through a single flat file, *hosts.txt*, which was copied around the Internet periodically. As the Net grew to thousands of hosts and managing that file became impossible, DNS was developed as a way to distribute the data sharing across the peer-to-peer Internet.

The namespace of DNS names is naturally hierarchical. For example, O'Reilly & Associates, Inc. owns the namespace *oreilly.com*: they are the sole authority for all names in their domain, such as *www.oreilly.com*. This built-in hierarchy yields a simple, natural way to delegate responsibility for serving part of the DNS database. Each domain has an *authority*, the name server of record for hosts in that domain. When a host on the Internet wants to know the address of a given name, it queries its nearest name server to ask for the address. If that server does not know the name, it delegates the query to the authority for that namespace. That query, in turn, may be delegated to a higher authority, all the way up to the root name servers for the Internet as a whole. As the answer propagates back down to the requestor, the result is cached along the way to the name servers so the next fetch can be more efficient. Name servers operate both as clients and as servers.

DNS as a whole works amazingly well, having scaled to 10,000 times its original size. There are several key design elements in DNS that are replicated in many distributed systems today. One element is that hosts can operate both as clients and as servers, propagating requests when need be. These hosts help make the network scale well by caching replies. The second element is a natural method of propagating data requests across the network. Any DNS server can query any other, but in normal operation there is a standard path up the chain of authority. The load is naturally distributed across the DNS network, so that any individual name server needs to serve only the needs of its clients and the namespace it individually manages.

So from its earliest stages, the Internet was built out of peer-to-peer communication patterns. One advantage of this history is that we have experience to draw from in how to design new peer-to-peer systems. The problems faced today by new peer-to-peer applications systems such as file sharing are quite similar to the problems that Usenet and DNS addressed 10 or 15 years ago.

The network model of the Internet explosion (1995–1999)

The explosion of the Internet in 1994 radically changed the shape of the Internet, turning it from a quiet geek utopia into a bustling mass medium. Millions of new people flocked to the Net. This wave represented a new kind of people— ordinary folks who were interested in the Internet as a way to send email, view web pages, and buy things, not computer scientists interested in the details of complex computer networks. The change of the Internet to a mass cultural phenomenon has had a far-reaching impact on the network architecture, an impact that directly affects our ability to create peer-to-peer applications in today's Internet. These changes are seen in the way we use the network, the breakdown of cooperation on the Net, the increasing deployment of firewalls on the Net, and the growth of asymmetric network links such as ADSL and cable modems.

The switch to client/server

The network model of user applications—not just their consumption of bandwidth, but also their methods of addressing and communicating with other machines—changed significantly with the rise of the commercial Internet and the advent of millions of home users in the 1990s. Modem connection protocols such as SLIP and PPP became more common, typical applications targeted slow-speed analog modems, and corporations began to manage their networks with firewalls and Network Address Translation (NAT). Many of these changes were built around the usage patterns common at the time, most of which involved downloading data, not publishing or uploading information.

The web browser, and many of the other applications that sprung up during the early commercialization of the Internet, were based around a simple client/server protocol: the client initiates a connection to a well-known server, downloads some data, and disconnects. When the user is finished with the data retrieved, the process is repeated. The model is simple and straightforward. It works for everything from browsing the Web to watching streaming video, and developers cram shopping carts, stock transactions, interactive games, and a host of other things into it. The machine running a web client doesn't need to have a permanent or well-known address. It doesn't need a continuous connection to the Internet. It doesn't need to accommodate multiple users. It just needs to know how to ask a question and listen for a response.

Not all of the applications used at home fit this model. Email, for instance, requires much more two-way communication between an email client and server. In these cases, though, the client is often talking to a server on the local network (either the ISP's mail server or a corporate one). Chat systems that achieved widespread usage, such as AOL's Instant Messenger, have similar "local" properties, and Usenet systems do as well. As a result, the typical ISP configuration instructions give detailed (and often misunderstood) instructions for email, news, and sometimes chat. These were the exceptions that were worth some manual configuration on the user's part. The "download" model is simpler and works without much configuration; the "two-way" model is used less frequently but perhaps to greater effect.

While early visions of the Web always called it a great equalizer of communications—a system that allowed every user to publish their viewpoints rather than simply consume media—the commercial explosion on the Internet quickly fit the majority of traffic into the downstream paradigm already used by television and newspapers. Architects of the systems that enabled the commercial expansion of the Net often took this model into account, assuming that it was here to stay. Peer-to-peer applications may require these systems to change.

The breakdown of cooperation

The early Internet was designed on principles of cooperation and good engineering. Everyone working on Internet design had the same goal: build a reliable, efficient, powerful network. As the Internet entered its current commercial phase, the incentive structures changed, resulting in a series of stresses that have highlighted the Internet's susceptibility to the tragedy of the commons. This phenomenon has shown itself in many ways, particularly the rise of spam on the Internet and the challenges of building efficient network protocols that correctly manage the common resource.

Spam: Uncooperative people

Spam, or unsolicited commercial messages, is now an everyday occurrence on the Internet. Back in the pre-commercial network, however, unsolicited advertisements were met with surprise and outrage. The end of innocence occurred on April 12, 1994, the day the infamous Canter and Seigel "green card spam" appeared on the Usenet. Their offense was an advertisement posted individually to every Usenet newsgroup, blanketing the whole world with a message advertising their services. At the time, this kind of action was unprecedented and engendered strong disapproval. Not only were most of the audience uninterested in the service, but many people felt that Canter and Seigel had stolen the Usenet's resources. The advertisers did not pay for the transmission of the advertisement; instead the costs were born by the Usenet as a whole.

In the contemporary Internet, spam does not seem surprising; Usenet has largely been given over to it, and ISPs now provide spam filtering services for their users' email both to help their users and in self-defense. Email and Usenet relied on individuals' cooperation to not flood the commons with junk mail, and that cooperation broke down. Today the Internet generally lacks effective technology to prevent spam.

The problem is the lack of accountability in the Internet architecture. Because any host can connect to any other host, and because connections are nearly anonymous, people can insert spam into the network at any point. There has been an arms race of trying to hold people accountable—closing down open sendmail relays, tracking sources of spam on Usenet, retaliation against spammers—but the battle has been lost, and today we have all learned to live with spam.

The lesson for peer-to-peer designers is that without accountability in a network, it is difficult to enforce rules of social responsibility. Just like Usenet and email, today's peer-to-peer systems run the risk of being overrun by unsolicited advertisements. It is difficult to design a system where socially inappropriate use is prevented. Technologies for accountability, such as cryptographic identification or reputation systems, can be valuable tools to help manage a peer-to-peer network. There have been proposals to retrofit these capabilities into Usenet and email, but none today are widespread; it is important to build these capabilities into the system from the beginning. Chapter 16, *Accountability*, discusses some techniques for controlling spam, but these are still arcane.

The TCP rate equation: Cooperative protocols

A fundamental design principle of the Internet is *best effort* packet delivery. "Best effort" means the Internet does not guarantee that a packet will get through, simply that the Net will do its best to get the packet to the destination. Higher-level protocols such as TCP create reliable connections by detecting when a packet gets lost and resending it. A major reason packets do not get delivered on the Internet is congestion: if a router in the network is overwhelmed, it will start dropping packets at random. TCP accounts for this by throttling the speed at which it sends data. When the network is congested, each individual TCP connection independently slows down, seeking to find the optimal rate while not losing too many packets. But not only do individual TCP connections optimize their bandwidth usage, TCP is also designed to make the Internet as a whole operate efficiently. The collective behavior of many individual TCP connections backing off independently results in a lessening of the congestion at the router, in a way that is exquisitely tuned to use the router's capacity efficiently. In essence, the TCP backoff algorithm is a way for individual peers to manage a shared resource without a central coordinator.

The problem is that the efficiency of TCP on the Internet scale fundamentally requires cooperation: each network user has to play by the same rules. The performance of an individual TCP connection is inversely proportional to the square root of the packet loss rate—part of the "TCP rate equation," a fundamental governing law of the Internet. Protocols that follow this law are known as "TCP-friendly protocols." It is possible to design other protocols that do not follow the TCP rate equation, ones that rudely try to consume more bandwidth than they should. Such protocols can wreak havoc on the Net, not only using more than their fair share but actually spoiling the common resource for all. This abstract networking problem is a classic example of a tragedy of the commons, and the Internet today is quite vulnerable to it.

The problem is not only theoretical, it is also quite practical. As protocols have been built in the past few years by companies with commercial demands, there has been growing concern that unfriendly protocols will begin to hurt the Internet.

An early example was a feature added by Netscape to their browser—the ability to download several files at the same time. The Netscape engineers discovered that if you downloaded embedded images in parallel, rather than one at a time, the whole page would load faster and users would be happier. But there was a question: was this usage of bandwidth fair? Not only does it tax the server to have to send out more images simultaneously, but it creates more TCP channels and sidesteps TCP's congestion algorithms. There was some controversy about this feature when Netscape first introduced it, a debate quelled only after Netscape released the client and people discovered in practice that the parallel download strategy did not unduly harm the Internet. Today this technique is standard in all browsers and goes unquestioned. The questions have reemerged at the new frontier of "download accelerator" programs that download different chunks of the same file simultaneously, again threatening to upset the delicate management of Internet congestion.

A more troubling concern about congestion management is the growth of bandwidth-hungry streaming broadband media. Typical streaming media applications do *not* use TCP, instead favoring custom UDP-based protocols with their own congestion control and failure handling strategies. Many of these protocols are proprietary; network engineers do not even have access to their implementations to examine if they are TCP-friendly. So far there has been no major problem. The streaming media vendors seem to be playing by the rules, and all is well. But fundamentally the system is brittle, and either through a mistake or through greed the Internet's current delicate cooperation could be toppled.

What do spam and the TCP rate algorithm have in common? They both demonstrate that the proper operation of the Internet is fragile and requires the cooperation of everyone involved. In the case of TCP, the system has mostly worked and the network has been preserved. In the case of spam, however, the battle has been lost and unsocial behavior is with us forever. The lesson for peer-to-peer system designers is to consider the issue of polite behavior up front. Either we must design systems that do not require cooperation to function correctly, or we must create incentives for cooperation by rewarding proper behavior or auditing usage so that misbehavior can be punished.

Firewalls, dynamic IP, NAT: The end of the open network

At the same time that the cooperative nature of the Internet was being threatened, network administrators implemented a variety of management measures that resulted in the Internet being a much less open network. In the early days of the Internet, all hosts were equal participants. The network was symmetric—if a host could reach the Net, everyone on the Net could reach that host. Every computer could equally be a client and a server. This capability began to erode in the mid-1990s with the deployment of firewalls, the rise of dynamic IP addresses, and the popularity of Network Address Translation (NAT).

As the Internet matured there came a need to secure the network, to protect individual hosts from unlimited access. By default, any host that can access the Internet can also *be accessed* on the Internet. Since average users could not handle the security risks that resulted from a symmetric design, network managers turned to firewalls as a tool to control access to their machines.

Firewalls stand at the gateway between the internal network and the Internet outside. They filter packets, choosing which traffic to let through and which to deny. A firewall changes the fundamental Internet model: some parts of the network cannot fully talk to other parts. Firewalls are a very useful security tool, but they pose a serious obstacle to peer-to-peer communication models.

A typical firewall works by allowing anyone inside the internal network to initiate a connection to anyone on the Internet, but it prevents random hosts on the Internet from initiating connections to hosts in the internal network. This kind of firewall is like a one-way gate: you can go out, but you cannot come in. A host protected in this way cannot easily function as a server; it can only be a client. In addition, outgoing connections may be restricted to certain applications like FTP and the Web by blocking traffic to certain ports at the firewall.

Allowing an Internet host to be only a client, not a server, is a theme that runs through a lot of the changes in the Internet after the consumer explosion. With the rise of modem users connecting to the Internet, the old practice of giving every Internet host a fixed IP address became impractical, because there were not enough IP addresses to go around. Dynamic IP address assignment is now the norm for many hosts on the Internet, where an individual computer's address may change every single day. Broadband providers are even finding dynamic IP useful for their "always on" services. The end result is that many hosts on the Internet are not easily reachable, because they keep moving around. Peer-to-peer applications such as instant messaging or file sharing have to work hard to circumvent this problem, building dynamic directories of hosts. In the early Internet, where hosts remained static, it was much simpler.

A final trend is to not even give a host a valid public Internet address at all, but instead to use NAT to hide the address of a host behind a firewall. NAT combines the problems of firewalls and dynamic IP addresses: not only is the host's true address unstable, it is not even reachable! All communication has to go through a fairly simple pattern that the NAT router can understand, resulting in a great loss of flexibility in applications communications. For example, many cooperative Internet games have trouble with NAT: every player in the game wants to be able to contact every other player, but the packets cannot get through the NAT router. The result is that a central server on the Internet has to act as an application-level message router, emulating the function that TCP/IP itself used to serve.

Firewalls, dynamic IP, and NAT grew out of a clear need in Internet architecture to make scalable, secure systems. They solved the problem of bringing millions of client computers onto the Internet quickly and manageably. But these same technologies have weakened the Internet infrastructure as a whole, relegating most computers to second-class status as clients only. New peer-to-peer applications challenge this architecture, demanding that participants serve resources as well as use them. As peer-to-peer applications become more common, there will be a need for common technical solutions to these problems.

Asymmetric bandwidth

A final Internet trend of the late 1990s that presents a challenge to peer-to-peer applications is the rise in asymmetric network connections such as ADSL and cable modems. In order to get the most efficiency out of available wiring, current broadband providers have chosen to provide asymmetric bandwidth. A typical ADSL or cable modem installation offers three to eight times more bandwidth when getting data from the Internet than when sending data to it, favoring client over server usage.

The reason this has been tolerated by most users is clear: the Web is the killer app for the Internet, and most users are only clients of the Web, not servers. Even users who publish their own web pages typically do not do so from a home broadband connection, but instead use third-party dedicated servers provided by companies like GeoCities or Exodus. In the early days of the Web it was not clear how this was going to work: could each user have a personal web server? But in the end most Web use is itself asymmetric—many clients, few servers—and most users are well served by asymmetric bandwidth.

The problem today is that peer-to-peer applications are changing the assumption that end users only want to download from the Internet, never upload to it. File-sharing applications such as Napster or Gnutella can reverse the bandwidth usage, making a machine serve many more files than it downloads. The upstream pipe cannot meet demand. Even worse, because of the details of TCP's rate control, if the upstream path is clogged, the downstream performance suffers as well. So if a computer is serving files on the slow side of a link, it cannot easily download simultaneously on the fast side.

ADSL and cable modems assume asymmetric bandwidth for an individual user. This assumption takes hold even more strongly inside ISP networks, which are engineered for bits to flow to the users, not from them. The end result is a network infrastructure that is optimized for computers that are only clients, not servers. But peer-to-peer technology generally makes every host act both as a client and a server; the asymmetric assumption is incorrect. There is not much an individual peer-to-peer application can do to work around asymmetric bandwidth; as peer-to-peer applications become more widespread, the network architecture is going to have to change to better handle the new traffic patterns.

Observations on the current crop of peer-to-peer applications (2000)

While the new breed of peer-to-peer applications can take lessons from earlier models, these applications also introduce new characteristics or features that are novel. Peer-to-peer allows us to separate the concepts of authoring information and publishing that same information. Peer-to-peer allows for decentralized application design, something that is both an opportunity and a challenge. And peer-to-peer applications place unique strains on firewalls, something well demonstrated by the current trend to use the HTTP port for operations other than web transactions.

Authoring is not the same as publishing

One of the promises of the Internet is that people are able to be their own publishers, for example, by using personal web sites to make their views and interests known. Self-publishing has certainly become more common with the commercialization of the Internet. More often, however, users spend most of their time reading (downloading) information and less time publishing, and as discussed previously, commercial providers of Internet access have structured their offering around this asymmetry.

The example of Napster creates an interesting middle ground between the ideal of "everyone publishes" and the seeming reality of "everyone consumes." Napster particularly (and famously) makes it very easy to *publish* data you did not *author*. In effect, your machine is being used as a repeater to retransmit data once it reaches you. A network designer, assuming that there are only so many authors in the world and therefore that asymmetric broadband is the perfect optimization, is confounded by this development. This is why many networks such as college campuses have banned Napster from use.

Napster changes the flow of data. The assumptions that servers would be owned by publishers and that publishers and authors would combine into a single network location have proven untrue. The same observation also applies to Gnutella, Freenet, and others. Users don't need to create content in order to want to publish it—in fact, the benefits of publication by the "reader" have been demonstrated by the scale some of these systems have been able to reach.

Decentralization

Peer-to-peer systems seem to go hand-in-hand with decentralized systems. In a fully decentralized system, not only is every host an equal participant, but there are *no* hosts with special facilitating or administrative roles. In practice, building fully decentralized systems can be difficult, and many peer-to-peer applications take hybrid approaches to solving problems. As we have already seen, DNS is peer-to-peer in protocol design but with a built-in sense of hierarchy. There are many other examples of systems that are peer-to-peer at the core and yet have some semi-centralized organization in application, such as Usenet, instant messaging, and Napster.

Usenet is an instructive example of the evolution of a decentralized system. Usenet propagation is symmetric: hosts share traffic. But because of the high cost of keeping a full news feed, in practice there is a backbone of hosts that carry all of the traffic and serve it to a large number of "leaf nodes" whose role is mostly to receive articles. Within Usenet, there was a natural trend toward making traffic propagation hierarchical, even though the underlying protocols do not demand it. This form of "soft centralization" may prove to be economic for many peer-to-peer systems with high-cost data transmission.

Many other current peer-to-peer applications present a decentralized face while relying on a central facilitator to coordinate operations. To a user of an instant messaging system, the application appears peer-to-peer, sending data directly to the friend being messaged. But all major instant messaging systems have some sort of server on the back end that facilitates nodes talking to each other. The server maintains an association between the user's name and his or her current IP address, buffers messages in case the user is offline, and routes messages to users behind firewalls. Some systems (such as ICQ) allow direct client-to-client communication when possible but have a server as a fallback. A fully decentralized approach to instant messaging would not work on today's Internet, but there are scaling advantages to allowing client-to-client communication when possible.

Napster is another example of a hybrid system. Napster's file sharing is decentralized: one Napster client downloads a file directly from another Napster client's machine. But the directory of files is centralized, with the Napster servers answering search queries and brokering client connections. This hybrid approach seems to scale well: the directory can be made efficient and uses low bandwidth, and the file sharing can happen on the edges of the network.

In practice, some applications might work better with a fully centralized design, not using any peer-to-peer technology at all. One example is a search on a large, relatively static database. Current web search engines are able to serve up to one billion pages all from a single place. Search algorithms have been highly optimized for centralized operation; there appears to be little benefit to spreading the search operation out on a peer-to-peer network (database generation, however, is another matter).

Also, applications that require centralized information sharing for accountability or correctness are hard to spread out on a decentralized network. For example, an auction site needs to guarantee that the best price wins; that can be difficult if the bidding process has been spread across many locations. Decentralization engenders a whole new area of network-related failures: unreliability, incorrect data synchronization, etc. Peer-to-peer designers need to balance the power of peer-to-peer models against the complications and limitations of decentralized systems.

Abusing port 80

One of the stranger phenomena in the current Internet is the abuse of port 80, the port that HTTP traffic uses when people browse the Web. Firewalls typically filter traffic based on the direction of traffic (incoming or outgoing) and the destination port of the traffic. Because the Web is a primary application of many Internet users, almost all firewalls allow outgoing connections on port 80 even if the firewall policy is otherwise very restrictive.

In the early days of the Internet, the port number usually indicated which application was using the network; the firewall could count on port 80 being only for Web traffic. But precisely because many firewalls allow connections to port 80, other application authors started routing traffic through that port. Streaming audio, instant messaging, remote method invocations, even whole mobile agents are being sent through port 80. Most current peer-to-peer applications have some way to use port 80 as well in order to circumvent network security policies. Naive firewalls are none the wiser; they are unaware that they are passing the exact sorts of traffic the network administrator intended to block.

The problem is twofold. First, there is no good way for a firewall to identify what applications are running through it. The port number has already been circumvented. Fancier firewalls can analyze the actual traffic going through the firewall and see if it is a legitimate HTTP stream, but that just encourages application designers to masquerade as HTTP, leading to an escalating arms race that benefits no one.

The second problem is that even if an application has a legitimate reason to go through the firewall, there is no simple way for the application to request permission. The firewall, as a network security measure, is outmoded. As long as a firewall allows some sort of traffic through, peer-to-peer applications will find a way to slip through that opening.

Peer-to-peer prescriptions (2001–?)

The story is clear: The Internet was designed with peer-to-peer applications in mind, but as it has grown the network has become more asymmetric. What can we do to permit new peer-to-peer applications to flourish while respecting the pressures that have shaped the Internet to date?

Technical solutions: Return to the old Internet

As we have seen, the explosion of the Internet into the consumer space brought with it changes that have made it difficult to do peer-to-peer networking. Firewalls make it hard to contact hosts; dynamic IP and NAT make it nearly impossible. Asymmetric bandwidth is holding users back from efficiently serving files on their systems. Current peer-to-peer applications generally would benefit from an Internet more like the original network, where these restrictions were not in place. How can we enable peer-to-peer applications to work better with the current technological situation?

Firewalls serve an important need: they allow administrators to express and enforce policies about the use of their networks. That need will not change with peer-to-peer applications. Neither application designers nor network security administrators are benefiting from the current state of affairs. The solution lies in making firewalls smarter so that peer-to-peer applications can cooperate with the firewall to allow traffic the administrator wants. Firewalls must become more sophisticated, allowing systems behind the firewall to ask permission to run a particular peer-to-peer application. Peer-to-peer designers must contribute to this design discussion, then enable their applications to use these mechanisms. There is a good start to this solution in the SOCKS protocol, but it needs to be expanded to be more flexible and more tied toward applications rather than simple port numbers.

The problems engendered by dynamic IP and NAT already have a technical solution: IPv6. This new version of IP, the next generation Internet protocol architecture, has a 128-bit address space—enough for every host on the Internet to have a permanent address. Eliminating address scarcity means that every host has a home and, in theory, can be reached. The main thing holding up the deployment of IPv6 is the complexity of the changeover. At this stage, it remains to be seen when or even if IPv6 will be commonly deployed, but without it peer-to-peer applications will continue to need to build alternate address spaces to work around the limitations set by NAT and dynamic IP.

Peer-to-peer applications stress the bandwidth usage of the current Internet. First, they break the assumption of asymmetry upon which today's ADSL and cable modem providers rely. There is no simple way that peer-to-peer applications can work around this problem; we simply must encourage broadband connections to catch up.

However, peer-to-peer applications can do several things to use the existing bandwidth more efficiently. First, data caching is a natural optimization for any peer-to-peer application that is transmitting bulk data; it would be a significant advance to make sure that a program does not have to retransmit or resend data to another host. Caching is a well understood technology: distributed caches like Squid have worked out many of the consistency and load sharing issues that peer-to-peer applications face.

Second, a peer-to-peer application must have effective means for allowing users to control the bandwidth the application uses. If I run a Gnutella node at home, I want to specify that it can use only 50% of my bandwidth. Current operating systems and programming libraries do not provide good tools for this kind of limitation, but as peer-to-peer applications start demanding more network resources from hosts, users will need tools to control that resource usage.

Social solutions: Engineer polite behavior

Technical measures can help create better peer-to-peer applications, but good system design can also yield social stability. A key challenge in creating peer-to-peer systems is to have a mechanism of accountability and the enforcement of community standards. Usenet breaks down because it is impossible to hold people accountable for their actions. If a system has a way to identify individuals (even pseudonymously, to preserve privacy), that system can be made more secure against antisocial behavior. Reputation tracking mechanisms, discussed in Chapter 16, and in Chapter 17, *Reputation*, are valuable tools here as well, to give the user community a collective memory about the behavior of individuals.

Peer-to-peer systems also present the challenge of integrating local administrative control with global system correctness. Usenet was successful at this goal. The local news administrator sets policy for his or her own site, allowing the application to be customized to each user group's needs. The shared communication channel of *news.admin* allows a community governance procedure for the entire Usenet community. These mechanisms of local and global control were built into Usenet from the beginning, setting the rules of correct behavior. New breed peer-to-peer applications should follow this lead, building in their own social expectations.

Conclusions

The Internet started out as a fully symmetric, peer-to-peer network of cooperating users. As the Net has grown to accommodate the millions of people flocking online, technologies have been put in place that have split the Net up into a system with relatively few servers and many clients. At the same time, some of the basic expectations of cooperation are showing the risk of breaking down, threatening the structure of the Net.

These phenomena pose challenges and obstacles to peer-to-peer applications: both the network and the applications have to be designed together to work in tandem. Application authors must design robust applications that can function in the complex Internet environment, and network designers must build in capabilities to handle new peer-to-peer applications. Fortunately, many of these issues are familiar from the experience of the early Internet; the lessons learned there can be brought forward to design tomorrow's systems.

chapter two

Listening to Napster

Clay Shirky, The Accelerator Group

Premature definition is a danger for any movement. Once a definitive label is applied to a new phenomenon, it invariably begins shaping—and possibly distorting—people's views. So it is with the present movement toward decentralized applications. After a year or so of attempting to describe the revolution in file sharing and related technologies, we have finally settled on *peer-to-peer* as a label for what's happening.*

Somehow, though, this label hasn't clarified things. Instead, it's distracted us from the phenomena that first excited us. Taken literally, servers talking to one another are peer-to-peer. The game Doom is peer-to-peer. There are even people applying the label to email and telephones. Meanwhile, Napster, which jump-started the conversation, is not peer-to-peer in the strictest sense, because it uses a centralized server to store pointers and resolve addresses.

If we treat peer-to-peer as a literal definition of what's happening, we end up with a phrase that describes Doom but not Napster and suggests that Alexander Graham Bell is a peer-to-peer engineer but Shawn Fanning is not. Eliminating Napster from the canon now that we have a definition we can apply literally is like saying, "Sure, it may work in practice, but it will never fly in theory."

This literal approach to peer-to-peer is plainly not helping us understand what makes it important. Merely having computers act as peers on the Internet is hardly novel. From the early days of PDP-11s and Vaxes to the Sun SPARCs and Windows 2000 systems of today, computers on the Internet have been peering

---

* Thanks to *Business 2.0*, where many of these ideas first appeared, and to Dan Gillmor of the *San Jose Mercury News*, for first pointing out the important relationship between P2P and the Domain Name System.

with each other. So peer-to-peer architecture itself can't be the explanation for the recent changes in Internet use.

What have changed are the nodes that make up these peer-to-peer systems—Internet-connected PCs, which formerly were relegated to being nothing but clients—and where these nodes are: at the edges of the Internet, cut off from the DNS (Domain Name System) because they have no fixed IP addresses.

Resource-centric addressing for unstable environments

Peer-to-peer is a class of applications that takes advantage of resources—storage, cycles, content, human presence—available at the edges of the Internet. Because accessing these decentralized resources means operating in an environment of unstable connectivity and unpredictable IP addresses, peer-to-peer nodes must operate outside the DNS and have significant or total autonomy from central servers.

That's it. That's what makes peer-to-peer distinctive.

Note that this isn't what makes peer-to-peer important. It's not the problem designers of peer-to-peer systems set out to solve, like aggregating CPU cycles, sharing files, or chatting. But it's a problem they all had to solve to get where they wanted to go.

What makes Napster and Popular Power and Freenet and AIMster and Groove similar is that they are all leveraging previously unused resources, by tolerating and even working with variable connectivity. This lets them make new, powerful use of the hundreds of millions of devices that have been connected to the edges of the Internet in the last few years.

One could argue that the need for peer-to-peer designers to solve connectivity problems is little more than an accident of history. But improving the way computers connect to one another was the rationale behind the 1984 design of the Internet Protocol (IP), and before that DNS, and before that the Transmission Control Protocol (TCP), and before that the Net itself. The Internet is made of such frozen accidents.

So if you're looking for a litmus test for peer-to-peer, this is it:

1. Does it allow for variable connectivity and temporary network addresses?
2. Does it give the nodes at the edges of the network significant autonomy?

If the answer to both of those questions is yes, the application is peer-to-peer. If the answer to either question is no, it's not peer-to-peer.

Another way to examine this distinction is to think about ownership. Instead of asking, "Can the nodes speak to one another?" ask, "Who owns the hardware that the service runs on?" The huge preponderance of the hardware that makes Yahoo! work is owned by Yahoo! and managed in Santa Clara. The huge preponderance of the hardware that makes Napster work is owned by Napster users and managed on tens of millions of individual desktops. Peer-to-peer is a way of decentralizing not just features, but costs and administration as well.

Peer-to-peer is as peer-to-peer does

Up until 1994, the Internet had one basic model of connectivity. Machines were assumed to be always on, always connected, and assigned permanent IP addresses. DNS was designed for this environment, in which a change in IP address was assumed to be abnormal and rare, and could take days to propagate through the system.

With the invention of Mosaic, another model began to spread. To run a web browser, a PC needed to be connected to the Internet over a modem, with its own IP address. This created a second class of connectivity, because PCs entered and left the network cloud frequently and unpredictably.

Furthermore, because there were not enough IP addresses available to handle the sudden demand caused by Mosaic, ISPs began to assign IP addresses dynamically. They gave each PC a different, possibly masked, IP address with each new session. This instability prevented PCs from having DNS entries, and therefore prevented PC users from hosting any data or applications that accepted connections from the Net.

For a few years, treating PCs as dumb but expensive clients worked well. PCs had never been designed to be part of the fabric of the Internet, and in the early days of the Web, the toy hardware and operating systems of the average PC made it an adequate life-support system for a browser but good for little else.

Over time, though, as hardware and software improved, the unused resources that existed behind this veil of second-class connectivity started to look like something worth getting at. At a conservative estimate—assuming only 100 million PCs among the Net's 300 million users, and only a 100 MHz chip and 100 MB drive on the average Net-connected PC—the world's Net-connected PCs presently host an aggregate 10 billion megahertz of processing power and 10 thousand terabytes of storage.

The veil is pierced

The launch of ICQ, the first PC-based chat system, in 1996 marked the first time those intermittently connected PCs became directly addressable by average users. Faced with the challenge of establishing portable presence, ICQ bypassed DNS in favor of creating its own directory of protocol-specific addresses that could update IP addresses in real time, a trick followed by Groove, Napster, and NetMeeting as well. (Not all peer-to-peer systems use this trick. Gnutella and Freenet, for example, bypass DNS the old-fashioned way, by relying on numeric IP addresses. United Devices and SETI@home bypass it by giving the nodes scheduled times to contact fixed addresses, at which times they deliver their current IP addresses.)

A run of *whois* counts 23 million domain names, built up in the 16 years since the inception of IP addresses in 1984. Napster alone has created more than 23 million non-DNS addresses in 16 *months*, and when you add in all the non-DNS instant messaging addresses, the number of peer-to-peer addresses designed to reach dynamic IP addresses tops 200 million. Even if you assume that the average DNS host has 10 additional addresses of the form *foo.host.com*, the total number of peer-to-peer addresses now, after only 4 years, is of the same order of magnitude as the total number of DNS addresses, and is growing faster than the DNS universe today.

As new kinds of Net-connected devices like wireless PDAs and digital video recorders such as TiVo and Replay proliferate, they will doubtless become an important part of the Internet as well. But for now, PCs make up the enormous majority of these untapped resources. PCs are the dark matter of the Internet, and their underused resources are fueling peer-to-peer.

Real solutions to real problems

Why do we have unpredictable IP addresses in the first place? Because there weren't enough to go around when the Web happened. It's tempting to think that when enough new IP addresses are created, the old "One Device/One Address" regime will be restored, and the Net will return to its pre–peer-to-peer architecture.

This won't happen, though, because no matter how many new IP addresses there are, peer-to-peer systems often create addresses for things that aren't machines. Freenet and Mojo Nation create addresses for content intentionally spread across multiple computers. AOL Instant Messenger (AIM) and ICQ create names that refer to human beings and not machines. Peer-to-peer is designed to handle unpredictability, and nothing is more unpredictable than the humans who use the network. As the Net becomes more human-centered, the need for addressing schemes that tolerate and even expect temporary and unstable patterns of use will grow.

Who's in and who's out?

Napster is peer-to-peer because the addresses of Napster nodes bypass DNS, and because once the Napster server resolves the IP addresses of the PCs hosting a particular song, it shifts control of the file transfers to the nodes. Furthermore, the ability of the Napster nodes to host the songs without central intervention lets Napster users get access to several terabytes of storage and bandwidth at no additional cost.

However, Intel's "server peer-to-peer" is not peer-to-peer, because servers have always been peers. Their fixed IP addresses and permanent connections present no new problems, and calling what they already do "peer-to-peer" presents no new solutions.

ICQ and Jabber are peer-to-peer, because they not only devolve connection management to the individual nodes after resolving the addresses, but they also violate the machine-centric worldview encoded in DNS. Your address has nothing to do with the DNS hierarchy, or even with a particular machine, except temporarily; your chat address travels with you. Furthermore, by mapping "presence"—whether you are at your computer at any given moment in time—chat turns the old idea of permanent connectivity and IP addresses on its head. Transient connectivity is not an annoying hurdle in the case of chat but an important contribution of the technology.

Email, which treats variable connectivity as the norm, nevertheless fails the peer-to-peer definition test because your address is machine-dependent. If you drop AOL in favor of another ISP, your AOL email address disappears as well, because it hangs off DNS. Interestingly, in the early days of the Internet, there was a suggestion to make the part of the email address before the @ globally unique, linking email to a person rather than to a person@machine. That would have been peer-to-peer in the current sense, but it was rejected in favor of a machine-centric view of the Internet.

Popular Power is peer-to-peer, because the distributed clients that contact the server need no fixed IP address and have a high degree of autonomy in performing and reporting their calculations. They can even be offline for long stretches while still doing work for the Popular Power network.

Dynamic DNS is not peer-to-peer, because it tries to retrofit PCs into traditional DNS.

And so on. This list of resources that current peer-to-peer systems take advantage of—storage, cycles, content, presence—is not necessarily complete. If there were some application that needed 30,000 separate video cards, or microphones, or speakers, a peer-to-peer system could be designed that used those resources as well.

Peer-to-peer is a horseless carriage

As with the "horseless" carriage or the "compact" disc, new technologies are often labeled according to some simple difference between them and what came before (horse-drawn carriages, non-compact records).

Calling this new class of applications peer-to-peer emphasizes their difference from the dominant client/server model. However, like the horselessness of the carriage or the compactness of the disc, the "peeriness" of peer-to-peer is more a label than a definition.

As we've learned from the history of the Internet, adoption is a better predictor of software longevity than elegant design. Users will not adopt peer-to-peer applications that embrace decentralization for decentralization's sake. Instead, they will adopt those applications that use just enough decentralization, in just the right way, to create novel functions or improve existing ones.

Follow the users

It seems obvious but bears repeating: Definitions are useful only as tools for sharpening one's perception of reality and improving one's ability to predict the future. Whatever one thinks of Napster's probable longevity, Napster is the killer app for this revolution.

If the Internet has taught technology watchers anything, it's that predictions of the future success of a particular software method or paradigm are of tenuous accuracy at best. Consider the history of "multimedia." If you had read almost any computer trade magazine or followed any technology analyst's predictions for the rise of multimedia in the early '90s, the future they predicted was one of top-down design, and this multimedia future was to be made up of professionally produced CD-ROMs and "walled garden" online services such as CompuServe and Delphi. And then the Web came along and let absolute amateurs build pages in HTML, a language that was laughably simple compared to the tools being developed for other multimedia services.

Users reward simplicity

HTML's simplicity, which let amateurs create content for little cost and little invested time, turned out to be HTML's long suit. Between 1993 and 1995, HTML went from an unknown protocol to the preeminent tool for designing electronic interfaces, decisively displacing almost all challengers and upstaging CD-ROMs, as well as online services and a dozen expensive and abortive experiments with interactive TV—and it did this while having no coordinated authority, no central R&D effort, and no discernible financial incentive for the majority of its initial participants.

What caught the tech watchers in the industry by surprise was that HTML was made a success not by corporations but by users. The obvious limitations of the Web for professional designers blinded many to HTML's ability to allow average users to create multimedia content.

HTML spread because it allowed ordinary users to build their own web pages, without requiring that they be software developers or even particularly savvy software users. All the confident predictions about the CD-ROM-driven multimedia future turned out to be meaningless in the face of user preference. This in turn led to network effects on adoption: once a certain number of users had adopted it, there were more people committed to making the Web better than there were people committed to making CD-ROM authoring easier for amateurs.

The lesson of HTML's astonishing rise for anyone trying to make sense of the social aspects of technology is simple: *follow the users*. Understand the theory, study the engineering, but most importantly, follow the adoption rate. The cleanest theory and the best engineering in the world mean nothing if the users don't use them, and understanding why some solution will never work in theory means nothing if users adopt it all the same.

Listen to Napster

In the present circumstance, the message that comes from paying attention to the users is simple: *Listen to Napster*.

Listen to what the rise of Napster is saying about peer-to-peer, because as important as Groove or Freenet or OpenCOLA may become, Napster is already a mainstream phenomenon. Napster has had over 40 million client downloads at the time of this writing. Its adoption rate has outstripped NCSA Mosaic, Hotmail, and even ICQ, the pioneer of P2P addressing. Because Napster is what the users are actually spending their time using, the lessons we can take from Napster are still our best guide to the kind of things that are becoming possible with the rise of peer-to-peer architecture.

It's the applications, stupid

The first lesson Napster holds is that it was written to solve a problem—limitations on file copying—and the technological solutions it adopted were derived from the needs of the application, not vice versa.

The fact that the limitations on file copying are legal ones matters little to the technological lessons to be learned from Napster, because technology is often brought to bear to solve nontechnological problems. In this case, the problem Shawn Fanning, Napster's creator, set out to solve was a gap between what was possible with digital songs (endless copying at a vanishingly small cost) and what was legal. The willingness of the major labels to destroy any file copying system they could reach made the classic Web model of central storage of data impractical, meaning Napster had to find a non-Web-like solution.

Decentralization is a tool, not a goal

The primary fault of much of the current thinking about peer-to-peer lies in an "if we build it, they will come" mentality, where interesting technological challenges of decentralizing applications are assumed to be the only criterion that a peer-to-peer system needs to address in order to succeed. The enthusiasm for peer-to-peer has led to a lot of incautious statements about the superiority of peer-to-peer for many, and possibly most, classes of networked applications.

In fact, peer-to-peer is distinctly bad for many classes of networked applications. Most search engines work best when they can search a central database rather than launch a meta-search of peers. Electronic marketplaces need to aggregate supply and demand in a single place at a single time in order to arrive at a single, transparent price. Any system that requires real-time group access or rapid searches through large sets of unique data will benefit from centralization in ways that will be difficult to duplicate in peer-to-peer systems.

The genius of Napster is that it understands and works within these limitations.

Napster mixes centralization and decentralization beautifully. As a search engine, it builds and maintains a master song list, adding and removing songs as individual users connect and disconnect their PCs. And because the search space for Napster—popular music—is well understood by all its users, and because there is massive redundancy in the millions of collections it indexes, the chances that any given popular song can be found are very high, even if the chances that any given user is online are low.

Like ants building an anthill, the contribution of any given individual to the system at any given moment is trivial, but the overlapping work of the group is remarkably powerful. By centralizing pointers and decentralizing content, Napster couples the strengths of a central database with the power of distributed storage. Napster has become the fastest-growing application in the Net's history in large part because it *isn't* pure peer-to-peer. Chapter 4, *The Cornucopia of the Commons*, explores this theme farther.

Where's the content?

Napster's success in pursuing this strategy is difficult to overstate. At any given moment, Napster servers keep track of thousands of PCs holding millions of songs comprising several terabytes of data. This is a complete violation of the Web's data model, "Content at the Center," and Napster's success in violating it could be labeled "Content at the Edges."

The content-at-the-center model has one significant flaw: most Internet content is created on the PCs at the edges, but for it to become universally accessible, it must be pushed to the center, to always-on, always-up web servers. As anyone who has ever spent time trying to upload material to a web site knows, the Web has made downloading trivially easy, but uploading is still needlessly hard. Napster dispenses with uploading and leaves the files on the PCs, merely brokering requests from one PC to another—the MP3 files do not have to travel through any central Napster server. Instead of trying to store these files in a central database, Napster took advantage of the largest pool of latent storage space in the world—the disks of the Napster users. And thus, Napster became the prime example of a new principle for Internet applications: Peer-to-peer services come into being by leveraging the untapped power of the millions of PCs that have been connected to the Internet in the last five years.

PCs are the dark matter of the Internet

Napster's popularity made it the proof-of-concept application for a new networking architecture based on the recognition that bandwidth to the desktop had become fast enough to allow PCs to serve data as well as request it, and that PCs are becoming powerful enough to fulfill this new role. Just as the application service provider (ASP) model is taking off, Napster's success represents the revenge of the PC. By removing the need to upload data (the single biggest bottleneck to the ASP model), Napster points the way to a reinvention of the desktop as the center of a user's data—only this time the user will no longer need physical access to the PC.

The latent capabilities of PC hardware made newly accessible represent a huge, untapped resource and form the fuel powering the current revolution in Internet use. No matter how it gets labeled, the thing that a file-sharing system like Gnutella and a distributed computing network like Data Synapse have in common is an ability to harness this dark matter, the otherwise underused hardware at the edges of the Net.

Promiscuous computers

While some press reports call the current trend the "Return of the PC," it's more than that. In these new models, PCs aren't just tools for personal use—they're promiscuous computers, hosting data the rest of the world has access to, and sometimes even hosting calculations that are of no use to the PC's owner at all, like Popular Power's influenza virus simulations.

Furthermore, the PCs themselves are being disaggregated: Popular Power will take as much CPU time as it can get but needs practically no storage, while Gnutella needs vast amounts of disk space but almost no CPU time. And neither kind of business particularly needs the operating system—since the important connection is often with the network rather than the local user, Intel and Seagate matter more to the peer-to-peer companies than do Microsoft or Apple.

It's too soon to understand how all these new services relate to one another, and the danger of the peer-to-peer label is that it may actually obscure the real engineering changes afoot. With improvements in hardware, connectivity, and sheer numbers still mounting rapidly, anyone who can figure out how to light up the Internet's dark matter gains access to a large and growing pool of computing resources, even if some of the functions are centralized.

It's also too soon to see who the major players will be, but don't place any bets on people or companies that reflexively use the peer-to-peer label. Bet instead on the people figuring out how to leverage the underused PC hardware, because the actual engineering challenges in taking advantage of the underused resources at the edges of the Net matter more—and will create more value—than merely taking on the theoretical challenges of peer-to-peer architecture.

Nothing succeeds like address, or, DNS isn't the only game in town

The early peer-to-peer designers, realizing that interesting services could be run off of PCs if only they had real addresses, simply ignored DNS and replaced the machine-centric model with a protocol-centric one. Protocol-centric addressing creates a parallel namespace for each piece of software. AIM and Napster user-names are mapped to temporary IP addresses not by the Net's DNS servers, but by privately owned servers dedicated to each protocol: the AIM server matches AIM names to the users' current IP addresses, and so on.

In Napster's case, protocol-centric addressing turns Napster into merely a customized FTP for music files. The real action in new addressing schemes lies in software like AIM, where the address points to a person, not a machine. When you log into AIM, the address points to you, no matter what machine you're sitting at, and no matter what IP address is presently assigned to that machine. This completely decouples what humans care about—*Can I find my friends and talk with them online?*—from how the machines go about it—*Route packet A to IP address X.*

This is analogous to the change in telephony brought about by mobile phones. In the same way that a phone number is no longer tied to a particular physical location but is dynamically mapped to the location of the phone's owner, an AIM address is mapped to you, not to a machine, no matter where you are.

An explosion of protocols

This does not mean that DNS is going away, any more than landlines went away with the invention of mobile telephony. It does mean that DNS is no longer the only game in town. The rush is now on, with instant messaging protocols, single sign-on and wallet applications, and the explosion in peer-to-peer businesses, to create and manage protocol-centric addresses that can be instantly updated.

Nor is this change in the direction of easier peer-to-peer addressing entirely to the good. While it is always refreshing to see people innovate their way around a bottleneck, sometimes bottlenecks are valuable. While AIM and Napster came to their addressing schemes honestly, any number of people have noticed how valuable it is to own a namespace, and many business plans making the rounds are just me-too copies of Napster or AIM. Eventually, the already growing list of kinds of addresses—phone, fax, email, URL, AIM, *ad nauseam*—could explode into meaninglessness.

Protocol-centric namespaces will also force the browser into lesser importance, as users return to the days when they managed multiple pieces of Internet software. Or it will mean that addresses like *aim://12345678* or *napster://green_day_fan* will have to be added to the browsers' repertoire of recognized URLs. Expect also the rise of "meta-address" servers, which offer to manage a user's addresses for all of these competing protocols, and even to translate from one kind of address to another. (These meta-address servers will, of course, need their own addresses as well.) Chapter 19, *Interoperability Through Gateways*, looks at some of the issues involved.

It's not clear what is going to happen to Internet addressing, but it is clear that it's going to get a lot more complicated before it gets simpler. Fortunately, both the underlying IP addressing system and the design of URLs can handle this explosion of new protocols and addresses. But that familiar DNS bit in the middle (which *really* put the dot in dot-com) will never recover the central position it has occupied for the last two decades, and that means that a critical piece of Internet infrastructure is now up for grabs.

An economic rather than legal challenge

Much has been made of the use of Napster for what the music industry would like to define as "piracy." Even though the dictionary definition of piracy is quite broad, this is something of a misnomer, because pirates are ordinarily in business to sell what they copy. Not only do Napster users not profit from making copies available, but Napster works precisely because the copies are free. (Its recent business decision to charge a monthly fee for access doesn't translate into profits for the putative "pirates" at the edges.)

What Napster does is more than just evade the law, it also upends the economics of the music industry. By extension, peer-to-peer systems are changing the economics of storing and transmitting intellectual property in general.

The resources Napster is brokering between users have one of two characteristics: they are either *replicable* or *replenishable*.

Replicable resources include the MP3 files themselves. "Taking" an MP3 from another user involves no loss (if I "take" an MP3 from you, it is not removed from your hard drive)—better yet, it actually adds resources to the Napster universe by allowing me to host an alternate copy. Even if I am a freeloader and don't let anyone else copy the MP3 from me, my act of taking an MP3 has still not caused any net loss of MP3s.

Other important resources, such as bandwidth and CPU cycles (as in the case of systems like SETI@home), are not replicable, but they are replenishable. The resources can be neither depleted nor conserved. Bandwidth and CPU cycles expire if they are not used, but they are immediately replenished. Thus they cannot be conserved in the present and saved for the future, but they can't be "used up" in any long-term sense either.

Because of these two economic characteristics, the exploitation of otherwise unused bandwidth to copy MP3s across the network means that additional music can be created at almost zero marginal cost to the user. It employs resources—storage, cycles, bandwidth—that the users have already paid for but are not fully using.

All you can eat

Economists call these kinds of valuable side effects "positive externalities." The canonical example of a positive externality is a shade tree. If you buy a tree large enough to shade your lawn, there is a good chance that for at least part of the day it will shade your neighbor's lawn as well. This free shade for your neighbor is a positive externality, a benefit to her that costs you nothing more than what you were willing to spend to shade your own lawn anyway.

Napster's signal economic genius is to coordinate such effects. Other than the central database of songs and user addresses, every resource within the Napster network is a positive externality. Furthermore, Napster coordinates these externalities in a way that encourages altruism. As long as Napster users are able to find the songs they want, they will continue to participate in the system, even if the people who download songs from them are not the same people they download songs from. And as long as even a small portion of the users accept this bargain, the system will grow, bringing in more users, who bring in more songs.

Thus Napster not only takes advantage of low marginal costs, it couldn't work without them. Imagine how few people would use Napster if it cost them even a penny every time someone else copied a song from them. As with other digital resources that used to be priced per unit but became too cheap to meter, such as connect time or per-email charges, the economic logic of infinitely copyable resources or non-conservable and non-depletable resources eventually leads to "all you can eat" business models.

Thus the shift from analog to digital data, in the form of CDs and then MP3s, is turning the music industry into a smorgasbord. Many companies in the traditional music business are not going quietly, however, but are trying to prevent these "all you can eat" models from spreading. Because they can't keep music entirely off the Internet, they are currently opting for the next best thing, which is trying to force digital data to behave like objects.

Yesterday's technology at tomorrow's prices, two days late

The music industry's set of schemes, called Digital Rights Management (DRM), is an attempt to force music files to behave less like ones and zeros and more like albums and tapes. The main DRM effort is the Secure Digital Music Initiative (SDMI), which aims to create a music file format that cannot be easily copied or transferred between devices—to bring the inconvenience of the physical world to the Internet, in other words.

This in turn has led the industry to make the argument that the music-loving public should be willing to pay the same price for a song whether delivered on CD or downloaded, because it is costing the industry so much money to make the downloaded file as inconvenient as the CD. When faced with the unsurprising hostility this argument engendered, the industry has suggested that matters will go their way once users are sufficiently "educated."

Unfortunately for the music industry, the issue here is not education. In the analog world, it costs money to make a copy of something. In the digital world, it costs money to prevent copies from being made. Napster has demonstrated that systems that work with the economic logic of the Internet rather than against it can have astonishing growth characteristics, and no amount of user education will reverse that.

30 million Britney fans does not a revolution make

Within this economic inevitability, however, lies the industry's salvation, because despite the rants of a few artists and techno-anarchists who believed that Napster users were willing to go to the ramparts for the cause, large-scale civil disobedience against things like Prohibition or the 55 MPH speed limit has usually been about relaxing restrictions, not repealing them.

Despite the fact that it is still possible to make gin in your bathtub, no one does it anymore, because after Prohibition ended high-quality gin became legally available at a price and with restrictions people could live with. Legal and commercial controls did not collapse, but were merely altered.

To take a more recent example, the civil disobedience against the 55 MPH speed limit did not mean that drivers were committed to having no speed limit whatsoever; they simply wanted a higher one.

So it will be with the music industry. The present civil disobedience is against a refusal by the music industry to adapt to Internet economics. But the refusal of users to countenance per-unit prices does not mean they will never pay for music at all, merely that the economic logic of digital data—its replicability and replenishability—must be respected. Once the industry adopts economic models that do, whether through advertising or sponsorship or subscription pricing, the civil disobedience will largely subside, and we will be on the way to a new speed limit.

In other words, the music industry as we know it is not finished. On the contrary, all of their functions other than the direct production of the CDs themselves will become more important in a world where Napster economics prevail. Music labels don't just produce CDs; they find, bankroll, and publicize the musicians themselves. Once they accept that Napster has destroyed the bottleneck of distribution, there will be more music to produce and promote, not less.

Peer-to-peer architecture and second-class status

With this change in addressing schemes and the renewed importance of the PC chassis, peer-to-peer is not merely erasing the distinction between client and server. It's erasing the distinction between consumer and provider as well. You can see the threat to the established order in a recent legal action: a San Diego cable ISP, Cox@Home, ordered several hundred customers to stop running Napster not because they were violating copyright laws, but because Napster leads Cox subscribers to use too much of its cable network bandwidth.

Cox built its service on the current web architecture, where producers serve content from always-connected servers at the Internet's center and consumers consume from intermittently connected client PCs at the edges. Napster, on the other hand, inaugurated a model where PCs are always on and always connected, where content is increasingly stored and served from the edges of the network, and where the distinction between client and server is erased. *Cox v. Napster* isn't just a legal fight; it's a fight between a vision of helpless, passive consumers and a vision where people at the network's edges can both consume and produce.

Users as consumers, users as providers

The question of the day is, "Can Cox (or any media business) force its users to retain their second-class status as mere consumers of information?" To judge by Napster's growth, the answer is "No."

The split between consumers and providers of information has its roots in the Internet's addressing scheme. Cox assumed that the model ushered in by the Web—in which users never have a fixed IP address, so they can consume data stored elsewhere but never provide anything from their own PCs—was a permanent feature of the landscape. This division wasn't part of the Internet's original architecture, and the proposed fix (the next generation of IP, called IPv6) has been coming Real Soon Now for a long time. In the meantime, services like Cox have been built with the expectation that this consumer/provider split would remain in effect for the foreseeable future.

How short the foreseeable future sometimes is. When Napster turned the Domain Name System inside out, it became trivially easy to host content on a home PC, which destroys the asymmetry where end users consume but can't provide. If your computer is online, it can be reached even without a permanent IP address, and any material you decide to host on your PC can become globally accessible. Napster-style architecture erases the people-based distinction between provider and consumer just as surely as it erases the computer-based distinction between server and client.

There could not be worse news for any ISP that wants to limit upstream bandwidth on the expectation that edges of the network host nothing but passive consumers. The limitations of cable ISPs (and Asymmetric Digital Subscriber Line, or ADSL) become apparent only if its users actually want to do something useful with their upstream bandwidth. The technical design of the cable network that hamstrings its upstream speed (upstream speed is less than a tenth of Cox's downstream) just makes the cable networks the canary in the coal mine.

New winners and losers

Any media business that relies on a neat division between information consumer and provider will be affected by roving, peer-to-peer applications. Sites like GeoCities, which made their money providing fixed addresses for end user content, may find that users are perfectly content to use their PCs as that fixed address. Copyright holders who have assumed up until now that only a handful of relatively identifiable and central locations were capable of large-scale serving of material are suddenly going to find that the Net has sprung another million leaks.

Meanwhile, the rise of the end user as information provider will be good news for other businesses. DSL companies (using relatively symmetric technologies) will have a huge advantage in the race to provide fast upstream bandwidth; Apple may find that the ability to stream home movies over the Net from a PC at home drives adoption of Mac hardware and software; and of course companies that provide the Napster-style service of matching dynamic IP addresses with fixed names will have just the sort of sticky relationship with their users that venture capitalists slaver over.

Real technological revolutions are human revolutions as well. The architecture of the Internet has effected the largest transfer of power from organizations to individuals the world has ever seen, and it is only getting started. Napster's destruction of the serving limitations on end users shows how temporary such bottlenecks can be. Power is gradually shifting to the individual for things like stock brokering and buying airline tickets. Media businesses that have assumed such shifts wouldn't affect them are going to be taken by surprise when millions of passive consumers are replaced by millions of one-person media channels.

This is not to say that all content is going to the edges of the Net, or that every user is going to be an enthusiastic media outlet. But enough consumers will become providers as well to blur present distinctions between producer and consumer. This social shift will make the next generation of the Internet, currently being assembled, a place with greater space for individual contributions than people accustomed to the current split between client and server, and therefore provider and consumer, had ever imagined.

chapter three

Remaking the Peer-to-Peer Meme

Tim O'Reilly, O'Reilly & Associates

On September 18, 2000, I organized a so-called "peer-to-peer summit" to explore the bounds of peer-to-peer networking. In my invitation to the attendees, I set out three goals:

1. To make a statement, by their very coming together, about the nature of peer-to-peer and what kinds of technologies people should think of when they hear the term.

2. To make some introductions among people whom I like and respect and who are working on different aspects of what could be seen as the same problem—peer-to-peer solutions to big problems—in order to create some additional connections between technical communities that ought to be talking to and learning from each other.

3. To do some brainstorming about the issues each of us are uncovering, so we can keep projects from reinventing the wheel and foster cooperation to accelerate mutual growth.

In organizing the summit, I was thinking of the free software (open source) summit I held a few years back. Like free software at that time, peer-to-peer currently has image problems and a difficulty developing synergy. The people I was talking to all knew that peer-to-peer is more than just swapping music files, but the wider world was still focusing largely on the threats to copyright. Even people working in the field of peer-to-peer have trouble seeing how far its innovations can extend; it would benefit them to learn how many different types of technologies share the same potential and the same problems.

This is exactly what we did with the open source summit. By bringing together people from a whole lot of projects, we were able to get the world to recognize that free software was more than GNU and Linux; we introduced a lot of people, many of whom, remarkably, had never met; we talked shop; and ultimately, we crafted a new "meme" that completely reshaped the way people thought about the space.

The people I invited to the peer-to-peer summit tell part of the story. Gene Kan from Gnutella (*http://gnutella.wego.com*) and Ian Clarke from Freenet (*http://freenet.sourceforge.net*) were obvious choices. They matched the current industry buzz about peer-to-peer file sharing. Similarly, Marc Hedlund and Nelson Minar from Popular Power (*http://www.popularpower.com*) made sense, because there was already a sense of some kind of connection between distributed computation and file sharing.

But why did I invite Jeremie Miller of Jabber and Ray Ozzie of Groove, Ken Arnold from Sun's Jini project and Michael Tiemann of Red Hat, Marshall Rose (author of BXXP and IMXP), Rael Dornfest of meerkat and RSS 1.0, Dave Stutz of Microsoft, Andy Hertzfeld of Eazel, Don Box (one of the authors of SOAP) and Steve Burbeck (one of the authors of UDDI)? (Note that not all of these people made it to the summit; Ian Clarke sent Scott Miller in his stead, and Ken Arnold and Don Box had to cancel at the last minute.) As I said in my invitation:

> [I've invited] a group of people who collectively bracket what I consider a new paradigm, which could perhaps best be summarized by Sun's slogan, "The Network is the Computer." They're all working on parts of what I consider the next-generation Net story.

This chapter reports on some of the ideas discussed at the summit. It continues the job of trying to reshape the way people think about that "next-generation Net story" and the role of peer-to-peer in telling that story. It also shows one of the tools I used at the meeting—something I'll call a "meme map"—and presents the results of the meeting in that form.

The concepts we bear in our minds are, at bottom, maps of reality. Bad maps lead to bad decisions. If we believe peer-to-peer is about illegal sharing of copyrighted material, we'll continue to see rhetoric about copyright and censorship at the heart of the debate, and may push for ill-advised legal restrictions on the use of the technology. If we believe it's about a wider class of decentralized networking applications, we'll focus instead on understanding what those applications are good for and on advancing the state of the art.

The meme map we developed at the peer-to-peer summit has two main benefits. First, the peer-to-peer community can use it to organize itself—to understand who is doing related work and identify areas where developers can learn from each other. Second, the meme map helps the community influence outsiders. It can create excitement where there previously was indifference and turn negative impressions into positive ones. Tangentially, the map is also useful in understanding the thinking behind the O'Reilly Network's P2P directory, a recent version of which is republished in this book as an appendix.

First, though, a bit of background.

From business models to meme maps

Recently, I started working with Dan and Meredith Beam of Beam, Inc., a strategy consulting firm. Dan and Meredith help companies build their "business models"—one page pictures that describe "how all the elements of a business work together to build marketplace advantage and company value." It's easy to conclude that two companies selling similar products and services are in the same business, but the Beams think otherwise.

For example, O'Reilly and IDG compete in the computer book publishing business, but we have completely different business models. Their strategic positioning is to appeal to the "dummy" who needs to learn about computers but doesn't really want to. Ours is to appeal to the people who love computers and want to go as deep as possible. Their marketing strategy is to build a widely recognized consumer brand, and then dominate retail outlets and "big box" stores in hopes of putting product in front of consumers who might happen to walk by in search of any book on a given subject. Our marketing strategy is to build awareness of our brand and products in the core developer and user communities, who then buy directly or drive traffic to retail outlets. The former strategy pushes product into distribution channels in an aggressive bid to reach unknown consumers; the latter pulls products into distribution channels as they are requested by consumers who are already looking for the product. Both companies are extremely successful, but our different business models require different competencies. I won't say more lest this chapter turn into a lesson for O'Reilly competitors, but hopefully I have said enough to get the idea across.

Boiling all the elements of your business down into a one-page picture is a really useful exercise. But what is even more useful is that Dan and Meredith have you run the exercise twice, once to describe your present business, and once to describe it as you want it to be.

At any rate, fresh from the strategic planning process at O'Reilly, it struck me that an adaptation of this idea would be useful preparation for the summit. We weren't modeling a single business but a technology space—the key projects, concepts, and messages associated with it.

I call these pictures "meme maps" rather than "business models" in honor of Richard Dawkins' wonderful contribution to cultural studies. He formulated the idea of "memes" as ideas that spread and reproduce themselves, passed on from mind to mind. Just as gene engineering allows us to artificially shape genes, meme engineering lets us organize and shape ideas so that they can be transmitted more effectively, and have the desired effect once they are transmitted. That's what I hoped to touch off at the summit, using a single picture that shows how a set of technologies fit together and demonstrates a few central themes.

A success story: From free software to open source

In order to illustrate the idea of a meme map to the attendees at the peer-to-peer summit, I drew some maps of free software versus open source. I presented these images at the summit as a way of kickstarting the discussion. Let's look at those here as well, since it's a lot easier to demonstrate the concept than it is to explain it in the abstract.

I built the free software map in Figure 3-1 by picking out key messages from the Free Software Foundation (FSF) web site, *http://www.fsf.org*. I also added a few things (the darker ovals in the lower right quadrant of the picture) to show common misconceptions that were typically applied to free software. This figure, and the others in this chapter are slightly edited versions of slides used at the summit.

Please note that this diagram should not be taken as a complete representation of the beliefs of the Free Software Foundation. I simply summarized my interpretation of the attitudes and positioning I found on their web site. No one from the Free Software Foundation has reviewed this figure, and they might well highlight very different points if given the chance to do so.

There are a couple of things to note about the diagram. The ovals at the top represent the outward face of the movement—the projects or activities that the movement considers *canonical* in defining itself. In the case of the Free Software Foundation, these are programs like *gcc* (the GNU C Compiler), GNU Emacs, GhostScript (a free PostScript display tool), and the GNU General Public License, or GPL.

The box in the center lists the strategic positioning, the key perceived user benefit, and the core competencies. The strategic goal I chose came right up front on the Free Software Foundation web site: to build a complete free replacement for the Unix operating system. The user benefit is sold as one of standing up for what's right, even if there would be practical benefits in compromising. The web site shows little sense of what the core competencies of the free software movement might be, other than that they have right on their side, along with the goodwill of talented programmers.

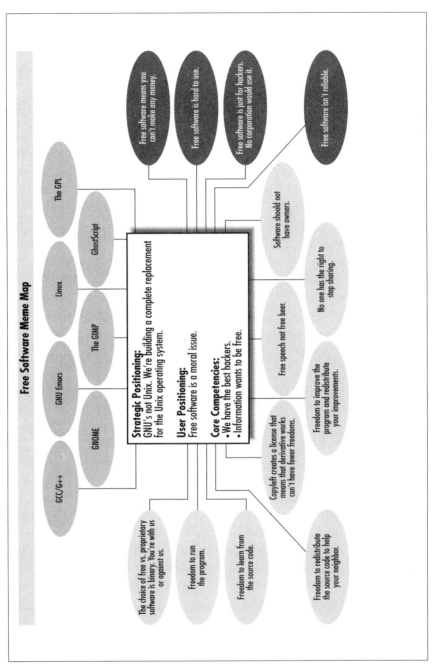

Figure 3-1. Map of the old free software meme

In the Beam models, the ovals at the bottom of the picture represent internal activities of the business; for my purposes, I used them to represent guiding principles and key messages. I used dark ovals to represent undesirable messages that others might be creating and applying to the subject of the meme map.

As you can see, the primary messages of the free software movement, thought-provoking and well articulated as they are, don't address the negative public perceptions that are spread by opponents of the movement.

Now take a look at the diagram I drew for open source—the alternative term for free software that was invented shortly before we held our open source summit in April 1998. The content of this diagram, shown in Figure 3-2, was taken partly from the Open Source Initiative web site *http://www.opensource.org*, but also from the discussions at the summit and from my own thinking and speaking about open source in the years since. Take the time to read the diagram carefully; it should be fairly self-explanatory, but I'll offer some insights into a few subtleties. The figure demonstrates what a well-formed strategic meme map ought to look like.

As you can see by comparing the two diagrams, they put a completely different spin on what formerly might have been considered the same space. We did more than just change the name that we used to describe a collection of projects from "free software" to "open source." In addition:

- We changed the canonical list of projects that we wanted to hold up as exemplars of the movement. (Even though BIND and sendmail and Apache and Perl are "free software" by the Free Software Foundation's definition, they aren't central to its free software "meme map" in the way that we made them for open source; even today, they are not touted on the Free Software Foundation web site.) What's more, I've included a tag line that explains why each project is significant. For example, BIND isn't just another free software program; it's the heart of the Domain Name System and the single most mission-critical program on the Internet. Apache is the dominant web server on the market, sendmail routes most Internet email and Linux is more reliable than Windows. The Free Software Foundation's GNU tools are still in the picture, but they are no longer at its heart.

- The strategic positioning is much clearer. Open source is not about creating a free replacement for Unix. It's about making better software through sharing source code and using the Internet for collaboration. The user positioning (the benefit to the user) was best articulated by Bob Young of Red Hat, who insisted that what Red Hat Linux offers to its customers is control over their own destiny.

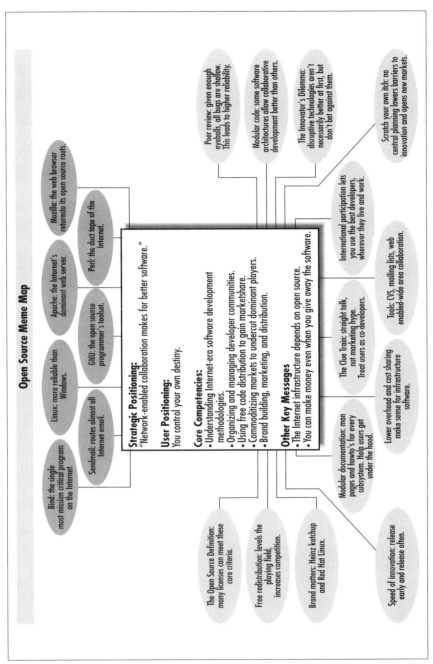

Figure 3-2. Map of the new open source meme

- The list of core competencies is much more focused and actionable. The most successful open source communities do in fact understand something about distributed software development in the age of the Internet, organizing developer communities, using free distribution to gain market share, commoditizing markets to undercut dominant players, and creating powerful brands for their software. Any aspiring open source player needs to be good at all of these things.

- We've replaced the negative messages used against free software with directly competing messages that counter them. For instance, where free software was mischaracterized as unreliable, we set out very explicitly to demonstrate that everyone counts on open source programs, and that the peer review process actually improves reliability and support.

- We've identified a set of guiding principles that can be used by open source projects and companies to see if they're hitting all the key points, or that can be used to explain why some projects have failed to gain as much traction as expected. For example, Mozilla's initial lack of modular code, weak documentation, and long release cycles hampered its quick uptake as an open source project. (That being said, key portions of Mozilla code are finally starting to appear in a variety of other open source projects, such as ActiveState's Komodo development environment and Eazel's Nautilus file manager.)

- We made connections between open source and related concepts that help to place it in context. For example, the concept from *The ClueTrain Manifesto* of open interaction with customers, and the idea of "disruptive technologies" from Clayton Christenson's book *The Innovator's Dilemma*, link open source to trends in business management.

While some further discussion of the open source meme map might be worthwhile in another context, I present it here mainly to clarify the use of meme maps to create a single unifying vision of a set of related technologies.

The current peer-to-peer meme map

The meme map for peer-to-peer is still very unformed, and consists largely of ideas applied by the media and other outsiders.

Figure 3-3 is the slide I showed to the group at the summit. Things have evolved somewhat since that time, partly as a result of efforts such as ours to correct common misconceptions, but this picture still represents the view being bandied about by industries that feel threatened by peer-to-peer technologies.

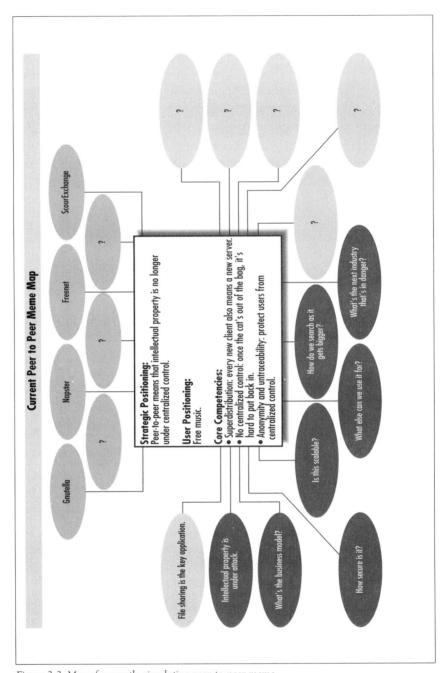

Current Peer to Peer Meme Map

Strategic Positioning:
Peer-to-peer means that intellectual property is no longer under centralized control.

User Positioning:
Free music.

Core Competencies:
- Superdistribution: every new client also means a new server.
- No centralized control: once the cat's out of the bag, it's hard to put back in.
- Anonymity and untraceability: protect users from centralized control.

Gnutella

Napster

Freenet

ScourExchange

?

?

?

?

?

?

?

?

File sharing is the key application.

Intellectual property is under attack.

What's the business model?

How secure is it?

Is this scalable?

How do we search as it gets bigger?

What else can we use it for?

What's the next industry that's in danger?

Figure 3-3. Map of currently circulating peer-to-peer meme

Not a pretty picture. The canonical projects all feed the idea that peer-to-peer is about the subversion of intellectual property. The chief benefit presented to users is that of free music (or other copyrighted material). The core competencies of peer-to-peer projects are assumed to be superdistribution, the lack of any central control point, and anonymity as a tool to protect the system from attempts at control.

Clearly, these are characteristics of the systems that put the peer-to-peer buzzword onto everyone's radar. But are they really the key points? Will they help peer-to-peer developers work together, identify problems, develop new technologies, and win the public over to those technologies?

A map is useful only to the extent that it reflects underlying reality. A bad map gets you lost; a good one helps you find your way through unfamiliar territory. Therefore, one major goal for the summit was to develop a better map for the uncharted peer-to-peer space.

The new peer-to-peer meme map

In a space as vaguely defined as peer-to-peer, we need to consider many angles at once in order to come up with an accurate picture of what the technology is and what is possible. Our summit looked at many projects from different sources, often apparently unrelated. We spent a few hours brainstorming about important applications of peer-to-peer technology, key principles, and so on. I've tried to capture the results of that brainstorming session in the same form that I used to spark the discussion, as the meme map in Figure 3-4. Note that this is what I took away personally from the meeting. The actual map below wasn't fully developed or approved there.

A quick walkthrough of the various projects and how they fit together leads us to a new understanding of the strategic positioning and core competencies for peer-to-peer projects. In the course of this walkthrough, I'll also talk about some of the guiding principles that we can derive from studying each project, which are captured in the ovals at the top of the diagram. This discussion is necessarily quite superficial, but suggests directions for further study.

File sharing: Napster and successors

One of the most obvious things about the map I've drawn of the peer-to-peer space is that file-sharing applications such as Napster, Gnutella, and Freenet are only a small part of the picture, even though they have received the lion's share of the attention to date. Nonetheless, Napster (*http://www.napster.com*), as the application whose rapid uptake and enormous impact on the music industry sparked the furor over peer-to-peer, deserves some significant discussion.

copies of the same song, and that they aren't all the same?" Her answer—that neither of these things bothered her in the slightest—seemed to him to illustrate the gulf between the traditional computer scientist's concern for reliability and orthogonality and the user's indifference for these issues.

Another important lesson from Napster is that free riders, "super peers" providing more or better resources, and other variations in peer participation will ultimately decrease the system's decentralization. Experience is already showing that a hierarchy is starting to emerge. Some users turn off file sharing. Even among those who don't, some have more files, and some have better bandwidth. As in Orwell's *Animal Farm*, all animals are equal, but some are more equal than others. While this idea is anathema to those wedded to the theory of radical decentralization, in practice, it is this very feature that gives rise to many of the business opportunities in the peer-to-peer space. It should give great relief to those who fear that peer-to-peer will lead to the leveling of all hierarchy and the end of industries that depend on it. The most effective way for the music industry to fight what they fear from Napster is to join the trend, and provide sites that become the best source for high-quality music downloads.

Even on Gnutella, the concept of super peers is starting to emerge. The service DSS (Distributed Search Solutions) from Clip2.com, Inc. (*http://dss.clip2.com*) has developed a program that they call a Gnutella "Reflector." This is a proxy and index server designed to make Gnutella more scalable. According to Kelly Truelove of Clip2, "Multiple users connect to such a Reflector as they might connect to a Napster central server, yet, unlike such a central server, the Reflector itself can function as a peer, making outgoing connections to other peers on the network."

Mixing centralization and decentralization: Usenet, email, and IP routing

Not coincidentally, this evolution from a pure peer-to-peer network to one in which peer-to-peer and centralized architectures overlap echoes the evolution of Usenet. This history also shows that peer-to-peer and client/server (which can also be called decentralization and centralization) are not mutually exclusive.

Usenet was originally carried over the informal, peer-to-peer, dial-up network known as UUCPnet. Sites agreed to phone each other, and passed mail and news from site to site in a store-and-forward network. Over time, though, it became clear that some sites were better connected than others; they came to form a kind of de facto "Usenet backbone." One of the chief sites, seismo, a computer at the U.S. Geological Society, was run by Rick Adams. By 1987, the load on seismo had become so great that Rick formed a separate company, called UUnet (*http://www.uu.net*), to provide connectivity services for a monthly fee.

As the UUCPnet was replaced by the newly commercialized Internet, UUnet added TCP/IP services and became the first commercial Internet service provider. ISPs create a layer of hierarchy and centralization even though the IP routing infrastructure of the Internet is still peer-to-peer. Internet routers act as peers in finding the best route from one point on the Net to another, but users don't find each other directly any more. They get their Internet connectivity from ISPs, who in turn connect to each other in asymmetric hierarchies that are hidden from the end user. Yet beneath the surface, each of those ISPs still depends on the same peer-to-peer architecture.

Similarly, email is routed by a network of peered mail servers, and while it appears peer-to-peer from the user point of view, those users are in fact aggregated into clusters by the servers that route their mail and the organizations that operate those servers.

Centralization and decentralization are never so clearly separable as anyone fixated on buzzwords might like.

Maximizing use of far-flung resources: Distributed computation

Some of the earliest projects that excited the public about the potential for coordinating peers were distributed computation programs like SETI@home. This project is described by one of its founders in Chapter 5. Served from the Space Sciences Lab at U.C. Berkeley, SETI@home runs as a screensaver that uses the "spare cycles" from more than 1 million PCs to process radio telescope data in search of signs of extraterrestrial intelligence.

Viewed from one angle, distributed computation programs are not at all peer-to-peer. After all, they use an old-style, asymmetric, client/server architecture, in which the million independent computational clients download their data sets and upload their computed results to the central repository at the Space Sciences Lab. The clients don't peer with each other in any way.

But look a little deeper, and something else emerges: the clients are active participants, not just passive "browsers." What's more, the project uses the massive redundancy of computing resources to work around problems such as reliability and network availability of any one resource.

But even more importantly, look further down the development timeline when startups such as United Devices, Popular Power, Parabon, and others have their services in the market. At that point, the "ecology" of distributed computation is going to be much more complex. There will be thousands (and ultimately, perhaps millions) of compute-intensive tasks looking for spare cycles. At what point does it make sense to design a specialized architecture that facilitates a two-way flow of tasks and compute cycles?

Further, many of the key principles of Napster are also at play in distributed computation. Both Napster and SETI@home need to create and manage metadata about a large community of distributed participants. Both need to make it incredibly simple to participate.

Finally, both Napster and SETI@Home have tried to exploit what Clay Shirky (who contributed Chapter 2, *Listening to Napster*, to this book) memorably called "the dark matter of the Internet"—the hundreds of millions of interconnected PCs that have hitherto been largely passive participants in the network.

Already, startups like Mojo Nation (*http://www.mojonation.net*) are making a link between file sharing and distributed computation. In the end, both distributed file sharing and distributed computation are aspects of a new world where individual computer systems take on their most important role as part of a network—where the whole is much greater than the sum of its parts.

Immediate information sharing: The new instant messaging services

Napster could be characterized as a "brokered peer-to-peer system," in which a central addressing authority connects end points, and then gets out of the way.

Once you realize this, it becomes clear just how similar the Napster model is to instant messaging. In each case, a central authority manages an addressing system and a namespace that allows the unique identification of each user. These are employed by the system to connect end users. In some ways, Napster can be thought of as an instant messaging system in which the question isn't, "Are you online and do you want to chat?" but, "Are you online and do you have this song?"

Not surprisingly, a project like AIMster (*http://www.aimster.com*) makes explicit use of this insight to build a file-sharing network that uses the AOL Instant Messenger (AIM) protocol. This brings IM features such as buddy lists into the file-sharing arena.

The Jabber instant messaging platform (*http://www.jabbercentral.com*) takes things even further. An open source project, Jabber started out as a switching system between incompatible instant messaging protocols; it is evolving into a general XML routing system and a basis for applications that allow users and their computers to ask each other even more interesting questions.

Ray Ozzie's Groove Networks (*http://www.groove.net*) is an even more mature expression of the same insight. It provides a kind of groupware dial tone or "LAN on demand" for ad hoc groups of peers. Like Jabber, it provides an XML routing infrastructure that allows for the formation of ad hoc peer groups. These can share not only files and chat, but a wide variety of applications. Replication, security, and so on are taken care of automatically by the underlying Groove system.

If systems like AIMster, Jabber, and Groove deliver what they promise, we can see peer-to-peer as a solution to the IT bottleneck, allowing users to interact more directly with each other in networks that can span organizational boundaries. Beyond the potential efficiency of such networks, peer-to-peer systems can help people share ideas and viewpoints more easily, ultimately helping the formation of online communities.

The writable Web

The Web started out as a participatory groupware system. It was originally designed by Tim Berners-Lee as a way for high-energy physicists to share their research data and conclusions. Only later was it recast into a publishing medium, in which sites seek to produce content that attracts millions of passive consumers.

To this day, there is a strong peer-to-peer element at the very heart of the Web's architecture: the hyperlink. A web hyperlink can point to any other site on the network, without any central intervention, and without the permission of the site being pointed to. What's more, hyperlinks can point to a variety of resources, not just web pages. Part of the Web's explosive growth, as compared to other early Internet information services, was that the web browser became a kind of universal client that was able to link to any kind of Internet resource. Initially, these resources were competing services such as FTP, Gopher, and WAIS. But eventually, through CGI, the Web became an interface to virtually any information resource that anyone wanted to make available. Mailto and news links even provide gateways to mail and Usenet.

There's still a fundamental flaw in the Web as it has been deployed, though. Tim Berners-Lee created both a web server and a web browser, but he didn't join them at the hip the way Napster did. And as the Buddhist Dhammapadda says, "If the gap between heaven and earth is as wide as a barleycorn, it is as wide as all heaven and earth." Before long, the asymmetry between clients and servers had grown wide enough to drive a truck through.

Browsers were made freely available to anyone who wanted to download one, but servers were seen as a high-priced revenue opportunity, and were far less widely deployed. There were free Unix servers available (including the NCSA server, which eventually morphed into Apache), but by 1995, 95% of Web users were on Windows, and there was no web server at all available to them! In 1995, in an attempt to turn the tide, O'Reilly introduced Website. The first web server for Windows, it tried to push the market forward with the slogan "Everyone who has a web browser ought to have a web server." But by then, the market was fixated on the idea of the web server as a centralized publishing tool. Microsoft eventually offered PWS, or Personal Web Server, bundled with Windows, but it was clearly a low-powered, second-class offering.

Perhaps even more importantly, as several authors in this book point out, the rise of dynamic IP addressing made it increasingly difficult for individuals to publish to the Web from their desktops. As a result, the original "Two-Way Web" became something closer to television, a medium in which most of the participants are consumers, and only a relatively small number are producers.

Web site hosting services and participatory sites like GeoCities made it somewhat easier to participate, but these services were outside the mainstream of web development, with a consumer positioning and nonstandard tools.

Recently, there's been a new emphasis on the "writable Web," with projects like Dave Winer's EditThisPage.Com (*http://www.editthispage.com*), Dan Bricklin's Trellix (*http://www.trellix.com*), and Pyra's Blogger (*http://www.blogger.com*) making it easy for anyone to host their own site and discussion area. Wiki (*http://c2.com/cgi/wiki?WikiWikiWeb*) is an even more extreme innovation, creating web sites that are writable by anyone in an area set aside for public comment on a given topic. Wiki has actually been around for about six or seven years, but has suddenly started to catch on.

The writable Web is only one way that the Web is recapturing its peer-to-peer roots. Content syndication with Rich Site Summary (RSS), which I'll describe in the following section, and web services built with protocols like XML-RPC and SOAP allow sites to reference each other more fully than is possible with a hyperlink alone.

Web services and content syndication

I asked above, "At what point does it make sense to have an architecture that allows a two-way flow of tasks and compute cycles?" That's actually a pretty good description of SOAP and other web services architectures.

The contribution of SOAP is to formalize something that sophisticated programmers have been doing for years. It's been relatively easy, using Perl and a library like libwww-perl, to build interfaces to web sites that do "screen scraping" and then reformulate and reuse the data in ways that the original web developers didn't intend. Jon Udell (co-author of Chapter 18, *Security*) demonstrated that one could even take data from one web site and pass it to another for further processing, in a web equivalent to the Unix pipeline.

SOAP makes this process more explicit, turning web sites into peers that can provide more complex services than simple CGI forms to their users. The next generation of web applications won't consist of single-point conversations between a single server and a single browser, but a multipoint conversation between cooperating programs.

One of the key issues that comes up, once you start thinking about more complex interactions between sites on the Net, is that metadata management is critical. In order for web clients and servers to use others as resources, they need a standard way to *discover* each other, the way Java-enabled devices discover each other through Jini. An initiative called Universal Description, Discovery, and Integration, or UDDI (*http://www.uddi.org*) represents a first step in this direction.

Similarly, content syndication formats like RSS allow web sites to cooperate in delivering content. By publishing RSS feeds, sites enable other sites to automatically pick up data about their stories. For instance, the O'Reilly Network home page is updated automatically out of a set of RSS news feeds from a web of cooperating sites.

Right now, RSS provides only the simplest of metadata about web pages, useful for simple syndication applications like creating news digest pages. But the RSS 1.0 proposal (*http://www.xml.com/pub/r/810*) will allow for more complex applications based on distributed data.

Peer-to-peer and devices

We've all heard popular descriptions of technologies such as BlueTooth and Jini. I walk into a room with my wireless laptop, and it queries other devices: "Hey, are there any printers here that can print a PostScript file?"

If this isn't peer-to-peer, what is? As we have billions of computing devices, some fixed, some mobile, some embedded in a variety of appliances (even in our clothing), we'll need technologies that allow the formation of ad hoc peer groups between devices.

As you look at these technologies, you see a great deal of overlap between the kinds of problems that need to be solved for peer-to-peer devices and for peer-to-peer network applications ranging from web services to file sharing. Key technologies include resource discovery, reliability through redundancy, synchronization, and replication.

Strategic positioning and core competencies

The whirlwind tour of canonical projects we've just been through weaves a story about peer-to-peer that's very different from the one we started with. Not only is peer-to-peer fundamental to the architecture of the existing Internet, but it is showing us important directions in the future evolution of the Net. In some ways, you can argue that the Net is reaching a kind of critical mass, in which the network itself is the platform, more important than the operating system running on the individual nodes.

Sun first articulated this vision many years ago with the slogan "The Network is the Computer," but that slogan is only now coming true. And if the network is the computer, the projects under the peer-to-peer umbrella are collectively involved in defining the operating system for that emergent global computer.

That positioning guides technology developers. But there is a story for users too: you and your computer are more powerful than you think. In the peer-to-peer vision of the global network, a PC and its users aren't just passive consumers of data created at other central sites.

Since the most promising peer-to-peer applications of the near future are only beginning to be developed, it's crucial to provide a vision of the core competencies that peer-to-peer projects will need to bring to the table.

High on the list is metadata management, which is the subject of Chapter 13, *Metadata*. Whether you're dealing with networked devices, file sharing, distributed computation, or web services, users need to find each other and what they offer. While we don't have a clear winner in the resource discovery area, XML has emerged as an important component in the puzzle.

What do we mean by metadata? In the case of Napster, metadata means the combination of artist and song names that users search for. It also includes additional data managed by the central Napster server, such as the names and Internet addresses of users, the size of the music files, and the reported amount of bandwidth of the user's Internet link. (You can think of this information as the Napster "namespace," a privately-managed metadata directory that gives Napster the ability to link users and their files with each other.)

In considering Napster, it's worth noting that it chose an easy information domain because the "namespace" of popular music is simple and well-known. The Napster model breaks down in cases where more complex metadata is required to find a given piece of data. For example, in the case of classical music, an artist/song combination is often insufficient, since the same piece may be performed by various combinations of artists.

A related observation, which Darren New of Invisible Worlds (*http:// www.invisible.net*) made at the summit, is that Napster depends on the music industry itself to "market its namespace." Without preexisting knowledge of song titles and artists, there is nothing for the Napster user to search for. This will lead to additional centralization layers as unknown artists try to provide additional information to help users find their work. This is much the same thing that happened on the Web, as a class of portals such as Yahoo! grew up to categorize and market information about the peer-to-peer world of hyperlinked web pages.

It's easy to see, then, how understanding and managing namespaces and other forms of metadata becomes central to peer-to-peer applications. What's more, it is also the key to many peer-to-peer business models. Controlling namespaces and resource discovery has turned out to be one of the key battlegrounds of the Web. From Network Solutions (which largely controls DNS registration) to Yahoo! and search engines, identifying and capitalizing on the ways that central-ization impacts even radically decentralized systems has turned out to be one key to financial success.

Instant messaging turns out to tell a similar story. The namespace of an instant messaging system, and the mapping of identity onto user addresses, is the key to those systems. You have only to witness the efforts of AOL to keep other instant messaging vendors from reaching its customers to understand just how impor-tant this is.

Note, however, that in the end, an open namespace with multiple providers will create a more powerful network than a closed one, just as the open Web trumped closed information services like AOL and MSN. AOL now succeeds for its customers as a "first among equals" rather than as a completely closed system.

In the case of a distributed computation application, metadata might mean some identifier that allows the distributed data elements to be reassembled, and the address of the user who is working on a particular segment. SETI@home tracks user identity as a way of providing a game-like environment in which users and companies compete to contribute the most cycles. Startups aiming to compensate users for their spare compute cycles will need to track how much is contributed.

Depending on the type of problem to be computed, they might want to know more about the resources being offered, such as the speed of the computer, the amount of available memory, and the bandwidth of the connection. Some of the technical means used to track and reward users are explored in Chapter 16, *Accountability*.

We can see, then, that some of the key battlegrounds for peer-to-peer as a business proposition will be the standards for metadata, the protocols for describing and discovering network-based resources and services, and ownership of the namespaces that are used to identify those resources.

Returning to Napster, though, it's also clear that the core competencies required of successful peer-to-peer projects will include seamless communication and connectivity, facilities that support self-organizing systems, and the management of trust and expectations.

Ultimately, peer-to-peer is about overcoming the barriers to the formation of ad hoc communities, whether of people, of programs, of devices, or of distributed resources. It's about decoupling people, data, and services from specific machines, using redundancy to replace reliability of connections as the key to consistency. If we get it right, peer-to-peer can help to break the IT bottleneck that comes with centralized services. Decentralization and user empowerment enable greater productivity. Edge services allow more effective use of Internet resources.

We're just at the beginning of a process of discovery. To get this right, we'll need a lot of experimentation. But if we can learn lessons from Internet history, we also need to remember to focus on the *interoperability* of many systems, rather than treating this as a winner-takes-all game in which a single vendor can establish the standard for the network platform.

The peer-to-peer landscape is changing daily. New companies, applications, and projects appear faster than they can be catalogued. Especially with all the hype around peer-to-peer, the connections between these projects can be fairly tenuous. Is it marketing buzz or substance, when everyone tries to join the parade?

While there's a danger in casting the net too widely, there's also a danger in limiting it. I believe that the story I've told here gives us a good starting point in understanding an emergent phenomenon: the kind of computing that results when networking is pervasive, resources are abundant (and redundant), and the barriers are low to equal participation by any individual network node.

chapter four

The Cornucopia of the Commons

Dan Bricklin, Cocreator of Visicalc

Let's get to the bottom of the Napster phenomenon—why is this music trading service so popular? One could say, trivially, that Napster is successful because you can find what you want (a particular song) and get it easily. It's also pretty obvious that songs are easy to find because so many of them are available through Napster. If Napster let me get only a few popular songs, once I downloaded those I'd lose interest fast.

But what's the root cause? Why are so many songs available? Hint: *It has nothing to do with peer-to-peer*. Peer-to-peer is plumbing, and most people don't care about plumbing. While the "look into other people's computers and copy directly" method has some psychological benefit to people who understand what's going on (as indicated by thinkers such as Tom Matrullo and Dave Winer), I think the peer-to-peer aspects actually get in the way of Napster.

Let's be blunt: Napster would operate much better if, when you logged in, it uploaded all the songs from your disk that weren't already in the Napster database. If the songs were copied to a master server, rather than just the names of the songs and who was currently logged in, the same songs would be available for download provided by the same people, but at all times (not just when the "owner" happened to be connected to the Internet), and probably through more reliable and higher-speed connections to the Internet. (Akamai provides the kind of redundancy and efficiency that Napster currently relies on its worldwide network of users to provide.) Napster could at least maintain the list of who has what songs better than they do now.

Napster doesn't work this way partly because peer-to-peer may be more legal (or so they argue) and harder to litigate against. But other applications may not have

Napster's legal problems and would therefore benefit from more centralized servers. While I'm a strong proponent for peer-to-peer for some things, I don't think architecture is the main issue driving new services.

The issue is whether you get what you want from the application: "Is the data I want in the database?" What's interesting about Napster is where its data ultimately comes from—the users—not when or how it's transferred. So in this chapter, I'm going to examine how a service can fill a database with lots of whatever people want.

Ways to fill shared databases

There are three common ways to fill a shared database: *organized manual, organized mechanical*, and *volunteer manual*.

The classic case of an organized manual database is the original Yahoo! directory. This database was filled by organizing an army of people to put in data manually. Another example is the old legal databases where armies of typists were paid to retype printed material into computers.

The original AltaVista is an example of an organized mechanical database. A program running on powerful computers followed links and domain names and spidered the Web, saving the information as it went. Many databases on the Web today are mechanically created by getting access to somebody else's data, sometimes for a fee. Examples include databases of street maps and the status of airline flights. Some of those databases are by-products of automated processes.

Finally, Usenet newsgroups and threaded discussions like Slashdot are examples of volunteer databases, where interested individuals provide the data because they feel passionate enough about doing so. Amazon.com's well-known reviews are created through a mixture of organized manual and volunteer manual techniques: the company recruits some reviews and readers spontaneously put up others.

CDDB: A case study in how to get a manually created database

The most interesting databases (for the purposes of this chapter) are the ones that involve manual creation. When we look closely at some of them, we find some very clever techniques for getting data that are very specific to the subjects they cover and the users they serve. Let's focus on one service that employs a very unusual technique to aggregate its data: the CDDB service offered by Gracenote to organize information about music CDs (*http://www.cddb.com*).

The CDDB database has information that allows your computer to identify a particular music CD in the CD drive and list its album title and track titles. Their service is used by RealJukebox, MusicMatch, Winamp, and others. What's interesting is how they accumulate this information that so many users rely on without even thinking about it.

Most CDs do not store title information. The only information on the CD, aside from the audio tracks themselves, is the number of tracks (songs) and the length of each one. This is the information your CD player displays. What CDDB does is let the software on your PC take that track information, send a CD signature to CDDB through Internet protocols (if you're connected), and get back the titles.

CDDB works because songs are of relatively random length. The chances are good almost all albums are unique. To understand this point, figure there are about 10 songs on an album, and that they each run from about a minute and a half to about three and a half minutes in length. The times for each song therefore vary by 100 seconds. There are $100 \times 100 \times ... \times 100 = 100^{10} = 10^{11} = 100$ billion = an awful lot of possible combinations. So an album is identified by a signature that is a special arithmetic combination of the times of all the tracks.

You'd figure that CDDB just bought a standard database with all the times and titles. Well, there wasn't one. What they did was accept postings over the Internet that contained track timing information and titles typed in by volunteers. Software for playing music CDs on personal computers was developed that let people type in that information if CDDB didn't have it. As people noticed that their albums failed to come up with titles when they played them on their PCs, many cared enough to type in the information. They benefited personally from typing the information because they could then more easily make their own playlists, but in the process they happened also to update the shared database. The database could be built even if only one person was willing to do this for each album (even an obscure album).

If you loved your CD collection, you'd want all the albums represented—or at least some people did. Some people are the type who like to be organized and label everything. Not everybody needed to be this type, just enough people to fill the database. Also, the CDDB site needed this volunteer (user) labor only until the database got big enough that it was valuable enough for other companies to pay for access.

CDDB is not run on a peer-to-peer architecture. Their database is on dedicated servers that they control. Their web site says:

> CDDB is now a totally secure and reliable service which is provided to users worldwide via a network of high availability, mirrored servers which each have multiple, high bandwidth connections to the Internet... boasting a database of nearly 620,000 album titles and over 7.5 million tracks.

So CDDB succeeded not through peer-to-peer networking—it succeeded by harnessing the energy of its users.

Napster: Harnessing the power of personal selfishness

Napster is a manually created database built on work by volunteers. It gets bigger when one of its users buys (or borrows) a copy of a CD, converts it to MP3, and stores it in his or her shared music directory. It can also be enlarged when somebody creates an MP3 of their own performance that they want to share. But Napster cleverly provides a short-circuit around the process of manually creating data: In both cases, *storing the copy in the shared music directory can be a natural by-product of the user's normal work with the songs.* It can be done as part of downloading songs to a portable music player or burning a personal mix CD. Whenever the users are connected to the Internet and to the Napster server, songs in the shared directory are then available to the world.

Of course, the user may not be connected to the Napster server all the time, so the song is not fully available to all who want it (a perennial problem with peer-to-peer systems). However, Napster overcomes this problem too, by exploiting the everyday activities of its users. Whenever someone downloads a song using Napster and leaves the file in his or her shared music directory, that person is increasing the number of Napster users who have that song, increasing the chances you will find someone with the song logged in to Napster when you want your copy. So again, the value of the database increases through normal use. (The same kind of replication is achieved in a more formal way by Freenet through its unique protocol, but Napster gets the same effect more simply—its protocol is just the decision of a user to do a download.)

The genius of Napster is that increasing the value of the database by adding more information is a natural by-product of each person using the tool for his or her own benefit. No altruistic sharing motives need be present, especially since sharing is the default. It isn't even like the old song about "leaving a cup with water by the pump to let the next person have something to prime it with." (I'll have to use Napster to find that song....) In other words, nobody has to think of being nice to the next guy or put in even a tiny bit of extra effort.

As Internet analyst Kevin Werbach wrote in Release 1.0, a monthly report on technology trends:

> What made Napster a threat to the record labels was its remarkable growth. That growth resulted from two things: Napster's user experience and its focus on music... What makes Napster different is that it's drop-dead simple to use. Its interface isn't pretty, but it achieves that magic resonance with user expectations that marks the most revolutionary software developments.

I would add that, in using that simple, desirable user interface, you also are *adding to the value of the database without doing any extra work*. I'd like to suggest that one can predict the success of a particular system for building a shared database by how much the database is aided through normal, selfish use.

The commons

We've heard plenty about the tragedy of the commons—in fact, it pops up in several other chapters of this book. In the 1968 essay that popularized the concept, "The Tragedy of the Commons," Garrett Hardin wrote:

> Therein is the tragedy. Each man is locked into a system that compels him to increase his herd without limit—in a world that is limited. Ruin is the destination toward which all men rush, each pursuing his own best interest in a society that believes in the freedom of the commons. Freedom in a commons brings ruin to all.

In the case of certain ingeniously planned services, we find a contrasting *cornucopia of the commons*: use brings overflowing abundance. Peer-to-peer architectures and technologies may have their benefits, but I think the historical lesson is clear: concentrate on what you can get from users, and use whatever protocol can maximize their voluntary contributions. That seems to be where the greatest promise lies for the new kinds of collaborative environments.

part two

Projects

This part of the book offers a look at several current systems, giving a sense of what actual peer-to-peer systems look like and how they behave.

chapter five

SETI@home

David Anderson, SETI@home

It was January 1986, and I was sitting in a cafe on Berkeley, California's Telegraph Avenue. Looking up, I recognized a student in the graduate course I was teaching that semester at the university. We talked. His name was David Gedye, and he had just arrived from Australia. Our conversation revealed many common interests, both within and outside of computer science. This chance meeting led, twelve years later, to a project that may revolutionize computing and science: SETI@home.

Gedye and I became running partners. Our long forays into the hills above the Berkeley campus occasioned many far-ranging discussions about the universe and our imperfect understanding of it. I enjoyed these times. But all good things must end, and in 1989 Gedye left Berkeley with a master's degree. He worked in Silicon Valley for a few years, then moved to Seattle and started a family. I also left academia, but remained in the Bay Area.

In 1995 Gedye visited me in Berkeley, and we returned to the hills, this time for a leisurely walk. He was bursting with excitement about a new idea. It sounded crazy at first: He proposed using the computing power of home PCs to search for radio signals from extraterrestrial civilizations. But Gedye was serious. He had contacted Woody Sullivan, an astronomy professor at the University of Washington and an expert in the theory behind SETI, the Search for Extraterrestrial Intelligence. Woody had steered him to Dan Werthimer, a SETI researcher at UC Berkeley.

The four of us—Gedye, Werthimer, Sullivan, and I—met several times over the next year, trying to assess the viability of Gedye's idea. We decided that existing technology was sufficient, though just barely, for recording radio data and distributing it over the Internet. And if we managed to get 100,000 people to participate, the aggregate computing power would let us search for fainter signals, and more types of signals, than had ever been done before. But could we get that many people interested? We decided to try it and find out.

Radio SETI

SETI is a scientific research area whose goal is to detect intelligent life outside the Earth. In 1959, Phil Morrison and Giuseppe Cocconi proposed listening for signals with narrow frequency bandwidth, like our own television and radar emissions, but unlike the noise emanating from stars and other natural sources. Such signals would be evidence of technology, and therefore of life.

The first radio SETI experiment was conducted in 1960 by Frank Drake, who pointed an 85-foot radio telescope in West Virginia at two nearby stars. Drake didn't detect an extraterrestrial signal, but he and other researchers have continued to listen. Since 1960 there have been tremendous advances in technology, especially in the digital technology at the heart of radio SETI. The systems that analyze radio signals use the Fast Fourier Transform (FFT), an algorithm that divides signals into their component frequencies. Most SETI projects have built special-purpose FFT supercomputers, but are limited to fairly simple types of analysis.

There are also larger and more sensitive radio telescopes. The largest is Arecibo, a 1,000-foot aluminum dish set into a natural hollow in the hills of northern Puerto Rico. A movable antenna platform is suspended 700 feet above the center of the dish. By moving the antenna, one can effectively point the telescope anywhere in a band of sky from the celestial equator to 38 degrees north. The telescope doesn't form an image like optical telescopes. It's more like a highly directional microphone. It sees a fuzzy disk (a *beam*) about 1/10 of a degree in diameter, or about 1/5 the diameter of the moon.

Arecibo's size and excellent electronics let it hear very faint signals. The telescope is used for many scientific purposes: looking for pulsars, imaging asteroids and planets by bouncing radio waves off them, and studying the upper atmosphere. Observation time on Arecibo is a precious commodity.

In 1992, Dan Werthimer devised a way for his SETI project, SERENDIP, to use Arecibo all the time—even while other projects are using it. He mounted a secondary antenna at the opposite end of the platform from the main antenna. While the main antenna tracks a fixed point in the sky (as it normally does) this secondary antenna moves slowly in an arc about 6 degrees away. SERENDIP observers have no control over where the scope points, but over long periods of time their beam covers the entire band of sky visible from Arecibo. SERENDIP is thus a *sky survey*: It covers lots of stars but doesn't spend much time on each star. Other radio SETI projects use *targeted search*: they look at specific stars for longer periods, which gives them more sensitivity. No one knows which approach is better, or even if radio signals are the right thing to look for. The best bet, SETI experts agree, is to try everything.

How SETI@home works

We decided that SETI@home would use SERENDIP's antenna. Like all previous radio SETI projects, SERENDIP analyzes its signal using a dedicated supercomputer at the telescope; it doesn't record the signal. For SETI@home, we needed to digitally record the signal and transport it to our computers at Berkeley. The network connection from Arecibo to the mainland is too slow. Instead, we record the data on digital tapes and mail them to Berkeley. The largest-capacity digital tape available in 1998 was the 35-GB digital linear tape (DLT).

We had to decide what frequency range to record. Covering a wide range is good from a scientific point of view, but it means more tapes and more network bandwidth. We decided to record a 2.5 MHz frequency band. Using 1-bit samples, this gives a data rate of 5 Mbps, meaning that a tape fills up in about 16 hours. Like most radio SETI projects, we centered our band at the *hydrogen line*, 1.42 GHz. This is the resonant frequency of the hydrogen molecules that fill interstellar space. Since hydrogen is the most abundant element in the universe, we hope that if aliens are sending an intentional signal, they will use this frequency. Our 2.5 MHz band is wide enough to contain Doppler shifts (frequency shifts due to relative motion) corresponding to any likely velocity of a transmitter in our galaxy.

SETI@home and SERENDIP are complementary: SETI@home looks at a narrower frequency range than SERENDIP (2.5 MHz versus 140 MHz) but does better signal analysis. SETI@home will record data for two years, during which time we'll cover Arecibo's visible band about four times.

Every week about ten newly-recorded tapes arrive from Arecibo. These tapes are catalogued and stored. Next, the data is divided into *work units*, the pieces that are sent to clients. The data is divided along two dimensions: time and frequency. We decided that work units should be about 0.3 MB—large enough to keep a computer busy for a while, but small enough so that, even over a 28.8-Kbps modem, the transmission time is only a few minutes. We wanted each work unit to cover several times the *beam period* (the time it takes for the beam to move across a point in the sky, typically about 20 seconds). To accomplish this, we divide the data into 256 frequency bands, each about 10 KHz wide. We then slice each band into pieces 256,000 samples long—about 107 seconds of recording time. Work units in a given band are overlapped in time by 20 seconds, ensuring that each beam period is contained entirely in at least one work unit.

The task of splitting data tapes into work units is itself computationally intensive—enough so that we considered making it a distributed task unto itself. In the end we assembled a group of six workstations, each equipped with a DLT tape drive, running the splitter program full-time.

Work units are stored on a computer with about 300 GB of disk space. Ideally, each work unit should remain in storage until a result for it has been returned. However, with 50 GB of data pouring in from Arecibo every day, and with some slow computers taking a week or more to complete a work unit, this can lead to a situation where we run out of space for new work units. Our current policy is to delete work units even if no result has been returned yet.

A relational database keeps track of everything: tapes, work units, results, users, and so on. This database has grown to several hundred gigabytes, and we place a tremendous load on it. Although we have spread it across two large server machines, it is frequently a performance bottleneck.

The most visible component of SETI@home is the client program. For Windows and Macintosh users, this program is a screensaver: it only does its work when the computer isn't being used. The client sets up an Internet connection to the SETI@home data distribution server, obtains a work unit, and closes the connection. It then processes the data; this may take anywhere from an hour to several days, depending on the speed of the computer. When it's finished, the client reconnects to the server, sends back the results, and gets a new work unit. Every few minutes the program writes a "checkpoint" file to disk, so that it can pick up where it left off in case the user turns off the computer.

The SETI@home data distribution server accepts connections from clients, collects their results, and sends them new data. The data server may send either new work units or previously sent work units that are still on disk. Many connections may arrive each second, and it may take several minutes (e.g., over a modem connection) to handle a request. So the server uses a large number of processes; in many respects it is like a web server such as Apache. The server system also uses several other programs, such as a "garbage collector" that removes work units for which results have been received.

If a transmitter and/or receiver is accelerated (e.g., because of planetary rotation or orbit), a signal sent at a constant frequency will be heard as drifting in frequency. SETI@home uses a technique called "coherent integration" for detecting drifting signals. SETI@home examines about 50,000 drift rates, ranging from −50 to +50 Hz/sec. For each drift rate, the client program transforms the data to remove the drift and then looks for signals at constant frequency. This gives about 10 times better sensitivity than looking for drifting signals directly.

For a given drift rate, the program uses 15 different FFT lengths, or frequency resolutions. A mathematical theorem called the Heisenberg Uncertainty Principle says that you can examine a signal with high frequency resolution or high time resolution, but not both. Since we don't know what characteristics an alien signal might have, we explore the full range of this trade-off.

For a given drift rate and FFT length, the program computes the time-varying power spectrum of the signal. This produces an array whose dimensions are time and frequency, and whose value is the power (the SETI@home graphics show a 3-D color graph of this array). The power array is analyzed, looking for several types of signals:

Spikes
> Power values much higher than the local average.

Gaussians
> Ridges in the data, along the time axis, whose shape matches the bell-shaped curve (called a "Gaussian") of the telescope beam.

Pulses
> Signals at a constant frequency that cycle on and off, with a Gaussian envelope. The pulse rate, phase, and duty cycle are not known in advance. We use an algorithm called Fast Folding, originally developed for finding pulsars, that efficiently covers a wide range of possibilities.

Triplets
> Groups of three evenly spaced spikes at the same frequency.

Signals that exceed predefined thresholds are returned to the server and added to the database. The client doesn't have a flashing light that goes off when an ET signal is found; this isn't possible. Man-made "radio frequency interference" (RFI), coming from TV stations, cell phones, and car ignitions, leaks into the radio telescope and is often indistinguishable from an ET signal. RFI rejection is a hard problem for radio SETI. Our approach is to check our database of candidate signals for two or more signals at the same frequency and sky position, but at different times. Man-made interference changes from one month to the next, but (hopefully) alien signals will remain unchanged.

So SETI@home's detection of an extraterrestrial signal, if it happens, will show up first on a computer screen at Berkeley, sometime towards the end of the project. But our database will have a complete record of the users whose PCs contributed to the detection, and they'll share in the credit.

SETI@home's web site (*http://setiathome.berkeley.edu*) plays an important role in the project. At the site, people can download the client program, learn about SETI@home and radio SETI, and create and join teams. The web site also shows current statistics and "leader boards:" lists of users and teams, ordered by number of work units completed. These pages are generated by programs that obtain the latest information from the database.

Trials and tribulations

SETI@home has faced many difficulties and challenges. Server performance, for example, has been a major problem. As more and more people downloaded and ran the client, the stream of client requests grew from a trickle to a torrent. At first, our server system consisted of three pieces: an Informix database server, the data distribution server, and an Apache web server. These ran on three Sun workstations, which also served as our personal computers.

In the first week the server system quickly was overwhelmed. Client connections were being turned away, resulting in irritating error messages being displayed to users, and hence a torrent of email.

We scrambled to fix these problems by modifying the software. For example, we realized that much of the load on the database server was due to updating lots of accounting records (for countries, CPU types, teams, etc.) for each result received. We hastily revised the system to update the accounting records off-line, combining thousands of database writes into a single write. This offline system quickly fell behind, producing yet another wave of irate email, but at least the data distribution server now kept up.

It quickly became clear that we needed more powerful server hardware. Sun Microsystems came to our rescue, and over the next year they donated several of their high-performance server machines. Even with these improvements, server performance continues to be an issue. Resources in general, especially funding and manpower, have been a problem. We've received funds from a variety of private donors and a grant from the University of California. This money has been enough to hire about three full-time employees. A project of similar magnitude in the private sector would probably employ 20 or 30 people. We've had to cut corners in many areas (for example, there is no customer support), and some tasks have fallen far behind schedule.

Another problem area involved processor-specific optimizations. The SETI@home client is written in C++, and we compile it using standard compilers such as Microsoft VC++ and Gnu's *gcc*. Performance-conscious users disassembled the inner loops of the program and figured out that it was doing FFTs and that the code was non-optimal on many processors. For example, several variants of the x86 architecture, such as AMD's 3DNow, have instructions that can do FFTs faster. This led to demands from 3DNow enthusiasts that we release a version optimized for 3DNow. Similar requests came from Altivec, MIPS, and Alpha owners.

We didn't have the manpower to maintain lots of processor-specific versions of the code. However, several people figured out how to replace the FFT routine at the heart of SETI@home with a faster routine. Some of them did this incorrectly, producing clients that returned incorrect results.

Doctored versions of the program were just one of many security challenges. Most of the problems involved "credit cheating" by, for example, returning the same result file over and over. People also doctored their result files, making it appear that their computers had found a strong signal. It's not clear what motivated these activities—after all, there are no financial rewards for work done. We invested a large amount of effort in making a more secure version of the client, which uses cryptographic checksumming to detect tampering with result files and with the program itself.

Some people feel that SETI@home should be an "open source" project, that we should distribute the source code and solicit the help of volunteer programmers to fix bugs and make enhancements. Indeed, we tried this for a short period and (perhaps due to our inexperience managing open source projects) were quickly inundated with code that, for various reasons, was unusable. We were also concerned that someone might substitute their own signal detection algorithm, announce a signal discovery, and destroy our project's credibility. When we launched the project as non–open source, a vocal group of critics created a web site calling for a boycott of SETI@home and attacking us for not being "free software." (Many people have interpreted this as meaning that we charge money for the client software, which is not the case.)

Human factors

Early in 1998, we launched a SETI@home web site describing the idea and letting people sign up. It was a good time to start a project like SETI@home. Public interest in SETI had been stirred by the movie *Contact*, which was released in

July 1997. This movie, based on a novel by Carl Sagan, describes radio SETI in reasonably accurate terms, and parts of it were filmed at Arecibo.

It became clear that there would be no shortage of participants—over 400,000 people signed up at the web site. After a long period of development and testing, we released the client software on May 17, 1999. In the first week after the launch, over 200,000 people downloaded and ran the client. This number has grown to 2,400,000 as of October 2000. People in 226 countries around the world run SETI@home. 50% of them are outside the U.S.; there are even 73 in Antarctica.

People have helped SETI@home in every way imaginable. People upgrade their computers, or buy new computers, just to run SETI@home faster. In Europe, people run SETI@home in spite of expensive Internet connection setup charges. Volunteers translated the web site into about 30 foreign languages. A number of people have written programs that track their work in elaborate detail. Graphic artists sent us dozens of banner and link graphics; one of these was so attractive that it replaced Gedye's original planet-and-wave image (which he threw together in PowerPoint) as our logo.

When it became clear that SETI@home was being widely embraced by the public, several questions arose. How was the word about SETI@home being spread? Why were people running SETI@home? Were they leaving their computers on longer, or buying faster computers, because of SETI@home?

We've heard the following "viral marketing" scenario from many sources: one person in an office starts running SETI@home; people see the screensaver graphics, ask about it, hear the explanation of the project, and try it themselves. Soon the entire office is running it.

In search of more quantitative information, we ran a poll on our web site, with questions involving demographics and attitudes about SETI and distributed computing. Some of the results were surprising; for example, only 7% of the respondents are female. We learned that our users are sober in their expectations: Only 10% think that a signal will be detected within the two-year duration of the project.

The world's most powerful computer

Scientific computations are often measured in units of *floating-point operations*—additions and multiplications of numbers with fractional parts, like 42.0 or 3.14159. A common unit of supercomputer speed is trillions of floating-point operations per second, or TFLOPS.

The 1.0 TFLOPS barrier has been broken only in the last year or so. The fastest supercomputer is currently the ASCI White, built by IBM for the U.S. Department of Energy. It costs $110 million, weighs 106 tons, and has a peak performance of 12.3 TFLOPS.

SETI@home is faster than ASCI White, at less than 1% of the cost. The FFT computations for each SETI@home work unit require 3.1 trillion floating-point operations. In a typical day, SETI@home clients process about 700,000 work units. This works out to over 20 TFLOPS. It has cost about $500,000, plus another $200,000 or so in donated hardware, to develop SETI@home and operate it for a year. Of course, the cost of the one million PCs running SETI@home greatly exceeds that of ASCI White—but these PCs were bought and paid for before SETI@home and would exist even without it.

As of October 2000, SETI@home has received 200 million results, for a total of 4×10^{20} floating-point operations. We believe that this is the largest computation ever performed. And in terms of the potential of the Internet for scientific computing, SETI@home is the tip of the iceberg. There are projected to be one billion Internet-connected computers by 2003. If 10% of them participate in distributed computing projects, there will be enough computing power for 100 projects the size of SETI@home.

To what range of problems is this power applicable? Certainly not all problems. It must be possible to factor the problem into a large number of pieces that can be handled in parallel, with few or no interdependencies between the pieces. The ratio between communication and computation must be fairly low: for example, it mustn't take an hour to transfer the data for one second of computing.

Surprisingly many problems meet these criteria. Some of them, such as mathematical problems, are of academic interest; others are in areas of commercial importance, such as genetic analysis. The range of feasible problems will increase along with communication speed and capacity; for example, it may soon be feasible to do computer graphics rendering for movies.

The peer-to-peer paradigm

In the brief history of computer technology, there have been several stages in the way computer systems are structured. The dominant paradigm today is called *client/server*: Information is concentrated in centrally located *server* computers and distributed through networks to *client* computers that act primarily as user interface devices. Client/server is a successor to the earlier *desktop computing* and *mainframe* paradigms.

Today's typical personal computer has a very fast processor, lots of unused disk space, and the ability to send data on the Internet—the same capabilities required of server computers. The sheer quantity of Internet-connected computers suggests a new paradigm in which tasks currently handled by central servers (such as supercomputing and data serving) are spread across large numbers of personal computers. In effect, the personal computer acts as both client and server. This new paradigm has been dubbed *peer-to-peer* (P2P). SETI@home and Napster (a program, released about the same time as SETI@home, that allows people to share sound files over the Internet) are often cited as the first major examples of P2P systems.

The huge number of computers participating in a P2P system can overcome the fact that individual computers may be only sporadically available (i.e., their owners may turn them off or disconnect them from the Internet). Software techniques such as data replication can combine a large number of slow, unreliable components into a fast, highly reliable system.

The P2P paradigm has a human as well as a technical side—it shifts power, and therefore control, away from organizations and toward individuals. This might lead, for example, to a music distribution system that efficiently matches musicians and listeners, eliminating the dilution and homogenization of mass marketing. For scientific computing, it could contribute to a democratization of science: a research project that needs massive supercomputing will have to explain its research to the public and argue the merit of the research. This, I believe, is a worthwhile goal and will be a significant accomplishment for SETI@home even if no extraterrestrial signal is found.

chapter six

Jabber

Conversational Technologies

Jeremie Miller, Jabber

Conversations are an important part of our daily lives. For most people, in fact, they are the most important way to acquire and spread knowledge during a normal working day.

Conversations provide a comfortable medium in which knowledge flows in both directions, and where contributors share an inherent context through their subjects and relationships. In addition to old forms of conversations—direct interaction and communication over the phone and in person—conversations are becoming an increasingly important part of the networked world. Witness the popularity of email, chat, and instant messaging, which enable users to increase the range and scope of their conversations to reach those that they may not have before.

Still, little attention has been paid in recent years to the popular Internet channels that most naturally support conversations. Instead, most people see the Web as the driving force, and they view it as a content delivery platform rather than as a place for exchanges among equals. The dominance of the Web has come about because it has succeeded in becoming a fundamentally unifying technology that provides access to content in all forms and formats. However, it tends toward being a traditional one-way broadcast medium, with the largest base of users being passive recipients of content.

Conversations have a stubborn way of reemerging in any human activity, however. Recently, much of the excitement and buzz around the Web have centered on sites that use it as a conversational medium. These conversations take place within a particular web site (Slashdot, eBay, Amazon.com) or an application (Napster, AIM/ICQ, Netshow).

And repeating the history of the pre-Web Internet, the new conversations sprout up in a disjointed, chaotic variety where the left hand doesn't know what the right hand is doing. The Web was a godsend for lowering the barrier to access information; it increased the value of all content by unifying the technologies that described and delivered that content. In the same way, Internet conversations stand to benefit significantly by the introduction of a common platform designed to support the rich dynamic and flexible nature of a conversation.

Jabber could well become this platform. It's not a single application (although Jabber clients can be downloaded and used right now) nor even a protocol. Instead, using XML, Jabber serves as a glue that can tie together an unlimited range of applications that tie together people and services. Thus, it will support and encourage the growth of diverse conversational systems—and this moment in Internet history is a ripe one for such innovations.

Conversations and peers

So what really is a conversation? A quick search using Dictionary.com reveals the following:

> con·ver·sa·tion (kän-ver-'sā-shən) n. 1. A spoken exchange of thoughts, opinions, and feelings; a talk. 2. An informal discussion of a matter by representatives of governments, institutions, or organizations. 3. *Computer Science*. A real-time interaction with a computer.

Essentially, a conversation is the rapid transfer of information between two or more parties. A conversation is usually characterized by three simple traits: it happens spontaneously, it is transient (lasting a short time), and it occurs among peers—that is, all sides are equal contributors.

Let's turn then to the last trait. The term "peer" is defined by Dictionary.com:

> peer (pîr) n. 1. A person who has equal standing with another or others, as in rank, class, or age; *children who are easily influenced by their peers*.

The Internet expands this definition to include both people (P) and applications (A). Inherently, when peers exchange information, it is a conversation, since both sides are equal and are transiently exchanging information with each other. Person-to-person conversations (P-P) include email, chat, and message boards. But crucial conversations also include application-to-application (A-A) ones such as web services, IP routing, and UUCP. Least common, but most intriguing for future possibilities, are person-to-application (P-A) conversations such as smart agents and bots.

It's interesting to take a step back and look at the existing conversations happening on the Internet today. How well does each technology map to the kind of natural conversational style we know from real life? Let's identify a few important metrics to help evaluate these traditional forms of Internet communication as conversational channels:

Time
>   The more rapidly messages can be created and delivered, and the more rapidly the recipient can respond, the more productive the conversation is for both participants.

P-A
>   A technology provides greater potential for future innovation if it inherently supports applications as well as people.

Peers
>   Participants in a conversation should be equal and the conversation bidirectional.

Distributed
>   Conversations may be constrained if there is a central form of control or authority.

We can now evaluate a few technologies along some of the metrics just defined.

Email comes to mind first as the most popular form of conversation now happening on the Internet. It is relatively fast, each message taking typically between 30 seconds and a few days to deliver, but certainly not real-time. It is predominantly P-P, with some P-A applications, but it is not a very natural use for A-A, because it provides no structure for content. *Usenet* is similar to email but is focused on group discussions. Both are innately distributed, and participants are peers.

Internet Relay Chat (IRC) is a very popular conversational medium, primarily supporting real-time group discussions. As with email, it's primarily P-P with some P-A and very little A-A. Participants are peers. IRC is a distributed application within a network of groups, but it is restricted to that particular network—it does not extend beyond a single collection of groups.

The traditional *Web* is real-time, but in a strict sense it does not support conversations, because the participants are not peers. The content may be produced by a person, but it has a natural flow in only one direction. Applications that support conversations can be built and made available on the Web, but they are pretty rigid—each conversation is specific and centralized to that application.

The *next-generation Web*—also called the *Two-Way Web* by visionary developer Dave Winer—is represented by Microsoft's .NET; and it tries to solve the short-comings in the evolution of the Web. It involves personal/fractional-horsepower (specialized) HTTP and DAV servers. These systems more naturally support peers and conversations than the traditional Web, but the conversations between these peers are still predominantly one-way (consumer or producer) and are often centralized based on the application or content.

Traditional *instant messaging* services, such as AOL Instant Messenger, ICQ, Yahoo! Messenger, and MSN Messenger, come the closest to a real-world con-versation yet, and that is the reason for their soaring popularity. They unfortu-nately focus primarily on P-P. The most significant drawback is that they are commercial and completely centralized around a single closed service. You must be part of the service to communicate with others on it.

None of these existing technologies provides a common platform for Internet conversations as the Web does for content. Each is either limited in some impor-tant dimension or is specific to one application.

What could people do with an ideal, standardized conversational platform open to applications that can cross boundaries and access end user content? Here are some fanciful future possibilities:

- I could ask a coworker's word processor or source editor what documents they are editing and discuss revisions.

- My spell checker could ask the entire department to check the validity of unknown acronyms and project or employee names.

- Instead of trying to combine the details of everybody's lives in a central address book or schedule, each application that needs to discover this infor-mation could ask other peers for it. Different conversations could be with different communities I define, such as my department, my family (for holi-day card or birthday lists), or my friends (for event invitations).

- My television set or video recorder could ask my friends what programs they are watching and use their recorders' extra space to save the programs in case I want to watch them too. With broadband, the television sets could have a conversation exchanging the actual video.

- My games could exchange scores and playing levels with my friends' games and schedule times to play collaboratively (possibly invoking some of the other peers above to schedule conversations). I could also ask another game to deliver an important message or to join a game.

- Businesses could reproduce some of the warmth and responsiveness of a phone conversation online, replacing the cold, faceless e-commerce store or customer support site that serves to drive us to our phones. The new sites could combine a rich context and content with the kind of conversational medium we all like to have.

Evolving toward the ideal

A look back at a bit of the World Wide Web's brief history proves quite interesting and enlightening. Back in its pioneering days, the Web was idealized as a revolutionary peer platform that would enable anyone on the Internet to become a publisher and editor. It empowered individuals to publish their unique collections of knowledge so that they were accessible by anyone. The vision was of a worldwide conversation where everyone could be both a voice and a resource. Here are a few quotes from Tim Berners-Lee to pique your interest:

> The World Wide Web was designed originally as an interactive world of shared information through which people could communicate with each other and with machines (*http://www.w3.org/People/Berners-Lee/1996/ppf.html*).

> I had (and still have) a dream that the web could be less of a television channel and more of an interactive sea of shared knowledge. I imagine it immersing us as a warm, friendly environment made of the things we and our friends have seen, heard, believe or have figured out. I would like it to bring our friends and colleagues closer, in that by working on this knowledge together we can come to better understandings (*http://www.w3.org/Talks/9510_Bush/Talk.html*).

Although the Web fulfills this vision for many people, it has quickly evolved into a traditional consumer/producer relationship. If it had instead evolved as intended, we might be in a different world today. Instead of passively receiving content, we might be empowered individuals collectively producing content, publishing parts of ourselves online to our family and friends, and collectively editing the shared knowledge within our communities.

So where did it go wrong in this respect? It could be argued that the problem was technological, in that the available tools were browsing-centric, and it wasn't easy to become an editor or publisher. A more thought-provoking answer might be that the problem was social, in that there was little demand for those empowering tools. Perhaps only a few people were ready to become individual publishers, and the rest of society wasn't ready to take that step.

The Web did not stagnate, however. It continued to evolve from a content distribution medium to an application distribution medium. Few users are publishing content, but a huge number of companies, groups, and talented individuals are building dynamic applications with new characteristics that reach beyond the original design of the Web. The most exciting of these exhibit characteristics of a peer medium and empower individuals to become producers as well as consumers. Examples include eBay, Slashdot, IMDB, and MP3.com. Although the applications provide a new medium for conversations between P-P peers, the mechanisms for doing so are application-specific. These new web-driven peer applications also have the drawbacks of being centralized, of not being real-time in the sense of a conversation, and of requiring their own form of internal addressing.

So instead of the Web being used primarily as a peer publishing medium, it has become a client/server application medium upon which a breed of peer applications are being built.

Elsewhere in the computer field we can find still other examples of systems that are incorporating greater interactivity. Existing desktop applications are evolving in that direction. They are becoming Internet-aware as they face competition from web sites, so that they can take advantage of the Internet in order to remain competitive and provide utility to the user. Thus, they are evolving from static, standalone, self-contained applications into dynamic, networked, componentized services.

Microsoft, recognizing the importance of staying competitive with online services, is pushing the evolution of desktop applications with their .NET endeavor. By turning applications into networked services, .NET blurs the lines even further between the desktop and the Internet.

The evolution of the Web and the desktop shows a definite trend towards applications becoming peers and having conversations with other applications, services, and people. The common language of conversations in both mediums is XML. As a way of providing a hierarchical structure and a meaningful context for data, XML is being adopted worldwide as the *de facto* language for moving this data between disparate applications. As Tim Bray puts it, "XML is the ASCII of the future."

Jabber is created

To fully realize the potential for unifying the conversations ranging throughout the Internet today, and enabling applications and services to run on top of a common platform, a community of developers worldwide has developed a set of technologies collectively known as Jabber (*http://jabber.org*). Jabber was designed from the get-go for peer conversations, both P-P and particularly A-A, and for real-time as well as asynchronous/offline conversations. Jabber is fully distributed, while allowing a corporation or service to manage its own namespace. Its design is a response to the popularity of the closed IM services. We are trying to create a simple and manageable platform that offers the conversational traits described earlier in this chapter, traits that none of the existing systems come close to providing in full.

Jabber began in early 1998 out of a desire to create a truly open, distributed platform for instant messaging and to break free from the centralized, commercial IM services. The design began with XML, which we exploited for its extensibility and for its ability to encapsulate data, which lowers the barrier to accessing it. The use of XML is pervasive across Jabber, allowing new protocols to be transparently implemented on top of a deployed network of servers and applications. XML is used for the native protocol, translated to other formats as necessary in order to communicate between Jabber applications and other messaging protocols.

The Jabber project emerged from that early open collaboration of numerous individuals and companies worldwide. The name Jabber symbolizes its existence as numerous independent projects sharing common goals, each building a part of the overall architecture. These projects include:

- A modular open source server written in C
- Numerous open source and commercial clients for nearly every platform
- Gateways to most existing IM services and Internet messaging protocols
- Libraries for nearly every programming language
- Specialized agents and services such as RSS and language translations

Jabber is simply a set of common technologies that all of these projects agree on collaboratively when building tools for peer-to-peer systems. One important focus of Jabber is to empower conversations between both people *and* applications.

The Jabber team hopes to create an open medium in which the user has choice and flexibility in the software used to manage conversations, instead of being hindered by the features provided by a closed, commercial service. We hope to accelerate the development of peer applications built on an open foundation, by enabling them to have intelligent conversations with other people and applications, and by providing a common underlying foundation that facilitates conversations and the accessibility of dynamic data from different services.

The centrality of XML

Fundamentally, Jabber enables software to have conversations in XML. When people use Jabber-based software as a messaging platform to have conversations with other people, data exchanges use XML under the surface. Applications use Jabber as an XML storage and exchange service on behalf of their users.

XML is not only the core format for encoding data in Jabber; it is also the protocol, the transport layer between peers, the storage format, and the internal data model within most applications. XML permeates every conversation.

The Jabber architecture is also aware of XML namespaces, which permit different groups of people to define different sets of XML tags to represent data. Thus, using a namespace, one group (Dublin Core) has developed a set of tags for talking about the titles, authors, and other elements of a document. Another group might define a namespace for describing music. An instant messaging community using Jabber could combine the two namespaces to exchange information on books about music. Chapter 13, *Metadata*, looks at the promise of Dublin Core and other namespaces for peer-to-peer applications.

Here is a simple message using Jabber's XML format:

```
<message to="hamlet@denmark" from="horatio@denmark" type="chat">
  <body>Here, sweet lord, at your service.</body>
</message>
```

And here's a hypothetical message with additional data in a namespace included:

```
<message to="horatio@denmark" from="hamlet@denmark">
  <body>Angels and Ministers of Grace, defend us!</body>
  <prayer xmlns="http://www.grace.org">
    <verse>...</verse>
  </prayer>
</message>
```

By supporting namespaces, Jabber enables the inclusion of any XML data in any namespace anywhere within the conversation. This allows applications and services to include, intercept, and modify their own XML data at any point. Jabber is thus reduced to serving as a conduit between peers. Ironically, this lowly status provides the power that Jabber offers to Internet conversations.

Pieces of the infrastructure

While the goal of Jabber is to support other naming conventions and protocols, rather than to create brand-new ones, it depends on certain new concepts that require new types of syntax and binding technologies. These help create a common architecture.

Identity

Naming is at the heart of any system—each resource must have a unique identity. In Jabber, each resource is identified by a three-part name consisting of a *user*, a *server*, and a *resource*.

The user is often an individual, and the server is a system that runs a Jabber-based application. In a name, the user and server are formatted just like email, *user@server*. This provides a general way to pass identification between people that is already well understood and socially accepted. Since the server resolves the username, the format also allows a user's identity to be managed by a service or corporation the way America Online and Napster manage their usernames. This is an important point for Internet services that are providing a public utility to consumers or companies, and especially for corporations that want to or are required to manage their identities very carefully. This also allows any user to use a third party, such as Dynamic DNS Network Services (*http://dyndns.org*), for transient access to a permanent hostname so as not to be forced to rely on someone else's identity.

The server component of the identity could also provide a community aspect to naming, as it may be shared between a small group of friends, a family, or a special interest group. The name then stands out and identifies the user's relationship as part of that community.

The third part of the identity is the resource. As in a Unix filename or URL, the resource follows the server and is delimited by a slash, as in *user@server/resource*. Outside Jabber, the name is formatted like a combination of an email address and a web URL: *jabber://user@server/resource/data*.

This third aspect of the identity, the resource, allows any Jabber application to provide public access to any data within itself, analogous to a web server providing access to any file it can serve. It also serves to identify different applications that might be operating for a single user. For example, my Jabber ID is *jer@jabber.org*, and when I'm online at home my client application might be identified as *jer@jabber.org/desktop*.

Presence

Presence is a concept fundamental to conversations, because it supports the arbitrary coming and going of participants. Technically, presence is simply a state that a user or application is in. Traditional states in instant messaging include online, offline, and somewhere in between (away, do not disturb, sleeping, etc.). The Jabber architecture automatically manages presence information for users and applications, distributing the information as needed while strictly protecting privacy. It is often this single characteristic that adds the most value to the peers in a conversation: just knowing that the other peer is available to have a conversation.

Presence can go beyond simple online/offline state information. XML could be used to convey location, activity, and contextual (work/project) or application-specific data. Presence information itself provides an inherent context for P-P conversations, as well as status and location context for A-A conversations.

Here is a simple presence example in XML:

```
<presence from="hamlet@denmark">
  <show>away</show>
  <status>Gone to England</status>
</presence>
```

Roster

Another powerful feature of a traditional instant messaging service is the *buddy list* or *roster*. The importance of this list is often underestimated. It is a valuable part of the user's reality that they've stored and made available to their applications.

In social terms, each user's roster is his or her community. It defines the participants in this community or relationships to larger communities. A roster is an actualization of personal trust and relationships with peers. Applications should use this list intelligently to share their functionality and filter conversations.

The circle of trust in which a user has chosen to include his or her computer is a starting point for applications to locate other devices the user utilizes. It should also be used for choosing to collaborate with the resources available from trusted peers. This single, simple feature begins to open the door to the future possibilities mentioned near the beginning of this chapter, and it forms a step toward the warm, friendly environment envisioned by Tim Berners-Lee for the World Wide Web.

Architecture

The Jabber architecture closely resembles email. Peers are connected and route data in a chain until it reaches the desired recipient. A client is connected to its server only, and its server is responsible for negotiating the delivery and receipt of that client's data with other servers or networks using whatever protocol is available. All data within the architecture is processed immediately and passed on to the next peer, or stored offline for immediate delivery once that peer is available again.

Peers can play traditional client and server roles within the Jabber architecture. Every server acts as a peer with respect to another server, using SRV DNS records to locate the actual server. Servers also use hostname dialback, independently contacting the sending server to validate incoming data. This prevents spoofing and helps ensure an overall more reliable and secure trust system.

All clients are peers with respect to other clients, and, after establishing a conversation with their servers, are able to establish real-time conversations in XML with any other client. Clients can also include or embed a server internally so that they can operate in any role and provide additional flexibility and security.

Protocols

Along with support for all major instant messaging services (AIM, ICQ, MSN, Yahoo!), Jabber is also protocol agnostic. It uses a variety of applications between the endpoints of the conversations to transparently translate the XML data to and from another protocol. In its immediate applications, Jabber's translation capabilities let it support P-P relationships across traditional instant messaging services, IRC, and email. But the same flexibility also allows the construction of A-A bridges, such as transparent access to SIP, IMXP, and PAM applications, as well as access to Jabber's native presence and messaging functionality from those protocols.

Finally, the protocol-agnostic design of Jabber allows it to participate in the exciting evolution of the Web mentioned earlier in the section "Evolving toward the ideal": An evolution including such technologies as WebDAV, the use of XML over HTTP in the SOAP protocol, the RSS service that broadcasts information about available content, and other web services. We hope to set up revolving door access so that HTTP applications can access native Jabber functionality and so that Jabber applications can transparently access conversations happening over HTTP.

Browsing

A recent addition to Jabber is browsing, which is similar to the feature of the same name in the Network Neighborhood on Microsoft systems. Browsing lets users retrieve lists of peers from other peers and establish relationships between peers. It can be used to see what services might be available from a server, as well as what applications and paths of communication a user has made available to other users and their applications.

Peers that a user might make available could include their normal instant messaging client (home, work, laptop, etc.), a pager transport, an offline inbox, a cell phone, a PDA, a TV, a scheduling application, a 3-D game, or a word processor. Additionally, XML information can be made browsable by a user or application, so that a user's vCard (verification information), public key, personal recipes, music list, bookmarks, or other XML information could be read by both people and applications. Browsing also allows people and applications to locate public peers, such as other messaging gateways mentioned earlier, web services, group chats, and agents (searching, translation, fortune, announcements, Eliza).

Conversation management

By centralizing and coordinating all of your conversations via a central identity, the software managing that identity for you may be empowered to act upon incoming conversations and intelligently filter them. This feature can be used to modify the content of a transmission or, even more often, to make decisions about what to do with a conversation when you're not available (store it offline, copy it to a pager, forward it to another account, etc.). The same feature is also useful to manage the conversations between applications. For instance, if you maintain a personal peer and a work-scheduling peer, conversation management software can redirect incoming conversations to the correct agent based on the relationship to the sender stored in the roster. When you have all of your conversations managed by a common identity, they can be managed directly from one single point, enabling you to have more control over your conversations.

Conclusion

For more information about Jabber, or to become involved in the project (we openly welcome anyone interested), visit *http://jabber.org* or contact the core team at *team@jabber.org*. The 1.0 server was released in May of 2000 and rapidly evolved into a 1.2 release in October, due to popularity and demand. The development focus is now on helping the architecture mature and further developing many of the ideas mentioned here. The development team is collaborating to quickly realize the future possibilities described in this paper, so that they're not so "future" after all.

chapter seven

Mixmaster Remailers

Adam Langley, Freenet

Remailers are one of the older peer-to-peer technologies, but they have stood the test of time. Work done on them has helped or motivated much of the current work in the P2P field. Furthermore, they can be valuable to users who want to access many of the systems described in other chapters of this book by providing a reasonable degree of anonymity during this access, as explained in Chapter 15, *Trust.*

Anonymous remailers allow people to send mail or post to newsgroups while hiding their identities. There are many reasons why people might want to act anonymously. Maybe they fear for their safety if they are linked to what they post (a concern of the authors of the Federalist Papers), maybe they think people will prejudge what they have to say, or maybe they just prefer to keep their public lives separate from their private lives. Whatever the reason, anonymous posting is quite difficult on the Internet. Every email has, in its headers, a list of every computer it passed through. Armed with that knowledge, an attacker could backtrack an email to you. If, however, you use a good remailer network, you make that task orders of magnitude harder.

Mixmasters (also known as Type 2 remailers) are the most common type of remailer. The Type 1 remailers are technically inferior and no longer used, though Mixmasters provide backward compatibility with them. The first stable, public release of Mixmaster was on May 3, 1995, by Lance Cottrell. The current version is 2.0.3, released on July 4, 1996. Don't be put off by the old release date; Mixmasters are still the best remailers.

A simple example of remailers

In order to demonstrate the basics of remailers, I'll start with the Type 1 system. The Type 2 system builds on it, adding some extra assurances that messages cannot be traced.

If you wanted to mail something anonymously to *alice@world.net*, you could send the following message to a Mixmaster remailer:

```
::
Anon-To: alice@world.net
Latent-Time: +1:30

I have some important information for you. I hope you understand why
I've taken the precautions I have to keep my identity a secret.
```

The remailer would hold this message for one and a half hours—to throw off track anyone who might be sniffing traffic and trying to match your incoming message to the remailer's outgoing message—and then strip all the headers except the subject and forward the mail to Alice. Alice would see that the mail had come from the remailer and would have no idea who actually sent it.

However, this system does have problems. First, the remailer knows the destination and source of the message and could be compromised. Second, while your message is in transit to the remailer, anyone with privileged access to your local area network or an intervening mail hub can see that you are sending anonymous messages to Alice. Finally, Alice has no easy way to reply to you.

In order to hide the fact that you are sending anonymous messages to Alice, you can encrypt the message to the remailer. This assumes that you know the public key of the remailer, and while these public keys are widely known, key management is always a weak spot.

Encryption stops anyone who views the message in transit to the remailer from seeing the message and destination. (It should be noted that this doesn't hide the fact that you are sending anonymous messages, and even that snippet of information could land you in trouble in some places.) To anyone who saw it, the message would look like this:

```
::
Encrypted: PGP

-----BEGIN PGP MESSAGE-----
Version: 5
Comment: The following is encrypted data

mQGiBDmG74kRBACzWRoHjjbTrgGxp7275Caldaol72oWkPgj6xxHl2KNnDyvSyNi
D+PDQUkOW86EXTr9fR8mi8V8yDzSuUQCthoD8UPf7Kk/HtR//lCGWRhoN81ynrsm
FLVhGSR5n4lgf6oNUeIObKYYOWmXzjtKCkgAUtbsImOd8/5hm7zKCQl/LwCgveTW
```

```
3bcbQ+A02SMlrxUZcx4qCfUD/1RRuZsdsJFsX9N/tBDLclqtepGQbtwJG02QSCMa
ut8ls+WEytb+l/jqBP/qN9Rry3YUtuRXmjjiYFQ8l3JWA5kd4VxzKP6nBTZfggEW
6BrGB8wDuhqTVL7SqivqrDdgB7S3WQIuZz17Vs1A1wzc37vDmHkw50wshTuvT0Pw
-----END PGP MESSAGE-----
```

This also solves the third problem of Alice needing to reply. You can give Alice a block, encrypted to the remailer, which contains your email address. If Alice then puts the encrypted block at the top of her reply and sends it to the same remailer, the remailer can decrypt it and forward it back to you. Alice can send messages to you without any way of knowing where they actually go. Thus, she has no way of tracing you.

That leaves the second problem, namely that the remailer is the weak link. If Alice, or anyone else, can compromise it, the whole project falls apart. The solution is a simple extension of the basic idea. Instead of the remailer sending the message to Alice, it sends it to another remailer. That remailer then sends it to another, and so on, until the last remailer in the chain sends it to Alice. Thus, no remailer in the chain knows both the source and the destination of the message.

Onion routing

If any remailer reads the contents of your message, it will know who is receiving it at the end. The solution to this involves a series of encryptions that hide the information from remailers in the middle.

Thus, when you send your message, you add an instruction to send it to *alice@world.net*, but you encrypt this recipient information using a key from the last remailer in the chain. So only this last remailer can determine her address. You then add instructions to send the mail to the last remailer and encrypt *that* information so that only the second-to-last remailer can read it, and so on. You thus form an "onion" of messages. Each remailer can remove a skin (one layer of encryption) and send the message to the next remailer, and no remailer knows anything more than what is under the skin they can remove. The layers are illustrated in Figure 7-1.

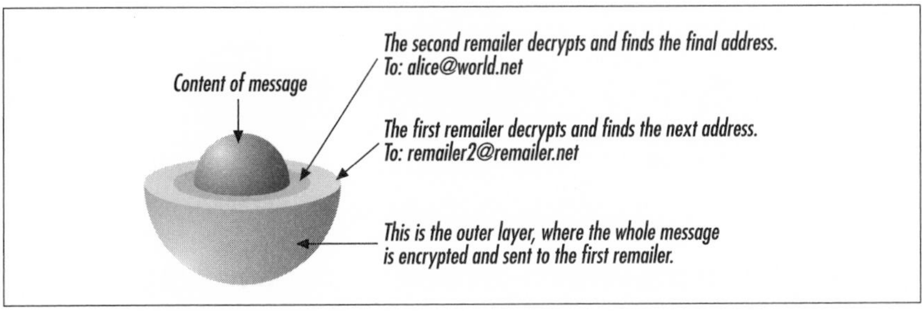

Figure 7-1. An onion of encrypted messages

You construct a reply block for Alice in the same fashion, an onion of encrypted messages. Alice, or anyone else, would then need to compromise every remailer in the chain in order to remove every skin of the onion and trace you.

How Type 2 remailers differ from Type 1 remailers

Type 2 remailers were designed to fix some of the problems with the Type 1 system above. Even though the Type 1 system seems very good, there are a number of weaknesses that a powerful attacker could use. Most of these weaknesses come from being able to do traffic analysis.

Traffic analysis means capturing the bits that cross a communications channel so as to see every packet that passes around a network—where it came from and where it's going. It is not necessary for the snooper to be able to read the contents of every packet; a lot of useful information can be gathered just from TCP and IP headers sent in the clear, or, as you will see, just from incidental characteristics such as the length of a message.

In order to hide the connection between your incoming message and the Mixmaster's outgoing message, each message must appear to the attacker exactly the same as every other message in the system. The most basic difference between messages is their length. (Remember that the message is multiply encrypted, so the contents don't count.) If an attacker can see a certain sized message going into a remailer and then see a message of a very similar size going out again, he or she can follow the message. Even though the message changes size at each remailer because a skin is peeled off, this doesn't provide much protection. The change in size as the skins are removed is small and easily calculated.

In order to make all messages the same size and frustrate traffic analysis, every Mixmaster message is the same length. This is done by breaking the message into pieces and adding padding to the last part to make it the same size. Each part is sent separately and has enough information for the last remailer in the chain to reassemble them. Only the last remailer in the chain knows what messages go together, because the information is only on the last skin. To every other remailer, each part looks like a different message.

The next identifying mark that needs to be removed is the time. If a message enters a remailer and another leaves immediately after, an attacker knows where the message is going and can trace it. This is a more difficult problem to solve than it seems at first. Simply reordering messages, or delaying them for a time, doesn't work. If the number of other messages is low, or if the attacker can stop other messages from reaching the remailer, your message will still stand out.

Mixmasters try to solve this problem by sending out a random selection of messages periodically, while always keeping a certain sized pool of messages. This makes it very difficult to match up outgoing messages with incoming ones, but still not impossible. However, if the traffic on the Mixmaster network is high enough, tracing the message over the whole chain of remailers becomes a massive challenge for an attacker.

Finally, an attacker can capture your message and attempt to replay it through a remailer. Since your message has the encrypted address of the next remailer, by sending many copies of it an attacker can watch for an unusually large number of outgoing messages to a certain address. That address is likely to be the next remailer in the chain (or the final destination). The attacker can then repeat this for each remailer in the chain.

To stop this, every skin has a random ID number. A remailer will not forward a message with the same ID number twice, so all the cloned messages will be dropped and no extra traffic will come out. An attacker cannot change the ID number of a message because it is encrypted along with everything else.

General discussion

Mixmasters have taken remailing to a fine art and are very good at it. They are an interesting study in peer-to-peer networks in which security is the absolute priority. Unlike many peer-to-peer networks, the Mixmaster user must have knowledge of the network in order to build the onion. This means that Mixmaster nodes are publicly known. It is possible to have a private remailer by simply not telling anyone about it, but this would leave the traffic level very low and thus reduce security.

Unfortunately, Mixmasters themselves are often the target of attacks by people who, for one reason or another, disagree that people have a right to anonymity. It has been known for people to send death threats to themselves to try to get remailers shut down. The public nature of remailers makes such attacks easier.

Life can be very hard for a Mixmaster administrator, because he has to explain to angry people why he can't give them the email address of someone who has used his remailer. This goes some way to explaining why there are only about 20–30 active Mixmasters and serves as a warning to other peer-to-peer projects that provide anonymity.

chapter eight

Gnutella

Gene Kan, Gnutella and GoneSilent.com

> When forced to assume [self-government], we were novices in its science.
> Its principles and forms had entered little into our former education. We
> established, however, some, although not all its important principles.
>
> —*Thomas Jefferson, 1824*

> Liberty means responsibility. That is why most men dread it.
>
> —*George Bernard Shaw*

Gnutella is among the first of many decentralized technologies that will reshape
the Internet and reshape the way we think about network applications. The traditional knee-jerk reaction to create a hierarchical client/server system for any
kind of networked application is being rethought. Decentralized technologies
harbor many desirable qualities, and Gnutella is a point of proof that such technologies, while young, are viable.

It is possible that Gnutella has walked the Earth before. Certainly many of the
concepts it uses—even the unconventional ones—were pioneered long ago. It's
tricky to determine what's brand-new and what's not, but this is for certain:
Gnutella is the successful combination of many technologies and concepts at the
right time.

Gnutella in a gnutshell

Gnutella is a citizen of two different worlds. In the popular consciousness, Gnutella is a peer-to-peer, techno-chic alternative to Napster, the popular Internet
music swapping service. To those who look past the Napster association, Gnutella is a landscape-altering technology in and of itself. Gnutella turned every

academically correct notion of computer science on its head and became the first large-scale, fully decentralized system running on the wild and untamed public Internet.

Roughly, Gnutella is an Internet potluck party. The virtual world's equivalents of biscuits and cheese are CPU power, network capacity, and disk space. Add a few MP3s and MPEGs, and the potluck becomes a kegger.

On the technical side, Gnutella brings together a strange mix of CDMA, TCP/IP, and lossy message routing over a reliable connection. It's a really strange concept.

Contrary to popular belief, Gnutella is not branded software. It's not like Microsoft Word. In fact, Gnutella is a language of communication, a protocol. Any software that speaks the language is Gnutella-compatible software. There are dozens of flavors of Gnutella compatibles these days, each catering to different users. Some run on Windows, others on Unix, and others are multi-platform Java or Perl. And as Gnutella's name implies, many of the authors of these Gnutella compatibles have contributed to the open source effort by making the source code of their projects freely available.

A brief history

Besides its impact on the future of intellectual property and network software technology, Gnutella has an interesting story, and it's worth spending a little time understanding how something this big happens with nobody writing any checks.

Gnutella's first breath

Gnutella was born sometime in early March 2000. Justin Frankel and Tom Pepper, working under the dot-com pen name of Gnullsoft, are Gnutella's inventors. Their last life-changing product, Winamp, was the beginning of a company called Nullsoft, which was purchased by America Online (AOL) in 1999. Winamp was developed primarily to play digital music files. According to Tom Pepper, Gnutella was developed primarily to share recipes.

Gnutella was developed in just fourteen days by two guys without college degrees. It was released as an experiment. Unfortunately, executives at AOL were not amenable to improving the state of recipe sharing and squashed the nascent Gnutella just hours after its birth. What was supposed to be a GNU General Public License product when it matured to Version 1.0 was never allowed to grow beyond Version 0.56. Certainly if Gnutella were allowed to develop further under the hands of Frankel and Pepper, this chapter would look a lot different.

Cocktail party	Gnutella
You enter at the foyer and say hello to the closest person.	You connect to a Gnutella host and issue a PING message.
Shortly, your friends see you and come to say hello.	Your PING message is broadcast to the Gnutella hosts in your immediate vicinity. When they receive your PING, they respond with a PONG, essentially saying, "Hello, pleased to meet you."
You would like to find the tray of sushi, so you ask your nearby friends.	You would like to find the recipe for strawberry rhubarb pie, so you ask the Gnutella nodes you've encountered.
None of your drunken friends seem to know where the sushi is, but they ask the people standing nearby. Those people in turn ask the people near them, and so on, until the request makes its way around the room.	One of the Gnutella nodes you're connected to has a recipe for strawberry rhubarb pie and lets you know. Just in case others have a better recipe, your request is passed on to other hosts, which repeat the question to all hosts known to them. Eventually the entire network is canvassed.
A handful of partygoers a few meters away have the tray. They pass back the knowledge of its location by word of mouth.	You get several replies, or "hits," routed back to you.
You walk over to the keepers of the tray and partake of their sushi.	There are dozens of recipes to choose from. You double-click on one and a request is issued to download the recipe from the Gnutella node that has it.

A client/server cocktail party

In contrast, centralized systems don't make much sense in the real world. Napster is a good example of a client/server system, so let's look at how things would be if there were a real-life cocktail party that mimicked Napster's system:

Cocktail party	Napster
You enter at the foyer and the host of the party greets you. Around him are clustered thirty-five million of his closest friends.	You connect to Napster and upload a list of files that you are sharing. The file list is indexed and stored in the memory of the party host: the central server.
Your only friend at this party is the host.	The Napster server says, "File list successfully received."
You would like to find the tray of sushi, so you find your way back to the foyer and ask the host where exactly the tray has gone.	You would like to find the recipe for strawberry rhubarb pie. So you type "rhubarb" into the search box, and the request is delivered to the central server.

Cocktail party	Napster
The host says, "Oh, yes. It's over there."	You get several replies, or "hits," from the Napster server that match your request.
You hold the tray and choose your favorite sushi.	You decide which MP3 file you want to download and double-click. A request is issued to the Napster server for the file. The Napster server determines which file you desire and whose computer it is on, and brokers a download for you. Soon the download begins.

As you can see, the idea of a central authority brokering all interaction is very foreign to us. When I look at what computer science has espoused for decades in terms of real-world interactions, I wonder how we got so far off track. Computer science has defined a feudal system of servers and slaves, but technologies like Gnutella are turning that around at long last.

Client/server means control, and control means responsibility

As it relates to Napster, the server is at once a place to plant a business model and the mail slot for a summons. If Napster threw the switch for Napster subscriptions, they could force everyone to pay to use their service. And if the RIAA (Recording Industry Association of America) wins its lawsuit, Napster just might have to throw the switch the other way, stranding thirty-five million music swappers. We'll see how that suit goes, but whether or not Napster wins in United States Federal Court, it will still face suits in countless municipalities and overseas. It's the Internet equivalent of tobacco: the lawsuits will follow Napster like so many cartoon rain clouds.

Gnutella, on the other hand, is largely free of these burdens. In a decentralized world, it's tough to point fingers. No one entity is responsible for the operation of the Gnutella network. Any number of warrants, writs, and summons can be executed, and Gnutella will still be around to help you find recipes for strawberry rhubarb pie and "Oops, I Did It Again" MP3s.

Thomas Hale, CEO of WiredPlanet, said, "The only way to stop Gnutella is to turn off the Internet." Well, maybe it's not the only way, but it's really hard to think of a way to eliminate every single cell of Gnutella users, which is truly the only way to wipe Gnutella off the planet.

The client is the server is the network

Standard network applications comprise three discrete modules. There is the server, which is where you deposit all the intelligence—the equivalent of the television studio. There is the client, which typically renders the result of some action on the server for viewing by the user—the equivalent of the television. And there is the network, which is the conduit that connects the client and the server—the equivalent of the airwaves.

Gnutella blends all that into one. The client is the server is the network. The client and server are one, of course. That's mainly a function of simplification. There could be two processes, one to serve files and another to download files. But it's just easier to make those two applications one; easier for users and no more difficult for developers.

The interesting thing is that the network itself is embedded in each Gnutella node. Gnutella is an internet built on top of the Internet, entirely in software. The Gnutella network expands as more nodes connect to the network, and, likewise, it does not exist if no users run Gnutella nodes. This is effectively a software-based network infrastructure that comes and goes with its users. Instead of having specialized routers and switches and hubs that enable communication, Gnutella marries all those things into the node itself, ensuring that the communication facilities increase with demand. Gnutella makes the network's users the network's operators.

Distributed intelligence

The underlying notion that sets Gnutella apart from all other systems is that it is a system of distributed intelligence. The queries that are issued on the network are requests for a response, any kind of response.

Suppose you query the Gnutella network for "strawberry rhubarb pie." You expect a few results that let you download a recipe. That's what we expect from today's Gnutella system, but it actually doesn't capture the unique properties Gnutella offers. Remember, Gnutella is a distributed, real-time information retrieval system wherein your query is disseminated across the network in its raw form. That means that every node that receives your query can interpret your query however it wants and respond however it wants, in free form. In fact, Gnutella file-sharing software does just that.

Each flavor of Gnutella software interprets the search queries differently. Some Gnutella software looks inside the files you are sharing. Others look only at the filename. Others look at the names of the parent directories in which the file is contained. Some Gnutella software interprets multiword queries as conjunctions, while others look at multiword queries as disjunctions. Even the results returned by Gnutella file-sharing software are wildly different. Some return the full path of the shared file. Others return only the name of the file. Yet others return a short description extracted from the file. Advertisers and spammers took advantage of this by returning URLs to web sites completely unrelated to the search. Creative and annoying, yet demonstrative of Gnutella's power to aggregate a collective intelligence from distributed sources.

To prove the point once and for all that Gnutella could be used to all kinds of unimagined benefit, Yaroslav Faybishenko, Spencer Kimball, Tracy Scott, and I developed a prototype search engine powered by Gnutella that we called InfraSearch. The idea was that we could demonstrate Gnutella's broad power by building a search engine that accessed data in a nontraditional way while using nothing but pure Gnutella protocol. At the time, InfraSearch was conceived solely to give meat to what many Gnutella insiders were unable to successfully convey to journalists interested in Gnutella: that Gnutella reached beyond simple file swapping. To illustrate, I'll use the examples we used in our prototype.

InfraSearch was accessed through the World Wide Web using a standard web browser. Its interface was familiar to anyone who had used a traditional web search engine. What happened with the query was all Gnutella. When you typed a search query into InfraSearch, however, the query was not answered by looking in a database of keywords and HTML files. Instead, the query was broadcast on a private Gnutella network comprising a few nodes. The nodes themselves were a hodgepodge of variegated data sources. A short list of the notables: Online Photo Lab's image database, a calculator, a proxy for Yahoo! Finance, and an archive of MoreOver.com's news headlines.

When you typed in "MSFT" the query would be broadcast to all the nodes. Each node would evaluate the query in relation to its knowledge base and respond only if the node had relevant information to share. Typically, that would mean that the Yahoo! Finance node would return a result stating Microsoft's current stock price and the MoreOver.com node would return a list of news stories mentioning Microsoft. The results were just arbitrary snippets of HTML. The HTML fragments would be stitched together by a Gnutella node, which also doubled as a web server, and forwarded on to the web browser. Figure 8-1 shows the results of a search for "rose."

The real power of this paradigm showed itself when one entered an algebraic expression into the search box, say, "1+1*3" for instance. The query would be disseminated and most nodes would realize that they had nothing intelligent to

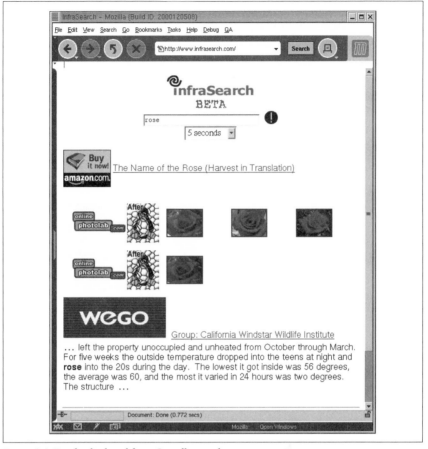

Figure 8-1. Results displayed from Gnutella search

say about such a strange question. All except the calculator node. The calculator was a GNU *bc* calculator hacked to make it speak Gnutella protocol. Every time the calculator received a query, it parsed the text to see if it was a valid algebraic expression. If it was not, then the calculator remained silent. If the query was an algebraic expression, however, the calculator evaluated the expression and returned the result. In this case, "1+1*3 = 4" would be the result.[*]

---

[*] Some creative users would search on ridiculously complex algebraic expressions, causing the calculator node to become overburdened. Gnutella would then simply discard further traffic to the calculator node until it recovered from figuring out what "98791283741984719798797971234*1234183743748845765" was. The other nodes continued on unaffected.

One potential application of this is to solve the dynamic page problem on the World Wide Web. Instead of trying to spider those pages as web search crawlers currently do, it would be possible to access the information databases directly and construct a response based upon data available at the time the query was issued. Possibilities that reach even further are within sight. The query could become structured or parameterized, making a huge body of data available through what effectively becomes a unified query interface. The possibilities for something like that in the enterprise are enormous. When peer-to-peer systems take off, accessing data across heterogeneous information stores will become a problem that Gnutella has already demonstrated it can solve.

What we realized is that this aggregation of intelligence maps very closely to the real world. When you ask a question of two different people, you expect two different answers. Asking a question about cars of a mechanic and a toy shop clerk would expectedly yield two very different answers. Yet both are valid, and each reflects a different sort of intelligence in relation to the topic. Traditional search technologies, however, apply only one intelligence to the body of data they search. Distributed search technologies such as Gnutella allow the personality of each information provider and software developer to show through undiluted.

Different from Freenet

Oftentimes Gnutella and Freenet are lumped together as decentralized alternatives to Napster. True, Gnutella and Freenet are decentralized. And it's true that one can share MP3 files using either Gnutella or Freenet. The technical similarities extend further in various ways, but the philosophical division between Gnutella and Freenet picks up right about here.

Freenet can really be described as a bandwidth- and disk space–sharing concept with the goal of promoting free speech. Gnutella is a searching and discovery network that promotes free interpretation and response to queries. With Freenet, one allocates a certain amount of one's hard drive to the task of carrying files which are in the Freenet. One shares bandwidth with others to facilitate the transport of files to their optimal localities in the Freenet. In a sense, Freenet creates a very large and geographically distributed hard drive with anonymous access. The network is optimized for computerized access to those files rather than human interaction. Each file is assigned a complex unique identification that is obscure in its interpretation. The only way to search for files is by searching via that unique identification code.

In contrast, Gnutella is a distributed searching system with obvious applications for humans and less obvious applications for automatons. Each Gnutella node is free to interpret the query as it wants, allowing Gnutella nodes to give hits in the form of filenames, advertising messages, URLs, graphics, and other arbitrary content. There is no such flexibility in the Freenet system. The Japanese Gnutella project, *http://jnutella.org*, is deploying Gnutella on i-Mode mobile phones, where the results of a search are tailored to mobile phone interfaces. Freenet's highly regimented system of file location based upon unique identification is about cooperative distribution of files. There is nothing wrong with this. It's just a different approach with different effects which I'll leave to Freenet's authors to explain.

Gnutella's communication system

With the basic understanding that Gnutella works the way real-world interpersonal communication works, let's take a look at the concepts that make it all possible in the virtual world. Many of these concepts are borrowed from other technologies, but their combination into one system makes for interesting results and traffic jams.

Message-based, application-level routing

Traditional application-level networks are circuit-based, while Gnutella is message-based. There is no idea of a persistent "connection," or circuit, between any two arbitrary hosts on the Gnutella network. They are both on the network but not directly connected to each other, and not even indirectly connected to each other in any predictable or stable fashion. Instead of forcing the determinism provided by circuit-based routing networks, messages are relayed by a computerized bucket-brigade which forms the Gnutella network. Each bucket is a message, and each brigadier is a host. The messages are handed from host to host willy-nilly, giving the network a unique interconnected and redundant topology.

TCP broadcast

Another unconventional approach that Gnutella uses is a broadcast communication model over unicast TCP. Contrast this to a traditional system such as Napster, where communication is carefully regulated to minimize traffic to its absolute lowest levels, and even then to only one or two concerned parties. Traditional networking models are highly regimented and about as natural as formal gardens.

The broadcast mechanism is extremely interesting, because it maps very closely to our everyday lives. Suppose you are standing at a bus stop and you ask a fellow when the next bus is to arrive: "Oi, mate! When's the next bus?" He may not know, but someone nearby who has heard you will hopefully chime in with the desired information. That is the strength behind Gnutella: it works like the real world.

One of the first questions I asked upon learning of Gnutella's TCP-based broadcast was, "Why not UDP?" The simple answer is that UDP is a pain. It doesn't play nicely with most firewall configurations and is tricky to code. Broadcasting on TCP is simple, and developers don't ask questions about how to assess "connection" status. Let's not even start on IP multicast.

Message broadcasting

Combining the two concepts of message-based routing and broadcast gives us what I'll term message broadcasting. Message broadcasting is perfect for situations where more than one network participant can provide a valid response to a request. This same sort of thing happens all the time. Auctions, for example, are an example of message broadcasting. The auctioneer asks for bids, and one person's bid is just as good as another's.

Gnutella's broadcasting mechanism elegantly avoids continuous echoing. Messages are assigned unique identifiers (128-bit unique identifiers, or UUIDs, as specified by Leach and Salz's 1997 *UUIDs and GUIDs Informational Draft* to the IETF). With millions of Gnutella nodes running around, it is probably worth answering the question, "How unique is a UUID?" Leach and Salz assert uniqueness until 3400 A.D. using their algorithm. Anyway, it's close enough that even if there were one or two duplicated UUIDs along the way nobody would notice.

Every time a message is delivered or originated, the UUID of the message is memorized by the host it passes through. If there are loops in the network then it is possible that a host could receive the same message twice. Normally, the host would be obligated to rebroadcast the message just like any other that it received. However, if the same message is received again at a later time (it will have the same UUID), it is not retransmitted. This explicitly prevents wasting network resources by sending a query to hosts that have already seen it.

Another interesting idea Gnutella implements is the idea of decay. Each message has with it a TTL* number, or time-to-live. Typically, a query starts life

---

* TTL is not unique to Gnutella. It is present in IP, where it is used in a similar manner.

with a TTL of 7. When it passes from host to host, the TTL is decremented. When the TTL reaches 0, the request has lived long enough and is not retransmitted again. The effect of this is to make a Gnutella request fan out from its originating source like ripples on a pond. Eventually the ripples die out.

Dynamic routing

Message broadcasting is useful for the query, but for the response, it makes more sense to route rather than to broadcast. Gnutella's broadcast mechanism allows a query to reach a large number of potential respondents. Along the way, the UUIDs that identify a message are memorized by the hosts it passes through. When Host A responds to a query, it looks in its memory and determines which host sent the query (Host B). It then responds with a reply message containing the same UUID as the request message. Host B receives the reply and looks in its memory to see which host sent the original request (Host C). And on down the line until we reach Host X, which remembers that it actually originated the query. The buck stops there, and Host X does something intelligent with the reply, like display it on the screen for the user to click on (see Figure 8-2).

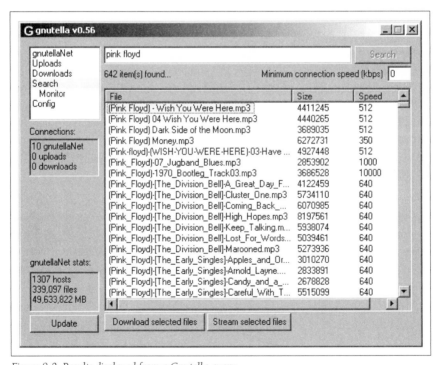

Figure 8-2. Results displayed from a Gnutella query

The idea to create an ephemeral route as the result of a broadcast for discovery is not necessarily novel, but it is interesting. Remember, a message is identified only by its UUID. It is not associated with its originator's IP address or anything of the sort, so without the UUID-based routes, there is no way for a reply to be delivered to the node that made the request.

This sort of dynamic routing is among the things that make Gnutella the intriguing technology that it is. Without it, there would need to be some kind of fixed Gnutella infrastructure. With dynamic routing, the infrastructure comes along with the nodes that join the network, in real time. A node brings with it some network capacity, which is instantly integrated into the routing fabric of the network at large.

When a node leaves the network, it does not leave the network at large in shambles, as is typical for the Internet. The nodes connected to the departing node simply clean up their memories to forget the departed node, and things continue without so much as a hiccup. Over time, the network adapts its shape to long-lived nodes, but even if the longest-lived, highest-capacity node were to disappear, there would be no lasting adverse effects.

Lossy transmission over reliable TCP

A further unconventional notion that is core to Gnutella's communication mechanisms is that the TCP connections that underlie the Gnutella network are not to be viewed as the totally reliable transports they are typically seen as. With Gnutella, when traffic rises beyond the capacity that a particular connection can cope with, the excess traffic is simply forgotten. It is not carefully buffered and preserved for future transmission as is typically done. Traffic isn't coddled on Gnutella. It's treated as the network baggage that it is.

The notion of using a reliable transport to unreliably deliver data is notable. In this case, it helps to preserve the near-real-time nature of the Gnutella network by preventing an overlong traffic backlog. It also creates an interesting problem wherein low-speed Gnutella nodes are at a significant disadvantage when they connect to high-speed Gnutella nodes. When that happens, it's like drinking from a fire hose, and much of the data is lost before it is delivered.

On the positive side, loss rates provide a simple metric for relative capacity. If the loss rate is consistently high, then it's a clear signal to find a different hose to drink from.

Organizing Gnutella

One of the ways Gnutella software copes with constantly changing infrastructure is by creating an ad hoc backbone. There is a large disparity in the speeds of Internet connections. Some users have 56-Kbps modems, and others have, say, T3 lines. The goal is that, over time, the T3-connected nodes migrate toward the center of the network and carry the bulk of the traffic, while the 56-Kbps nodes simultaneously move out toward the fringes of the network, where they will not carry as much of the traffic.

In network terms, the placement of a node on the network (in the middle or on the fringes) isn't determined geographically. It's determined in relation to the topology of the connections the node makes. So a high-speed node would end up being connected to potentially hundreds of other high-speed Gnutella nodes, acting as a huge hub, while a low-speed node would hopefully be connected to only a few other low-capacity nodes.

Over time this would lead the Gnutella network to have a high concentration of high-speed nodes in the middle of the network, surrounded by rings of nodes with progressively decreasing capacities.

Placing nodes on the network

When a Gnutella node connects to the network, it just sort of parachutes in blindly. It lands where it lands. How quickly it is able to become a productive member of Gnutella society is determined by the efficacy of its network analysis algorithms. In the same way that at a cocktail party you want to participate in conversations that interest you, that aren't too dull and aren't too deep, a Gnutella node wants to quickly determine which nodes to disconnect from and which nodes to maintain connections to, so that it isn't overwhelmed and isn't too bored.

It is unclear how much of this logic has been implemented in today's popular Gnutella client software (Gnotella, Furi, Toadnode, and Gnutella 0.56), but this is something that Gnutella developers have slowly educated themselves about over time. Early Gnutella software would obstinately maintain connections to nodes in spite of huge disparities in carrying capacity. The effect was that modem nodes acted as black holes into which packets were sent but from which nothing ever emerged.

One of the key things that we[*] did to serve the surges of users and new client software was to run high-speed nodes that were very aggressive in disconnecting nodes which were obviously bandwidth disadvantaged. After a short time, the only active connections were to nodes running on acceptably high-speed links. This kind of feedback system created an effective backbone that was captured in numerous early network maps. A portion of one is shown in Figure 8-3.

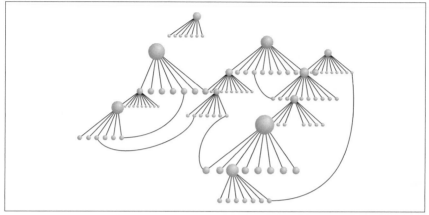

Figure 8-3. Snapshot of effective Gnutella network structure

Gnutella's analogues

The first thing that technologists say when they think about how Gnutella works is, "It can't possibly scale." But that is simply not the case. Gnutella is an unconventional system and as such requires unconventional metrics. Millions of users may be using Gnutella simultaneously, but they will not all be visible to one another. That is the basic nature of a public, purely peer-to-peer network. Because there is no way to guarantee the quality of service throughout the network, it is impossible to guarantee that every node on the network can be reached by every other node on the network. In spite of that, Gnutella has many existing analogues.

Of all the analogues that exist, the most interesting two are cellular telephony and Ethernet.

---

* Bob Schmidt, Ian Hall-Beyer, Nathan Moinvaziri, Tom Camarda, and countless others came to the rescue by running software which made the network work in its times of need. This software ranged from standard Gnutella software to host caches to so-called Mr. Clean nodes, which aggressively removed binary detritus from the network.

The Gnutella horizon

In Gnutella, there is a concept of a horizon. This is simply a restatement of the effect the TTL has on how far a packet can go before it dies, the attenuation of ripples on a pond. Gnutella's standard horizon is seven hops. That means that from where you stand, you can see out seven hops. How far is that? Typically, a seven-hop radius combined with network conditions means about ten thousand nodes are within sight.

When Gnutella was younger, and the pond analogy hadn't yet crossed my mind, I explained this effect as a horizon, because it was just like what happens when you are at the beach and the world seems to disappear after some distance (approximately five kilometers if you're two meters tall). Of course, that is due to the curvature of the earth, but it seemed like a pretty good analogy.

A slightly better one is what happens in a mob. Think first day of school at UC Berkeley, or the annual Love Parade in Germany. You stand there in the middle of the mob, and you can only see for a short distance around you. It's obvious that there are countless more people outside your immediate vision, but you can't tell how many. You don't even really know where you are in relation to the crowd, but you're certainly in the thick of it. That's Gnutella.

Each node can "see" a certain distance in all directions, and beyond that is a great unknown. Each node is situated slightly differently in the network and as a result sees a slightly different network. Over time, as nodes come and go and the network shifts and morphs, your node gets to see many different nodes as the network undulates around it. If you've used Gnutella, you've seen this happen. Initially, the host count increases very rapidly, but after a minute or two, it stabilizes and increases much more slowly than it did at the outset. That is because in the beginning your node discovers the network immediately surrounding it: the network it can see. Once that is done, your node discovers only the nodes that migrate through its field of view.

Cellular telephony and the Gnutella network

In the technological world, this concept is mirrored exactly by cellular telephony cell sites (cellular telephony towers). Each site has a predetermined effective radius. When a caller is outside that radius, his telephone cannot reach the site and must use another if a nearer one is available. And once the caller is outside the operating radius, the site cannot see the caller's telephone either. The effect is the irksome but familiar "no coverage" message on your phone.

Cellular network operators situate cell sites carefully to ensure that cell sites overlap one another to prevent no-coverage zones and dropped calls. A real coverage map looks like a Venn diagram gone mad. This is, in fact, a very close analogue of the Gnutella network. Each node is like a cell site in the sense that it has a limited coverage radius, and each node's coverage area overlaps with that of the nodes adjacent to it. The key to making cellular telephony systems scale is having enough cells and enough infrastructure to connect the cells. It's a similar story with Gnutella.

Cell sites are not all that one needs to build a successful cellular network. Behind all those cell towers is a complex high-bandwidth packet switching system, also much like Gnutella. In the cellular world, this network is very carefully thought out and is a piece of physical infrastructure. As with everything else, the infrastructure comes and goes in the Gnutella network, and things are constantly changing shape.

So then the goal is to find a way to create cells that are joined by a high-speed backbone. This is entirely what would happen in the early Gnutella network. Gnutella nodes would gather around a local hub, forming a cluster. There were numerous clusters interconnected by high-speed lines. All this happened in an unplanned and dynamic way.

Ethernet

Gnutella is also similar in function to Ethernet. In fact, Ethernet is a broadcast network where each message has a unique identifier. Like Gnutella, its scalability metrics are unconventional. The question most people ask about Gnutella is, "How many users are on Gnutella?" The answer is complicated.

Millions of users have Gnutella on their computers. One node can only see about ten thousand others from where it stands in the network. So what is the answer? Ten thousand, or several million?

We could ask the same question about Ethernet, and we'd get the same duality in answer. Hundreds of millions of computers have Ethernet, yet only a few dozen can share an Ethernet "segment" before causing network gridlock. The solution for Ethernet was to develop specialized hardware in the form of Ethernet bridges, switches, and routers. With that hardware, it became possible to squeeze all those millions of computers onto the same network: the Internet.

Cultivating the Gnutella network

Similar development is underway for Gnutella. Fundamentally, each Gnutella node can contain enough logic to make the Gnutella network grow immensely. Broadening the size of a Gnutella cell, or segment, is only a matter of reducing the network traffic. A minor reduction by each node can translate into a huge reduction in traffic over all nodes. That is what happens with distributed systems: a minor change can have a huge effect, once multiplied over the number of nodes.

There is at least one effort underway to create a specialized Gnutella node which outwardly mimics a standard Gnutella node but inwardly operates in a dramatically different manner. It is known as Reflector and is being developed by a company called Clip2. The Reflector is effectively a miniature Napster server. It maintains an index of the files stored on nodes to which it is connected. When a query is issued, the Reflector does not retransmit it. Rather, it answers the query from its own memory. That causes a huge reduction in network use.*

Anyone can run a Reflector, making it an ideal way to increase the size of a Gnutella cluster. Connecting Reflectors together to create a super high-capacity backbone is the obvious next step. Gnutella is essentially an application-level Internet, and with the development of the Gnutella equivalent of Cisco 12000s, Gnutella will really become what it has been likened to so many times: an internet on the Internet.

Gnutella's traffic problems

One place where the analogy drawn between Gnutella and cellular telephony and Ethernet holds true down to its last bits is how Gnutella suffers in cases of high traffic. We know this because the public Gnutella network at the time of this writing has a traffic problem that is systemic, rather than the standard transient attack. Cellular telephones show a weakness when the cell is too busy with active calls. Sometimes there is crosstalk; at other times calls are scratchy and low quality. Ethernet similarly reaches a point of saturation when there is too much traffic on the network, and, instead of coping gracefully, performance just degrades in a downward spiral. Gnutella is similar in almost every way.

---

* Depending on your view, the benefit, or unfortunate downside, of Reflector is that it makes Gnutella usable only in ways that Reflector explicitly enables. To date, Reflector is chiefly optimizing the network for file sharing, and because it removes the ability for hosts to respond free-form and in real time, it sacrifices one of the key ideas behind Gnutella.

In terms of solutions, the bottom line is that when too many conversations take place in one cell or segment the only way to stop the madness is to break up the cell.

On the Gnutella network, things started out pretty peacefully. First a few hundred users, then a few thousand, then a few hundred thousand. No big deal. The network just soldiered along. The real problem came along when host caches came into wide use.

Host caches

In the early days of Gnutella, the way you found your way onto the network was by word of mouth. You got onto IRC and asked for a host address to connect to. Or you checked one of the handful of web pages which maintained lists of hosts to connect to. You entered the hosts into your Gnutella software one by one until one worked. The the software took care of the rest. It was tedious, but it worked for a long while.

Before host caches, it was fairly random what part of the network you connected to. Ask two different people, and they would direct you to connect to hosts on opposite sides of the Gnutella network. Look at two different host lists, and it was difficult to find any hosts in common. Host lists encouraged sparseness and small clusters. It was difficult for too many new hosts to be concentrated into one cell. The cells were sparsely connected with one another, and there wasn't too much crosstalk. That created a nearly optimal network structure, where the Gnutella network looked like a land dotted by small cities and townships interconnected by only a few roads.

Users eventually became frustrated by the difficulties of getting onto Gnutella. Enter Bob Schmidt and Josh Pieper. Bob Schmidt is the author of GnuCache, a host caching program. Josh Pieper also included host caching logic in his popular Gnut software for Unix. Host caches provide a jumping off spot for Gnutella users, a host that's always up and running, that gives a place for your Gnutella software to connect to and find the rest of the Gnutella network.* The host cache greets your node by handing off a list of other hosts your node should connect to. This removes the uncertainty from connecting to Gnutella and provides a more friendly user experience. We were all very thankful for Schmidt and Pieper's efforts until host caches became a smashing success.

---

* Actually, Gnutella was born with a ready host cache located at *findshit.gnutella.org*. Unfortunately, the same people who took away Gnutella also took away *findshit.gnutella.org*, leaving us with a host-cacheless world until GnuCache and Pieper's Gnut software came along.

An unexpected consequence evidenced itself when waves of new Gnutella users logged on in the wake of the Napster injunction on July 26, 2000. Everyone started relying on host caches as their only means of getting onto the Gnutella network. Host caches were only telling new hosts about hosts they saw recently. By doing that, host caches caused Gnutella nodes to be closely clustered into the same little patch of turf on the Gnutella network. There was effectively only one tightly clustered and highly interconnected cell, because the host caches were doling out the same list of hosts to every new host that connected. What resulted was overcrowding of the Gnutella airwaves and a downward spiral of traffic.

Oh well. That's life in the rough-and-tumble world of technology innovation.

To draw an analogy, the Gnutella network became like a crowded room with lots of conversations. Sure, you can still have a conversation, but maybe only with one or two of your closest friends. And that is what has become frustrating for Gnutella users. Whereas the network used to have a huge breadth and countless well-performing cells of approximately ten thousand nodes each, the current network has one big cell in which there is so much noise that queries only make it one or two hops before drowning in overcrowded network connections.

Effectively, a crowded network means that cells are only a few dozen hosts in size. That makes the network a bear to use and gives a disappointing user experience.

Returning the network to its natural state

Host caches were essentially an unnatural addition to the Gnutella network, and the *law of unintended consequences* showed that it could apply to high technology, too. Improving the situation requires a restoration of the network to its original state, where it grew organically and, at first glance, inefficiently. Sometimes, minor inefficiency is good, and this is one of those cases.

Host lists, by enforcing a sparse network, made it so that the communities of Gnutella nodes that did exist were not overcrowded. Host caches created a tightly clustered network, which, while appearing more efficient, in fact led to a major degradation in overall performance. For host caches to improve the situation, they need only to encourage the sparseness that we know works well.

Sort of. An added complication is that each Gnutella host maintains a local host *catcher*, in which a long list of known hosts (all hosts encountered in the node's travels) is deposited for future reference. The first time one logs into the Gnutella network, a host list or a host cache must be used. For all future logins,

Gnutella softwares refer to their host catcher to connect into the Gnutella network. This creates a permanent instability in the network as nodes log on and connect to hosts they remember, irrespective of the fact that those hosts are often poor choices in terms of capacity and topology. The problem is compounded by the reluctance of most Gnutella software to "forget" hosts that are unsuitable.

Turning the network around is technically easy. Host caches can listen to the levels of traffic on each cell they want to serve and distribute new hosts among those cells until the traffic levels become high enough to warrant establishment of new cells. By purposely separating nodes into distinct cells, traffic in each cell can be reduced to a manageable level. With those well-planted seeds and periodic resets of the collective memories of host catchers to allow smart host caches to work their magic, the network can be optimized for performance. The trouble with host catchers, though, is that they are seldom reset, because that requires manual intervention as well as some understanding of the reset mechanism.

Private Gnutella networks

One feature that some Gnutella client software implements is the notion of private Gnutella networks. To join a private network, one needs to know the secret handshake or password. That enforces manageably-sized networks with a predetermined community membership, and it is a pretty good way to ensure a high quality of service no matter what is happening out in the wilds of the public Gnutella network.

Reducing broadcasts makes a significant impact

Broadcasts are simultaneously the most powerful and the most dangerous feature of the Gnutella protocol. Optimally, there are two broadcast packet types: PING and QUERY. PING packets are issued when a node greets the network and wants to learn what other nodes are available to connect to. QUERY packets are issued when a search is conducted. Some Gnutella developers also implemented the PUSH REQUEST packet as a broadcast packet type. PUSH REQUEST packets are used to request files from hosts which are protected by firewalls. The concept is one of the unsung heroes of Gnutella, making it work in all but the most adverse of Internet environments (the double firewall, arch enemy of productivity).

Unfortunately, the PUSH REQUEST packet should be implemented as a routed packet rather than a broadcast packet. At times, PUSH REQUEST packets comprised 50% of all Gnutella network traffic. Simply routing those packets rather than broadcasting them would reduce the overall network traffic dramatically.

Reductions can also be made in the number of queries that are broadcast to large expanses of the network by intelligently caching results from similar searches. Clip2's Reflector software is an example of such a product. Portions of Reflector can be integrated into each Gnutella client, leading to a small increase in the software's internal complexity (the user need not concern herself with this behind-the-scenes activity) in exchange for a massive improvement in network performance.

The final broadcast packet that was the carrier of some early abuses is the PING packet. In early Gnutella software, PING packets could have a payload, even though it was not clear what that payload might contain. It was subsequently abused by script kiddies to debilitate the Gnutella network. Gnutella developers responded immediately by altering their software to discard PING packets with payloads, causing a several thousand–fold traffic reduction on the Gnutella network and simultaneously foiling what amounted to a denial of service attack.

What developers have been debating ever since is how to reduce the level of traffic usurped by PING packets. Suggestions have ranged from eliminating PING packets to reducing the allowed number of retransmissions of a PING packet. Personally, I favor something in the middle, where every host on the network behaves as a miniature host cache for its locality, returning proxied greetings for a few nearby hosts in response to a PING and only occasionally retransmitting the PING. That would allow the PING to continue to serve its valuable duty in shaping the network's structure and connectivity, while reducing the network's traffic levels dramatically. Figure a thousand-fold reduction in traffic.

One thing to consider in distributed applications is that, no matter how difficult the code is to write and how much it bloats the code (within reason), it's worth the trouble, because the savings in network utilization pay dividends on every packet. As an example, just consider that if a PUSH REQUEST packet is broadcast, it may reach 1,000 hosts. If it is routed, it may reach four or five. That is a 200-fold reduction in traffic in exchange for a dozen lines of code.

The analogy that Gnutella is like an Internet potluck rings true. Everyone brings a dish when they join the Gnutella network. At a minimum, the one dish that everyone brings is network capacity. So then there is definitely enough bandwidth to go around. The only matter is to organize the combined capacity and manage the traffic to make sure the network operates within its limits.

We just covered what is probably Gnutella's biggest problem, so if this was a corporate memorandum, this would be the perfect point at which to introduce the engineering organization. This isn't a memo, but let's do it anyway. Keep in mind the Thomas Jefferson quotation at the beginning of the chapter: none of us knew what we were doing, but we got our hands dirty and took responsibility for what we did.

The policy debates

Napster and Gnutella have really been at the center of the policy debate surrounding the new breed of peer-to-peer technologies. For the moment, let's forget about the debate that's burning in the technology community about what is truly peer-to-peer. We'll get back to that later and tie all these policy questions back to the technology.

Napster wars

There is only one thing that gets people more riled up than religion, and that is money. In this case, the squabble is over money that may or may not be lost to online music swaps facilitated by services such as Napster and systems like the Gnutella network. This war is being fought by Napster and the RIAA, and what results could change the lives of everyone, at least in the United States.

Well, sort of. The idea that lawsuit or legislature can stop a service that everyone enjoys is certainly a false one. Prohibition was the last real effort (in the U.S.) by the few against the many, and it was a dismal failure that gave rise to real criminal activity and the law's eventual embarrassing repeal. We have an opportunity to see all that happen again, or the recording industry could look at what's coming down the road and figure out a way to cooperate with Napster before the industry gets run down by next-generation peer-to-peer technologies.

Napster, at least, provides a single place where file swappers can be taxed. With Gnutella and Freenet, there is no place to tax, no person to talk to about instituting a tax, and no kinds of controls. The recording industry may hope that Gnutella and Freenet will "just go away," but that hope will probably not materialize into reality.

Anonymity and peer-to-peer

One of the big ideas behind peer-to-peer systems is their potential to provide a cloak under which users can conduct information exchanges without revealing their identities or even the information they are exchanging. The possibility of anonymity in nearly every case stems from the distribution of information across the entire network, as well as the difficulty in tracking activities on the network as a whole.

Gnutella provides some degree of anonymity by enabling an essentially anonymous searching mechanism. It stops there, though. Gnutella reveals the IP address of a downloading host to the uploading host, and vice versa.

Gnutella pseudoanonymity

Gnutella is a prime example of peer-to-peer technology. It was, after all, the first successful, fully decentralized, peer-to-peer system. But in the policy debate, that's not a huge matter. What does matter is that Gnutella's message-based routing system affords its users a degree of anonymity by making request and response packets part of a crowd of similar packets issued by other participants in the network.

In most messages that are passed from node to node, there is no mention of anything that might tie a particular message to a particular user. On the Internet, identity is established using two points of data: An IP address and the time at which the packet containing the IP address was seen. Most Gnutella messages do not contain an IP address, so most messages are not useful in identifying Gnutella users. Also, Gnutella's routing system is not outwardly accessible. The routing tables are dynamic and stored in the memory of the countless Gnutella nodes for only a short time. It is therefore nearly impossible to learn which host originated a packet and which host is destined to receive it.

Furthermore, Gnutella's distributed nature means that there is no one place where an enforcement agency can plant a network monitor to spy on the system's communications. Gnutella is spread throughout the Internet, and the only way to monitor what is happening on the Gnutella network is to monitor what is happening on the entire Internet. Many are suspicious that such monitoring is possible, or even being done already. But given the vastness of today's Internet and its growing traffic, it's pretty unlikely.

What Gnutella does subject itself to, however, are things such as Zeropaid.com's Wall of Shame. The Wall of Shame, a Gnutella Trojan Horse, was an early attempt to nab alleged child pornography traffickers on the Gnutella network. This is how it worked: a few files with very suggestive filenames were shared by a special host. When someone attempted to download any of the files, the host would log the IP address of the downloader to a web page on the Wall of Shame. The host obtained the IP address of the downloader from its connection information.

That's where Gnutella's pseudoanonymity system breaks down. When you attempt to download, or when a host returns a result, identifying information is given out. Any host can be a decoy, logging that information. There are systems that are more interested in the anonymity aspects of peer-to-peer networking, and take steps such as proxied downloads to better protect the identities of the two endpoints. Those systems should be used if anonymity is a real concern.

The Wall of Shame met a rapid demise in a rather curious and very Internet way. Once news of its existence circulated on IRC, Gnutella users with disruptive senses of humor flooded the network with suggestive searches in their attempts to get their IP addresses on the Wall of Shame.

Downloads, now in the privacy of your own direct connection

So Gnutella's message-based routing system and its decentralization both give some anonymity to its users and make it difficult to track what exactly is happening. But what really confounds any attempt to learn who is actually sharing files is that downloads are a private transaction between only two hosts: the uploader and the downloader.

Instead of brokering a download through a central authority, Gnutella has sufficient information to reach out to the host that is sharing the desired file and grab it directly. With Napster, it's possible not only to learn what files are available on the host machines but what transactions are actually completed. All that can be done easily, within the warm confines of Napster's machine room.

With Gnutella, every router and cable on the Internet would need to be tapped to learn about transactions between Gnutella hosts or peers. When you double-click on a file, your Gnutella software establishes an HTTP connection directly to the host that holds the desired file. There is no brokering, even through the Gnutella network. In fact, the download itself has nothing to do with Gnutella: it's HTTP.

By being truly peer-to-peer, Gnutella gives no place to put the microscope. Gnutella doesn't have a mailing address, and, in fact, there isn't even anyone to whom to address the summons. But because of the breakdown in anonymity when a download is transacted, Gnutella could not be used as a system for publishing information anonymously. Not in its current form, anyway. So the argument that Gnutella provides anonymity from search through response through download is impossible to make.

Anonymous Gnutella chat

But then, Gnutella is not exclusively a file-sharing system. When there were fewer users on Gnutella, it was possible to use Gnutella's search monitor to chat with other Gnutella users. Since everyone could see the text of every search that was being issued on the network, users would type in searches that weren't searches at all: they were messages to other Gnutella users (see Figure 8-4).

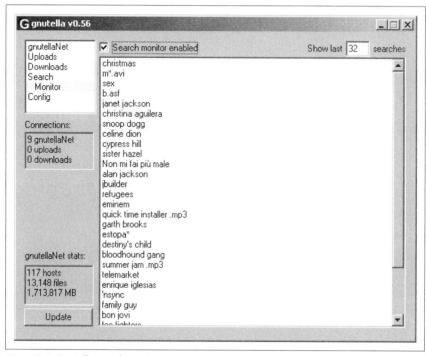

Figure 8-4. Gnutella search monitor

It was impossible to tell who was saying what, but conversations were taking place. If you weren't a part of the particular thread of discussion, the messages going by were meaningless to you. This is an excellent real-world example of the ideas behind Rivest's "Chaffing and Winnowing."* Just another message in a sea of messages. Keeping in mind that Gnutella gives total anonymity in searching, this search-based chat was in effect a totally anonymous chat! And we all thought we were just using Gnutella for small talk.

---

* Ronald L Rivest (1998), "Chaffing and Winnowing: Confidentiality without Encryption," http://www.toc.lcs.mit.edu/~rivest/chaffing.txt.

Next-generation peer-to-peer file-sharing technologies

No discussion about Gnutella, Napster, and Freenet is complete without at least a brief mention of the arms race and war of words between technologists and holders of intellectual property. What the recording industry is doing is sensitizing software developers and technologists to the legal ramifications of their inventions. Napster looked like a pretty good idea a year ago, but today Gnutella and Freenet look like much better ideas, technologically and politically. For anyone who isn't motivated by a business model, true peer-to-peer file-sharing technologies are the way to go.

It's easy to see where to put the toll booths in the Napster service, but taxing Gnutella is trickier. Not impossible, just trickier. Whatever tax system is successfully imposed on Gnutella, if any, will be voluntary and organic—in harmony with Gnutella, basically. The same will be true for next-generation peer-to-peer file-sharing systems, because they will surely be decentralized.

Predicting the future is impossible, but there are a few things that are set in concrete. If there is a successor to Gnutella, it will certainly learn from the lessons taught to Napster. It will learn from the problems that Gnutella has overcome and those that frustrate it today. For example, instead of the pseudoanonymity that Gnutella provides, next generation technologies may provide true anonymity through proxying and encryption. In the end, we can say with certainty that technology will outrun policy. It always has. The question is what impact that will have.

Gnutella's effects

Gnutella started the decentralized peer-to-peer revolution.* Before it, systems were centralized and boring. Innovation in software came mainly in the form of a novel business plan. But now, people are seriously thinking about how to turn the Internet upside down and see what benefits fall out.

Already, the effects of the peer-to-peer revolution are being felt. Peer-to-peer has captured the imagination of technologists, corporate strategists, and venture

---

* The earliest example of a peer-to-peer application that I can come up with is Zephyr chat, which resulted from MIT's Athena project in the early 1990s. Zephyr was succeeded by systems such as ICQ, which provided a commercialized, graphical, Windows-based instant messaging system along the lines of Zephyr. Next was Napster. And that is the last notable client/server-based, peer-to-peer system. Gnutella and Freenet were next, and they led the way in decentralized peer-to-peer systems.

capitalists alike. Peer-to-peer is even getting its own book. This isn't just a passing fad.

Certain aspects of peer-to-peer are mundane. Certain other aspects of it are so interesting as to get notables including George Colony, Andy Grove, and Marc Andreessen excited. That doesn't happen often. The power of peer-to-peer and its real innovation lies not just in its file-sharing applications and how well those applications can fly in the face of copyright holders while flying under the radar of legal responsibility. Its power also comes from its ability to do what makes plain sense and what has been overlooked for so long.

The basic premise underlying all peer-to-peer technologies is that individuals have something valuable to share. The gems may be computing power, network capacity, or information tucked away in files, databases, or other information repositories, but they are gems all the same. Successful peer-to-peer applications unlock those gems and share them with others in a way that makes sense in relation to the particular applications.

Tomorrow's Internet will look quite different than it does today. The World Wide Web is but a little blip on the timeline of technology development. It's only been a reality for the last six years! Think of the Web as the Internet equivalent of the telegraph: it's very useful and has taught us a lot, but it's pretty crude. Peer-to-peer technologies and the experience gained from Gnutella, Freenet, Napster, and instant messaging will reshape the Internet dramatically.

Unlike what many are saying today, I will posit the following: today's peer-to-peer applications are quite crude, but tomorrow's applications will not be strictly peer-to-peer or strictly client/server, or strictly anything for that matter. Today's peer-to-peer applications are necessarily overtly peer-to-peer (often to the users' chagrin) because they must provide application and infrastructure simultaneously due to the lack of preexisting peer-to-peer infrastructure. Such infrastructure will be put into place sooner than we think. Tomorrow's applications will take this infrastructure for granted and leverage it to provide more powerful software and a better user experience in much the same way modern Internet infrastructure has.

In the short term, decentralized peer-to-peer may spell the end of censorship and copyright. Looking out, peer-to-peer will enable crucial applications that are so useful and pervasive that we will take them for granted.

chapter nine

Freenet

Adam Langley, Freenet

Freenet is a decentralized system for distributing files that demonstrates a particularly strong form of peer-to-peer. It combines many of the benefits associated with other peer-to-peer models, including robustness, scalability, efficiency, and privacy.

In the case of Freenet, decentralization is pivotal to its goals, which are the following:

- Prevent censorship of documents
- Provide anonymity for users
- Remove any single point of failure or control
- Efficiently store and distribute documents
- Provide plausible deniability for node operators

Freenet grew out of work done by Ian Clarke when he was at the University of Edinburgh, Scotland, but it is now maintained by volunteers on several continents.

Some of the goals of Freenet are very difficult to bring together in one system. For example, efficient distribution of files has generally been done by a centralized system, and doing it with a decentralized system is hard.

However, decentralized networks have many advantages over centralized ones. The Web as it is today has many problems that can be traced to its client/server model. The Slashdot effect, whereby popular data becomes less accessible because of the load of the requests on a central server, is an obvious example.

Centralized client/server systems are also vulnerable to censorship and technical failure because they rely on a small number of very large servers.

Finally, privacy is a casualty of the structure of today's Web. Servers can tell who is accessing or posting a document because of the direct link to the reader/poster. By cross-linking the records of many servers, a large amount of information can be gathered about a user. For example, DoubleClick, Inc., is already doing this. By using direct marketing databases and information obtained through sites that display their advertisements, DoubleClick can gather very detailed and extensive information. In the United States there are essentially no laws protecting privacy online or requiring companies to handle information about people responsibly. Therefore, these companies are more or less free to do what they wish with the data.

We hope Freenet will solve some of these problems.

Freenet consists of nodes that pass messages to each other. A node is simply a computer that is running the Freenet software, and all nodes are treated as equals by the network. This removes any single point of failure or control. By following the Freenet protocol, many such nodes spontaneously organize themselves into an efficient network.

Requests

In order to make use of Freenet's distributed resources, a user must initiate a request. Requests are messages that can be forwarded through many different nodes. Initially the user forwards the request to a node that he or she knows about and trusts (usually one running on his or her own computer). If a node doesn't have the document that the requestor is looking for, it forwards the request to another node that, according to its information, is more likely to have the document. The messages form a chain as each node forwards the request to the next node. Messages time out after passing through a certain number of nodes, so that huge chains don't form. (The mechanism for dropping requests, called the hops-to-live count, is a simple system similar to that used for Internet routing.) The chain ends when the message times out or when a node replies with the data.

The reply is passed back though each node that forwarded the request, back to the original node that started the chain. Each node in the chain may cache the reply locally, so that it can reply immediately to any further requests for that particular document. This means that commonly requested documents are cached on more nodes, and thus there is no Slashdot effect whereby one node becomes overloaded.

The reply contains an address of one of the nodes that it came through, so that nodes can learn about other nodes over time. This means that Freenet becomes increasingly connected. Thus, you may end up getting data from a node you didn't even know about. In fact, you still might not know that that node exists after you get the answer to the request—each node knows only the ones it communicates with directly and possibly one other node in the chain.

Because no node can tell where a request came from beyond the node that forwarded the request to it, it is very difficult to find the person who started the request. This provides anonymity to the users who use Freenet.

Freenet doesn't provide perfect anonymity (like the Mixmaster network discussed in Chapter 7, *Mixmaster Remailers*) because it balances paranoia against efficiency and usability. If someone wants to find out exactly what you are doing, then given the resources, they will. Freenet does, however, seek to stop mass, indiscriminate surveillance of people.

A powerful attacker that can perform traffic analysis of the whole network could see who started a request, and if they controlled a significant number of nodes so that they could be confident that the request would pass through one of their nodes, they could also see what was being requested. However, the resources needed to do that would be incredible, and such an attacker could find better ways to snoop on users.

An attacker who simply controlled a few nodes, even large ones, couldn't find who was requesting documents and couldn't generate false documents (see "Key Types," later in this chapter). They couldn't gather information about people and they couldn't censor documents. It is these attackers that Freenet seeks to stop.

Detail of requests

Each request is given a unique ID number by the node that initiates it, and this serves to identify all messages generated by that request. If a node receives a message with the same unique ID as one it has already processed, it won't process it again. This keeps loops from forming in the network, which would congest the network and reduce overall system performance.

The two main types of requests are the *InsertRequest* and the *DataRequest*. The *DataRequest* simply asks that the data linked with a specified key is returned; these form the bulk of the requests on Freenet. *InsertRequests* act exactly like *DataRequests* except that an *InsertReply*, not a *TimedOut* message, is returned if the request times out.

This means that if an attacker tries to insert data which already exists on Freenet, the existing data will be returned (because it acts like a *DataRequest*), and the attacker will only succeed in spreading the existing data as nodes cache the reply.

If the data doesn't exist, an *InsertReply* is sent back, and the client can then send a *DataInsert* to actually insert the new document. The insert isn't routed like a normal message but follows the same route as the *InsertRequest* did. Intermediate nodes cache the new data. After a *DataInsert*, future *DataRequests* will return the document.

The data store

The major tasks each node must perform—deciding where to route requests, remembering where to return answers to requests, and choosing how long to store documents—revolve around a stack model. Figure 9-1 shows what a stack could contain.

KEY	DATA	ADDRESS
8e0109xb87wkhkujhs98k	99usbkjhgd7333khjgs763	tcp/5.34.27.4:6473
uushs89763kjhx7w732722	yy6254231gsyw4GGcwhgs	tcp/89.34.36.1:24855
kjhks872228x0982876jjhd	TTRas384hgygduybv1111n	tcp/194.44.62.66:9897
878772kx762776xbv8622		tcp/64.28.67.48:43653
222764kjhx8t63wkbkjs77w		tcp/4.18.49.35:65466
57765xkjhd72729jnbck01kj		tcp/55.18.4.1:3895

Figure 9-1. Stack used by a Freenet node

Each key in the data store is associated with the data itself and an address to the node where the data came from. Below a certain point the node no longer stores the data related to a key, only the address. Thus the most often requested data is kept locally. Documents that are requested more often are moved up in the stack, displacing the less requested ones. The distance that documents are moved is linked to the size, so that bigger documents are at a disadvantage. This gives people an incentive not to waste space on Freenet and so compress documents before inserting.

When a node receives a request for a key (or rather the document that is indexed by that key), it first looks to see if it has the data locally. If it does, the request is answered immediately. If not, the node searches the data store to find the key closest to the requested key (as I'll explain in a moment). The node referenced by the closest key is the one that the request is forwarded to. Thus nodes will forward to the node that has data closest to the requested key.

The exact closeness function used is complex and linked to details of the data store that are beyond this chapter. However, imagine the key being treated as a number, so that the closest key is defined as the one where the absolute difference between two keys is a minimum.

The closeness operation is the cornerstone of Freenet's routing, because it allows nodes to become biased toward a certain part of the keyspace. Through routine node interactions, certain nodes spontaneously emerge as the most often referenced nodes for data close to a certain key. Because those nodes will then frequently receive requests for a certain area of the keyspace, they will cache those documents. And then, because they are caching certain documents, other nodes will add more references to them for those documents, and so on, forming a positive feedback.

A node cannot decide what area of the keyspace it will specialize in because that depends on the references held by other nodes. If a node could decide what area of the keyspace it would be asked for, it could position itself as the preferred source for a certain document and then seek to deny access to it, thus censoring it.

For a more detailed discussion of the routing system, see Chapter 14, *Performance*. The routing of requests is the key to Freenet's scalability and efficiency. It also allows data to "move." If a document from North America is often requested in Europe, it is more likely to soon be on European servers, thus reducing expensive transatlantic traffic. (But neighboring nodes can be anywhere on the Internet. While it makes sense for performance reasons to connect to nodes that are geographically close, that is definitely not required.)

Because each node tries to forward the request closer and closer to the data, the search is many times more powerful than a linear search and much more efficient than a broadcast. It's like looking for a small village in medieval times. You would ask at each village you passed through for directions. Each time you passed through a village you would be sent closer and closer to your destination. This method (akin to Freenet's routing closer to data) is much quicker than the linear method of going to every village in turn until you found the right one. It also means that Freenet scales well as more nodes and data are added. It is also better than the Gnutella-like system of sending thousands of messengers to all the villages in the hope of finding the right one.

The stack model also provides the answer to the problem of culling data. Any storage system must remove documents when it is full, or reject all new data. Freenet nodes stop storing the data in a document when the document is pushed too far down the stack. The key and address are kept, however. This means that future requests for the document will be routed to the node that is most likely to have it.

This data-culling method allows Freenet to remove the least requested data, not the least agreeable data. If the most unpopular data was removed, this could be used to censor documents. The Freenet design is very careful not to allow this.

The distinction between unpopular and unwanted is important here. Unpopular data is disliked by a lot of people, and Freenet doesn't try to remove that because that would lead to a tyranny of the majority. Unwanted data is simply data that is not requested. It may be liked, it may not, but nobody is interested in it.

Every culling method has problems, and on balance this method has been selected as the best. We hope that the pressure for disk space won't be so high that documents are culled quickly. Storage capacity is increasing at an exponential rate, so Freenet's capacity should also. If an author wants to keep a document in Freenet, all he or she has to do is request or reinsert it every so often.

It should be noted that the culling is done individually by each node. If a document (say, a paper at a university) is of little interest globally, it can still be in local demand so that local nodes (say, the university's node) will keep it.

Keys

As has already been noted, every document is indexed by a key. But Freenet has more than one type of key—each with certain advantages and disadvantages.

Since individual nodes on Freenet are inherently untrusted, nodes must not be allowed to return false documents. Otherwise, those false documents will be cached and the false data will spread like a cancer. The main job of the key types is to prevent this cancer. Each node in a chain checks that the document is valid before forwarding it back toward the requester. If it finds that the document is invalid, it stops accepting traffic from the bad node and restarts the request.

Every key can be treated as an array of bytes, no matter which type it is. This is important because the closeness function, and thus the routing, treats them as equivalent. These functions are thus independent of key type.

Key types

Freenet defines a general Uniform Resource Indicator (URI) in the form:

freenet:keytype@data

where binary data is encoded using a slightly changed Base64 scheme. Each key type has its own interpretation of the *data* part of the URI, which is explained with the key type.

Documents can contain metadata that redirects clients to another key. In this way, keys can be chained to provide the advantages of more than one key type. The rest of this section describes the various types of keys.

Content Hash Keys (CHKs)

A CHK is formed from a hash of the data. A hash function takes any input and produces a fixed-length output, where finding two inputs that give the same output is computationally impossible. For further information on the purpose of hashes, see the section on "Message digest functions" in Chapter 15, *Trust*.

Since a document is returned in response to a request that includes its CHK, a node can check the integrity of the returned document by running the same hash function on it and comparing the resulting hash to the CHK provided. If the hashes match, it is the correct document. CHKs provide a unique and tamperproof key, and so the bulk of the data on Freenet is stored under CHKs. CHKs also reduce the redundancy of data, since the same data will have the same CHK and will collide on insertion. However, CHKs do not allow updating, nor are they memorable.

A CHK URI looks like the following example:

freenet:CHK@
DtqiMnTj8YbhScLp1BQoW9In9C4DAQ,2jmj7l5rSw0yVb-vlWAYkA

Keyword Signed Keys (KSKs)

KSKs appear as text strings to the user (for example, "text/books/1984.html"), and so are easy to remember. A common misunderstanding about Freenet, arising from the directory-like format of KSKs, is that there is a hierarchy. There isn't. It is only by convention that KSKs look like directory structures; they are actually freeform strings.

KSKs are transformed by clients into a binary key type. The transformation process makes it impractical to recover the string from the binary key. KSKs are based on a public key system where, in order to generate a valid KSK document, you need to know the original string. Thus, a node that sees only the binary form of the KSK does not know the string and cannot generate a cancerous reply that the requestor would accept.

KSKs are the weakest of the key types in this respect, as it is possible that a node could try many common human strings (such as "Democratic" and "China" in many different sentences) to find out what string produced a given KSK and then generate false replies.

KSKs can also clash as different people insert different data while trying to use the same string. For example, there are many versions of the Bible. Hopefully the Freenet caching system should cause the most requested version to become dominant. Tweaks to aid this solution are still under discussion.

A KSK URI looks like this:

freenet:KSK@text/books/1984.html

Signature Verification Keys (SVKs)

SVKs are based on the same public key system as KSKs but are purely binary. When an SVK is generated, the client calculates a private key to go with it. The point of SVKs is to provide something that can be updated by the owner of the private key but by no one else.

SVKs also allow people to make a subspace, which is a way of controlling a set of keys. This allows people to establish pseudonyms on Freenet. When people trust the owner of a subspace, documents in that subspace are also trusted while the owner's anonymity remains protected. Systems like Gnutella and Napster that don't have an anonymous trust capability are already finding that attackers flood the network with false documents.

Named SVKs can be inserted "under" another SVK, if one has its private key. This means you can generate an SVK and announce that it is yours (possibly under a pseudonym), and then insert documents under that subspace. People trust that the document was inserted by you, because only you know the private key and so only you can insert in that subspace. Since the documents have names, they are easy to remember (given that the user already has the base SVK, which is binary), and no one can insert a document with the same key before you, as they can with a KSK.

An SVK URI looks like this:

freenet:SVK@
XChKB7aBZAMIMK2cBArQRo7v05ECAQ,7SThKCDy~QCuODt8xP=KzHA

or for an SVK with a document name:

freenet:SSK@ U7MyLl0mHrjm6443k1svLUcLWFUQAgE/text/books/1984.html

Keys and redirects

Redirects use the best aspects of each kind of key. For example, if you wanted to insert the text of George Orwell's *1984* into Freenet, you would insert it as a CHK and then insert a KSK like "Orwell/1984" that redirects to that CHK. Recent Freenet clients will do this automatically for you. By doing this you have a unique key for the document that you can use in links (where people don't need to remember the key), and a memorable key that is valuable when people are either guessing the key or can't get the CHK.

All documents in Freenet are encrypted before insertion. The key is either random and distributed by the requestor along with the URI, or based on data that a node cannot know (like the string of a KSK). Either way, a node cannot tell what data is contained in a document. This has two effects. First, node operators cannot stop their nodes from caching or forwarding content that they object to, because they have no way of telling what the content of a document is. For example, a node operator cannot stop his or her node from carrying pro-Nazi propaganda, no matter how anti-Nazi he or she may be. It also means that a node operator cannot be responsible for what is on his or her node.

However, if a certain document became notorious, node operators could purge that document from their data stores and refuse to process requests for that key. If enough operators did this, the document could be effectively removed from Freenet. All it takes to bypass explicit censorship, though, is for an anonymous person to change one byte of the document and reinsert it. Since the document has been changed, it will have a different key. If an SVK is used, they needn't even change it at all because the key is random. So trying to remove documents from Freenet is futile.

Because a node that does not have a requested document will get the document from somewhere else (if it can), an attacker can never find which nodes store a document without spreading it. It is currently possible to send a request with a hops-to-live count of 1 to a node to bypass this protection, because the message goes to only one node and is not forwarded. Successful retrieval can tell the requestor that the document must be on that node.

Future releases will treat the hops-to-live as a probabilistic system to overcome this. In this system, there will be a certain probability that the hops-to-live count will be decremented, so an attacker can't know whether or not the message was forwarded.

Conclusions

In simulations, Freenet works well. The average number of hops for requests of random keys is about 10 and seems largely independent of network size. The simulated network is also resilient to node failure, as the number of hops remains below 20 even after 10% of nodes have failed. This suggests that Freenet will scale very well. More research on scaling is presented in Chapter 14.

At the time of writing, Freenet is still very much in development, and a number of central issues are yet to be decided. Because of Freenet's design, it is very difficult to know how many nodes are currently participating. But it seems to be working well at the moment.

Searching and updating are the major areas that need work right now. During searches, some method must be found whereby requests are routed closer and closer to the answer in order to maintain the efficiency of the network. But search requests are fuzzy, so the idea of routing by key breaks down here. It seems at this early stage that searching will be based on a different concept. Searching also calls for node-readable metadata in documents, so node operators would know what is on their nodes and could then be required to control it. Any searching system must counter this breach as best it can.

Even at this early stage, however, Freenet is solving many of the problems seen in centralized networks. Popular data, far from being less available as requests increase (the Slashdot effect), becomes more available as nodes cache it. This is, of course, the correct reaction of a network storage system to popular data. Freenet also removes the single point of attack for censors, the single point of technical failure, and the ability for people to gather large amounts of personal information about a reader.

chapter ten

Red Rover

Alan Brown, Red Rover

The success of Internet-based distributed computing will certainly cause head-aches for censors. Peer-to-peer technology can boast populations in the tens of millions, and the home user now has access to the world's most advanced cryptography. It's wonderful to see those who turned technology against free expression for so long now scrambling to catch up with those setting information free. But it's far too early to celebrate: What makes many of these systems so attractive in countries where the Internet is not heavily regulated is precisely what makes them the wrong tool for much of the world.

Red Rover was invented in recognition of the irony that the very people who would seem to benefit the most from these systems are in fact the least likely to be able to use them. A partial list of the reasons this is so includes the following:

The delivery of the client itself can be blocked
> The perfect stealth device does no good if you can't obtain it. Yet, in exactly those countries where user secrecy would be the most valuable, access to the client application is the most guarded. Once the state recognized the potential of the application, it would not hesitate to block web sites and FTP sites from which the application could be downloaded and, based on the application's various compressed and encrypted sizes, filter email that might be carrying it in.

Possession of the client is easily criminalized
> If a country is serious enough about curbing outside influence to block web sites, it will have no hesitation about criminalizing possession of any application that could challenge this control. This would fall under the ubiquitous legal category "threat to state security." It's a wonderful advance for technology that some peer-to-peer applications can pass messages even the

CIA can't read. But in some countries, being caught with a clever peer-to-peer application may mean you never see your family again. This is no exaggeration: in Burma, the possession of a modem—*even a broken one*—could land you in court.

Information trust requires knowing the origin of the information

Information on most peer-to-peer systems permits the dissemination of poisoned information as easily as it does reliable information. Some systems succeed in controlling disreputable transmissions. On most, though, there's an information free-for-all. With the difference between freedom and jail hinging on the reliability of information you receive, would you really trust a Wrapster file that could have originated with any one of 20 million peer clients?

Non-Web encryption is more suspicious

Encrypted information can be recognized because of its unnatural entropy values (that is, the frequencies with which characters appear are not what is normally expected in the user's language). It is generally tolerated when it comes from web sites, probably because no country is eager to hinder online financial transactions. But especially when more and more states are charging ISPs with legal responsibility for their customers' online activities, encrypted code from a non-Web source will attract suspicion. Encryption may keep someone from reading what's passing through a server, but it never stops him from logging it and confronting the end user with its existence. In a country with relative Internet freedom, this isn't much of a problem. In one without it, the cracking of your key is not the only thing to fear.

I emphasize these concerns because current peer-to-peer systems show marked signs of having been created in relatively free countries. They are not designed with particular sensitivity to users in countries where stealth activities are easily turned into charges of subverting the state. States where privacy is the most threatened are the very states where, for your own safety, you must not take on the government: if they want to block a web site, you need to let them do so for your own safety.

Many extant peer-to-peer approaches offer other ways to get at a site's information (web proxies, for example), but the information they provide tends to be untrustworthy and the method for obtaining it difficult or dangerous.

Red Rover offers the benefits of peer-to-peer technology while offering a clientless alternative to those taking the risk behind the firewall. The Red Rover anticensorship strategy does not require the information seeker to download any software, place any incriminating programs on her hard drive, or create any two-way electronic trails with information providers. The benefactor of Red Rover needs only to know how to count and how to operate a web browser to access a web-based email account.

Red Rover is technologically very "open" and will hopefully succeed at traversing censorship barriers not by electronic stealth but by simple brute force. The Red Rover distributed clients create a population of contraband providers which is far too large, changing, and growing for any nation's web-blocking software to keep up with.

Architecture

Red Rover is designed to keep a channel of information open to those behind censorship walls by exploiting some now mundane features of the Internet, such as dynamic IP addresses and the unbalanced ratio of Red Rover clients to censors. Operating out in the open at a low-tech level helps keep Red Rover's benefactors from appearing suspicious. In fact, Red Rover makes use of aspects of the current Internet that other projects consider liabilities, such as the impermanent connections of ordinary Internet users and the widespread use of free, web-based email services. The benefactors, those behind the censorship barrier (hereafter, "subscribers"), never even need to see a Red Rover client application: users of the client are in other countries.

The following description of the Red Rover strategy will be functional (i.e., top-down) because that is the best way to see the rationale behind decisions that make Red Rover unique among peer-to-peer projects. It will be clear that the Red Rover strategy openly and necessarily embraces human protocols, rather than performing all of its functions at the algorithmic level. The description is simplified in the interest of saving space.

The Red Rover application is not a proxy server, not a site mirror, and not a gate allowing someone to surf the Web through the client. The key elements of the system are hosts on ordinary dial-up connections run by Internet users who volunteer to download data that the Red Rover administrator wants to provide. Lists of these hosts and the content they offer, changing rapidly as the hosts come and go over the course of a day, are distributed by the Red Rover hub to the subscribers. The distribution mechanism is done in a way that minimizes the risk of attracting attention.

It should be clear, too, that Red Rover is a strategy, not just the software application that bears the name. Again, those who benefit the most from Red Rover will never see the program. The strategy is tripartite and can be summarized as follows. (The following sentence is deliberately awkward, for reasons explained in the next section.)

3 simple layers: the hub, the client, & sub scriber.

The hub

The hub is the server from which all information originates. It publishes two types of information.

First, the hub creates packages of HTML files containing the information the hub administrator wants to pass through the censorship barrier. These packages will go to the clients at a particular time. Second, the hub creates a plain text, email notification that explains what material is available at a particular time and which clients (listing their IP addresses) have the material. The information may be encoded in a nontraditional way that avoids attracting attention from software sniffers, as described later in this chapter.

The accuracy of these text messages is time-limited, because clients go on- and offline. A typical message will list perhaps 10 IP addresses of active clients, selected randomly from the hub's list of active clients for a particular time.

The hub distributes the HTML packages to the clients, which can be done in a straightforward manner. The next step is to get the text messages to the subscribers, which is much trickier because it has to be done in such a way as to avoid drawing the attention of authorities that might be checking all traffic.

The hub would never send a message directly to any subscriber, because the hub's IP address and domain name are presumed to be known to authorities engaged in censorship. Instead, the hub sends text messages to clients and asks them to forward them to the subscribers. Furthermore, the client that forwards this email would never be listed in its own outgoing email as a source for an HTML package. Instead, each client sends mail listing the IP addresses of *other* clients. The reason for this is that if a client sent out its own IP address and the subscriber were then to visit it, the authorities could detect evidence of two-way communication. It would be much safer if the notification letter and the subscriber's decision to surf took different routes.

The IP addresses on these lists are "encrypted" at the hub in some nonstandard manner that doesn't use hashing algorithms, so that they don't set off either entropy or pattern detectors. For example, that ungrammatical "3 simple layers" sentence at the end of the last section would reveal the IP address 166.33.36.137 to anyone who knew the convention for decoding it. The convention is that each digit in an IP address is represented by the number of letters in a word, and octets are separated by punctuation marks. Thus, since there is 1 letter in "3," 6 in "simple," and 6 in "layers," the phrase "3 simple layers" yields the octet 166 to someone who understands the convention.

Sending a list of 10 unencoded IP addresses to someone could easily be detected by a script. But by current standards, high-speed extraction of any email containing a sentence with bad grammar would result in an overwhelming flood of false positives. The "encryption" method, then, is invisible in its overtness. Practical detection would require a great expenditure of human effort, and for this reason, this method should succeed by its pure brute force. The IP addresses will get through.

The hub also keeps track of the following information about the subscriber:

* Her web-based email address, allowing her the option of proxy access to email and frequent address changes without overhead to the hub.

* The dates and times that she wishes to receive information (which she could revise during each Red Rover client visit, perhaps via SSL, in order to avoid identifiable patterns of online behavior).

* Her secret key, in case she prefers to take her chances with encrypted list notifications (an option Red Rover would offer).

The clients

The clients are free software applications that are run on computers around the world by ordinary, dial-up Internet users who volunteer to devote a bit of their system usage to Red Rover. Clients run in the background and act as both personal web servers and email notification relays. When the user on the client system logs on, the client sends its IP address to the hub, which registers it as active. For most dial-up accounts, this means that, statistically, the IP will differ from the one the client had for its last session. This simple fact plays an important role in client longevity, as discussed below.

Once the client is registered, the hub sends it two things. The first is an HTML package, which the client automatically posts for anyone accessing the IP address through a browser. (URL encryption would be a nice feature to offer here, but not an essential one.)

The second message from the hub is an email containing the IP list, plus some filler to make sure the size of the message is random. This email will be forwarded automatically from the receiving Red Rover client to a subscriber's web-based email account. These emails will be generated in random sizes as an added frustration to automated censors which hunt for packet sizes.

The email list, with its unhashed encryption of the IP addresses, is itself fully encrypted at the hub and decrypted by a client-specific key by the client just before mailing it to the subscriber. This way, the client user doesn't know anything about who she's sending mail to. The client will also forward the email with a spoofed originating IP address so that if the email is undelivered, it will not be returned to the sender. If it did return, it would be possible for a malicious user of the client (censors and police, for example) to determine the subscriber's email address simply by reading it off of the route-tracing information revealed by any of a variety of publicly available products. Together with the use of web-based accounts for subscriber email, rather than ISP accounts, subscriber privacy will benefit from these precautions.

The subscribers

The subscriber's role requires a good deal of caution, and anyone taking it on must understand how to make the safest use of Red Rover as well as the legal consequences of getting caught. The subscriber's actions should be assumed, after all, to be entirely logged by the state or its agents from start to finish.

The first task of the subscriber is to use a side channel (a friend visiting outside the country, for instance, or a phone call or postal letter) to give the hub the information needed to maintain contact. She also needs to open a free web-based email account in a country outside the area being censored. Then, after she puts in place any other optional precautions she feels will help keep her under the authorities' digital radar (and perhaps real-life radar), she can receive messages and download controversial material. Figure 10-1 shows how information travels between the hub, clients, and servers.

In particular, it is wise for subscribers to change their notification times frequently. This decreases the possibility of the authorities sending false information or attempting to entrap a subscriber by sending a forged IP notification email (containing only police IPs) at a time they suspect the subscriber expects notification. If the subscriber is diligent and creates new email addresses frequently, it is far less likely that a trap will succeed. The subscriber is also advised to ignore any notification sent even one second different from her requested subscription time. Safe subscription and subscription-changing protocols involve many interesting options, but these will not be detailed here.

When the client is closed or the computer disconnected, the change is registered by the hub, and that IP address is no longer included on outgoing notifications. Those subscribers who had already received an email with that IP address on it would find it did not serve Red Rover information, if indeed it worked at

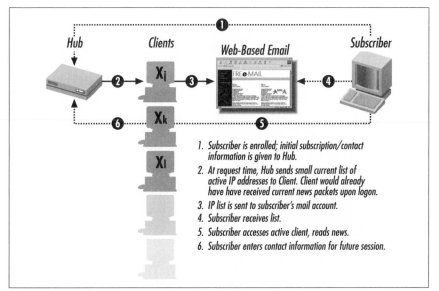

1. Subscriber is enrolled; initial subscription/contact information is given to Hub.
2. At request time, Hub sends small current list of active IP addresses to Client. Client would already have have received current news packets upon logon.
3. IP list is sent to subscriber's mail account.
4. Subscriber receives list.
5. Subscriber accesses active client, reads news.
6. Subscriber enters contact information for future session.

Figure 10-1. The flow of information between the hub, clients, and servers

all from the browser. The subscribers would then try the other IP addresses on the list. The information posted by the hub is identical on all clients, and the odds that the subscriber would find one that worked before all the clients on the list disconnect are quite high.

Client life cycle

Every peer-to-peer system has to deal with the possibility that clients will disappear unexpectedly, but senescence is actually assumed for Red Rover clients. Use it long enough and, just as with tax cheating, they'll probably catch up with you. In other words, the client's available IPs will eventually all be blocked by the authorities.

The predominant way nations block web sites is by IP address. This generally means all four octets are blocked, since C-class blocking (blocking any of the possibilities in the fourth octet of the IP address) could punish unrelated web sites. Detection has so far tended to result not in prosecution of the web visitor, but only in the blocking of the site. In China, for example, it will generally take several days, and often two weeks, for a "subversive" site to be blocked.

The nice thing about a personal web server is that when a user logs on to a dial-up account, the user will most likely be assigned a fourth octet different from the one she had in previous sessions. With most ISPs, odds are good of getting a different third octet as well. This means that a client can sustain a great number of blocks before becoming useless, and, depending on the government's methods (and human workload), many events are likely to evade any notice whatsoever. But whenever the adversary is successful in completely blocking a Red Rover client's accessible IP addresses, that's the end of that client's usefulness— at least until the user switches ISPs. (Hopefully she'll choose a new ISP that hasn't been blocked due to detection of *another* Red Rover client.) Some users can make their clients more mobile, and therefore harder to detect, by subscribing to a variety of free dial-up services.

A fact in our favor is that it is considered extremely unlikely that countries will ever massively block the largest ISPs. A great deal of damage to both commerce and communication would result from a country blocking a huge provider like, for example, America Online, which controls nearly a quarter of the American dial-up market. This means that even after many years of blocking Red Rovers, there will still always be virgin IPs for them. Or so we hope.

The Red Rover strategy depends upon a dynamic population. On one level, each user can stay active if she has access to abundant, constantly changing IP addresses. And at another level, Red Rover clients, after they become useless or discontinued, are refreshed by new users, compounding the frustration of would-be blockers.

The client will be distributed freely at software archives and partner web sites after its release, and will operate without user maintenance. A web site (see "Acknowledgments") is already live to provide updates and news about the strategy, as well as a downloadable client.

Putting low-tech "weaknesses" into perspective

Red Rover creates a high-tech relationship between the hub and the client (using SL and strong encryption) and a low-tech relationship between the client and the subscriber. Accordingly, this latter relationship is inherently vulnerable to security-related difficulties. Since we receive many questions challenging the viability of Red Rover, we present below in dialogue form our responses to some of these questions in the hope of putting these security "weaknesses" into perspective.

Skeptic:

> I understand that the subscriber could change subscription times and addresses during a Red Rover visit. But how would anyone *initially* subscribe? If subscription is done online or to an email site, nothing would pre-

vent *those* sites from being blocked. The prospective subscriber may even be at risk for *trying* to subscribe.

Red Rover:

True, the low-tech relationship between Red Rover and the client means that Red Rover must leave many of the steps of the strategy to the subscriber. As we've said above, another channel such as a letter or phone call (not web or email communication) will eventually be necessary to initiate contact since the Red Rover site and sites which mirror it will inevitably be victims of blocking. But this requirement is no different than other modern security systems. SSL depends on the user downloading a browser from a trusted location; digital signatures require out-of-band techniques for a certificate authority to verify the person requesting the digital signature.

This is *not* a weakness; it is a strength. By permitting a diversity of solutions on the part of the subscribers, we make it much harder for a government to stop subscription traffic. It also lets the user determine the solution ingredients she believes are safest for her, whether public key cryptography (legal, for now, in many blocking countries), intercession by friends who are living in or visiting countries where subscribing would not be risky, proxy-served requests to forward email to organizations likely to cooperate, etc.

We are confident that word of mouth and other means will spread the news of the availability of Red Rover. It is up to the subscriber, though, to first offer her invitation to crash the censorship barrier. For many, subscribing may not be worth the risk. But for every subscriber who gets information from Red Rover, word of mouth can also help hundreds to learn of the content.

If this response is not as systematic as desired, remember that prospective subscribers face vastly different risks based on their country, profession, technical background, criminal history, dependents, and other factors. Where a problem is not recursively enumerable, the best solution to it will rarely be an algorithm. A variety of subscription opportunities, combined with non-patterned choices by each subscriber, leads to the same kind of protection that encryption offers in computing: Both benefit from increased entropy.

Skeptic:

What is to stop a government from cracking the client and cloning their own application to entrap subscribers or send altered information?

Red Rover:

Red Rover has to address this problem at both the high-tech and low-tech levels. I can't cover all strategies available to combat counterfeiting, but I can lay out what we've accomplished in our design.

At the high-tech level, we have to make sure the hub can't be spoofed, that the client knows if some other source is sending data and pretending to be the hub. This is a problem *any* secure distributed system must address, and a number of successful peer-to-peer systems have already led the way in solving this problem. Red Rover can adopt one of these solutions for the relationship between the hub and clients. This aspect of Red Rover does not need to be novel.

Addressing this question for the low-tech relationship is far more interesting. An alert subscriber will know, to the second, what time she is to receive email notifications. This information is sent and recorded using an SSL-like solution, so if that time (and perhaps other clues) isn't present on the email, the subscriber will know to ignore any IP addresses encoded in it.

Skeptic:

Ah, but what stops the government from intercepting the IP list, altering it to reflect different IP addresses, and *then* forwarding it to the subscriber? After all, you don't use standard encryption and digest techniques to secure the list.

Red Rover:

First, we have taken many precautions to make it hard for surveillance personnel to actually notice or suspect the email containing the IP list. Second, remember that we told the subscribers to choose web-based email accounts outside the boundaries of the censoring country. If the email is waiting at a web-based site in the United States, the censoring government would have to intercept a message during the subscriber's download, determine that it contained a Red Rover IP address (which we've encoded in a low-tech manner to make it hard to recognize), substitute their own encoded IP address, and finish delivering the message to the subscriber. All this would have to be done in the amount of time it takes for mail to download, so as not to make the subscriber suspicious. It would be statistically incredible to expect such an event to occur.

Skeptic:

But the government could hack the web-based mail site and change the email content without the subscriber knowing. So there wouldn't be any delay.

Red Rover:

Even if this happened, the government wouldn't know when to expect the email to arrive, since this information was passed from the subscriber to the client via SSL. And if the government examined and counterfeited every unread email waiting for the subscriber, the subscriber would know from our instructions that any email which is not received "immediately" (in some sense based on experience) should be distrusted. It is in the subscriber's interest to be prompt in retrieving the web pages from the clients anyway, since the longer the delay, the greater the chance that the client's IP address will become inactive. Still, stagnant IP lists are far more likely to be useless than dangerous.

Skeptic:

A social engineering question, then. Why would anyone want to run this client? They don't get free music, and it doesn't phone E.T. Aren't you counting a little too much on people's good will to assume they'll sacrifice their valuable RAM for advancing human rights?

Red Rover:

This has been under some debate. Options always include adding file server functions or IRC capability to entice users into spending a lot of time at the sponsor's site. Another thought was letting users add their own, client-specific customized page to the HTML offering, one which would appear last so as not to interfere with the often slow downloading of the primary content by subscribers in countries with stiff Internet and phone rates and slow modems. This customized page could be pictures of their dog, editorials, or, sadly but perhaps crucially, advertising. Companies could even pay Red Rover users to post their ads, an obvious incentive. But many team members are rightfully concerned that if Red Rover becomes viewed as a mercantile tool, it would repel both subscribers and client users. These discussions continue.

Skeptic:

Where does the name "Red Rover" come from?

Red Rover:

Red Rover is a playground game analogous to the strategy we adopted for our anti-censorship system. Children form two equal lines, facing each other. One side invites an attacker from the other, yelling to the opposing line: "Red Rover, Red Rover, send Lena right over." Lena then runs at full speed at the line of children who issued the challenge, and her goal is to break through the barrier of joined arms and cut the line. If Lena breaks through, she takes a child back with her to her line; if she fails, she joins that line. The two sides alternate challenges until one of the lines is completely absorbed by the other.

It is a game, ultimately, with no losers. Except, of course, the kid who stayed too rigid when Lena rammed him and ended up with a dislocated shoulder.

We hope Red Rover leads to similar results.

Acknowledgments

The author is grateful to the following individuals for discussions and feedback on Red Rover: Erich Moechel, Gus Hosein, Richard Long, Sergei Smirnov, Andrey Kuvshinov, Lance Cottrell, Otmar Lendl, Roger Dingledine, David Molnar, and two anonymous reviewers. All errors are the author's.

Red Rover was unveiled in April 2000 at *Outlook on Freedom*, Moscow, sponsored by the Human Rights Organization (Russia) and the National Press Institute, in a talk entitled "A Functional Strategy for an Online Anti-Blocking Remedy," delivered by the author. Red Rover's current partners include Anonymizer, Free Haven, Quintessenz, and VIP Reference. Updates about production progress and contact information about Red Rover will be posted at *http://redrover.org*.

chapter eleven

Publius

Marc Waldman, Lorrie Faith Cranor,
and Avi Rubin, AT&T Labs-Research

Publius is a web-based publishing system that resists censorship and tampering. A file published with Publius is replicated across many servers, making it very hard for any individual or organized group to destroy the document. Distributing the document also provides resistance to so-called distributed denial of service (DDoS) attacks, which have been used in highly publicized incidents to make a resource unavailable. Another key feature of Publius is that it allows an individual to publish a document without providing information that links the document to any particular computer. Therefore, the publisher of a document can remain anonymous.

Publius has been designed with ease of access for end users in mind. HTML pages, images, or any other type of file can be published with the system. Documents published with Publius can be read with a standard web browser in combination with an HTTP proxy that can run locally or remotely. Files published with Publius are assigned a URL that can be entered into a web browser or embedded in a hyperlink.

The current architecture of the World Wide Web does not lend itself easily to censorship-resistant, anonymous publication. Published documents have a URL that can be traced back to a specific Internet host and usually a specific file owner. However, there are many reasons why someone might wish to publish something anonymously. Among the nobler of these reasons is political dissent or "whistleblowing." It is for these reasons that we designed Publius. Chapter 12 covers Free Haven, a project with some similarities, and provides more background on anonymity.

Anonymous publishing played an important role in the early history of the United States. James Madison, Alexander Hamilton, and John Jay collectively wrote the Federalist Papers under the pen name Publius. This collection of 85 articles, published pseudonymously in New York State newspapers from October 1787 through May 1788, was influential in convincing New York voters to ratify the proposed United States Constitution. It is from these distinguished authors that our system gets its name.

Like many of the other systems in this book, Publius is seen from the outside as a unified system that works as a monolithic service, not as a set of individual Internet hosts. However, Publius consists of a set of servers that host content. These servers are collectively referred to as Publius Servers. The Publius Servers are independently owned and operated by volunteers located throughout the world. The system resists attack because Publius as a whole is robust enough to continue serving files even when many of the hosts go offline.

Publius uses two main pieces of software. The first is the server software, which runs on every Publius server. The second piece of software is the client software. This software consists of a special HTTP proxy that interfaces with a web browser and allows an individual to publish and retrieve files. In this chapter we use the terms proxy and client software interchangeably, as they both refer to the HTTP proxy. In order to use Publius an individual runs the proxy on their computer or connects to a proxy running on someone else's computer.

Why censorship-resistant anonymous publishing?

The publication of written words has long been a tool for spreading new (and sometimes controversial) ideas, often with the goal of bringing about social change. Thus the printing press, and more recently, the World Wide Web, are powerful revolutionary tools. But those who seek to suppress revolutions possess powerful tools of their own. These tools give them the ability to stop publication, destroy published materials, or prevent the distribution of publications. And even if they cannot successfully censor the publication, they may intimidate and physically or financially harm the author or publisher in order to send a message to other would-be revolutionaries that they would be well advised to consider an alternative occupation. Even without a threat of personal harm, authors may wish to publish their works anonymously or pseudonymously because they believe they will be more readily accepted if not associated with a person of their gender, race, ethnic background, or other characteristics.

Publius and other systems in this book

The focus of this book is peer-to-peer systems. While Publius is not a pure peer-to-peer system, it does share many characteristics with such systems. In addition, Publius provides unique and useful solutions to many of the problems faced by users and designers of such systems.

Distributed publishing tools and peer-to-peer file-sharing tools are still in their infancy. Many of these systems are changing very rapidly—each system continually gains new features or improves on old ones. This complicates any sort of direct comparison. However, in certain areas Publius does have some advantages over other file-sharing systems described in this book, such as Gnutella and Freenet. This is not to say that Publius is necessarily better than other systems. Indeed, in certain areas other systems offer marked advantages over Publius. Each system has its strengths and weaknesses.

One of Publius' strengths is that it allows a publisher (and only the publisher) to update previously published material in such a way that anyone retrieving the old version is automatically redirected to the newly updated document. Publius also allows a publisher to delete a published document from all of the servers it is stored on. Safeguards are in place to prevent anyone but the publisher from deleting or updating the published document. A tamper-check mechanism is built into the Publius URL. This allows the Publius client to verify that a retrieved document has not been tampered with.

Publius is one of a handful of file-sharing and publishing systems that are entirely implemented on top of the standard HTTP protocol. This makes Publius portable and simplifies installation as it easily interfaces with a standard web browser. By portable we mean that Publius can run on a variety of different operating systems with little or no modification. Of course, as with everything in life, there is a trade-off. Implementing Publius over HTTP means that Publius is not as fast as it could be. There is a slight overhead in using HTTP as opposed to implementing the communication between server and browser directly.

System architecture

The Publius system consists of a collection of web servers called Publius Servers. The list of web servers, called the Publius Server List, is known to all Publius clients. An individual can publish a document using the client software.

The first part of the publication process involves using the Publius client software to encrypt the document with a key. This key is split into many pieces, called shares, such that only a small number of shares are required to form the key. For example, the key can be split into 30 shares such that any 3 of these shares can be used to form the key. But anyone combining fewer than 3 shares has no hint as to the value of the key. The choice of 3 shares is arbitrary, as is the choice of 30. The only constraint is that the number of shares required to form the key must be less than or equal to the total number of shares.

The client software then chooses a large subset of the servers listed in the Publius Server List and uploads the document to each one. It places the complete encrypted document and a single share on each server; each server has a different share of the key. The encrypted file and a share are typically stored on at least 20 servers. Three shares from any of these servers are enough to form the key.

A special URL called the Publius URL is created for each published document. The Publius URL is needed to retrieve the document from the various servers. This URL tells the client software where to look for the encrypted document and associated shares.

Upon receiving a Publius URL, the client software randomly retrieves three shares from the servers indicated by the URL. The shares are then combined to form the key. The client software also retrieves one copy of the encrypted file from one of the servers. The key is used to decrypt the file and a tamper check is then performed. If the document successfully passes the tamper check, it is displayed in the browser; otherwise, a new set of shares and a new encrypted document are retrieved from another set of servers.

The encryption prevents Publius server administrators from reading the documents stored on their servers. It is assumed that if server administrators don't know what is stored on their servers they are less likely to censor them. Only the publisher knows the Publius URL—it is formed by the client software and displayed in the publisher's web browser. Publishers can do what they wish with their URLs. They can post them to Usenet news, send them to reporters, or simply place them in a safe deposit box. To protect their identities, publishers may wish to use anonymous remailers when communicating these URLs.

The Publius client software is implemented as an HTTP proxy. Most web browsers can be configured to send web requests to an HTTP proxy, which retrieves the requested document (usually performing some extra service, such as caching, in the process) and returns it to the web browser. The HTTP proxy may be located on the user's computer or on some other computer on the Internet. In the case of Publius, the HTTP proxy is able to interpret Publius URLs, fetch the necessary shares and encrypted documents, and return a decrypted document to the user's web browser.

Cryptography fundamentals

Before describing the Publius operations, we briefly introduce some cryptographic topics that are essential to all Publius operations. For more information about these cryptographic topics see an introductory cryptography text.[*]

Encryption and decryption

Encryption is the process of hiding a message's true content. An unencrypted message is called a *plaintext*, while a message in encrypted form is called a *ciphertext*.

A *cipher* is a function that converts plaintext to ciphertext or ciphertext back to plaintext. Rijndael, the Advanced Encryption Standard, is an example of a well-known cipher. Decryption is the process of converting ciphertext back to plaintext. The encryption and decryption processes require a key. Trying to decrypt a message with the wrong key results in gibberish, but when the correct key is used, the original plaintext is revealed. Therefore it is important to keep the key secret and to make sure it is virtually impossible for an adversary to guess.

Ciphers that use the same key to encrypt and decrypt messages are called *symmetric ciphers*. These are the type of ciphers used in Publius.

Secret sharing

A message can be divided into a number of pieces in such a way that combining only a fraction of those pieces results in the original message. Any combination of pieces is sufficient, so long as you have the minimum number required.

An algorithm that divides data in such a manner is called a secret sharing algorithm. The secret sharing algorithm takes three parameters: the message to divide, the number of pieces to divide the message into, and the number of pieces needed to reconstruct the message. The individual pieces are called shares. Publius uses Shamir's secret sharing algorithm. Other secret sharing algorithms also exist.

---

[*] See, for example, Bruce Schneier (1996), *Applied Cryptography Protocols, Algorithms, and Source Code in C, 2nd Edition,* John Wiley & Sons.

Hash functions

A hash function takes a variable-length input and returns a fixed-length output. Publius uses the cryptographically strong hash functions MD5 and SHA-1. Cryptographically strong hash functions possess two properties. First, the hash function is hard to invert—that is, if someone is told the hash value, it is hard to find a message that produces that hash value. Second, it is hard to find two messages that produce the same hash value. By hard we mean that it is not feasible, even using massive amounts of computing power, to accomplish the specified task.

The slightest change to a file completely changes the value of the hash produced. This characteristic makes hash functions ideal for checking whether the content of a message has been changed. The MD5 hash function produces a 128-bit output and SHA-1 produces a 160-bit output.

Publius operations

Given the previous description of Publius-related cryptographic functions, we now describe the Publius operations Publish, Retrieve, Update, and Delete.

Publish operation

Suppose that we wish to publish the file *homepage.html* with Publius. The accompanying sidebar outlines the steps the Publius proxy follows to publish a file. First, a key is created from the MD5 and SHA-1 hash of the contents of the file *homepage.html*. This key is then used to encrypt the file, producing a new file we will call *homepage.enc*. Using Shamir's secret sharing algorithm, the key is split into 30 shares such that any 3 of these shares can be used to reconstruct the key. The first share is named *Share_1*, the second *Share_2*, and so on. The MD5 hash of the contents of *homepage.html* and *Share_1* is calculated. This MD5 hash results in a 128-bit number. An operation is performed on this number to determine an index into the Publius Server List. The Publius Server List is essentially just a numbered table of web servers, each running the Publius server software. The index is used to locate a particular server. For instance, the index value 5 corresponds to the 5th entry in the Publius Server List. You will recall that all Publius client software has the same list, and therefore the 5th server is the same for everyone.

For the sake of argument let's assume that our index number is 5 and that the 5th server is named *www.nyu.edu*. The proxy now attempts to store the file *homepage.enc* and *Share_1* on *www.nyu.edu*. The files are stored in a directory derived from the previously calculated MD5 hash of *homepage.html* and *Share_1*. The file *homepage.enc* is stored in a file named *file* and *Share_1* is stored in a file named *share*. These same two names are used for every piece of content published with Publius, regardless of the type of the file. One of the reasons for storing *homepage.enc* as *file* rather than as *homepage.enc* is that we don't want to give anyone even a hint as to the type of file being stored. The neutrality of the name, along with the use of encryption so that no one can read the file without the key, allows Publius server administrators to plausibly deny any knowledge of the content of the files being hosted on the Publius server. While each server possesses a part of the encryption key, it is of no value by itself for decrypting the file. We thus expect that server administrators have little motive to delete, and thereby censor, files stored on their servers.

The whole process of performing the MD5 hash and storing the files on a Publius server is repeated for each of the 30 shares. A file is stored on a particular server only once—if Publius generates the same index number more than once, the corresponding share is discarded.

Each time a file and share are stored on a Publius server, the file and share's corresponding MD5 hash (calculated in line 5 of the sidebar "Process for publishing the file homepage.html in Publius") is used in the formation of the Publius URL. A Publius URL has the following form:

http://!publius!/ options MD5_hash MD5_hash MD5_hash...MD5_hash

where each *MD5_hash* is the hash defined in line 5 of the sidebar. Each *MD5_hash* is Base64-encoded to generate an ASCII representation of the hash value. Here is an example of a Publius URL:

http://!publius!/010310023/
VYimRS+9ajc=B20wYdxGsPk=kMCiu9dzSHg=xPTuzOyUnNk=/
O5uFb3KaC8I=MONUMmecuCE=P5WY8LS8HGY=KLQGrFwTcuE=/
kJyiXge4S7g=6I7LBrYWAV0=

The *options* part of the Publius URL is made up of several flags that specify how the proxy should interpret the URL. The options section includes a "do not update" flag, the number of shares needed to form the key, and the version number of the Publius client that published the URL.

The version number allows us to add new features to future versions of Publius while at the same time retaining backward compatibility.

The update flag determines whether the update operation can be performed on the Publius content represented by the URL. If the update flag is 1, the retrieval of updated content may be performed when update URLs are discovered. If the

Process for publishing the file homepage.html in Publius

1. Generate a key.
2. Using the key, encrypt file *homepage.html* to produce *homepage.enc*.
3. Perform Shamir's secret sharing algorithm on the key.
   This produces *Share_1, Share_2...Share_30*.
   Any three shares can be used to form the key.
4. Set *share* to *Share_1*.
5. Set *h* as the MD5 hash of *share* appended to content of file *homepage.html*.
6. Set *index* to *h* mod (the number of entries in the Publius Server List).
7. Set *server* to the Publius server at the location specified by *index*.
8. On *server*: Create a directory derived from *h*. In this directory store the contents of *homepage.enc* into a file named *file* and *share* into a file named *share*.

Repeat steps 4 through 8 once for each of the remaining shares (*Share_2... Share_30*), setting the variable *share* appropriately before each repetition.

update flag is 0, however, the client ignores update URLs sent by Publius servers in response to share and encrypted file requests.

The options part of the Publius URL also includes a number that indicates the size of the Publius Server List at the time the file was published. The Publius Server List is not static—it can grow over time. Servers can be added without affecting previously published files. The index calculation performed on line 6 of the Publius Publish algorithm (see the sidebar "Process for publishing the file homepage.html in Publius") depends on the size of the Publius Server List. Changes to this value change the computed index location. Therefore it is necessary to store this value in the URL. When interpreting a given Publius URL, the proxy essentially ignores all entries in the server list with index greater than the one stored in the Publius URL. This ensures that the proxy will calculate the correct index value for every server hosting the shares and encrypted file.

Retrieve operation

Upon receiving a request to retrieve a Publius URL, the proxy first breaks the URL into its MD5 hash components. As the size of each MD5 hash is exactly 128 bits, this is an easy task. As you may recall, each of these hash values determines which servers in the Publius Server List are storing the encrypted file and a share. In order to retrieve the encrypted file and share, the proxy randomly selects one of the hash values and performs the same operation performed by the Publish operation (line 6 in the sidebar). The value returned is used as an index into the Publius Server List, revealing the name of the server. The proxy retrieves the encrypted file and share file from the server. Recall that the file named *file* contains the encrypted version of the published file and the file named *share* contains a single share. In order to form the key, the proxy needs to find two additional shares. Thus, the client selects two other MD5 hash values randomly from the Publius URL and performs the same operation as before on each. This reveals two other servers that in turn lead to two more shares. The 3 shares can now be combined to form the key used to encrypt the file.

During the Publish operation, the key was broken into 30 shares. Assume that after testing each of these shares, the proxy ends up storing the encrypted file and a corresponding share on 20 servers. This means that 20 MD5 hashes appear in the Publius URL. During the retrieval process only 3 of these 20 shares are needed. Publius derives its fault-tolerant and censorship-resistant properties from the storage of these additional shares and encrypted files. By fault tolerant we mean that if for some reason several servers are unavailable, the proxy can still successfully retrieve the Publius document. In fact, if the file is stored on 20 servers, even if 17 servers are unavailable we can successfully retrieve the Publius document. However, if 18 Publius servers are unavailable, the Publius document cannot be retrieved because 2 shares are not enough to form the key needed to decrypt the content.

The additional copies also provide censorship resistance—if several Publius server administrators decide to delete the encrypted files and shares corresponding to a particular Publius file, the file can still be retrieved if at least three servers still contain the shares and encrypted file. With Publius servers located throughout the world, it becomes increasingly difficult to force Publius server administrators to delete files corresponding to a particular Publius URL, by legal or other means.

Many of the other systems in this book also have fault-tolerant features. However, most of these systems focus on maintaining a network of nodes with variable connectivity and temporary network addresses. Publius does not address the use of servers with temporary network addresses.

Once the key has been reconstructed from the shares, it can be used to decrypt the file. The decrypted file can now be displayed in the web browser. However, just before the file is displayed in the web browser, a tamper check is initiated. The tamper check verifies that the file has not changed since the time it was initially published. The MD5 hashes stored in the URL are used to perform the tamper check. The hash was formed from the unencrypted file and a share—both of which are now available. Therefore, the client recalculates the MD5 hash of the unencrypted file and of each share (as in line 5 in the sidebar). If the calculated hashes do not match the corresponding hashes stored in the URL, the file has been tampered with or corrupted. In this case, the proxy simply throws away the encrypted file and shares and tries another set of encrypted files and shares. If a tamper check is successfully performed, the file is sent to the web browser. If the proxy runs out of share and encrypted file combinations, a message appears in the browser stating that the file could not be retrieved.

Update operation

Files, especially web pages, change over time. An individual may find a particular web document interesting and add it to his collection of bookmarks or link to it from a web page. The problem with linking to a Publius URL is that if anyone changes the document and tries to republish it, a new Publius URL is generated for the document. Therefore, anyone linking to the old document may never learn that the document has been updated because the link or bookmark still points to the older Publius document.

To remedy this situation, Publius supports an Update operation. The operation allows the publisher of a document to replace an older version of the Publius document with a newer one while still retaining the old URL. This is accomplished by allowing a Publius URL to be stored in a file called *update* in the same directory where the old version of the file resided.

For example, let's say that one encrypted file and share are stored on *www.nyu.edu* in directory *pubdir*. Upon receiving the update command, the proxy contacts the server *www.nyu.edu*, deletes the files named *file* and *share* from the directory *pubdir*, and places the new Publius URL in a file named *update*. Of course, the Update command is issued to all servers holding copies of the file to be updated.

Now, whenever *www.nyu.edu* receives a request for the encrypted file or share in the directory *pubdir*, the server sends the new Publius URL found in the *update* file. If several of the queried Publius servers also respond with this same Publius URL, the proxy retrieves the document referenced by the new Publius URL. Therefore, whenever a proxy requests the old file it is automatically redirected to the updated version of the file.

Of course, we want only the publisher of the document to be able to perform the Update command. In order to enforce this, the Publish operation allows a password to be specified. This password is stored in the file *password* and is checked by the server during an Update operation. In order for this scheme to work, the password must be stored on each server so that the server can check that the password sent with the Update command matches the stored password. However, simply storing the password on the server would be dangerous, because it would permit Publius server administrators to update the document on all servers if they discover the corresponding URL. This is essentially a form of censorship, as the original file would no longer be accessible. So instead of simply storing the password, we store the MD5 hash of the password appended to the domain name of the particular server. The server stores this value in the password file associated with the particular document. The hash by itself provides no clues as to the actual value of the password, so it cannot be used to update the document on all of the servers.

Delete operation

There are circumstances in which a publisher may wish to delete a document from Publius. Publius therefore supports the Delete operation. Only the publisher may delete the document. The same password that controls the Update operation also ensures that only the publisher can perform the Delete operation.

The ability to delete Publius documents gives an adversary the option of trying to force the publisher of a Publius document to delete it. In order to prevent this scenario, Publius provides a "do not delete" option during the Publish operation. This option allows someone to publish a document in such a way that Publius servers deny requests to delete the document.

Of course, nothing stops a Publius server administrator from deleting the document from her own server, but the safeguards in this section do prevent a single person from deleting the Publius file from all the servers at once.

Both the Delete and Update commands attempt to make the required changes on all of the relevant servers. For example, the Update command tries to update every server storing a particular document. However, this may not always be possible due to a server being down or otherwise unavailable. This could lead to an inconsistent state in which some servers are updated and others are not. Although Publius does not currently deal with the problem of an inconsistent state, it does report the names of the servers on which the operation failed. At a later time, the Update command can be executed again in an attempt to contact the servers that failed to get updated. The same is true for the Delete command.

Publius implementation

Publius is a working system that has been in operation since August 2000. In the following sections, we describe several important aspects of the implementation. As you will recall, Publius consists of both client and server software. All Publius servers run the server software. The client software consists of a special HTTP proxy that interfaces with any standard web browser. This special proxy handles all Publius commands and therefore interacts with the Publius servers. Upon connecting to the proxy, the web browser displays the Publius User Interface. This user interface is essentially an HTML form that allows an individual to select a Publius operation (Delete, Publish, or Update). This form is not required for the Retrieve operation as it is the default operation.

User interface

The web browser interface, as shown in Figure 11-1, allows someone to select the Publius operation (Delete, Publish, or Update) and enter the operation's required parameters such as the URL and password. Each Publius operation is bound to a special *!publius!* URL that is recognized by the proxy. For example, the Publish URL is *http://!publius!PUBLISH*. The operation's parameters are sent in the body of the HTTP POST request to the corresponding *!publius!* URL. The proxy parses the parameters and executes the corresponding Publius operation. An HTML message indicating the success or failure of the operation is returned. If the Retrieve operation is requested and is successful, the requested document is displayed in a new web browser window.

Server software

To participate as a Publius server, one needs to install the Publius CGI script on a system running an HTTP server. The client software communicates with the server by executing an HTTP POST operation on the URL corresponding to the server's CGI script. The requested operation (Retrieve, Update, Publish, or Delete), the filename, the password, and any other required information is passed to the server in the body of the POST request.

Client software

The client software consists of the special HTTP proxy. The proxy transparently sends non-Publius URLs to the appropriate servers and passes the returned content back to the browser. Upon receiving a request for a Publius URL, the proxy retrieves the encrypted document and shares, as described in the "Retrieve operation" section earlier. The proxy also handles the Delete, Publish, and Update commands.

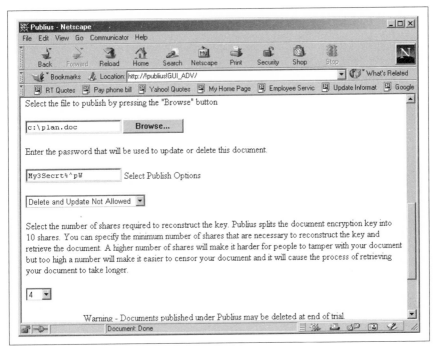

Figure 11-1. User interface for publishing a Publius document

Publius MIME type

The filename extension of a particular file usually determines the way in which a web browser or other software interprets the file's content. For example, a file that has a name ending with the extension *.html* usually contains HTML. Similarly, a file that has a name ending with the extension *.jpg* usually contains a JPEG image. The Publius URL does not retain the file extension of the file it represents. So the Publius URL gives no hint to the browser, or anyone else for that matter, as to the type of file it points to. However, in order for the browser to correctly interpret the byte stream sent to it by the proxy, the proxy must properly identify the type of data it is sending. Therefore, before publishing a file, Publius prepends the first three-letters of the file's name extension to the file. The file is then published as described earlier, in the section "Publish operation." When the proxy is ready to send the requested file back to the browser, the three-letter extension is removed from the file and checked to determine an appropriate MIME type for the document. The MIME type is sent in an HTTP Content-type header. If the three-letter extension is not helpful in determining the MIME type, a default type of *text/plain* is sent for text files. The default MIME type for binary files is *octet/stream*.

Publius in a nutshell

Documents are published in a censorship-resistant manner
This is partially achieved by storing the encrypted document and a share on a large number of servers.

Retrieved documents can be tamper-checked
The Publius URL is made up of MD5 hashes that allow the document to be checked for changes since publication.

Published documents can be updated
Any requests for the previous document are redirected to the new document.

Published documents can be securely deleted
A password mechanism is utilized for the Delete and Update commands.

A document can be anonymously published
Once the document is published there is no way to directly link the document to the publisher. However, indirect mechanisms of identification may exist, so one may wish to use an anonymizing proxy or publish the file in a cyber café or library.

The stored document is resistant to distributed denial of service attacks
The published file can still be retrieved even if a large number of servers are unavailable.

The Publius web site is *http://www.cs.nyu.edu/waldman/publius*. The source code, a technical paper describing Publius, and instructions for using Publius are available at this site.

chapter twelve

Free Haven

Roger Dingledine, Reputation Technologies, Inc., Michael J. Freedman, MIT, and David Molnar, Harvard University

The Free Haven Project is dedicated to designing a system of anonymous storage that resists the attempts of powerful adversaries to find or destroy any stored data. Our goals include the following:

Anonymity
> We try to meet this goal for all parties: the publishers that insert documents, the readers that retrieve documents, and the servers that store documents.

Persistence
> The publisher of a document—not the servers holding the document—determines its lifetime.

Flexibility
> The system functions smoothly as servers are added or remove themselves.

Accountability
> We apply a reputation system to servers that attempts to limit the damage done by those that misbehave.

In this chapter, we'll show how Free Haven tries to meet these goals. We spend a particularly large amount of time on anonymity. It is not adequate to speak of "anonymity" as a monolithic concept. In the section "Anonymity for anonymous storage," we'll enumerate the many different kinds of anonymity that are important to protect participants in the system.

Free Haven differs from the other projects in this book in the wide range of difficult goals we have taken on. We try to assure anonymity, server accountability, and persistent storage for data independent of its popularity, all at the same time. Here are some comparisons to other projects:

Gnutella

> The strength of Gnutella is its extremely flexible network design. But when a search is performed, servers respond with an external IP address or URL where the user can download the document. Since this actual retrieval is done without any privacy protection, using Gnutella is not a good choice if publishers or readers want anonymity. Further, documents in the Gnutella network last only as long as their host servers; when a user logs out for the night, all of his files leave with him.

Freenet and Mojo Nation

> These systems make files highly accessible and offer some level of anonymity. But since the choice to drop a file is a purely local decision, and since files that aren't requested for some time tend to disappear automatically, these systems don't guarantee a specified lifetime for a document. Indeed, we expect that Freenet will provide a very convenient service for porn and popular audio files, but anything less popular will be driven off the system.

Publius

> This project is closest to ours, because it addresses file storage rather than easy accessibility. But Publius provides no smooth decentralized support for adding new servers and excising dead or malicious servers. More importantly, Publius provides no accountability—there is no way to prevent publishers from entirely filling the system with garbage data.

Currently, Free Haven sacrifices efficiency and convenience to achieve its design requirements. Free Haven is designed more for anonymity and persistence of documents than for frequent querying. We expect that interesting material will be retrieved from the system and published in a more accessible fashion (such as in Freenet or normal web pages). Then the document in Free Haven will only need to be accessed if the other sources are shut down or the reader requires stronger anonymity. For more discussion of such "gatewaying" issues, refer to Chapter 19, *Interoperability Through Gateways*.

Privacy in data-sharing systems

Privacy is a term with positive connotations that every person can appreciate. One key way to achieve privacy, however—anonymity—is widely misunderstood both in daily life and in computer networking. The media and politicians stress socially disapproved activities (such as the exchange of unauthorized music files or erotic pictures involving children) and ignore the important contributions that anonymity provides. Anonymity is used on an everyday basis in forums ranging from radio shows to Usenet newsgroups, by people who suffer from child abuse, drug dependency, or other social problems.

Anonymous publication and storage services allow individuals to speak freely without fear of persecution. Political dissidents must publish their views in order to reach enough people for their criticisms of a regime to be effective, yet they and their readers require anonymity at the same time. Less extreme examples involve cases in which a large and powerful private organization attempts to silence its critics by attacking either the critics themselves or those who make the criticism publicly available.

Developers and potential users of other peer-to-peer systems should be interested in the techniques we are developing to preserve anonymity in Free Haven, because they may prove useful in protecting the privacy of users in other systems as well. Many people would like to participate in communities and share information without revealing who they are. Their reasons may range from the trivial—such as avoiding spam—to deep social concerns. It is time to face these concerns directly so solutions can be designed fundamentally into peer-to-peer systems.

Peer-to-peer systems that attempt to address anonymity are just starting to be deployed, and the exact requirements and design choices are not yet clear. Recent events have highlighted some shortcomings of current systems. For instance, the limitations of Gnutella were dramatized by the Gnutella Wall of Shame, where someone lured readers to a web site by claiming to offer child pornography and then published each visitor's IP address. While Napster allowed people with MP3 files to find each other, it also made it easy for the band Metallica to find people who were offering unauthorized copies of Metallica songs and force them off the system.

These shortcomings cause people to look toward a new generation of anonymous publication services that address anonymity. In developing Free Haven, we hope to clarify some of the requirements for such systems and highlight the design choices.

Reliability with anonymity

In the physical world, people use safety deposit boxes to protect valuable items. Everything from passports to house titles to krugerrands—if it's important, it goes in the box, which is kept at the local bank. The bank has armed guards, smiling tellers, and a history going back to the Knights Templar. Now suppose someone suggested to you that instead of going to the bank, it would be a better idea to hand your gold bars to the next guy on the street and ask him to "just hold these for a bit." You'd look at a person with such notions as though he had three heads... yet in some sense, this is exactly what distributed peer-to-peer file-sharing systems like Free Haven ask you to do.

The critical point is that for a safety deposit box, the only thing that really matters is reliability and availability: can you get your items when you want them? The rest is irrelevant. If the guy on the street could guarantee that you'll get your gold back and follow through, he would be "just as good" as the bank. In fact, if you're interested in protecting your privacy, the guy on the street may be better—he doesn't know or care who you really are. Of course, in the physical world, it's still a bad idea to give gold bars to random people on the street. Online, however, cryptography allows things to work out differently.

Many systems in addition to Free Haven need reliability, particularly peer-to-peer systems that ask people to share resources. When offering and retrieving resources, users want to preserve their privacy. When evaluating whether to transfer custody of their resources to another party on the system, users want to know whether that party can be trusted.

Initially these goals seem mutually exclusive, but the solution is to allow users to have *pseudonyms*, and to assign a *reputation* to each pseudonym. Free Haven differs from other systems in that the servers in the Free Haven system are known only by their pseudonyms, and we provide an automated system to track reputations (honesty and performance) for each server. A server's reputation influences how much data it can store in Free Haven and provides an incentive to act correctly. Reputation can be a complex matter—just think of all the reader reviews and "People also bought..." ratings on the Amazon.com retail site—so we'll leave its discussion to Chapter 16, *Accountability*, and Chapter 17, *Reputation*. Establishing trust through the use of pseudonyms is covered in Chapter 15, *Trust*.

What lets a malicious adversary find a person in real life? One way is to know his or her *true name*, a term first used in a short story by fiction author Vernor Vinge[*] and popularized by Tim May.[†] The true name is the legal identity of an

---

[*] Vernor Vinge (1987), *True Names... and Other Dangers*, Baen.

[†] Tim May, *Cyphernomicon*, http://www-swiss.ai.mit.edu/6805/articles/crypto/cypherpunks/cyphernomicon.

individual and can be used to find an address or other real-life connection. Obviously, a pseudonym should not be traceable to a true name.

As an author can use a pseudonym to protect his or her true name, in a computerized storage system a user can employ a pseudonym to protect another form of identity called *location*. This is an IP address or some other aspect of the person's physical connection to the computer system. In a successful system, a pseudonym always reflects the activities of one particular entity—but no one can learn the true name or location of the entity. The ability to link many different activities to a pseudonym is the key to supporting reputations.

Anonymity for anonymous storage

The word "anonymous" can mean many different things. Indeed, some systems claim "anonymity" without specifying a precise definition. This introduces a great deal of confusion when users are trying to evaluate and compare publishing systems to understand what protections they can expect from each system.

A publishing situation creates many types of anonymity—many requirements that a system has to meet in order to protect the privacy of both content providers and users. Here, we'll define the *author* of a document as whoever initially created it. The author may be the same as or different from the *publisher*, who places the document into Free Haven or another storage system. Documents may have *readers*, who retrieve the document from the system. And many systems, including Free Haven, have *servers*, who provide the resources for the system, such as disk space and bandwidth.

Free Haven tries to make sure that no one can trace a document back to any of these people—or trace any of them forward to a document. In addition, we want to prevent adversaries who are watching both a user and a document from learning anything that might convince them that the user is connected to that document. Learning some information that might imply a connection allows "linking" the user to that action or document. Thus, we define the following types of anonymity:

Author-anonymity
> A system is author-anonymous if an adversary cannot link an author to a document.

Publisher-anonymity
> A system is publisher-anonymous if it prevents an adversary from linking a publisher to a document.

Reader-anonymity

To say that a system has reader-anonymity means that a document cannot be linked with its readers. Reader-anonymity protects the privacy of a system's users.

Server-anonymity

Server-anonymity means no server can be linked to a document. Here, the adversary always picks the document first. That is, given a document's name or other identifier, an adversary is no closer to knowing which server or servers on the network currently possess this document.

Document-anonymity

Document-anonymity means that a server does not know which documents it is storing. Document-anonymity is crucial if mere possession of some file is cause for action against the server, because it provides protection to a server operator even after his or her machine has been seized by an adversary. This notion is sometimes also known as "plausible deniability," but see below under query-anonymity. There are two types of document-anonymity: isolated-server and connected-server.

Passive-server document-anonymity means that if the server is allowed to look only at the data that it is storing, it is unable to figure out the contents of the document. This can be achieved via some sort of secret sharing mechanism. That is, multiple servers split up either the document or an encryption key that recreates the document (or both). An alternative approach is to encrypt the document before publishing, using some key which is external to the server—Freenet takes this approach. Mojo Nation takes a different approach to get the same end: it uses a "two-layer" publishing system, in which documents are split up into shares, and then a separate "share map" is similarly split and distributed to participants called *content trackers*. In this way, servers holding shares of a document cannot easily locate the share map for that document, so they cannot determine which document it is.

Active-server document-anonymity refers to the situation in which the server is allowed to communicate and compare data with all other servers. Since an active server may act as a reader and do document requests itself, active-server document-anonymity seems difficult to achieve without some trusted party that can distinguish server requests from "ordinary" reader requests.

Query-anonymity

Query-anonymity means that the server cannot determine which document it is serving when satisfying a reader's request. A weaker form of query-anonymity is *server deniability*—the server knows the identity of the requested document, but no third party can be sure of its identity. Query-anonymity can provide another aspect of plausible deniability.

Partial anonymity

Often an adversary can gain some partial information about the users of a system, such as the fact that they have high-bandwidth connections or all live in California. Preventing an adversary from obtaining *any* such information may be impossible. Instead of asking "Is the system anonymous?" the question shifts to "Is it anonymous enough?"

We might say that a system is *partially anonymous* if an adversary can only narrow down a search for a user to one of a "set of suspects." If the set is large enough, it is impractical for an adversary to act as if any single suspect were guilty. On the other hand, when the set of suspects is small, mere suspicion may cause an adversary to take action against all of them.

The design of Free Haven

Free Haven offers a community of servers called the *servnet*. Despite the name, all servers count the same, and within the servnet Free Haven is a peer-to-peer system. There are no "clients" in the old client/server sense; the closest approximation are users looking for files and potential publishers. Users query the entire servnet at once, not any single server in particular. Potential publishers do convince a single server to publish a document, but the actual publishing of a document is done by a server itself in a peer-to-peer fashion.

All of these entities—server, reader, and publisher—make up the Free Haven players. Thanks to pseudonymity, nobody knows where any server is located—including the one they use as their entry point to the system. Users query the system via broadcast.

Servers don't have to accept just any document that publishers upload to them. That would permit selfish or malicious people to fill up the available disk space. Instead, servers form contracts to store each other's material for a certain period of time.

Successfully fulfilling a contract increases a server's reputation and thus its ability to store some of its own data on other servers. This gives an incentive for each server to behave well, as long as cheating servers can be identified. We illustrate a technique for identifying cheating servers in the section "Accountability and the buddy system." In the section "Reputation system," we discuss the system that keeps track of trust in each server.

Some of these contracts are formed when a user inserts new data into the servnet through a server she operates. Most of them, however, are formed when two servers swap parts of documents (shares) by *trading*. Trading allows the servnet to be *dynamic* in the sense that servers can join and leave easily and without special treatment. To join, a server starts building up a reputation by storing shares for others—we provide a system where certain servers can act as *introducers* in order to smoothly add new servers. To leave, a server trades away all of its shares for short-lived shares, and then waits for them to expire. The benefits and mechanisms of trading are described in the later section "Trading."

The following sections explain how the design of Free Haven allows it to accomplish its goals. "Elements of the system" describes the design of the Free Haven system and the operations that it supports, including the insertion and retrieval of documents. We describe some potential attacks in the section "Attacks on Free Haven" and show how well the design does (or does not) resist each attack. We then compare our design to other systems aimed at anonymous storage and publication using the kinds of anonymity described in the section "An analysis of anonymity," allowing us to distinguish systems that at first glance look very similar. We conclude with a list of challenges for anonymous publication and storage systems, each of which reflects a limitation in the current Free Haven design.

Elements of the system

This chapter focuses on Free Haven's publication system, which is responsible for storing and serving documents. Free Haven also has a communications channel, which is responsible for providing confidential and anonymous communications between parties. Since this communications channel is implemented using preexisting systems that are fairly well known in the privacy community, we won't discuss it here. On the other hand, the currently available systems are largely insufficient for our accountability requirements; see Chapter 16.

The agents in our publication system are the author, publisher, server, and reader. As we stated in the section "Anonymity for anonymous storage," authors are agents that produce documents and wish to store them in the service, publishers place the documents in the storage system, servers are computers that store data for authors, and readers are people who retrieve documents from the service.

These agents know each other only by their pseudonyms and communicate only using the secure communications channel. Currently, the pseudonyms are provided by the Cypherpunks remailer network,[*] and the communications channel consists of remailer reply blocks provided by that network. Each server has a public key and one or more reply blocks, which together can be used to provide secure, authenticated, pseudonymous communication with that server. Every machine in the servnet has a database that contains the public keys and reply blocks of other servers in the servnet.

As we said in the section "The design of Free Haven," documents are split into pieces and stored on different servers; each piece of a document is called a *share*. Unlike Publius or Freenet, servers in Free Haven give up something (disk space) and get other servers' disk space in return. In other words, you earn the right to store your data on the rest of the servnet after you offer to store data provided by the rest of the servnet.

The servnet is dynamic: shares move from one server to another every so often, based on each server's trust of the others. The only way to introduce a new file into the system is for a server to use (and thus provide) more space on its local system. This new file will migrate to other servers by the process of trading.

Publishers assign an expiration date to documents when they are published; servers make a promise to keep their shares of a given document until its expiration date is reached. To encourage honest behavior, some servers check whether other servers "drop" data early and decrease their trust of such servers. This trust is monitored and updated by use of a reputation system. Each server maintains a database containing its perceived reputation of the other servers.

Storage

When an author (call her Alice) wishes to store a new document in Free Haven, she must first identify a Free Haven server that's willing to store the document for her. Alice might do this by running a server herself. Alternatively, some servers might have public interfaces or publicly available reply blocks and be willing to publish data for others.

Publication

To introduce a file *f* into the servnet, the publishing server first splits it into shares. Like the Publius algorithm described in Chapter 11, *Publius*, we use an algorithm that creates a large number (*n*) of shares but allows the complete

---

[*] David Mazieres and M. Frans Kaashoek (1998), "The Design and Operation of an E-mail Pseudonym Server," *5th ACM Conference on Computer and Communications Security*.

document to be recreated using a smaller number (k) of those shares. We use Rabin's information dispersal algorithm (IDA)[*] to break the file into shares $f_1...f_n$. (For any integer i, the notation f_i indicates share i of document f.)

The server then generates a key pair (PK_{doc}, SK_{doc}), constructs and signs a data segment for each share, and inserts these shares into its local server space. Attributes in each share include a timestamp, expiration information, hash(PK_{doc}) (a message digest or hash of the public key from the key pair[†]), information about share numbering, and the signature itself.

The robustness parameter k should be chosen based on some compromise between the importance of the file and the size and available space. A large value of k relative to n makes the file more brittle, because it will be unrecoverable after a few shares are lost. On the other hand, a smaller value of k implies a larger share size, since more data is stored in each share.

We maintain a content-neutral policy toward documents in the Free Haven system. That is, each server agrees to store data for the other servers without regard for the legal or moral issues for that data in any given jurisdiction. For more discussion of the significant moral and legal issues that anonymous systems raise, see the first author's master's degree thesis.[‡]

Retrieval

Documents in Free Haven are indexed by the public key PK_{doc} from the key pair that was used to sign the shares of the document. Readers must locate (or be running) a server that performs the document request. The reader generates a key pair (PK_{client}, SK_{client}) for this transaction, as well as a one-time remailer reply block. The servnet server broadcasts a request containing a message digest or hash of the document's public key, hash(PK_{doc}), along with the client's public key, PK_{client}, and the reply block. This request goes to all the other servers that the initial server knows about. These broadcasts can be queued and then sent out in bulk to conserve bandwidth.

---

[*] Michael O. Rabin (1989), "Efficient Dispersal of Information for Security, Load Balancing, and Fault Tolerance," *Journal of the ACM*, vol. 36, no. 2, pp. 335–348.

[†] Chapter 15 describes the purpose of message digests. Briefly, the digest of any data item can be used to prove that the data item has not been modified. However, no one can regenerate the data item from the digest, so the data item itself remains private to its owner.

[‡] Roger Dingledine (2000), *The Free Haven Project*, MIT master's degree thesis, *http://freehaven.net/papers.html*.

Each server that receives the query checks to see if it has any shares with the requested hash of PK_{doc}. If it does, it encrypts each share using the public key PK_{client} enclosed in the request and then sends the encrypted share through the remailer to the enclosed address. These shares will magically arrive out of the ether at their destination; once enough shares arrive (k or more), the client recreates the file and is done.

Share expiration

Each share includes an expiration date chosen at share creation time. This is an absolute (as opposed to relative) timestamp indicating the time after which the hosting server may delete the share with no ill consequences. Expiration dates should be chosen based on how long the publisher wants the data to last; the publisher has to consider the file size and likelihood of finding a server willing to make the trade.

By allowing the publisher of the document to set its expiration time, Free Haven distinguishes itself from related works such as Freenet and Mojo Nation that favor frequently requested documents. We think this is the most useful approach to a persistent, anonymous data storage service. For example, Yugoslav phone books are currently being collected "to document residency for the close to one million people forced to evacuate Kosovo";* those phone books might not have survived a popularity contest. The Free Haven system is designed to provide privacy for its users. Rather than being a publication system aimed at convenience like Freenet, it is designed to be a private, low-profile storage system.

Document revocation

Some publishing systems, notably Publius, allow for documents to be "unpublished" or *revoked*. Revocation has some benefits. It allows the implementation of a read/write filesystem, and published documents can be updated as newer versions became available.

Revocation could be implemented by allowing the author to come up with a random private value x and then publishing a hash of it inside each share. To revoke the document, the author could broadcast his original value x to all servers as a signal to delete the document.

---

* University of Michigan News and Information Services, "Yugoslav Phone Books: Perhaps the Last Record of a People," *http://www.umich.edu/~newsinfo/Releases/2000/Jan00/r012000e.html*.

On the other hand, revocation allows new attacks on the system. Firstly, it complicates accountability. Revocation requests may not reach all shares of a file, due either to a poor communication channel or to a malicious adversary who sends unpublishing requests only to some members of the servnet. Secondly, authors might use the same hash for new shares and thus "link" documents. Adversaries might do the same to make it appear that the same author published two unrelated documents. Thirdly, the presence of the hash in a share assigns "ownership" to a share that is not present otherwise. An author who remembers his x has evidence that he was associated with that share, thus leaving open the possibility that such evidence could be discovered and used against him later.

One of the most serious arguments against revocation was raised by Ross Anderson.[*] If the capability to revoke exists, an adversary has incentive to find who controls this capability and threaten or torture him until he revokes the document.

We could address this problem by making revocation optional: the share itself could make it clear whether that share can be unpublished. If no unpublishing tag is present, there would be no reason to track down the author. (This solution is used in Publius.) But this too is subject to attack: If an adversary wishes to create a pretext to hunt down the publisher of a document, he can republish the document *with* a revocation tag and use that as "reasonable cause" to target the suspected publisher.

Because the ability to revoke shares may put the original publisher in increased physical danger, as well as allow new attacks on the system, we chose to leave revocation out of the current design.

Trading

In the Free Haven design, servers periodically trade shares with each other. There are a number of reasons why servers trade:

To provide a cover for publishing
> If trades are common, there is no reason to assume that somebody offering a trade is the publisher of a share. Publisher-anonymity is enhanced.

To let servers join and leave
> Trading allows servers to exit the servnet gracefully by trading for short-lived shares and then waiting for them to expire. This support for a dynamic network is crucial, since many of the participants in Free Haven

---

[*] Ross Anderson, "The Eternity Service," *http://www.cl.cam.ac.uk/users/rja14/eternity/eternity.html.*

will be well-behaved but transient relative to the duration of the longer-lived shares.

To permit longer expiration dates

Long-lasting shares would be rare if trading them involved finding a server that promised to be available for the next several years.

To accommodate ethical concerns of server operators

Frequent trading makes it easy and unsuspicious for server operators to trade away a particular piece of data with which they do not wish to be associated. If the Catholic Church distributes a list of discouraged documents, server operators can use the hash of the public key in each share to determine if that document is in the list and then trade away the share without compromising either their reputation as a server or the availability of the document. In a non-dynamic environment, the server would suffer a reputation hit if it chose not to keep the document. While we do not currently offer this functionality, trading allows this flexibility if we need it down the road. In particular, the idea of servers getting an "ISP exemption" for documents they hold currently seems very dubious.

To provide a moving target

Encouraging shares to move from server to server through the servnet means that there is never any specific, static target to attack.

The frequency of trading should be a parameter set by the server operator. When server *Alice* wants to make a trade, it chooses another server, *Bob* from its list of known servers (based on reputation) and offers a share x and a request for size or duration of a return share. If *Bob* is interested, it responds with a share y of its own.

Trades are considered "fair" based on the two-dimensional currency of *size* × *duration*. That is, the bigger the size and the longer the document is to be held, the more expensive the trade becomes. The price is adjusted based on the preferences of the servers involved in the trade.

The negotiation is finalized by each server sending an acknowledgment of the trade (including a receipt, as described in the next section, "Receipts") to the other. In addition, each server sends a receipt to both the buddy of the share it is sending and the buddy of the share it is receiving; buddies and the accountability they provide are described later in the section "Accountability and the buddy system." Thus, the entire trading handshake takes four rounds: the first two to exchange the shares themselves, and the next two to exchange receipts while at the same time sending receipts to the buddies.

By providing the receipt on the third round of the trading handshake, *Alice* makes a commitment to store the share y. Similarly, the receipt that *Bob* generates on the fourth round represents a commitment to store the share x. *Bob* could cheat *Alice* by failing to continue the protocol after the third step; in this case, *Alice* has committed to keeping the share from *Bob*, but *Bob* has not committed to anything. At this point, *Alice's* only recourse is to broadcast a complaint against *Bob* and hope that the reputation system causes others to recognize that *Bob* has misbehaved. The alternative is to use a fair exchange protocol, which is unreasonably communications-intensive without a trusted third party.

When *Alice* trades a share to server *Bob*, *Alice* should keep a copy of the share around for a while, just in case *Bob* proves untrustworthy. This will increase the amount of overhead in the system by a factor of two or so (depending on duration), but provides greatly increased robustness. In this case, when a query is done for a share, the system responding should include a flag for whether it believes itself to be the "primary provider" of the data or just happens to have a copy still lying around. The optimum amount of time requires further study.

A diagram describing a trade is given in Figure 12-1. In this diagram, server *Alice* starts out in possession of share $Gita_w$—that is, share w of document *Gita*—and server *Bob* starts out in possession of document $Tune_y$. In this case, server *Charlie* has share x of document *Gita*, and server *David* has share z of document *Tune*. w and x are buddies, and y and z are buddies.

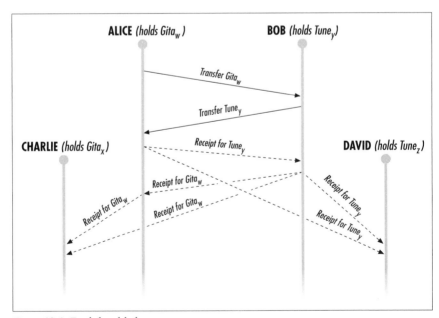

Figure 12-1. Trade handshake

Receipts

A receipt contains a hash of the public keys for the source server and the destination server, information about the share traded away, information about the share received, and a timestamp. For each share, it includes a hash of that document's key, which share number it was, its expiration date, and its size.

This entire set of information about the transaction is signed by server A. If B (or any other server) has to broadcast a complaint about the way A handled the transaction, furnishing this receipt along with the complaint will provide some rudimentary level of "proof" that B is not fabricating its complaint. Note that the expiration date of both shares is included within the receipt, and the signature makes this value immutable. Thus, other servers observing a receipt can easily tell whether the receipt is still "valid"—that is, they can check to see whether the share is still supposed to be kept on A. The size of each share is also included, so other servers can make an informed decision about how influential this transaction should be on their perceived reputation of the two servers involved in the trade.

We really aren't treating the receipt as proof of a transaction, but rather as proof of *half* of a transaction—an indication of a commitment to keep a given share safe. This is because the trading protocol is not bulletproof: The fact that Alice has a receipt from Bob could mean that they performed a transaction, or it could mean that they performed 3 out of the 4 steps of the transaction, and then Alice cheated Bob and never gave him a receipt. Thus, the most a given server can do when it detects a misbehaving server is broadcast a complaint and hope the reputation system handles it correctly.

Accountability and the buddy system

Malicious servers can accept document shares and then fail to store them. If enough shares are lost, the document is unrecoverable. Malicious servers can continue their malicious behavior unless there are mechanisms in place for identifying and excising them.

We've designed a *buddy system* that creates an association between two shares within a given document. Each share is responsible for maintaining information about the location of the other share, or *buddy*. When a share moves, it notifies its buddy,* as described in the earlier section "Trading."

---

* More precisely, it notifies both the server it's moving from and the server it's moving to.

Periodically, a server holding a given share should query for its buddy, to make sure its buddy is still alive. Should the server that is supposed to contain its buddy stop responding, the server with the share making the query is responsible for reporting an anomaly. This server announces which server had responsibility for the missing share when it disappeared. The results of this announcement are described later in this chapter in the section "Reputation system."

We considered allowing abandoned shares to optionally spawn a new share if their buddies disappear, but we discarded this notion. Buddy spawning would make the service much more robust, since lost shares could be regenerated. However, such spawning could cause an exponential population explosion of shares for the wrong reasons. If two servers are out of touch for a little while but are not misbehaving or dead, both shares will end up spawning new copies of themselves. This is a strong argument for not letting shares replicate.

When a share x moves to a new machine, there are two "buddy notifications" sent to its buddy x'. But since the communications channel we have chosen currently has significant latency, a notification to x' might arrive after x' has already been traded to a new server. The old server is then responsible for forwarding these buddy notifications to the new server that it believes currently holds x'. Since the old server keeps a receipt as a record of the transaction, it can use this information to remember the new location of x'. The receipt, and thus the forwarding address, is kept by the old server until the share's expiration date has passed.

When a buddy notification comes in, the forwarder is checked and the notification is forwarded if appropriate. This forwarding is *not* done in the case of a document request, since this document request has presumably been broadcast to all servers in the servnet.

We have attempted to distinguish between the design goals of robustness and accountability. The system is quite robust, because a document cannot be lost until a high threshold of its shares has been lost. Accountability, in turn, is provided by the buddy checking and notification system among shares, which protects against malicious or otherwise ill-behaving servers. Designers can choose the desired levels of robustness and accountability independently.

Communications channel

The Free Haven design requires a means of anonymously passing information between agents. One such means is the remailer network, including the Mixmaster remailers first designed by Lance Cottrell. This system is described in fairly nontechnical terminology in Chapter 7, *Mixmaster Remailers*.

Other examples of anonymous communication channels are Onion Routing[*] and Zero-Knowledge Systems' Freedom.[†] David Martin's doctoral thesis offers a comprehensive overview of anonymous channels in theory and practice.[‡]

The first implementation of the Free Haven design will use the Cypherpunks and Mixmaster remailers as its anonymous channel.

Reputation system

The reputation system in Free Haven is responsible for creating accountability. Accountability in a system so committed to anonymity is a difficult task. There are many opportunities to try to take advantage of other servers, such as neglecting to send a receipt after a trade or wrongly accusing another server of losing a share. Some of the attacks are quite insidious and complex. The history and issues to consider when developing a reputation system can be found in much more detail in Chapter 16.

Careful trust management should enable each server to keep track of which servers it trusts. Given the large number of shares into which documents are divided—and the relatively few shares required to reconstitute a document—no document should be irretrievably lost unless an astoundingly large number of the servers prove evil.

Each server needs to keep two values that describe each other server it knows about: reputation and credibility. Reputation signifies a belief that the server in question will obey the Free Haven Protocol. Credibility represents a belief that the utterances of that server are valuable information. For each of these two values, each server also needs to maintain a confidence rating. This represents the "stiffness" of the reputation and credibility values.

Servers should broadcast referrals in several circumstances, such as when they log the honest completion of a trade, when they suspect that a buddy of a share they hold has been lost, and when the reputation or credibility values for a server change substantially.

---

[*] P.F. Syverson, D.M. Goldschlag, and M.G. Reed (1997), "Anonymous Connections and Onion Routing," *Proceedings of the 1997 IEEE Symposium on Security and Privacy.*

[†] Ian Goldberg and Adam Shostack (1999), *Freedom Network 1.0 Architecture.*

[‡] David Michael Martin (2000), "Network Anonymity," Boston University Ph.D. thesis, *http:// www.cs.du.edu/~dm/anon.html.*

Introducers

Document request operations are done via broadcast. Each server wants to store its documents on a lot of servers, and if it finds a misbehaving server it wants to complain to as many as possible. But how do Free Haven servers discover each other?

The reputation system provides an easy method of adding new servers and removing inactive ones. Servers that have already established a good reputation act as *introducers*. New servers can contact these introducers via the anonymous communication channel; the introducers will then broadcast referrals of this new server. This broadcast by itself does not imply an endorsement of the new server's honesty or performance; it is simply an indication that the new server is interested in performing some trades to increase its reputation. Likewise, a server may mark another as "dormant" given some threshold of unanswered requests. Dormant servers are not included in broadcasts or trade requests. If a dormant server starts initiating requests again, the other servers conclude it is not actually dormant and resume sending broadcasts and offering trades to this server.

Implementation status

The Free Haven Project is still in its design stages. Although we have a basic proof-of-concept implementation, we still wish to firm up our design, primarily in the areas of accountability and bandwidth overhead. Before deploying any implementation, we want to convince ourselves that the Free Haven system offers better anonymity than current systems. Still, the design is sufficiently simple and modular, allowing both a straightforward basic implementation and easy extensibility.

Attacks on Free Haven

Anonymous publishing and storage systems will have adversaries. The attacks and pressures that these adversaries employ might be technical, legal, political, or social in nature. The system's design and the nature of anonymity it provides also affect the success of nontechnical attacks.

We now consider possible attacks on the Free Haven system based on their respective targets: the availability of documents and servnet operation, the accountability offered by the reputation system, and the various aspects of anonymity relevant to anonymous storage and publication, as described in the earlier section "Anonymity for anonymous storage." For a more in-depth consideration of attacks, we refer to Dingledine's thesis.*

This list of attacks is not complete. In particular, we do not have a systematic discussion of what *kinds* of adversaries we expect. Such a discussion would begin with the most powerful adversaries possible, asking questions like, "What if the adversary controls all but one of the servers in the servnet?" and scaling back from there. In analyzing systems like Free Haven, it is not enough to look at the everyday, plausible scenarios—every effort must be made to provide security against adversaries more powerful than the designers ever expect, because in real life, adversaries have a way of being more powerful than anyone ever expects.

Attacks on documents or the servnet

We've considered a wide variety of ways for adversaries to stop Free Haven or make it less effective, and some ways that we might prevent such attacks:

Physical attack
Destroy a server.

Prevention: Because we are breaking documents into shares, and only k of n shares are required to reconstruct the document, an adversary must find and destroy many servers before availability is compromised.

Legal action
Find a physical server and prosecute the owner based on its contents.

Prevention: Because of the passive-server document-anonymity property that the Free Haven design provides, the servnet operator may be able to plausibly deny knowledge of the data stored on his computer. This depends on the laws of the country in question.

Social pressure
Bring various forms of social pressure against server administrators. Claim that the design is patented or otherwise illegal. Sue the Free Haven Project and any known server administrators. Conspire to make a cause "unpopular," convincing administrators that they should manually prune their data. Allege that they "aid child pornographers" and other socially unacceptable activities.

Prevention: We rely on the notion of jurisdictional arbitrage. Information illegal in one place is frequently legal in others. Free Haven's content-neutral policies mean that there is no reason to expect that the server operator

---

* Dingledine, *op. cit.*

has looked at the data she holds, which might make it more difficult to prosecute. We further rely on having enough servers in enough different jurisdictions that organizations cannot conspire to bully a sufficient fraction of servers to make Free Haven unusable.

Denial of service

Attack the servnet by continued flooding of queries for data or requests to join the servnet. These queries may use up all available bandwidth and processing power for a server.

Prevention: We must assume that our communications channel has adequate protection and buffering against this attack, such as the use of client puzzles or other protections described in Chapter 16. Most communications channels we are likely to choose will not protect against this attack. This is a real problem.

Data flooding

Attempt to flood the servnet with shares, to use up available resources.

Prevention: The trading protocol implicitly protects against this type of denial of service attack against storage resources. The ability to insert shares, whether "false" or valid, is restricted to trading: that server must find another that trusts its ability to provide space for the share it would receive in return.

Similarly, the design provides protection against the corrupting of shares. Altering (or "spoofing") a share cannot be done, because the share contains a particular public key and is signed by the corresponding private key. Without knowledge of the original key that was used to create a set of shares, an adversary cannot forge new shares for a given document.

Share hoarding

Trade until a sufficient fraction of an objectionable document is controlled by a group of collaborating servers, and then destroy this document. Likewise, a sufficiently wealthy adversary could purchase a series of servers with very large drives and join the servnet, trading away garbage for "valuable data." He can trade away enough garbage to have a significant portion of all the data in the servnet on his drives, subject to deletion.

Prevention: We rely on the overall size of the servnet to make it unlikely or prohibitively expensive for any given server or group of collaborating servers to obtain a sufficient fraction of the shares of any given document. The failure of this assumption would leave us with no real defense.

Attacks on the reputation system

While attacks against the reputation system* are related to attacks directly against servers, their goal is not to directly affect document availability or servnet operation. Rather, these attacks seek to compromise the means by which we provide accountability for malicious or otherwise misbehaving servers.

Some of these attacks, such as temporary denials of service, have negative repercussions on the reputation of a server. These repercussions might be qualified as "unfair," but are best considered in the following light: if a server is vulnerable to these attacks, it may not be capable of meeting the specifications of the Free Haven Protocol. Such a server is not worthy of trust to meet those specifications. The reputation system does not judge intent, merely actions. Following are some possible attacks on the reputation system, and ways that we might prevent such attacks:

Simple betrayal

An adversary may become part of the servnet, act correctly long enough to gain a good reputation, and then betray this trust by deleting files before their expiration dates.

Prevention: The reputation economy is designed to make this unprofitable. In order to obtain enough "currency" to store data, a server must reliably store data for others. Because a corrupt server must store at least as much data for others as the amount of data it deletes, such an adversary at worst does no overall harm to the system and may even help.

A server that engages in this behavior should be caught by the buddy system when it deletes each share.

Buddy coopting

If a corrupt server (or group of colluding servers) can gain control of both a share and its buddy, it can delete both of them without repercussions.

Prevention: We assume a large quantity of shares in the servnet, making buddy capture more difficult. Servers also can modify reputation ratings if precise trading parameters, or constant trading, suggests an attempt to capture buddies. More concretely, a possible work-around involves separating the reply-block addresses for trading and for buddy checking, preventing corrupt servers from acquiring the buddies of the shares they already have. Such an approach adds complexity and possibly opens other avenues for attack.

---

* Parts of this section were originally written by Brian T. Sniffen in "Trust Economies in the Free Haven Project," May 2000, *http://theory.lcs.mit.edu/~cis/cis-theses.html*.

False referrals

An adversary can broadcast false referrals, or even send them only to selected servers.

Prevention: The confidence rating of credibility can provide a guard against false referrals, combined with a single-reporting policy (i.e., at most one referral per target per source is used for reputation calculations).

Trading receipt games

While we believe that the signed timestamps attest to who did what and when, receipt-based accountability may be vulnerable to some attacks. Most likely, these will involve multiserver adversaries engaging in coordinated bait-and-switch games with target servers.

Entrapment

There are several ways in which an adversary can appear to violate the protocols. When another server points them out, the adversary can present receipts that show her wrong and can accuse her of sending false referrals. A more thorough system of attestations and protests is necessary to defend against and account for this type of attack.

Attacks on anonymity

There are a number of attacks that might be used to determine more information about the identity of some entity in the system:

Attacks on reader-anonymity

An adversary might develop and publish on Free Haven a customized virus that automatically contacts a given host upon execution. A special case of this attack would be to include mime-encoded URLs in a document to exploit reader software that automatically loads URLs. Another approach might be to become a server on both the servnet and the mix net and attempt an end-to-end attack, such as correlating message timing with document requests. Indeed, servers could claim to have a document and see who requests it, or simply monitor queries and record the source of each query. Sophisticated servers might attempt to correlate readers based on the material they download and then try to build statistical profiles and match them to people (outside Free Haven) based on activity and preferences. We prevent this attack by using each reply block for only one transaction.

Attacks on server-anonymity

Adversaries might create unusually large shares and try to reduce the set of known servers that might have the capacity to store such shares. This attacks the partial anonymity of these servers. An adversary could become a server and then collect routine status and participation information (such as server lists) from other servers. This information might be combined with extensive knowledge of the bandwidth characteristics and limitations of the Internet to map servnet topology. By joining the mix net, an adversary might correlate message timing with trade requests or reputation broadcasts. An alternate approach is simply to spread a Trojan Horse or worm that looks for Free Haven servers and reports which shares they are currently storing.

Attacks on publisher-anonymity

An adversary could become a server and log publishing acts, and then attempt to correlate source or timing. Alternatively, he might look at servers that recently have published a document and try to determine who has been communicating with them recently.

There are also entirely social attacks that can be very successful, such as offering a large sum of money for information leading to the current location of a given document, server, reader, etc.

We avoid or reduce the threat of many of these attacks by using an anonymous channel that supports pseudonyms for our communications. This prevents most or all adversaries from being able to determine the source or destination of a given message or establish linkability between each endpoint of a set of messages. Even if server administrators are subpoenaed or otherwise pressured to release information about these entities, they can openly disclaim any knowledge.

An analysis of anonymity

We describe the protections offered for each of the broad categories of anonymity. In Table 12-1, we provide an overview of Free Haven and the different publishing systems that we examined. We consider the level of privacy provided—computational (C) and perfect-forward (P-F) anonymity—by the various systems.

Table 12-1. Anonymity properties of publishing systems

Project	Publisher		Reader		Server		Document	Query
	C	P-F	C	P-F	C	P-F	C	C
Gnutella								
Eternity Usenet	✓	✓	?				✓	
Freenet	✓	✓	?				✓	
Mojo Nation	?	?					✓	
Publius	✓	✓					✓	
Free Haven	✓	✓	✓	✓	✓		✓	

Computational anonymity means that an adversary with "reasonable" computing resources and knowledge is unable to break the anonymity involved. The adversary may do anything it likes to try to break the system but is limited in how much power it has; for example, it may not be able to break the cryptography involved in building a system or be able to break into the computers of every single machine running the system.

Perfect-forward anonymity is analogous to perfect-forward secrecy: A system is perfect-forward anonymous if no information remains after a transaction is completed that could later identify the participants if one side or the other is compromised. This notion is a little bit trickier—think of it from the perspective of an adversary watching the system over a long period of time. Is there anything that the adversary can discover from watching several transactions that he can't discover from watching a single transaction?

Free Haven provides computational and perfect-forward author-anonymity, because authors communicate with publishers via an anonymous channel. Servers trade with other servers via pseudonyms, providing computational but not perfect-forward anonymity, as the pseudonyms can be broken later. Because trading is constant, however, Free Haven achieves publisher-anonymity for publishers trying to trade away all shares of the same document. The use of IDA to split documents provides passive-server document-anonymity, but the public key embedded in each share (which we require for authenticating buddy messages) makes it trivial for active servers to discover what they are storing. Because requests are broadcast via an anonymous channel, Free Haven provides computational reader-anonymity, and different reply blocks used and then destroyed after each request provide perfect-forward reader-anonymity.

Gnutella fails to provide publisher-anonymity, reader-anonymity, or server-anonymity because of the direct connections for actual file transfer. Because Gnutella servers start out knowing the intended contents of each document they are offering, they also fail to provide document-anonymity.

Eternity Usenet provides publisher-anonymity via the use of one-way anonymous remailers. Server-anonymity is not provided, because every Usenet server that carries the Eternity newsgroup is a server. Anonymity expert Adam Back, designer of the Eternity Usenet service, has pointed out that passive-server document-anonymity can be provided by encrypting files with a key derived from the URL; active servers might find the key and attempt to decrypt stored documents. Reader-anonymity is not provided by open public proxies unless the reader uses an anonymous channel, because the proxy can see what a user queries or downloads, and at what time. For local proxies, which connect to a separate news server, however, the situation is better because the news server knows only what the user downloads. Even so, this is not quite satisfactory, because the user can be tied by the server to the contents of the Eternity newsgroup at a certain time.

Freenet achieves passive-server document-anonymity because servers are unable to reverse the hash of the document name to determine the key with which to decrypt the document. For active-server document-anonymity, the servers can check whether they are carrying a particular key but cannot easily match a stored document to a key due to the hash function. Server-anonymity is not provided because, given a document key, it is very easy to locate a server that is carrying that document—querying any server at all will result in that server carrying the document! Because of the TTL and Hops fields for both reading and publishing, it is also not clear that Freenet achieves publisher- or reader-anonymity, although it is much better in these regards than Gnutella. We note that the most recent Freenet design introduces randomized TTL and Hops fields in each request, and plans are in the works to allow a Publish or Retrieve operation to traverse a mix net chain before entering the Freenet system. These protections will make attacks based on tracking queries much more difficult.

Mojo Nation achieves document-anonymity, as described earlier, because the server holding a share doesn't know how to reconstruct that document. The Mojo Nation design is amenable to integrating publisher-anonymity down the road—a publisher can increase her anonymity by paying more Mojo and chaining requests through participants that act as "relays." The specifics of prepaying the path through the relays are not currently being designed. It seems possible that this technique could be used to ensure reader-anonymity as well, but the payment issues are even more complex. Indeed, the supplied digital cash model is not even anonymous currently; users need to uncomment a few lines in the source, and this action breaks Chaum's patents.

Publius achieves document-anonymity because the key is split between n servers, and without sufficient shares of the key, a server is unable to decrypt the document that it stores. The secret sharing algorithm provides a stronger form of this anonymity (albeit in a storage-intensive manner), since a passive server really can learn nothing at all about the contents of a document that it is helping to store. Because documents are published to Publius through a one-way anonymous remailer, it provides publisher-anonymity. Publius provides no support for protecting readers by itself, however, and the servers containing a given file are clearly marked in the URL used for retrieving that file. Readers can use a system such as ZKS Freedom or Onion Routing to protect themselves, but servers may still be liable for storing "bad" data.

We see that systems can often provide publisher-anonymity via one-way communication channels, effectively removing any linkability; removing the need for a reply pseudonym on the anonymous channel means that there is "nothing to crack." The idea of employing a common mix net as a communication channel for each of these publication systems is very appealing. We could leave most of the anonymity concerns to the communication channel itself and provide a simple backend filesystem or equivalent service to transfer documents between agents. Thus the design of the backend system could be based primarily on addressing other issues such as availability of documents, protections against flooding and denial of service attacks, and accountability in the face of this anonymity.

Future work

Our experience designing Free Haven revealed several problems that have no simple solutions; further research is surely required. We state some of these problems here and refer to Dingledine's thesis[*] for in-depth consideration:

Deployed free low-latency pseudonymous channel

Free Haven requires pseudonyms in order to create server reputations. The only current widely deployed channels that support pseudonyms seem to be the Cypherpunk remailer network and ZKS Freedom mail. The Cypherpunk and ZKS Version 1 networks run over SMTP and consequently have high latency. This high latency complicates protocol design. The recently announced Version 2 of ZKS Freedom mail runs over POP and may offer more opportunity for the kind of channel we desire.

Modelling and metrics

When designing Free Haven, we made some choices, such as the choice to include trading, based on only our intuition of what would make a robust, anonymous system. A mathematical model of anonymous storage would allow us to test this intuition and run simulations. We also need *metrics*: Specific quantities that can be measured and compared to determine which designs are better. For example, we might ask, "How many servers must be compromised by an adversary for how long before any document's availability is compromised? Before a specific targeted document's availability is compromised?" or, "How many servers must be compromised by an adversary for how long before the adversary can link a document and a publisher?" This modelling could draw from a wide variety of previous work.

---

[*] Dingledine, *op. cit.*

Formal definition of anonymity

Closely related to the last point is the need to formalize the kinds of anonymity presented in the section "Anonymity for anonymous storage." By formally defining anonymity, we can move closer to providing meaningful *proofs* that a particular system provides the anonymity we desire. We might leverage our experience with cryptographic definitions of semantic security and nonmalleability to produce similar definitions and proofs.[*] A first step in this direction might be to carefully explore the connection remarked upon by Simon and Rackoff between secure multiparty computation and anonymous protocols.[†]

Usability requirements and interface

We stated in the introduction that we began the Free Haven Project out of concern for the rights of political dissidents. Unfortunately, at this stage of the project, we have contacted few political dissidents and, as a consequence, do not have a clear idea of the usability and interface requirements for an anonymous storage system. Our concern is heightened by a recent paper which points out serious deficiencies in PGP's user interface.[‡]

Efficiency

It seems like nearly everyone is doing a peer-to-peer system or WWW replacement these days. Which one will win? Adam Back pointed out that in many cases, the efficiency and perceived benefit of the system is more important to an end user than its anonymity properties. This is a major problem with the current Free Haven design: we emphasize a quality relatively few potential users care about at the expense of something nearly everyone cares about. Is there a way to create an anonymous system with a tolerable loss of perceived efficiency compared to its non-anonymous counterpart? And what does "tolerable" mean, exactly?

We consider the above to be "challenge problems" for anonymous publication and storage systems.

---

[*] Oded Goldreich (1999). *Modern Cryptography, Probabilistic Proofs, and Pseudo-Randomness.* Springer-Verlag.

[†] Simon and Rackoff (1993), "Cryptographic Defense Against Traffic Analysis," *STOC 1993*, pp. 672–681.

[‡] Alma Whitten and J.D. Tygar (1999), "Why Johnny Can't Encrypt," *USENIX Security 1999*, *http://www.usenix.org/publications/library/proceedings/sec99/whitten.html.*

Conclusion

Free Haven aims to solve a problem that no other system currently addresses—creating a decentralized storage service that at the same time protects the anonymity of publishers, readers, and servers, provides a dynamic network, and ensures the availability of each document for a publisher-specified lifetime. We have made progress in identifying the requirements for each of these goals and designing solutions that meet them.

The current Free Haven design is unfortunately unsuitable for wide deployment, because of several remaining problems. The primary problem is efficiency—unless we can provide a sufficiently friendly and efficient interface to the documents stored in the system, we will find ourselves with very few servers. Indeed, since we need systems that are relatively reliable, we can't make as good use of typical end-user machines as a system like Freenet can. This small number of servers will in turn decrease the amount of robustness that our system offers.

Free Haven uses inefficient broadcasts for communication. A large step to address this problem is coupling Free Haven with a widely deployed efficient file-sharing service such as Freenet or Mojo Nation. Popular files will be highly accessible from within the faster service; Free Haven will answer queries for less popular documents that have expired in this service.

Free Haven sets out to accomplish several goals not considered *en masse* by other peer-to-peer publishing/storage systems: Flexibility, anonymity for all parties, content-neutral persistence of data, and accountability. These ambitious goals are the root cause of existing design difficulties. Without the requirement of long-term persistent storage, strong accountability measures are not as necessary. Without these measures, computational overhead can be greatly lowered, making unnecessary many communications that are used to manage reputation metrics. And without the requirement for such anonymity and the resulting latency from the communications channel, readers could enjoy much faster document retrieval. Yet, the study and emphasis of these ambitious goals are Free Haven's contribution and importance in a rapidly evolving peer-to-peer digital world.

Acknowledgments

Professor Ronald Rivest provided invaluable assistance reviewing Roger's master's thesis and as Michael's bachelor's thesis advisor and caused us to think hard about our design decisions. Professor Michael Mitzenmacher made possible

David's involvement in this project and provided insightful comments on information dispersal and trading. Beyond many suggestions for overall design details, Brian Sniffen provided the background for the reputation system (which we followed up with the discussion of reputation systems in Chapter 16), and Joseph Sokol-Margolis was helpful in considering attacks on the system. Andy Oram, our editor, was instrumental in turning this from an academic paper into something that is actually readable. Adam Back and Theodore Hong commented on our assessment of their systems and made our related work section much better. Furthermore, we thank Susan Born, Nathan Mahn, Jean-François Raymond, Anna Lysyanskaya, Adam Smith, and Brett Woolsridge for further insight and feedback.

part three

Technical Topics

In this part, project leaders choose various key topics in order to focus on the problems, purposes, and promises of peer-to-peer technologies.

chapter thirteen

Metadata

*Rael Dornfest, O'Reilly Network, and
Dan Brickley, ILRT and RDFWeb*

Today's Web is a great, big, glorious mess. Spiders, robots, screen-scraping, and plaintext searches are standard practices that indicate a desperate attempt to draw arbitrary distinctions between needles and hay. And they go only so far as the data we've taken the trouble to make available online.

Now peer-to-peer promises to turn your desktop, laptop, palmtop, and fridge into peers, chattering away with one another and making swaths of their data stores available online. Of course, if every single device on the network exposes even a small percentage of the resources it manages, it will exacerbate the problem by piling on more hay and needles in heaps. How will we cope with the sudden logarithmic influx of disparate data sources?

The new protocols being developed at breakneck speed for peer-to-peer applications also add to the mess by disconnecting data from the fairly bounded arena of the Web and the ubiquitous port 80. Loosening the hyperlinks that bind all these various resources together threatens to scatter hay and needles to the winds. Where previously we had application user interfaces for each and every information system, the Web gave us a single user interface—the browser— along with an organizing principle—the hyperlink—that allowed us to reach all the material, at least in theory. Peer-to-peer might undo all this good and throw us back into the dark ages of one application for each application type or application service. We already have Napster for MP3s and work has begun on Docster for documents—can JPEGster and Palmster be very far off?

And how shall we search these disparate, transitory clumps of data, winking in and out of existence as our devices go on and offline, to say nothing of finding the clumps in the first place? Napster is held up as a reassurance that everything can work out on its own. The inherent ubiquity of any one MP3 track gets around the problem of resource transience. However, isn't this abundance simply the direct result of its rather constrained problem space? MP3 files are popular, and MP3 rippers make it easy for huge numbers of people to create decent-quality files. As industry attention turns to peer-to-peer technologies, and as the content within these systems becomes more heterogeneous, the technology will have to accommodate content that is harder to accumulate and less popular; the critical mass of replicated files will not be attained. Familiar problems associated with finding a particular item may reemerge, this time in a decentralized environment rather than around the familiar Web hub.

Whether or not peer-to-peer fares any better than the Web, it certainly presents a new challenge for people concerned with describing and classifying information resources. Peer-to-peer provides a rich environment and a promising early stage for putting in place all we've learned about metadata over the past decade.

So, before we go much further, what exactly *is* metadata?

Data about data

Metadata is the stuff of card catalogues, television guides, Rolodexes, taxonomies, tables of contents—to borrow a Zen concept, the finger pointing at the moon. It is labels like "title," "author," "type," "height," and "language" used to describe a book, person, television program, species, etc. Metadata is, quite simply, data about data.

There are communities of specialists who have spent years working on—and indeed solving some of—the hard problems of categorizing, cataloguing, and making it possible to find things. Even in the early days of the Web, developers enlisted the help of these information scientists and architects, realizing that otherwise we'd be in for quite a mess. The Dublin Core Metadata Initiative (DMCI)* is just such an effort. An interdisciplinary, international group founded in 1994, the DCMI's charter is to use a minimal set of metadata constructs to make it easier to find things on the Web. We'll take a closer look at Dublin Core in a moment.

Yet, while well-understood systems exist for cataloguing and classifying some classic types of information, such as books (e.g., MARC records and the Dewey Decimal System), equivalent facilities were late to arrive on the Web—some

---

* Dublin Core Metadata Initiative, *http://www.dublincore.org*; "Metadata With a Mission: Dublin Core", *http://www.xml.com/pub/2000/10/25*; Dublin Core Metadata Element Set, Version 1.1, *http://purl.org/dc/elements/1.1*.

would say far too late. They are emerging, however, just in time for peer-to-peer.

Metadata lessons from the Web

Peer-to-peer's power lies in its willingness to rethink old assumptions and reinvent the way we do things. This can be quite constructive, even revolutionary, but it also risks being hugely destructive in that we can throw out lessons previously learned from the web experience. In particular, we know that the Web suffered because metadata infrastructure was added relatively late (1997+), an add-on situation that had an impact on various levels.

The Web burst onto the scene before we managed to agree on common descriptive practices—ways of describing "stuff." Consequently, the vast majority of web-related tools lack any common infrastructure for specifying or using the properties of web content. WYSIWYG HTML editors don't go out of their way to make their metadata support (if any) visible, nor do they request metadata for a document when authors press the "Save" button. Search engines provide little room for registering metadata along with their associated sites. Robots and spiders often discard any metadata in the form of HTML <meta> tags they might find. This has resulted in an enormous hodgepodge of a data set with little rhyme or reason. The Web is hardly the intricately organized masterpiece represented by its namesake in nature.

Early peer-to-peer applications come from relatively limited spheres (MP3 filesharing, messaging, Weblogs, groupware, etc.) with pretty well understood semantics and implicit metadata—we know it's an MP3 because it's in Napster. These communities have the opportunity, before heterogeneity and ubiquity muddy the waters, to describe and codify their semantics to allow for better organization, extraction, and search functionality down the road. Yet even at this early stage, we're already seeing the same mistakes creeping in.

Resource description

Until recently, the means available to content providers for describing the resources they make available on the Web have been inconsistent at best. About the only consistent metadata in an HTML document is the <title> element, which provides only a hint at best as to the content of the page. HTML's <meta> element is supposed to provide a method for embedding arbitrary metadata—but that creates more of a problem than a solution, because applications, books, articles, tutorials, and standards bodies alike express little guidance as to what good metadata should look like and how best to express it.

The work of the aforementioned Dublin Core offers a wonderful start. The Dublin Core Metadata Element Set is a set of 15 elements (title, description, creator, date, publisher, etc.) that are useful in describing almost any web resource. Rather than attempt to define semantics for specific instances and situations, the DCMI focused on the commonalities found in resources of various shapes and flavors. The Dublin Core may just as easily be used to describe "a journal article in PDF format," "an MPEG encoding of an episode of *Buffy the Vampire Slayer* recorded on a hacked TiVO," or "a healthcare speech given by the U.S. President on March 2, 2000."

Example 13-1 shows a typical appearance of Dublin Core metadata in a fragment of HTML. Each <meta> tag contains an element of metadata defined by Dublin Core.

Example 13-1. Dublin Core metadata in an HTML document

```
<html>
  <head>
    <title>Distributed Metadata</title>
    <meta name="description" content="This article addresses...">
    <meta name="subject" content="metadata, rdf, peer-to-peer">
    <meta name="creator" content="Dan Brickley and Rael Dornfest">
    <meta name="publisher" content="O'Reilly & Associates">
    <meta name="date" content="2000-10-29T00:34:00+00:00">
    <meta name="type" content="article">
    <meta name="language" content="en-us">
    <meta name="rights" content="Copyright 2000, O'Reilly & Associates,
Inc.">
    ...
  </head>
  ...
```

While useful up to a point, the original HTML mechanism for embedding metadata has proven limited. There is no built-in convention to control the names given to the various embedded metadata fields. As a consequence, HTML <meta> tags can be ambiguous: we don't know which sense of "title" or "date" is being used.

XML represents another evolution in web architecture, and along with XML come namespaces. Example 13-2 illustrates some namespaces in use. Like peer-to-peer, namespaces exemplify decentralization. We can now mix descriptive elements defined by independent communities, without fear of naming clashes, since each piece of data is tied a URI that provides a context and definition for it.

Example 13-2. Dublin Core metadata in an XML document

```
<?xml version="1.0" encoding="iso-8859-1"?>

<rdf:RDF
  xmlns:rdf="http://www.w3.org/1999/02/22-rdf-syntax-ns#"
  xmlns:dc="http://purl.org/dc/elements/1.1/"
  xmlns="http://purl.org/rss/1.0/"
>
...
  <item rdf:about="http://www.oreillynet.com/.../metadata.html">
    <title>Distributed Metadata</title>
    <link>http://www.oreillynet.com/.../metadata.html </link>
    <dc:description>This article addresses...</dc:description>
    <dc:subject>metadata, rdf, peer-to-peer </dc:subject>
    <dc:creator>Dan Brickley and Rael Dornfest </dc:creator>
    <dc:publisher>O'Reilly & Associates</dc:publisher>
    <dc:date>2000-10-29T00:34:00+00:00</dc:date>
    <dc:type>article</dc:type>
    <dc:language>en-us</dc:language>
    <dc:format>text/html</dc:format>
    <dc:rights>Copyright 2000, O'Reilly & Associates, Inc.</dc:rights>
    ...
  </item>
  ...
```

In the example above, Dublin Core elements are prepended by the namespace name "dc:". The name is associated with the URI *http://purl.org/dc/elements/1.1* by the "xmlns:dc" construct at the beginning of the document. "dc:subject" is therefore understood to mean "the subject element in the dc namespace as defined at *http://purl.org/dc/elements/1.1*."

Namespaces let each author weave additional semantics required by particular types of resources or appropriate to a specific realm with the more general resource description such as that provided by the Dublin Core. In the book world, an additional definition might be the ISBN or Library of Congress number, while in the music world, it might be some form of compact disc identifier.

Now, we're not insisting that each and every document be described using all 15 Dublin Core elements and along various other lines as well. Something to keep in mind, however, is that every bit of metadata provides a logarithmic increase in available semantics, making resources less ambiguous and easier to find. Peer-to-peer application developers may then use the descriptions provided by a resource rather than having to resort to guesswork or such extremes as sequestering resources of a certain type to their own network.

Searching

Searching is the bane of the Web's existence, despite the plethora of search tools—Yahoo currently lists 193 registered web search engines.* Search engines typically suffer from a lack of semantics on both the gathering and querying ends. On the gathering side, search engines typically utilize one of two methods:

1. Internet directories typically ask content providers to register their web sites through an online form. Unfortunately, such forms don't provide slots for metadata such as publisher, author, subject keywords, etc.

2. Search engines scour the Web with armies of agents/spiders, scraping pages and following links for hints at semantics. Sadly, even if a site does embed metadata (such as HTML's `<meta>` tags) in its documents, this information is often ignored.

On the querying end, while some sites do make an attempt to narrow the context for particular word searches (using such categories as "all the words," "any of the words," or "in the title"), successful searching still comes down to keywords and best guess. It's virtually impossible to disambiguate between concepts like "by" and "about"—"find me all articles written *by* Andy Oram" versus "find me anything *about* Andy Oram." Queries like "find me anything on Perl written by the person whose email address is *larry@wall.org*" are out of the question.

While the needs of users clearly call for semantically rich queries, some peer-to-peer applications and systems are doing little to provide even the simplest of keyword searches. The categories "artist" and "title," which may be enough within Napster, will fold up and collapse in more heterogeneous peer-to-peer environments populated by MP3s, documents, images, and the various other data types found on the Web today. While Freenet does provide the boon of an optional accompanying metadata file to accompany any resource added to the cloud, this is currently of minimal use for a couple of reasons: a) No guidance exists on what this metadata file should contain, and b) There is currently no search functionality. Gnutella's InfraSearch allows for a wonderfully diverse interpretation and subsequent processing of search terms: While a dictionary node sees "country" as a term to be looked up, an MP3 node may see it as a music genre. Unfortunately, however, the InfraSearch user interface still provides only a simple text entry field and little chance for the user to be an active participant in defining the parameters of his or her search.

---

* Yahoo!'s "Search Engines" category, *http://dir.yahoo.com/computers_and_internet/internet/world_wide_web/searching_the_web/search_engines*.

Hopefully we'll see peer-to-peer applications emerging that empower both the content provider and end user by providing semantically rich environments for the description and subsequent retrieval of content. This should be reflected both in the user interface and in the engine itself.

Resources and relationships: A historical overview

So where does this all leave us? How do we infuse our peer-to-peer applications with the metadata lessons learned from the Web?

The core of the World Wide Web Consortium's (W3C) metadata vision is a concept known as the *Semantic Web*. This is not a separate Web from the one we currently weave and wander, but a layer of metadata providing richer relationships between the ostensibly disparate resources we visit with our mouse clicks. While HTML's hyperlinks are simple linear paths lacking any obvious meaning, such semantics do exist and need only a means of expression.

Enter the *Resource Description Framework* (RDF),* a data model and XML serialization syntax for describing resources both on and off the Web. RDF turns those flat hyperlinks into arcs, allowing us to label not only the endpoints, but the arc itself—in other words, ascribe meaning to the relationship between the two resources at hand. A simple link between Andy Oram's home page and an article on the O'Reilly Network provides little insight into the relationship between the two. RDF disambiguates the relationship: "Andy wrote this particular article" versus "this is an article about Andy" versus "Andy found this article rather interesting."

RDF's history itself shows how emerging peer-to-peer applications can benefit from a generalized and consistent metadata framework. RDF has roots in an earlier effort, the *Platform for Internet Content Selection*, or PICS. One of the original goals for PICS was to facilitate a wide range of rating and filtering services, particularly in the areas of child protection and filtering of pornographic content. It defined a simple metadata "label" format that could encode a variety of classification and rating vocabularies (e.g., RSACi, MedPICS†). It included the goal of allowing diverse communities to create their own content rating languages and networked metadata services for distributing these descriptive labels. While

---

* Resource Description Framework, *http://www.w3.org/RDF*.

† Links to PICS vocabularies and W3C specifications, *http://www.w3.org/PICS*; "Metadata, PICS and Quality" (1997), *http://www.ariadne.ac.uk/issue9/pics*.

originally it defined a pretty comprehensive set of tools for rating and filtering systems, PICS as initially defined did not play well with other metadata applications. The protocols, data formats, and accompanying infrastructure were too tightly coupled to one narrow application—it wasn't general enough to be useful for everyone.

One critical piece PICS lacked was a namespaces mechanism that would allow a single PICS label to draw upon multiple, independently managed vocabularies. The designers of PICS eventually realized that all the work they had put into a well-designed query protocol, a digital signatures system, vocabularies, and so forth risked being reinvented for various other, non-PICS-specific metadata applications.

The threat of such duplication led to the invention of RDF. Unlike PICS, RDF has a highly general information model designed from the ground up to allow diverse applications to create data that can be easily intermingled. However diverse, RDF applications all share a common strategy: they talk about unambiguously named properties of unambiguously named resources. To eliminate ambiguous interpretations of properties such as "type" or "format," RDF rests on unique identifiers.

Foundations of resource description: Unique identifiers

Unique identification is the critical empowering technology for metadata. We benefit from having unique identifiers for both the things we describe (*resources*), and the ways we describe them (*properties*). In RDF, we call the things we're describing resources regardless of whether they're people, places, documents, movies, images, databases, etc. All RDF applications adopt a common convention for identifying these things (regardless of what else they disagree about!).

We identify the things we're describing with Uniform Resource Identifiers, or URIs.[*] You're most probably familiar with one subset of URIs, the Uniform Resource Locator, or URL. While URLs are concerned with the location and retrieval of resources, URIs more generally are unique identifiers for things that may not necessarily be retrievable.

We also need clarity concerning properties, which are how we describe our resources. To say that something is of a particular type, or has a certain relationship to another resource, or has some specified attribute, we need to uniquely

---

[*] URI defines a simple text syntax for URLs, URNs and similar controlled names for use on the Internet, *http://www.w3.org/Addressing*.

identify our descriptive concepts. RDF uses URIs for these too. Different communities can invent new descriptive properties (such as person, employee, price, and classification) and assign URIs to these properties.

Since the assignment of URIs is decentralized, we can be sure that uniquely named descriptive properties don't get mixed up when we integrate metadata from multiple sources. An auto-maker's concept of "type" is different from that of a cheese-maker's. The use of URIs such as *http://webuildcars.org/descriptions/types* and *http://weagecheese.org/descriptions/type* serves to uniquely identify the particular "type" we're using to describe a resource.

One critical lesson we can take away from the PICS story is that, when it comes to metadata, it is very hard to partition the problem space. The things we want to describe, the things we want to say about them, and the things we want to do with this data are all deeply entangled. RDF is an attempt to provide a generalized framework for all types of metadata. By providing a consistent abstraction layer that goes below surface differences, we gain an elegant core architecture on which to build. There is no limit to the material or applications RDF supports: through different URIs and namespaces, different groups can extend the common RDF model to describe the needs of the peer-to-peer application at hand. No standards committee or centralized initiative gets to decide how we describe things. Applications can draw upon multiple descriptive vocabularies in a consistent, principled manner. The combination of these two attributes—consistent framework and decentralized descriptive concepts—is a powerful architecture for the peer-to-peer applications being built today.

When it comes to metadata, the network becomes a poorer information resource whenever we create artificial boundaries between metadata applications. The Web's own metadata system, RDF, was built in acknowledgment of this. There is little reason to suppose peer-to-peer content is different in this regard since we're talking about pretty much the same kind of content, albeit in a radically new environment.

A contrasting evolution: MP3 and the metadata marketplace

The alternatives to erecting a rigorous metadata architecture like RDF can be illustrated by the most popular decentralized activity on the Internet today: MP3 file exchange.

How do people find out the names of songs on the CDs they're playing on their networked PCs? One immediate problem is that there is nothing resembling a URI scheme for naming CDs; this makes it difficult to agree on a protocol for querying metadata servers about the properties of those CDs. While one might imagine taking one of the various CDDB-like algorithms and proposing a URI scheme for universal adoption (for instance, cd:894120720878192091), in practice this would be time-consuming and somewhat politicized. Meanwhile, peer-to-peer developers just want to build killer apps; they don't want to spend 18 months on a standards committee specifying the identifiers for compact discs (or people or films...). Most of us can't afford the time to create metadata tags, and if we could, we'd doubtless think of more interesting ways of using that time.

What to do? Having just stressed the importance of unique names when describing content, can we get by without them? Actually, it appears so.

Every day thousands of MP3 users work around the unique identification problem without realizing it. Their CD rippers inspect the CD, compute one of several identifying properties for the CD they're digitizing, and use this uniquely identifying property to consult a networked metadata service. This is metadata in action on a massive scale. But it also smacks of the PICS problem. MP3 listeners have settled on an application-specific piece of infrastructure rather than a more useful, generalized approach.

These metadata services exist and operate very successfully today, despite the lack of any canonical "standard" identifier syntax for compact discs. The technique they use to work around the standards bottleneck is simple, being much the same as saying things like "the person whose personal mailbox is..." or "the company whose corporate homepage is...". Being simple, it can (and should) be applied in other contexts where peer-to-peer and web applications want to query networked services for metadata. There's no reason to use a different protocol when asking for a CD track list and when asking for metadata describing any other kind of thing.

The basic protocol being used in CD metadata query is both simple and general: "tell me what you know about the resource whose CD checksum is some-huge-number"—a protocol reminiscent of the PICS label bureau protocol. The MP3 community could build enormously useful services on top of this, even without adopting a more general framework such as that provided by RDF, but they have stopped short of the next step.

On the contrary, while MP3 CD rippers currently embed lots of descriptive information (track listings) right into the encoding, they omit the most crucial piece of data from a fan's point of view: the CD and track identifiers. The simple unique identifier for a song on a CD, while only a tiny fragment of data, could allow both peer-to-peer and web applications to hook into a marketplace of descriptive services. How could MP3 services use this information?

One application is to update the metadata inside MP3 files, either to correct errors or to add additional information. If we don't know which CD an MP3 file was derived from, it becomes hard to know which MP3 files to update when we learn more about that CD. MP3s of collected works (i.e., compilations) typically have very poor embedded metadata. Artist names often appear inside the track name, for example. This makes for difficulties in finding information: If I want to generate a browsable listing organized alphabetically by artist, I don't want half the songs filed away under "Various Artists," nor do I want to find dozens of artist names in the "By Track Title" listings. Embedding unique identifiers in MP3s would allow this mess to be fixed at a later date.

Another example can be found in the practice of sharing playlists: Given some convention for identifying songs and tracks, we can describe virtual, personalized compilation albums that another listener can recreate on his personal system by asking a peer-to-peer network for files representing those tracks. Unique identification strategies would provide the architectural glue that would allow us to reconnect fragmented information resources. Were someone to put a unique identification service in place, we could soon expect all kinds of new applications built on top:

- Collaborative filtering ("Who likes songs that I like?")
- E-commerce ("Where can I can I buy this T-shirt, CD, or book?" or "Is there a compilation album containing these tracks?")
- Discovery ("What are the words to this song?" or "Where can I find other offerings by this artist?")

The lesson for peer-to-peer metadata architecture is simple. Unique identifiers create markets. If you want to build interesting peer-to-peer applications that hook into a wide range of additional services, adopt the same strategy for uniquely identifying things that others are using.

Conclusion

Metadata applied at a fundamental level, early in the game, will provide rich semantics upon which innovators can build peer-to-peer applications that will amaze us with their flexibility. While the symmetry of peer-to-peer brings about a host of new and interesting ways of interacting, there's no substitute for taking the opportunity to rethink our assumptions and learn from the mistakes made on the Web. Let's not continue the screen-scraping modus operandi; rather, let's replace extrapolation with forethought and rich assertions.

To summarize with a call to action for peer-to-peer architects, project leaders, developers, and end users:

- Use a single, coherent metadata framework such as that provided by RDF. When it comes to metadata, the network becomes a poorer information resource whenever we create artificial boundaries between metadata applications.

- Work on the commonalities between seemingly disparate data sources and formats. Work in your community to agree on some sort of common descriptive concepts. If such concepts already exist, borrow them.

- Describe your resources well, in a standard way, getting involved in this standardization process itself where necessary. Be sure to make as much of this description as possible available to peer applications and end users through clear semantics and simple APIs.

- Design ways of searching for (and finding) resources on the Net that take full advantage of any exposed metadata.

chapter fourteen

Performance

Theodore Hong, Imperial College of Science, Technology, and Medicine

We live in the era of speed. Practically as a matter of course, we expect each day to bring faster disks, faster networks, and above all, faster processors. Recently, a research group at the University of Arizona even published a tongue-in-cheek article arguing that large calculations could be done more quickly by slacking off for a few months first, then buying a faster computer:

> [B]y fine tuning your slacktitude you can actually accomplish more than either the lazy bum at the beach for two years or the hard working sucker who got started immediately. Indeed with a little bit of algebra we convince ourselves that there exists an optimal slack time s★.[*]

In a world like this, one might well wonder whether performance is worth paying attention to anymore. For peer-to-peer file-sharing systems, the answer is a definite yes, for reasons I will explain in the next section.

Let me first emphasize that by performance, I don't mean abstract numerical benchmarks such as, "How many milliseconds will it take to render this many millions of polygons?" Rather, I want to know the answers to questions such as, "How long will it take to retrieve this file?" or "How much bandwidth will this query consume?" These answers will have a direct impact on the success and usability of a system.

Fault tolerance is another significant concern. Peer-to-peer operates in an inherently unreliable environment, since it depends on the personal resources of ordinary individual users. These resources may become unexpectedly unavailable at any time, for a variety of reasons ranging from users disconnecting from

---

[*] C. Gottbrath, J. Bailin, C. Meakin, T. Thompson, and J.J. Charfman (1999), "The Effects of Moore's Law and Slacking on Large Computations," arXiv:astro-ph/9912202.

the network or powering off a machine to users simply deciding not to participate any longer. In addition to these essentially random failures, personal
machines tend to be more vulnerable than dedicated servers to directed hack-
ing attacks or even legal action against their operators. Therefore, peer-to-peer
systems need to anticipate failures as ordinary, rather than extraordinary, occur-
rences, and must be designed in a way that promotes redundancy and graceful
degradation of performance.

Scaling is a third important consideration. The massive user bases of Napster
and of the Web have clearly shown how huge the demand on a successful
information-sharing system can potentially be. A designer of a new peer-to-peer
system must think optimistically and plan for how it might scale under strains
orders of magnitude larger in the future. If local indices of data are kept, will
they overflow? If broadcasts are used, will they saturate the network? Scalability will also be influenced by performance: some design inefficiencies may pass
unnoticed with ten thousand users, but what happens when the user base hits
ten million or more? A recent report from Gnutella analysts Clip2, indicating
that Gnutella may already be encountering a scaling barrier, should serve to
sound a note of warning.

A note on terminology

We can classify peer-to-peer systems into three main categories, broadly speaking: centrally coordinated, hierarchical, and decentralized.

In a centrally coordinated system, coordination between peers is controlled and
mediated by a central server, although peers may later act on information
received from the central server to contact one another directly. Napster and
SETI@home fall into this category.

A hierarchical peer-to-peer system devolves some or all of the coordination
responsibility down from the center to a tree of coordinators. In this arrangement, peers are organized into hierarchies of groups, where communication
between peers in the same group is mediated by a local coordinator, but communication between peers in different groups is passed upwards to a higher-
level coordinator. Some examples are the Domain Name System (DNS) and the
Squid web proxy cache.

Finally, completely decentralized peer-to-peer systems have no notion of global
coordination at all. Communication is handled entirely by peers operating at a
local level. This usually implies some type of forwarding mechanism in which

peers forward messages on behalf of other peers. Freenet and Gnutella are examples in this last category.

In this chapter, when I refer to peer-to-peer systems, I will be talking only about decentralized peer-to-peer. Since the performance issues of centralized systems have been discussed so much, it will be interesting to look at the issues of a fully decentralized system.

Why performance matters

Several factors combine to make decentralized peer-to-peer systems more sensitive to performance issues than other types of software. First, the essential characteristic of such systems is communication—a characteristic that makes them fundamentally dependent on the network. In network communication, as every dial-up user knows, connection speed dominates processor and I/O speed as the bottleneck. Since this situation will most likely persist into the foreseeable future, Moore's Law (so helpful elsewhere) provides little comfort. The problem is compounded by the highly parallel nature of peer-to-peer: A connection fast enough to talk to one remote peer quickly becomes much less so for ten trying to connect simultaneously. Thus, traffic minimization and load balancing become important considerations.

Second, decentralized systems like Freenet and Gnutella need to use messages that are forwarded over many hops from one peer to the next. Since there is no central server to maintain a master index, it necessarily takes more effort to search through the system to find out where data is. Each hop not only adds to the total bandwidth load but also increases the time needed to perform a query, since it takes a nontrivial amount of time to set up a connection to the next peer or to discover that it is down. As mentioned previously, the latter occurrence can be extremely common in peer-to-peer environments. If a peer is unreachable, TCP/IP can take up to several minutes to time out the connection. Multiply that by several times for retries to other peers and add the time needed to actually send the message over a possibly slow dial-up connection, and the elapsed time per hop can get quite high. It is therefore important to cut down on the number of hops that messages travel.

Third, the balance between resource providers and consumers must be considered. Like their counterparts in the real world, peer-to-peer communities depend on the presence of a sufficient base of communal participation and cooperation in order to function successfully.

However, there will always be those who consume resources without giving any back. Recent analysis by Eytan Adar and Bernardo Huberman at Xerox PARC[*] indicates that as many as 70% of current Gnutella users may be sharing no files at all.

If a high enough proportion of users are free riders, performance degrades for those who do contribute. A substantial decline in performance may impel some contributors to pull out of the system altogether. Their withdrawal worsens the situation further for the remainder, who will have even less incentive to stay, leading to a downward spiral (the well-known "tragedy of the commons").

To avoid this outcome, system designers must take into account the impact of free riding on performance and devise strategies to encourage higher rates of community participation. Some such strategies are discussed in Chapter 16, *Accountability*.

Bandwidth barriers

There has been some progress on the network speed front, of course. Today's 56-Kbps dial-up lines are a huge improvement on the 300-baud modems of yore. Still, true broadband has been slow to arrive.

Clip2's analysis of Gnutella is instructive in showing how bandwidth limitations can affect system capabilities. Based on a series of measurements over a period of a month, Clip2 noted an apparent scalability barrier of substantial performance degradation when query rates went above 10 queries per second. To explain this, they proposed the following model. A typical Gnutella query message is about 560 bits long, including TCP/IP headers. Clip2 observed that queries made up approximately a quarter of all message traffic, with another half being pings and the remainder miscellaneous messages. At any given time, Gnutella peers were seen to have an average of three remote peers actively connected simultaneously. Taking these numbers together, we get the following average burden on a user's link:

> 10 queries per second
> × 560 bits per query
> × 4 to account for the other three-quarters of message traffic
> × 3 simultaneous connections
> _____
> 67,200 bits per second

---

[*] E. Adar and B.A. Huberman (2000), "Free Riding on Gnutella," *First Monday* 5(10), *http://firstmonday.org/issues/issue5_10/adar/index.html*.

That's more than enough to saturate a 56-Kbps link. This calculation suggests that 10 queries per second is the maximum rate the system can handle in the presence of a significant population of dial-up users.

Even when broadband finally becomes widespread, it is unlikely to eliminate the importance of conserving bandwidth and usher in a new era of plenty. Just as building more highways failed to decrease traffic congestion because people drove more, adding more bandwidth just causes people to send larger files. Today's kilobit audio swapping becomes tomorrow's megabit video swapping. Hence, bandwidth conservation is likely to remain important for quite some time in the foreseeable future.

It's a small, small world

In 1967, Harvard professor Stanley Milgram mailed 160 letters to a set of randomly chosen people living in Omaha, Nebraska. He asked them to participate in an unusual social experiment in which they were to try to pass these letters to a given target person, a stockbroker working in Boston, Massachusetts, using only intermediaries known to one another on a first-name basis. That is, each person would pass her letter to a friend whom she thought might bring the letter closest to the target; the friend would then pass it on to another friend, and so on until the letter reached someone who knew the target personally and could give it to him. For example, an engineer in Omaha, on receiving the letter, passed it to a transplanted New Englander living in Bellevue, Nebraska, who passed it to a math teacher in Littleton, Massachusetts, who passed it to a school principal in a Boston suburb, who passed it to a local storekeeper, who gave it to a surprised stockbroker.

In all, 42 letters made it through, via a median number of just 5.5 intermediaries. Such a surprisingly low number, compared to the then-U.S. population of 200 million, demonstrated concretely for the first time what has become popularly known as the *small-world effect*. This phenomenon is familiar to anyone who has exclaimed "Small world, isn't it!" upon discovering a mutual acquaintance shared with a stranger.

Milgram's experiment was designed to explore the properties of *social networks*: the interconnecting bonds of friendship among individuals in a society. One way we can think about social networks is to use the mathematical discipline of *graph theory*. Formally, a *graph* is defined as a collection of points (called *vertices*) that are connected in pairs by lines (called *edges*).* Figure 14-1 shows an example of a graph.

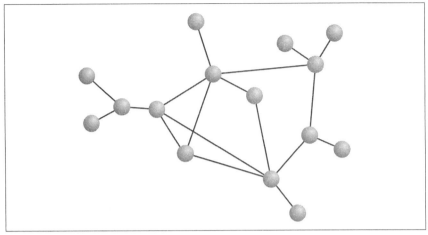

Figure 14-1. An example of a graph

How are graphs related to social networks? We can represent a social network as a graph by creating a vertex for each individual in the group and adding an edge between two vertices whenever the corresponding individuals know one another. Each vertex will have a different number of edges connected to it going to different places, depending on how wide that person's circle of acquaintances is. The resulting structure is likely to be extremely complex; for example, a graph for the United States would contain over 280 million vertices connected by a finely tangled web of edges.

Computer networks bear a strong resemblance to social networks and can be represented by graphs in a similar way. In fact, you've probably seen such a graph already if you've ever looked at a connectivity map for a LAN or WAN, although you might not have thought of it that way. In these maps, points representing individual computers or routers are equivalent to graph vertices, and lines representing physical links between machines are edges.

Another electronic analogue to a social network is the World Wide Web. The Web can be viewed as a graph in which web pages are vertices and hyperlinks are edges. Just as friendship links in a social network tend to connect members

---

* By the way, these graphs have nothing to do with the familiar graphs of equations used in algebra.

of the same social circle, hyperlinks frequently connect web pages that share a common theme or topic.

There is a slight complication because (unlike friendships) hyperlinks are one-way; that is, you can follow a hyperlink from a source page to a target page but not the reverse. For Web links, properly speaking, we need to use a *directed graph*, which is a graph in which edges point from a source vertex to a target vertex, rather than connecting vertices symmetrically. Directed graphs are usually represented by drawing their edges as arrows rather than lines, as shown in Figure 14-2.

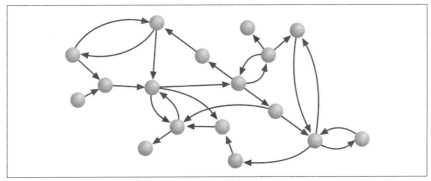

Figure 14-2. A directed graph

Most importantly for our purposes, peer-to-peer networks can be regarded as graphs as well. We can create a Freenet graph, for example, by creating a vertex for each computer running a Freenet node and linking each node by a directed edge to every node referenced in its data store. Similarly, a Gnutella graph would have a vertex for each computer running a Gnutella "servent" and edges linking servents that are connected to each other. These graphs form a useful abstract representation of the underlying networks. By analyzing them mathematically, we ought to be able to gain some insight into the functioning of the corresponding systems.

An excursion into graph theory

There are a number of interesting questions you can ask about graphs. One immediate question to ask is whether or not it is *connected*. That is, is it always possible to get from any vertex (or individual) to any other via some chain of intermediaries? Or are there some groups which are completely isolated from one another, and never the twain shall meet?

An important property to note in connection with this question is that paths in a graph are *transitive*. This means that if there is a path from point A to point B, and also a path from point B to point C, then there must be a path from A to C. This fact might seem too obvious to need stating, but it has broader consequences. Suppose there are two separate groups of vertices forming two subgraphs, each connected within itself but disconnected from the other. Then adding just one edge from any vertex V in one group to any vertex W in the other, as in Figure 14-3, will make the graph as a whole connected. This follows from transitivity: by assumption there is a path from every vertex in the first group to V, and a path from W to every vertex in the second group, so adding an edge between V and W will complete a path from every vertex in the first group to every vertex in the second (and vice versa). Conversely, deleting one critical edge may cause a graph to become disconnected, a topic we will return to later in the context of network robustness.

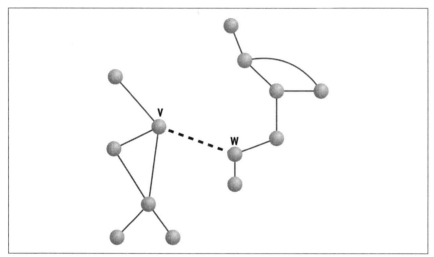

Figure 14-3. Adding an edge between V and W connects the two subgraphs

If it is possible to get from any vertex to any other by some path, a natural follow-up question to ask is how long these paths are. One useful measure to consider is the following: for each pair of vertices in the graph, find the length of the shortest path between them; then, take the average over all pairs. This number, which we'll call the *characteristic pathlength* of the graph, gives a sense of how far apart points are in the network.

In the networking context, the relevance of these two questions is immediately apparent. For example, performing a *traceroute* from one machine to another is equivalent to finding a path between two vertices in the corresponding graph.

Finding out whether a route exists, and how many hops it takes, are basic questions in network analysis and troubleshooting.

For decentralized peer-to-peer networks, these two questions have a similar significance. The first tells us which peers can communicate with one another (via some message-forwarding route); the second, how much effort is involved in doing so. To see how we can get a handle on these questions, let's return to the letter-passing experiment in more depth. Then we'll see if we can apply any insights to the peer-to-peer situation.

The small-world model

The success of Milgram's volunteers in moving letters between the seemingly disparate worlds of rural heartland and urban metropolis suggests that the social network of the United States is indeed connected. Its characteristic pathlength corresponds to the median number of intermediaries needed to complete a chain, measured to be about six.

Intuitively, it seems that the pathlength of such a large network ought to be much higher. Most people's social circles are highly cliquish or clustered; that is, most of the people whom you know also know each other. Equivalently, many of the friends of your friends are people whom you know already. So taking additional hops may not increase the number of people within reach by much. It seems that a large number of hops would be necessary to break out of one social circle, travel across the country, and reach another, particularly given the size of the U.S. How then can we explain Milgram's measurement?

The key to understanding the result lies in the distribution of links within social networks. In any social grouping, some acquaintances will be relatively isolated and contribute few new contacts, whereas others will have more wide-ranging connections and be able to serve as bridges between far-flung social clusters. These bridging vertices play a critical role in bringing the network closer together. In the Milgram experiment, for example, a quarter of all the chains reaching the target person passed through a single person, a local storekeeper. Half the chains were mediated by just three people, who collectively acted as gateways between the target and the wider world.

It turns out that the presence of even a small number of bridges can dramatically reduce the lengths of paths in a graph, as shown by a recent paper by Duncan Watts and Steven Strogatz in the journal *Nature*.* They began by considering a

---

* D.J. Watts and S.H. Strogatz (1998), "Collective Dynamics of 'Small-World' Networks," *Nature* 393, p.440.

simple type of graph called a *regular graph*, which consists of a ring of *n* vertices, each of which is connected to its nearest *k* neighbors. For example, if *k* is 4, each vertex is connected to its nearest two neighbors on each side (four in total), giving a graph such as the one shown in Figure 14-4.

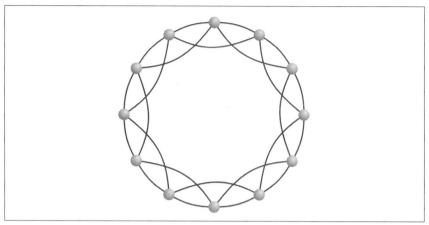

Figure 14-4. A regular graph

If we look at large regular graphs in which *n* is much larger than *k*, which in turn is much larger than 1, the pathlength can be shown to be approximately *n*/2*k*. For example, if *n* is 4,096 and *k* is 8, then *n*/2*k* is 256—a very large number of hops to take to get where you're going! (Informally, we can justify the formula *n*/2*k* by noticing that it equals half the number of hops it takes to get to the opposite side of the ring. We say only half because we are averaging over all pairs, some of which will be close neighbors and some of which will be on opposite sides.)

Another property of regular graphs is that they are highly clustered, since all of their links are contained within local neighborhoods. To make this notion more precise, we can define a measure of clustering as follows. For the *k* neighbors of a given vertex, the total number of possible connections among them is $k \times (k-1)/2$. Let's define the *clustering coefficient* of a vertex as the proportion (between 0 and 1) of these possible links that are actually present in the graph. For example, in the regular graph of Figure 14-4, each vertex has four neighbors. There are a total of $(4 \times 3)/2 = 6$ possible connections among the four neighbors (not counting the original vertex itself), of which 3 are present in the graph. Therefore the clustering coefficient of each vertex is 3/6 = 0.5.

In social terms, this coefficient can be thought of as counting the number of connections among a person's friends—a measure of the cliquishness of a group.

If we do the math, it can be shown that as the number of vertices in the graph increases, the clustering coefficient approaches a constant value of 0.75 (very cliquish).

More generally, in a non-regular graph, different vertices will have different coefficients. So we define the clustering coefficient of a whole graph as the average of all the clustering coefficients of the individual vertices.

The opposite of the completely ordered regular graph is the *random graph*. This is just a graph whose vertices are connected to each other at random. Random graphs can be categorized by the number of vertices n and the average number of edges per vertex k. Notice that a random graph and a regular graph having the same values for n and k will be comparable in the sense that both will have the same total number of vertices and edges. For example, the random graph shown in Figure 14-5 has the same number of vertices (12) and edges (24) as the regular graph in Figure 14-4. It turns out that for large random graphs, the pathlength is approximately log n/log k, while the clustering coefficient is approximately k/n. So using our previous example, where n was 4,096 and k was 8, the pathlength would be log 4,096/log 8 = 4—much better than the 256 hops for the regular graph!

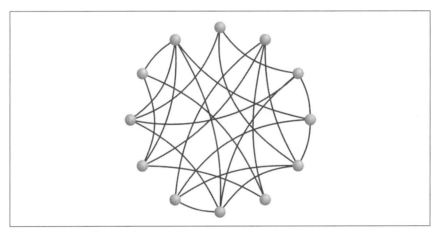

Figure 14-5. A random graph

On the other hand, the clustering coefficient would be 8/4,096 ≈ 0.002—much less than the regular graph's 0.75. In fact, as n gets larger, the clustering coefficient becomes practically 0.

If we compare these two extremes, we can see that the regular graph has high clustering and a high pathlength, whereas the random graph has very low clustering and a comparatively low pathlength. (To be more precise, the pathlength of the regular graph grows linearly as n gets larger, but the pathlength of the random graph grows only logarithmically.)

What about intermediate cases? Most real-world networks, whether social networks or peer-to-peer networks, lie somewhere in between—neither completely regular nor completely random. How will they behave in terms of clustering and pathlength?

Watts and Strogatz used a clever trick to explore the in-between region. Starting with a 1000-node regular graph with k equal to 10, they "rewired" it by taking each edge in turn and, with probability p, moving it to connect to a different, randomly chosen vertex. When p is 0, the regular graph remains unchanged; when p is 1, a random graph results. The region we are interested in is the region where p is between 0 and 1. Figure 14-6 shows one possible rewiring of Figure 14-4 with p set to 0.5.

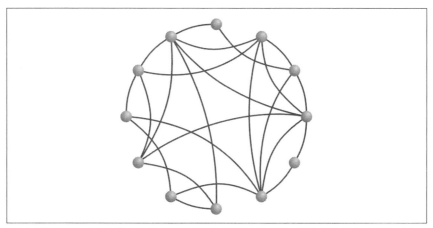

Figure 14-6. A rewiring of a regular graph

Surprisingly, what they found was that with larger p, clustering remains high but pathlength drops precipitously, as shown in Figure 14-7. Rewiring with p as low as 0.001 (that is, rewiring only about 0.1% of the edges) cuts the pathlength in half while leaving clustering virtually unchanged. At a p value of 0.01, the graph has taken on hybrid characteristics. Locally, its clustering coefficient still looks essentially like that of the regular graph. Globally, however, its pathlength has nearly dropped to the random-graph level. Watts and Strogatz dubbed graphs with this combination of high local clustering and short global pathlengths *small-world graphs*.

Two important implications can be seen. First, only a small amount of rewiring is needed to promote the small-world transition. Second, the transition is barely

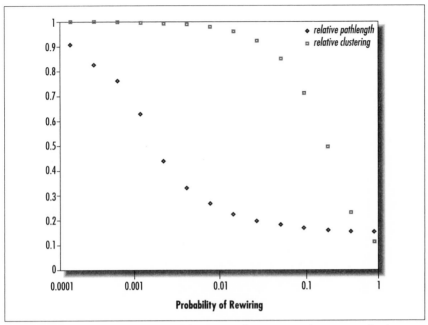

Figure 14-7. Evolution of pathlength and clustering under rewiring, relative to initial values

noticeable at the local level. Hence it is difficult to tell whether or not your world is a small world, although it won't take much effort to turn it into one if it isn't.

These results can explain the small-world characteristics of the U.S. social network. Even if local groups are highly clustered, as long as a small fraction (1% or even fewer) of individuals have long-range connections outside the group, pathlengths will be low. This happens because transitivity causes such individuals to act as shortcuts linking entire communities together. A shortcut doesn't benefit just a single individual, but also everyone linked to her, and everyone linked to those who are linked to her, and so on. All can take advantage of the shortcut, greatly shortening the characteristic pathlength. On the other hand, changing one local connection to a long-range one has only a small effect on the clustering coefficient.

Let's now look at how we can apply some of the concepts of the small-world model to peer-to-peer by considering a pair of case studies.

Case study 1: Freenet

The small-world effect is fundamental to Freenet's operation. As with Milgram's letters, Freenet queries are forwarded from one peer to the next according to local decisions about which potential recipient might make the most progress towards the target. Unlike Milgram's letters, however, Freenet messages are not targeted to a specific named peer but toward any peer having a desired file in its data store.

To take a concrete example, suppose I were trying to obtain a copy of *Peer-to-Peer*. Using Milgram's method, I could do this by trying to get a letter to Tim O'Reilly asking for a copy of the book. I might begin by passing it to my friend Dan (who lives in Boston), who might pass it to his friend James (who works in computers), who might pass it to his friend Andy (who works for Tim), who could pass it to Tim himself. Using Freenet's algorithm, I don't try to contact a particular person. Instead, I might ask my friend Alison (who I know has other O'Reilly books) if she has a copy. If she didn't, she might similarly ask her friend Helena, and so on. Freenet's routing is based on evaluating peers' bookshelves rather than their contacts—any peer owning a copy can reply, not just Tim O'Reilly specifically.

For the Freenet algorithm to work, we need two properties to hold. First, the Freenet graph must be connected, so that it is possible for any request to eventually reach some peer where the data is stored. (This assumes, of course, that the data does exist on Freenet somewhere.) Second, despite the large size of the network, short routes must exist between any two arbitrary peers, making it possible to pass messages between them in a reasonable number of hops. In other words, we want Freenet to be a small world.

The first property is easy. Connectedness can be achieved by growing the network incrementally from some initial core. If each new node starts off by linking itself to one or more introductory nodes already known to be reachable from the core, transitivity will assure a single network rather than several disconnected ones. There is a potential problem, however: If the introductory node fails or drops out, the new node and later nodes connected to it might become stranded.

Freenet's request and insert mechanisms combat this problem by adding additional redundant links to the network over time. Even if a new node starts with only a single reference to an introductory node, each successful request will cause it to gain more references to other nodes. These references will provide more links into the network, alleviating the dependence on the introductory node. Conversely, performing inserts creates links in the opposite direction, as nodes deeper in the network gain references to the inserting node. Nonetheless, the effect of node failures needs to be examined more closely. We will return to this subject later.

The second property presents more of a challenge. As we saw earlier, it is difficult to tell from local examination alone whether or not the global network is a small world, and Freenet's anonymity properties deliberately prevent us from measuring the global network directly. For example, it is impossible to even find out how many nodes there are. Nor do we know precisely which files are stored in the network or where, so it is hard to infer much from local request outcomes. We therefore turn to simulation.

Initial experiments

Fortunately, simulation indicates that Freenet networks do evolve small-world characteristics. Following Watts and Strogatz, we can initialize a simulated Freenet network with a regular topology and see how it behaves over time. Suppose we create a network of 1,000 identical nodes having initially empty data stores with a capacity of 50 data items and 200 additional references each. To minimally bootstrap the network's connectivity, let's number the nodes and give each node references to 2 nodes immediately before and after it numerically (modulo 1,000). For example, node 0 would be connected to nodes 998, 999, 1, and 2. We have to associate keys with these references, so for convenience we'll use a hash of the referenced node number as the key. Using a hash has the advantage of yielding a key that is both random and consistent across the network (that is, every node having a reference to node 0 will assign the same key to the reference, namely $hash(0)$). Figure 14-8 shows some of the resulting data stores. Topologically, this network is equivalent to a directed regular graph in which n is 1,000 and k is 4.

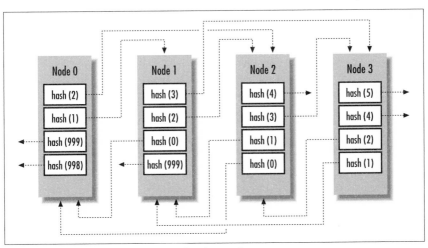

Figure 14-8. Initial data stores for a simulated network

What are the initial characteristics of this network? Well, from the earlier discussion of regular graphs, we know that its pathlength is $n/2k$, or $1,000/8 = 125$. Each node has four neighbors—for example, node 2 is connected to nodes 0, 1, 3, and 4. Of the 12 possible directed edges among these neighbors, 6 are present (from 0 to 1, 1 to 3, and 3 to 4, and from 1 to 0, 3 to 1, and 4 to 3), so the clustering coefficient is $6/12 = 0.5$.

A comparable random graph, on the other hand, would have a pathlength of log $1,000/\log 4 \approx 5$ and a clustering coefficient of $4/1,000 = 0.004$.

Now let's simulate a simple network usage model. At each time step, pick a node at random and flip a coin to decide whether to perform a request or an insert from that node. If requesting, randomly choose a key to request from those known to be present in the network; if inserting, randomly choose a key to insert from the set of all possible keys. Somewhat arbitrarily, let's set the hops-to-live to 20 on both insert and request.

Every 100 time steps, measure the state of the network. We can directly calculate its clustering coefficient and characteristic pathlength by examining the data stores of each node to determine which other nodes it is connected to and then performing a breadth-first search on the resulting graph.

Figure 14-9 shows the results of simulating this model. Ten trials were taken, each lasting 5,000 time steps, and the results were averaged over all trials.

As we can see, the pathlength rapidly decreases by a factor of 20 within the first 500 time steps or so before leveling off. On the other hand, the clustering coefficient decreases only slowly over the entire simulation period. The final pathlength hovers slightly above 2, while the final clustering is about 0.22. If we compare these figures to the values calculated earlier for the corresponding regular graph (125 pathlength and 0.5 clustering) and random graph (5 pathlength and 0.004 clustering), we can see the small-world effect: Freenet's pathlength approximates the random graph's pathlength while its clustering coefficient is of the same order of magnitude as the regular graph.

Does the small-world effect translate into real performance, however? To answer this question, let's look at the request performance of the network over time. Every 100 time steps, we probe the network by simulating 300 requests from randomly chosen nodes in the network. During this probe period, the network is frozen so that no data is cached and no links are altered. The keys requested are chosen randomly from those known to be stored in the network and the hops-to-live is set to 500. By looking at the number of hops actually taken, we can measure the distance that a request needs to travel before finding data. For our purposes, a request that fails will be treated as taking 500 hops. At each

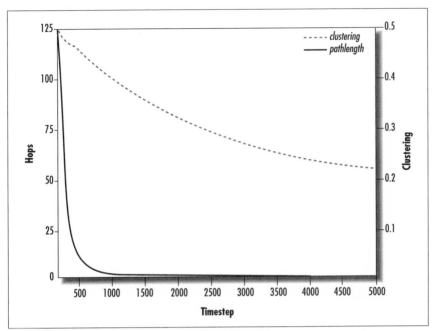

Figure 14-9. Evolution of pathlength and clustering over time in a Freenet network

snapshot, we'll plot the median pathlength of all requests (that is, the top 50% fastest requests).

These measurements are plotted in Figures 14-10 and 14-11. Reassuringly, the results indicate that Freenet does actually work. The median pathlength for requests drops from 500 at the outset to about 6 as the network converges to a stable state. That is, half of all requests in the mature network succeed within six hops. A quarter of requests succeed within just three hops or fewer.

Note that the median request pathlength of 6 is somewhat higher than the characteristic pathlength of 2. This occurs because the characteristic pathlength measures the distance along the *optimal* path between any pair of nodes. Freenet's local routing cannot always choose the globally optimal route, of course, but it manages to get close most of the time.

On the other hand, if we look at the complete distribution of final pathlengths, as shown in Figure 14-12, there are some requests that take a disproportionately long time. That is, Freenet has good average performance but poor worst-case performance, because a few bad routing choices can throw a request completely off the track.

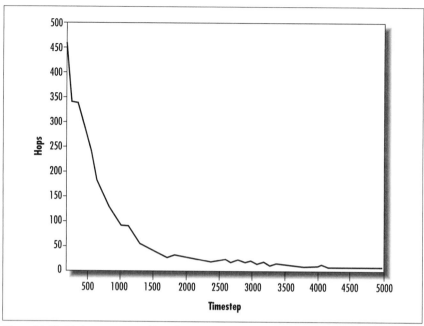

Figure 14-10. Median request pathlength over time (linear scale)

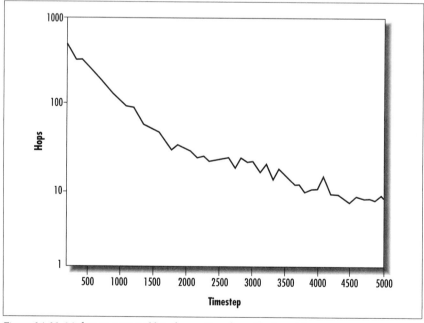

Figure 14-11. Median request pathlength over time (logarithmic scale)

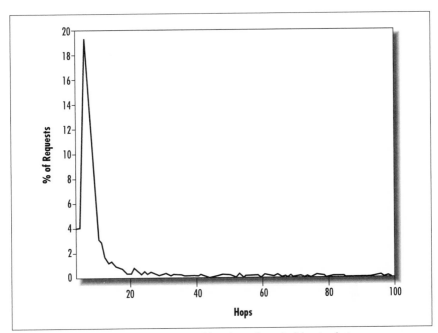

Figure 14-12. Distribution of all request pathlengths at the end of the simulation

Indeed, local routing decisions are extremely important. Although the small-world effect tells us that short routes exist between any pair of vertices in a small-world network, the tricky part is actually finding these short routes.

To illustrate this point, consider a Freenet-like system in which nodes forward query messages to some peer randomly chosen from the data store, rather than the peer associated with the closest key to the query. Performing the same simulation on this system gives the measurements shown in Figure 14-13.

We see that the median request pathlength required now is nearly 50, although analysis of the network shows the characteristic pathlength to still be about 2. This request pathlength is too high to be of much use, as 50 hops would take forever to complete. So although short paths exist in this network, we are unable to make effective use of them.

These observations make sense if we think about our intuitive experience with another small-world domain, the Web. The process of navigating on the Web from some starting point to a desired destination by following hyperlinks is quite similar to the process of forwarding a request in Freenet. A recent paper in

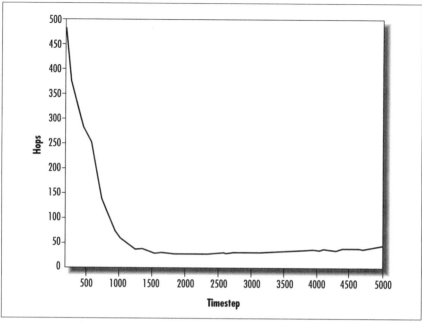

Figure 14-13. Median request pathlength under random routing

Nature by Réka Albert, Hawoong Jeong, and Albert-László Barabási[*] reported that the Web is a small-world network with a characteristic pathlength of 19. That is, from any given web page, it is possible to surf to any other one of the nearly 800 million reachable pages in existence with an average of 19 clicks.

However, such a path can be constructed only by an intelligent agent able to make accurate decisions about which link to follow next. Even humans often fail in this task, getting "lost in the Web." An unintelligent robot choosing links at random would clearly get nowhere. The only hope for such a robot is to apply brute-force indexing, and the force required is brute indeed: Albert *et al.* estimated that a robot attempting to locate a web page at a distance of 19 hops would need to index at least a full 10% of the Web, or some 80 million pages.

Simulating growth

Having taken a preliminary look at the evolution of a fixed Freenet network, let's now look at what happens in a network that grows over time. When a new node wants to join Freenet, it must first find (through out-of-band means) an initial

---

[*] R. Albert, H. Jeong, and A. Barabási (1999), "Diameter of the World-Wide Web," *Nature* 401, p.130.

introductory node that is already in the network. The new node then sends an announcement message to the introductory node, which forwards it into Freenet. Each node contacted adds a reference to the new node to its data store and sends back a reply containing its own address, before forwarding the announcement on to another node chosen randomly from its data store. In turn, the new node adds all of these replies to its data store. The net result is that a set of two-way links are established between the new node and some number of existing nodes, as shown in Figure 14-14.

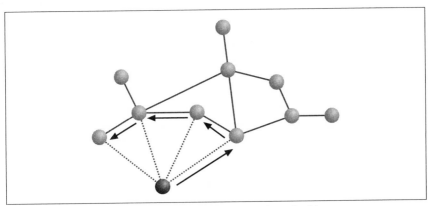

Figure 14-14. Adding a new node to Freenet (arrows show the path of the announcement message; dotted lines show the new links established)

We can simulate this evolution by the following procedure. Initialize the network with 20 nodes connected in a regular topology as before, so that we can continue to use a hops-to-live of 20 from the outset. Add a new node every 5 time steps until the network reaches a size of 1,000. When adding a new node, choose an introductory node at random and send an announcement message with hops-to-live 10. Meanwhile, inserts and requests continue on every time step as before, and probes every 100 time steps.

It might seem at first that this simulation won't realistically model the rate of growth of the network, since nodes are simply added linearly every five steps. However, simulation time need not correspond directly to real time. The effect of the model is essentially to interpose five requests between node additions, regardless of the rate of addition. In real time, we can expect that the number of requests per unit time will be proportional to the size of the network. If we assume that the rate at which new nodes join is also proportional to the size of the network, the linear ratio between request rate and joining rate is justified.

Figure 14-15 shows the results of simulating this model. As before, 10 trials were run and the results averaged over all trials.

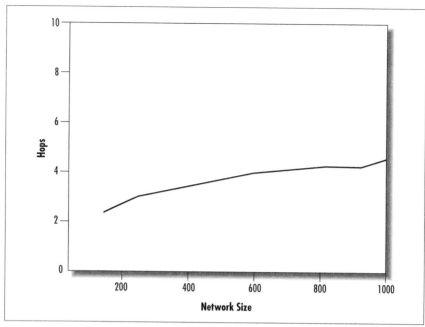

Figure 14-15. Median request pathlength in a growing network

The results are extremely promising. The request pathlength starts off low, unsurprisingly, since the network is so small initially that even random routing should find the data quickly. However, as the network grows, the request pathlength remains low.

By the end of the simulation, the network is performing even better than the fixed-size simulation having the same number of nodes. Now 50% of all requests succeed within just 5 hops or fewer, while 84% succeed within 20. Meanwhile, the characteristic pathlength and the clustering coefficient are not appreciably different from the fixed case—about 2.2 for the pathlength and about 0.25 for the clustering coefficient.

Simulating fault tolerance

Let's turn to some aspects of robustness. As mentioned earlier, an important challenge in designing a peer-to-peer system is coping with the unreliability of peers. Since peers tend to be personal machines rather than dedicated servers, they are often turned off or disconnected from the network at random. Another consideration for systems that may host content disapproved of by some group is the possibility of a deliberate attempt to bring the network down through technical or legal attacks.

Taking as a starting point the network grown in the second simulation, we can examine the effects of two node failure scenarios. One scenario is random failure, in which nodes are simply removed at random from the network. The other scenario is targeted attack, in which the most important nodes are targeted for removal. Here we follow the approach of another paper by Albert, Jeong, and Barabási on the fault tolerance of the Internet.[*]

We can model the random failure scenario by progressively removing more and more nodes selected at random from the network and watching how the system's performance holds up. Figure 14-16 shows the request pathlength plotted against the percentage of nodes failing. The network remains surprisingly usable, with the median request pathlength remaining below 20 even when up to 30% of nodes fail.

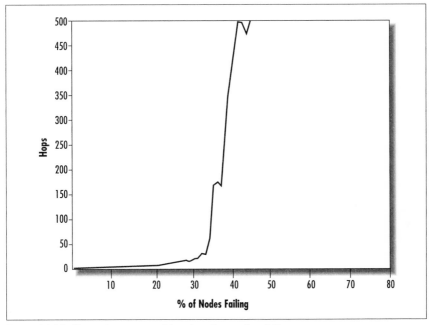

Figure 14-16. Change in request pathlength under random failure

An explanation can be offered by looking at the distribution of links within the network. If we draw a histogram of the proportion of nodes having different numbers of links, as shown in Figure 14-17, we can see that the distribution is highly skewed. Most nodes have only a few outgoing links, but a small number

---

[*] R. Albert, H. Jeong, and A. Barabási (2000), "Error and Attack Tolerance of Complex Networks," *Nature* 406, p.378.

of nodes toward the right side of the graph are very well-connected. (The unusually large column at 250 links is an artifact of the limited data store size of 250—when larger data stores are used, this column spreads out farther to the right.)

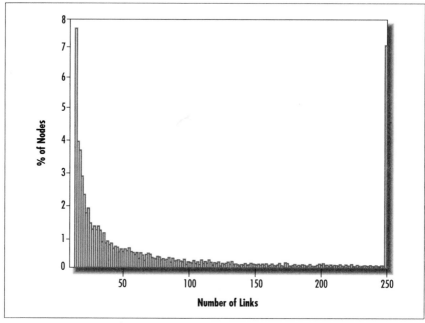

Figure 14-17. Histogram showing the proportion of nodes vs. the number of links

When nodes are randomly removed from the network, most of them will probably be nodes with few links, and thus their loss will not hurt the routing in the network much. The highly connected nodes in the right-hand tail will be able to keep the network connected. These nodes correspond to the shortcuts needed to make the small-world effect happen.

The attack scenario, on the other hand, is more dangerous. In this scenario, the most-connected nodes are preferentially removed first. Figure 14-18 shows the trend in the request pathlength as nodes are attacked. Now the network becomes unusable much more quickly, with the median request pathlength passing 20 at the 18% failure level. This demonstrates just how important those nodes in the tail are. When they are removed, the network starts to fall apart into disconnected fragments.

Figure 14-19 shows the contrast between the two failure modes in more detail, using a semi-log scale.

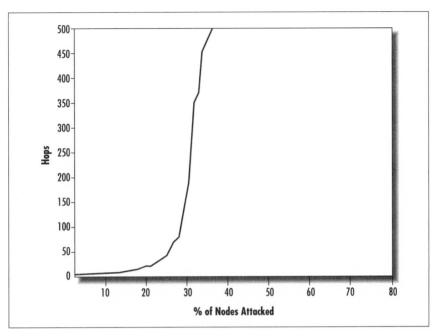

Figure 14-18. Change in request pathlength under targeted attack

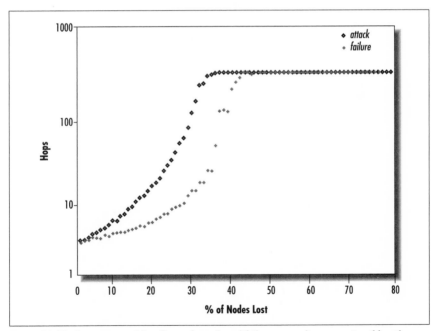

Figure 14-19. Comparison of the effects of attack and failure on median request pathlength

Link distribution in Freenet

Where do the highly connected nodes come from? We can get some hints by trying to fit a function to the observed distribution of links. If we redraw the histogram as a log-log plot, as shown in Figure 14-20, we can see that the distribution of link numbers roughly follows a straight line (except for the anomalous point at 250). Since the equation for a downward-sloping line is:

$$y = -kx + b$$

where k and b are constants, this means that the proportion of nodes p having a given number of links L satisfies the equation:

$$\log p = -k \log L + b$$

By exponentiating both sides, we can express this relationship in a more normal-looking way as:

$$p = A \times L^{-k}$$

This is called a *scale-free* relationship, since the total number of nodes doesn't appear in the equation. Therefore it holds regardless of the size of the network, big or small. In fact, scale-free link distributions are another characteristic often used to identify small-world networks.

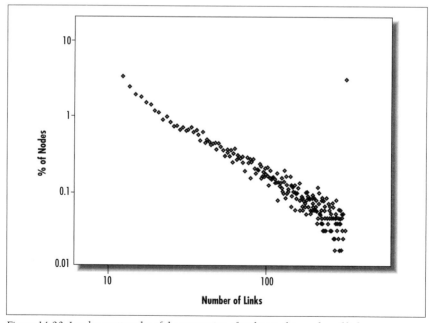

Figure 14-20. Log-log scatter plot of the proportion of nodes vs. the number of links

It turns out that this type of relationship arises naturally from the interaction of two processes: Growth and preferential attachment. Growth just means that new nodes are added over time. Preferential attachment means that new nodes tend to add links to nodes that have a lot of links already. This makes sense because nodes that are well known (i.e., have lots of links) will tend to see more requests and hence will tend to become even better connected.

The impact of free riding

In addition to being robust against node failures, peer-to-peer systems must be able to cope with free riders. Just as in any other social system, there are always those who take from the system without contributing anything back. In the peer-to-peer context, this might mean downloading files but not sharing any for upload, or initiating queries without forwarding or answering queries from others. At best, such behavior just means increased load for everyone else; at worst, it can significantly harm the functioning of the system.

Freenet deals with free riders by simply ignoring them. If a node never provides any files, no other nodes will gain references to it. To the rest of the network, it might as well not exist, so it won't have any effect on the pathlengths of others' requests. However, its own requests will contribute to the total bandwidth load on the network while providing no additional capacity. Similarly, if a node refuses to accept incoming connections, other nodes will treat it as though it were down and try elsewhere. Only if a node drops messages without responding will untoward things start to happen, although in that case it is behaving more like a malicious node than a free riding one.

Scalability

Finally, let's consider Freenet's scaling properties. In small-world graphs, the characteristic pathlength scales logarithmically with the size of the network, since it follows the random-graph pathlength of log n/log k. That is, a geometric increase in the number of vertices results in only a linear increase in the characteristic pathlength. This means that for example, if k is 3, increasing the size of the network by 10 times would increase the pathlength by just 2. If Freenet's routing continues to work in large networks, the request pathlength should scale similarly. (Remember that the correlation between the request pathlength and the characteristic pathlength depends on the accuracy of the routing.)

Figure 14-21 shows the results of extending our earlier growth simulation up to 200,000 nodes. As hoped, the request pathlength does appear to scale logarithmically.

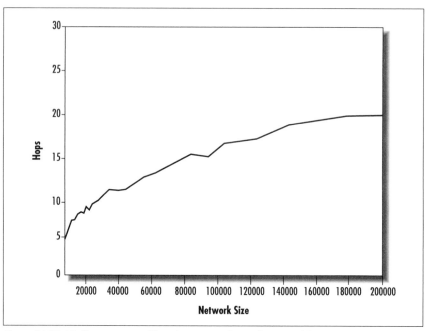

Figure 14-21. Median request pathlength vs. network size (linear scale)

We can see the scaling more clearly on the semi-log plot shown in Figure 14-22. On this plot, the data follow approximately straight lines, showing that pathlength is indeed roughly proportional to log(*size*). The median line has a "knee" where it changes slope at 50,000 nodes. This probably results from data stores becoming filled and could be corrected by creating larger data stores. Note that our data stores were limited to 250 links by the memory requirements of the simulation, whereas real Freenet nodes can easily hold thousands of references. In fact, if we recall the connectivity distribution shown in Figure 14-17, only a small number of high-capacity nodes should be necessary. Even with small data stores, the trend shows that Freenet scales very well: Doubling the network size brings a pathlength increase of only 4 hops.

The number of messages that must be transmitted per request is proportional to the request pathlength, since the latter indicates the number of times a request is forwarded. In turn, the bandwidth used is proportional to the number of messages sent. Thus, the bandwidth requirements of requests should also scale logarithmically in relation to the size of the network. Considering that, in general, the effort required to search for an item in a list grows logarithmically in relation to the size of the list, this is probably the best scaling that can be expected from a decentralized peer-to-peer system.

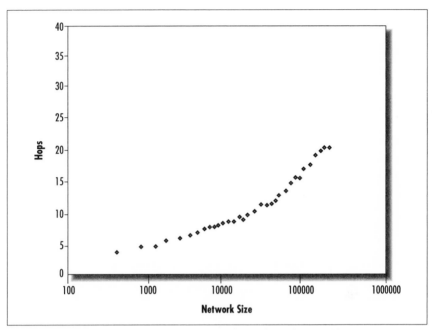

Figure 14-22. Median request pathlength vs. network size (logarithmic scale)

Case study 2: Gnutella

Gnutella uses a simple broadcast model to conduct queries, which does not invoke the small-world effect. Nonetheless, many of the concepts presented in this chapter can be taken as a useful framework for thinking about Gnutella's performance, which has been in the trade press so much recently.

In Gnutella, each peer tries to maintain a small minimum number (typically around three) of active simultaneous connections to other peers. These peers are selected from a locally maintained *host catcher* list containing the addresses of the other peers that this peer knows about. Peers can be discovered through a wide variety of mechanisms, such as watching for PING and PONG messages, noting the addresses of peers initiating queries, receiving incoming connections from previously unknown peers, or using out-of-band channels such as IRC and the Web. However, not all peers so discovered may accept new connections, since they may already have enough connections or be picky about the peers they will talk to. Establishing a good set of connections can in general be a somewhat haphazard process. Further, peers leaving the network will cause additional shuffling as the remaining peers try to replace lost connections.

It therefore seems reasonable to model a Gnutella network by a random graph with a k of 3. Note that such a graph does not necessarily have exactly three edges per vertex. Rather, there will be some distribution in which the probability of finding a vertex having a given number of edges peaks around 3 and decreases exponentially with increasing numbers of edges. We will have more to say about this later.

Gnutella queries propagate through the network as follows. Upon receiving a new query, a peer broadcasts it to every peer that it is currently connected to, each of which in turn will broadcast the query to the peers it is connected to, and so on, in the manner of a chain letter. If a peer has a file that matches the query, it sends an answer back to the originating peer, but still forwards the query anyway. This process continues up to a maximum depth (or "search horizon") specified by the time-to-live field in the query. Essentially, Gnutella queries perform breadth-first searches on the network graph, in which searches broaden out and progressively cover the vertices closest to the starting point first. (By contrast, Freenet's style is closer to depth-first search, in which searches are directed deeper into the graph first.)

As before, it is necessary for the network graph to be connected, so that it is possible for any query to eventually reach some peer having the desired data. Achieving complete connectivity is somewhat more difficult than in Freenet because of the random nature of Gnutella connectivity. We can imagine that a random assignment of connections might leave some subset of peers cut off from the rest. However, in practice connectedness appears to hold.

Second, there must again be short routes between arbitrary peers, so that queries will be able to reach their targets before exceeding their depth limits. We turn to simulation to explore these properties.

Initial experiments

Suppose we create a network of 1,000 identical nodes initially sharing no files. To model its connectivity, let's add 1,500 edges by picking random nodes to be connected, two at a time, and creating edges between them. Topologically, the resulting network will be equivalent to a random graph in which n is 1,000 and k is 3.

Now let's add data to fill the network, since Gnutella does not have an explicit "insert" or "publish" mechanism. To make this simulation broadly comparable to the Freenet simulation, we'll randomly generate data items to be stored on 20 nodes each (the equivalent of a Freenet insert with hops-to-live 20). This can be imagined as 20 users independently choosing to share the same file, perhaps a particular MP3. We set the number of different data items added to be the same as the number inserted over the course of the Freenet simulation—that is, about 2,500.

As before, we simulate a simple network usage model. Since a Gnutella network does not evolve organically over time the way a Freenet network does, a single set of probe measurements should suffice. Following our previous method, we perform 300 queries from randomly chosen nodes in the network. The keys requested are chosen randomly from those known to be stored in the network, and the time-to-live is set to infinity, so these queries will always succeed eventually. To gauge the distance a query must travel before finding data, we stop the query as soon as a hit is found and note the number of hops taken to that point. (In the real Gnutella, queries proceed in parallel on a large number of nodes, so it is not practicable to halt them after finding a match on one node.) Figure 14-23 shows the resulting distribution of query pathlengths.

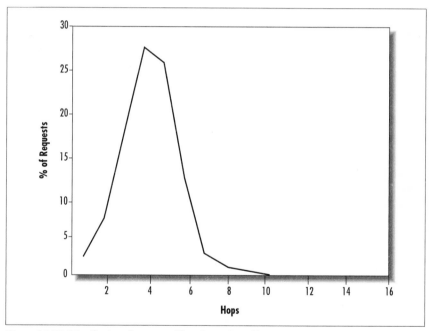

Figure 14-23. Distribution of query pathlengths in Gnutella

We see that Gnutella queries are satisfied extremely quickly, under both average-case and worst-case conditions. Indeed, the breadth-first search guarantees that the optimal shortest path to the data will always be found, making the query pathlength equal to the characteristic pathlength. However, this is not a true measure of the effort expended by the network as a whole, since queries are broadcast to so many nodes. A better measure is to consider the number of nodes contacted in the course of a query, as shown in Figure 14-24.

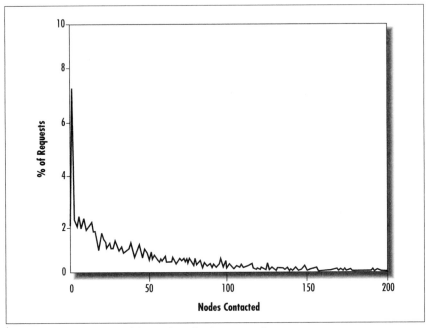

Figure 14-24. Distribution of the number of nodes contacted per query

A significant number of queries require the participation of 50 nodes, and many even call for 100 or more. It is apparent that the price paid for a quick result is a large expenditure of effort to exhaustively search a significant proportion of the network. Vis-à-vis Freenet, Gnutella makes a trade-off of much greater search effort in return for optimal paths and better worst-case performance.

Fault tolerance and link distribution in Gnutella

What are Gnutella's fault-tolerance characteristics? As before, we can consider its behavior under two node failure scenarios: random failure and targeted attack. The distribution of links in Freenet was an important factor in its robustness, so let's look at Gnutella's corresponding distribution, shown in Figure 14-25.

Mathematically, this is a "Poisson" distribution peaked around the average connectivity of 3. Its tail drops off exponentially, rather than according to a power law as Freenet's does. This can be seen more clearly in the log-log plot of Figure 14-26.

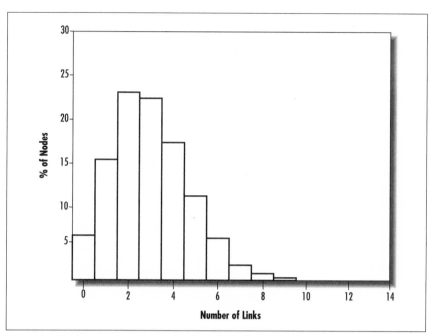

Figure 14-25. Histogram showing the distribution of links in Gnutella

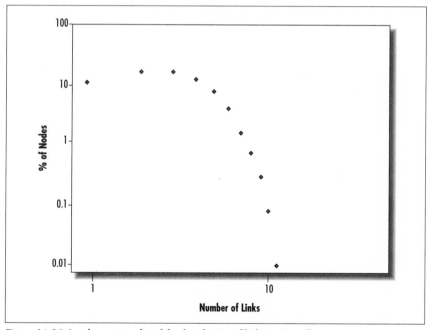

Figure 14-26. Log-log scatter plot of the distribution of links in Gnutella

Comparing this plot to Figure 14-20, we can see that Figure 14-26 drops off much more sharply at high link numbers. As a result, highly connected nodes are much less of a factor in Gnutella than they are in Freenet.

Let's see how Gnutella behaves under the targeted attack scenario, in which the most-connected nodes are removed first. Figure 14-27 shows the number of nodes contacted per query (as a percentage of the surviving nodes) versus the percentage of nodes attacked. (A request that fails is treated as a value of 100%.) If we compare this plot to Figure 14-18, we can see that Gnutella resists targeted attack better than Freenet does, since the highly connected nodes play less of a role.

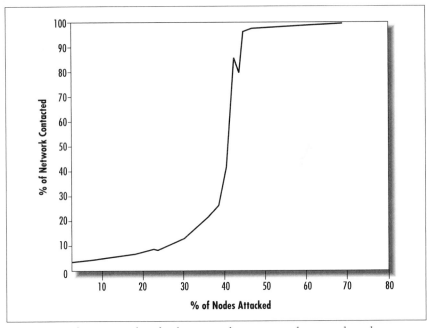

Figure 14-27. Change in number of nodes contacted per query, under targeted attack

On the other hand, the random failure scenario is the opposite. Figure 14-28 shows the number of nodes contacted versus the percentage of nodes failing. If we compare this to Figure 14-16, Freenet does better.

In fact, this occurs because Gnutella performs about the same under both random failure and targeted attack, as can be seen more clearly in Figure 14-29. Here again is a trade-off: Gnutella responds equally to failure and attack, since all of its nodes are roughly equivalent. Freenet's highly connected nodes enable it to better cope with random failure, but these then become points of vulnerability for targeted attack.

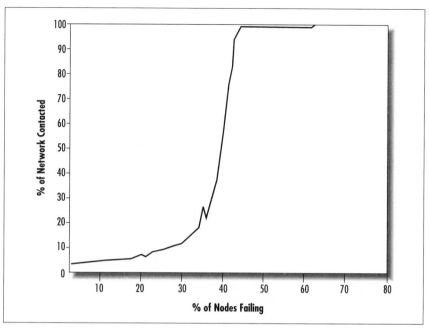

Figure 14-28. Change in number of nodes contacted per query, under random failure

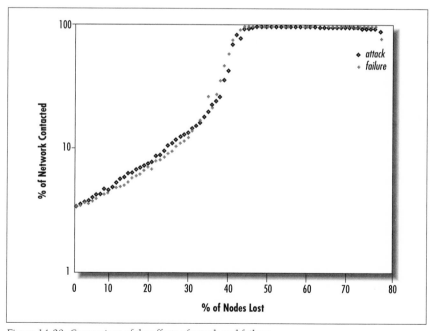

Figure 14-29. Comparison of the effects of attack and failure

This is brought out in more detail by Figure 14-30, which plots the four scenarios together using an arbitrary scale. We can see that the Freenet failure curve grows much more slowly than the Gnutella curves, while the Freenet attack curve shoots up sooner.

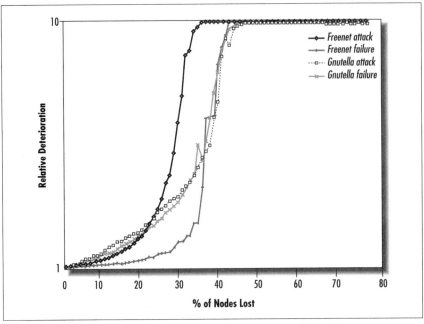

Figure 14-30. Comparison of attack and failure nodes in Freenet and Gnutella

The impact of free riding

Free riding in Gnutella is of more than merely theoretical interest, as indicated by the Xerox PARC paper mentioned earlier. Gnutella is vulnerable to free riders because its peers do not maintain any state information about other peers, so they cannot distinguish free riding from non–free riding peers. In particular, free riding peers will still have queries sent to them even if they never answer any. The presence of free riders will thus "dilute" the network, making queries travel farther before finding data. This can cause queries to fail if the desired data is pushed beyond the search horizon.

Ironically, it may be better for the network if free riding peers drop queries altogether instead of forwarding them, since queries will then simply flow around the free riders (unless portions of the network are completely cut off, of course). This is the opposite of the Freenet situation: Freenet free riders that drop queries are harmful since they kill off those queries, but those that forward queries unanswered actually help the network to route around them later on by propagating information about downstream peers.

Scalability

Finally, let's consider Gnutella's scalability. As a random graph, its characteristic pathlength scales logarithmically with the size of the network. Since its breadth-first search finds optimal paths, the request pathlength always equals the characteristic pathlength and also scales logarithmically. We have already seen that these pathlengths are quite low, so the amount of time taken by queries should be manageable up to very large network sizes. This does not accurately reflect their bandwidth usage, however.

The bandwidth used by a query is proportional to the number of messages sent, which in turn is proportional to the number of nodes that must be contacted before finding data. Actually, this is an underestimate, since many nodes will be sent the same query more than once and queries continue after finding data. Figure 14-31 shows the median number of nodes contacted per query versus network size, up to 200,000 nodes.

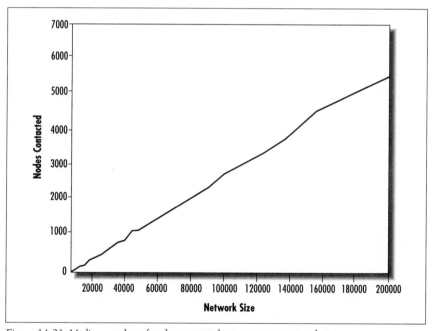

Figure 14-31. Median number of nodes contacted per query, vs. network size

We can see that the number of nodes that must be contacted scales essentially linearly, meaning that every doubling of network size will also double the bandwidth needed per query. An alternate way of looking at this is to see that if bandwidth usage is kept lower by limiting search depths, success rates will drop since queries will not be able to reach the data. This may pose a serious scalability problem.

One solution already being explored is to modify Gnutella from a pure decentralized peer-to-peer model to a partly hierarchical model by using *super peers*. These are special peers that act as aggregators for other peers located "behind" them in the manner of a firewall. Super peers maintain indices of all the files their subordinate peers are sharing, and appear to the rest of the network as though they were sharing those files themselves. When queried for a file, a super peer can route the query directly to the relevant peer without a broadcast. In addition, if one of its subordinates requests a file held by another subordinate, it can satisfy the request immediately without involving the wider network. Super peers thus reduce the effective size of the network by replacing a group of ordinary peers with a single super peer.

From there, it is a short step to imagine "super-super peers" that aggregate queries for super peers, "super-super-super peers," and so on. Taken to the extreme, this could yield a completely hierarchical search tree like DNS. Such an arrangement would place each peer in successively larger aggregate groups, ultimately ending in a root peer managing the entire network. Searches in such a tree would scale logarithmically; however, it implies a considerable loss of the autonomy promised by peer-to-peer.

Conclusions

Performance is likely to remain an important issue in peer-to-peer systems design well into the foreseeable future. Within the peer-to-peer model, a number of trade-offs can be used to tailor different sets of performance outcomes. Freenet, for example, emphasizes high scalability and efficient searches under average conditions while sacrificing worse-case performance. At the other end of the spectrum, Gnutella sacrifices efficiency for faster searches and better worst-case guarantees. Ideas drawn from graph theory and the small-world model can help to quantify these trade-offs and to analyze systems in concrete terms.

Fault tolerance and free riding are additional challenges to deal with, and here again we can see different approaches. Systems like Freenet that develop specialized nodes can improve their robustness under random failure, but more uniform systems like Gnutella can better cope with targeted attacks. Free riding, a different type of failure mode, needs to be addressed in terms of routing around or otherwise neutralizing uncooperative nodes.

Last but not least, scalability is a crucial concern for systems that hope to make the leap from conceptual demonstration to world-wide usage. For systems that do not inherently scale well, a further set of trade-offs can allow better scalability through a move toward a hierarchical peer-to-peer model, though at the expense of local autonomy.

The peer-to-peer model encompasses a diverse set of approaches. By recognizing the wide range of possibilities available, inventing new ideas and new combinations, and using analytical methods to evaluate their behaviors, system designers will be well-equipped to exploit the power of peer-to-peer.

Acknowledgments

I would like to thank Catherine Reive and the Marshall Aid Commemoration Commission for their help and support. Many thanks also to Ian Clarke for creating Freenet, to *Need to Know* for bringing it to my attention, to David Molnar for prompting a submission to the ICSI Workshop on Design Issues in Anonymity and Unobservability, and to Sammy Klein, Matt Bruce, and others for reviewing early drafts. Jon Kleinberg's influence in serendipitously publishing an article on navigation in small-world networks the very week I started writing this was invaluable. Thanks to my thesis advisor, Professor Keith Clark, for putting up with my extracurricular activities. Finally, big thanks go to Andy Oram for putting the whole thing together.

chapter fifteen

Trust

Marc Waldman, Lorrie Faith Cranor,
and Avi Rubin, AT&T Labs-Research

Trust plays a central role in many aspects of computing, especially those related to network use. Whether downloading and installing software, buying a product from a web site, or just surfing the Web, an individual is faced with trust issues. Does this piece of software really do what it says it does? Will the company I make purchases from sell my private information to other companies? Is my ISP logging all of my network traffic? All of these questions are central to the trust issue. In this chapter we discuss the areas of trust related to distributed systems—computers that communicate over a network and share information.

Trust in peer-to-peer, collaborative, or distributed systems presents its own challenges. Some systems, like Publius, deliberately disguise the source of data; all of the systems use computations or files provided by far-flung individuals who would be difficult to contact if something goes wrong—much less to hold responsible for any damage done.

Trust in real life, and its lessons for computer networks

In the physical world, when we talk about how much we trust someone, we often consider that person's reputation. We usually are willing to put great trust in someone whom we have personally observed to be highly capable and have a high level of integrity. In the absence of personal observation, the recommendation of a trusted friend can lead one to trust someone. When looking for someone to provide a service for us in which trust is an issue—whether a doctor, baby-sitter, or barber—we often ask our friends for recommendations or check with a trusted authority such as a childcare referral service. In real life, *trust is often increased by establishing positive reputations and networks for conveying these reputations.* This is true for computer networks as well. More will be said about this in Chapter 16, *Accountability,* and Chapter 17, *Reputation.* Once reputations are established, digital certificates and networks like the PGP web of trust (described later in this chapter) can be used to convey reputation information in a trustworthy way.

Information conveyed by a trusted person is itself seen to be trustworthy, especially if it is based on a personal observation by that person. Information conveyed via a long chain of people, trustworthy or not, is generally viewed to be less trustworthy—even if the entire chain is trustworthy, the fact that it was conveyed via a long chain introduces the possibility that somewhere along the way the facts may have been confused. So we may trust all of the people in the chain to be honest, but we may not trust all of them to accurately remember and convey every detail of a story told by someone else. If it is important to us to have confidence in the veracity of a piece of information, we may try to follow the chain back to its source. *Essentially, we are able to increase trust by reducing the number of people that must be trusted.* This applies to real life situations as well as computer networks.

We can also look at trust from a risk assessment perspective. We tend to be more willing to place trust in people when the risk of adverse consequences should our trust be misplaced is small. Likewise, even if there is high risk, if the potential consequences are not that bad, we may still be willing to trust. *Thus, we can also increase trust by reducing risk.* Just as in real life we may reduce risk by removing valuable items from a car before leaving it with a parking lot attendant, in a networked environment we may reduce risk by creating protected "sandboxes" where we can execute untrusted code without exposing critical systems to danger.

Sometimes we interact with people whose reputations are unknown to us, but they somehow seem worthy of our trust. We may talk about people who seem to have an honest face or a trustworthy demeanor. In the online world, a web site that looks very professional may also appear to be trustworthy, even if we do not know anything else about it. Clearly there are ways of changing perceptions about trust when our later experiences conflict with our first impressions. Indeed, many companies spend a lot of effort honing a marketing message or corporate image in an effort to convey more of an image of trustworthiness to consumers.

In this chapter, we are concerned less about perceptions of trustworthiness than we are about designing systems that rely as little as possible on trust. Ultimately, we would like to design systems that do not require anyone to trust any aspect of the system, because there is no uncertainty about how the system will behave. In this context, the ideal trusted system is one that everyone has confidence in because they do not have to trust it. Where that is impossible, we use techniques such as reputation building and risk reduction to build trust.

We first examine the issue of downloaded software. For the most part, the software described in this book can be downloaded from the Web. This simple act of downloading software and running it on your computer involves many trust-related issues. We then examine anonymous publishing systems. This discussion uses Publius as an example, but many of these issues apply to other systems as well. The last part of the chapter examines the trust issues involved in file sharing and search engines.

Trusting downloaded software

Trust issues exist even before an individual connects her computer to any network. Installing software supplied with your computer or that perhaps was bought in a retail store implies a level of trust—you trust that the software will work in the manner described and that it won't do anything malicious. By purchasing it from a "reputable" company, you believe that you know who wrote the software and what kind of reputation is associated with their software products. In addition, you may be able to take legal action if something goes horribly wrong.

The advent of the Internet changes this model. Now software can be downloaded directly onto your computer. You may not know who the author is and whether the software has been maliciously modified or really does what it claims. We have all heard stories of an individual receiving an attachment via email that, when executed, deleted files on the victim's hard drive.

Ideally, when downloading software from the Internet, we would like to have the same assurances that we have when we purchase the software directly from a store. One might think that simply downloading software from companies that one is already familiar with raises no trust issues. However, you can see from the sampling of potential problems in Table 15-1 this is really not true. The software you are downloading may have been modified by a malicious party before you even begin downloading it. Even if it begins its journey unmodified, it has to travel to you over an untrusted network—the Internet. The software, while it is traveling on the network, can be intercepted, modified, and then forwarded to you—all without your knowledge. Even if this doesn't happen, your Internet service provider (ISP) or another party could be logging the fact that you are downloading a particular piece of software or visiting a particular web site. This information can, for example, be used to target specific advertising at you. At the very least, this logging is an invasion of privacy. As we shall see there are ways of overcoming each of these problems.*

Table 15-1. Trust issues when downloading software

Risk	Solution	Trust principle
Software doesn't behave as advertised, and may even damage your computer system.	Only download software from companies or individuals who have established a good reputation, or those you know where to find should a problem occur.	Look for positive reputations.
Software is modified (on server or in transit).	Check for digital signature on message digest and verify signature against author's certificate.	Use tools that accurately convey reputations.
Your downloads (and other online behavior) are logged by your ISP or other parties.	Use an anonymity tool so other parties do not get access to information that might link you to a particular download.	Reduce risk.

Message digest functions

Almost all of the software described in this book is given away for free. The only way to acquire it is to download it—you can't walk into your local computer store and purchase it. We would like some way to verify that the downloaded files have not been tampered with in any way. This can be accomplished through the use of a *message digest function*, which is also known as a cryptographically secure hash function. A message digest function takes a variable-length input message and produces a fixed-length output. The same message will always produce the same output. If the input message is changed in any way, the digest function produces a different output value. This feature makes digest functions ideal for detecting file tampering.

Now that we have message digest functions, it looks like all of our tamper problems are solved—the author of a piece of software just places the value of the file's hash on the same web page that contains the file download link. After the user downloads the file, a separate program finds the digest of the file. This digest is then compared with the one on the web page. If the digests don't match the file has been tampered with; otherwise it is unchanged. Unfortunately things are not that simple. How do we know that the digest given on the web page is correct? Perhaps the server administrator or some malicious hacker changed the

---

* For a more comprehensive discussion of this topic, see Bruce Schneier (1999), *Secrets and Lies: Digital Security in a Networked World*, John Wiley & Sons.

software and placed the digest of the modified file on the web page. If someone downloaded the altered file and checked the replaced digest everything would look fine. The problem is that we do not have a mechanism to guarantee that the author of the file was the one who generated the particular digest. What we need is some way for the author to state the digest value so that someone else cannot change it.

Digital signatures

Public key cryptography and digital signatures can be used to help identify the author of a file. Although the mathematics behind public key cryptography are beyond the scope of this book, suffice it to say that a pair of keys can be generated in such a way that if one key is used to sign some piece of data, the other key can be used to verify the signed data. Keys are essentially large numbers that are needed for the signature and verification operations. One of these keys is kept secret and is therefore called the private key. The other key is made available to everyone and is called the public key. Someone can send you an authenticated message simply by signing the message with his private key. You can then use his public key to verify the signature on the message.

So it looks like our problem is almost solved. The author of the software generates a public and private key. The author then computes the digest of the software package. This digest is then signed using a private key. A file containing the signed digest is placed on the same web page as the file to be downloaded (the software package). After downloading the software an individual finds its digest. The signed digest file is downloaded from the web site and verified using the author's public key.

Digital certificates

The problem with the scheme is that we have no way of verifying the author's public key. How do we know that someone didn't just generate a public/private key pair, modify the file, and sign its digest with the private key just generated? The public key on the web site cannot necessarily be trusted. We need a way to certify that a particular public key does indeed belong to the author of the software. Digital certificates are meant to provide this binding of public keys to individuals or organizations.

Digital certificates are issued by companies called certifying authorities (CAs). These are organizations that mint digital certificates for a fee; they are often called *trusted third parties* because both you and your correspondent trust them. An individual or corporation requesting a certificate must supply the CA with the proper credentials. Once these credentials have been verified, the CA mints a new certificate in the name of the individual or corporation. The CA signs the certificate with its private key and this signature becomes part of the certificate. The CA signature guarantees its authenticity.

The certificate creation process just described is a simplification of the actual process. Different classes of certificates exist corresponding to the type of credentials presented when applying for the certificate. The more convincing the credentials, the more verification work is created for the CA, and therefore it assesses a higher annual fee on the individual or corporation applying for the certificate. Therefore, certain types of certificates are more trustworthy than others.

Signature verification

Now all the pieces are in place. The author of some software applies to a CA for a certificate. This certificate binds her to a public key—only she knows the associated private key. She signs her software using the method described above. The signed digest and a link to the software are placed on the author's web page. In addition, a link to the author's certificate is added to the web page. At some later time, an individual downloads the software and author's certificate. The digest function is performed on the file. The author's certificate is verified using the CA's public key, which is available on the CA's web page. Once verified, the author's public key is used to verify the signature on the digest. This digest is compared to the one just performed on the file. If the digests match, the file has not been tampered with. See Figure 15-1 for an illustration of the process.

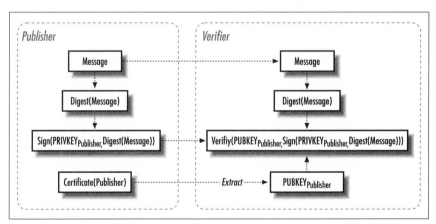

Figure 15-1. Digital signatures and how they are verified

This verification process provides assurance that the downloaded software is signed by someone who has a private key that was issued to a software author with a particular name. Of course, there is no guarantee that the software author did not let someone else use her key, or that the key was not stolen without her knowledge. Furthermore, if we don't know anything about the reputation of this particular software author, knowing her name may not give us any confidence in her software (although if we have confidence in the CA, we may at least believe that it might be possible to track her down later should her software prove destructive).

The previously described verification process is not performed by hand. A number of software products are available that automate the task.

Pretty Good Privacy (PGP) is a well-known tool for encrypting files and email. It also allows individuals to sign and verify files. Rather than having to trust a third party, the CA, PGP allows individuals to create their own certificates. These certificates by themselves are not very helpful when trying to verify someone's identity; however, other people can sign the certificates. People that know you can sign your certificate, and you in turn can sign their certificates. If you receive a certificate from someone you don't trust, you can check the signatures on the certificate and see if you trust any of them. Based on this information you can decide if you wish to trust the certificate. This is a trust system based on intermediaries, and it forms what is called the "web of trust." The web of trust can be thought of as a peer-to-peer certification system. No centralized certifying authority is needed. A free version of PGP is available for download at *http:// web.mit.edu/network/pgp.html*.

Unfortunately, digital certificates and signatures don't solve all of our problems. Not all software packages are signed. An author's private key can become compromised, allowing others to sign any piece of software with the compromised key. Just because software is signed doesn't mean that it doesn't have malicious intent. So one must still be vigilant when it comes to downloaded software.

Open source software

Much of the software available for download is available as source code, which needs to be compiled or interpreted in order to run on a specific computer. This means that one can examine the source code for any malicious intent. However, this is really practical only for rather small programs. This naturally leads to the question of whether it is possible to write a program that examines the source code of another program to determine if that program really does what it claims to do. Unfortunately, computer scientists have shown that, in general, it is impossible to determine if a program does what it claims to do.* However, we can build programs to monitor or constrain the behavior of other programs.

Sandboxing and wrappers

Programs that place limits on the behavior of other programs existed before the Internet. The most obvious example of this type of program is an operating system such as Unix or Windows NT. Such an operating system, for example, won't allow you to delete a file owned by someone else or read a file owned by another user unless that user has granted you permission. Today, programs exist that can constrain the behavior of programs you download while surfing the Web. When a web page contains a Java applet, that applet is downloaded and interpreted by another program running on your computer. This interpreter prevents the applet from performing operations that could possibly damage your computer, such as deleting files. The term used to describe the process of limiting the type of operations a program can perform is called sandboxing. The applet or other suspicious program is allowed to execute only in a small sandbox. Thus the risk of damage is reduced substantially. Programs called wrappers allow the behavior of CGI scripts to be constrained in a similar manner.

Trust in censorship-resistant publishing systems

We now examine trust issues specific to distributed file-sharing and publishing programs. We use Publius as an example; however, the problems and solutions discussed are applicable to many of the other programs discussed in this book.

Publius is a web-based publishing system that allows people to publish documents in such a way that they are resistant to censorship. For a full description of Publius, see Chapter 11.

Publius derives its censorship resistance in part from a collection of independently owned web servers. Each server donates a few hundred megabytes of disk space and runs a CGI script that allows it to store and retrieve Publius files. Since each server is independently owned, the server administrator has free rein over the server. This means the administrator can arbitrarily read, delete or modify any files on the server including the Publius files. Because the Publius

---

* Proving certain properties of programs can be reduced to proving the "Halting Problem." See, for example, Michael Sipser (1997). *Introduction to the Theory of Computation.* PWS Publishing Company.

files are encrypted, reading a file does not reveal anything interesting about the file (unless the server administrator knows the special Publius URL).

Publius in a nutshell

Before describing the trust issues involved in Publius, we briefly review the Publius publication process. When an individual publishes a file, the Publius client software generates a key that is used to encrypt the file. This key is split into a number of pieces called shares. Only a small number of these shares are required to reconstruct the key. For example, the key can be split into 30 shares such that any 3 shares are needed to reconstruct the document.

A large number of Publius servers—let's say 20—then store the file, each server taking one share of the key along with a complete copy of the encrypted file. Each server stores a different share, and no server holds more than one share. A special Publius URL is generated that encodes the location of the encrypted file and shares on the 20 servers. In order to read the document, the client software parses the special URL, randomly picks 3 of these 20 servers, and downloads the share stored on each of them. In addition, the client software downloads one copy of the encrypted file from one of the servers.

The client now combines the shares to form the key and uses the key to decrypt the file. A tamper check is performed to see if the file was changed in any way. If the file was changed, a new set of three shares and a new encrypted document are retrieved and tested. This continues until a file passes the tamper check or the system runs out of different encrypted file and share combinations.

Risks involved in web server logging

Most web servers keep a log of all files that have been requested from the server. These logs usually include the date, time, and the name of the file that was requested. In addition, these logs usually hold the IP address of the computer that made the request. This IP address can be considered a form of identification. While it may be difficult to directly link an individual to a particular IP address, it is not impossible.

Even if your IP address doesn't directly identify you, it certainly gives some information about you. For example, an IP address owned by an ISP appearing in some web server log indicates that an individual who uses that ISP visited the web site on a certain date and time. The ISP itself may keep logs as to who was using a particular IP address during a particular date and time. So while it may not be possible to directly link an individual to a web site visit, an indirect route may exist.

Web servers almost always log traffic for benign reasons. The company or individual who owns the server simply wishes to get an idea how many requests the web server is receiving. The logs may answer questions central to the company's business. However, as previously stated, these logs can also be used to identify someone. This is a problem faced by Publius and many of the other systems described in this book.

Why would someone want to be anonymous on the Internet? Well, suppose that you are working for a company that is polluting the environment by dumping toxic waste in a local river. You are outraged but know that if you say anything you will be fired from your job. Therefore you secretly create a web page documenting the abuses of the corporation. You then decide you want to publish this page with Publius. Publishing this page from your home computer could unwittingly identify you. Perhaps one or more of the Publius servers are run by friends of the very corporation that you are going to expose for its misdeeds. Those servers are logging IP addresses of all computers that store or read Publius documents. In order to avoid this possibility you can walk into a local cyber café or perhaps the local library and use their Internet connection to publish the web page with Publius. Now the IP address of the library or cyber café will be stored in the logs of the Publius servers. Therefore there is no longer a connection to your computer. This level of anonymity is still not as great as we would like. If you are one of a very few employees of the company living in a small town, the company may be able to figure out you leaked the information just by tracing the web page to a location in that town.

Going to a cyber café or library is one option to protect your privacy. Anonymizing software is another. Depending on your trust of the anonymity provided by the cyber café or library versus your trust of the anonymity provided by software, you may reach different conclusions about which technique provides a higher level of anonymity in your particular situation. Whether surfing the Web or publishing a document with Publius, anonymizing software can help you protect your privacy by making it difficult, if not impossible, to identify you on the Internet. Different types of anonymizing software offer varying degrees of anonymity and privacy protection. We now describe several anonymizing and privacy-protection systems.

Anonymizing proxies

The simplest type of anonymizing software is an anonymizing proxy. Several such anonymizing proxies are available today for individuals who wish to surf the Web with some degree of anonymity. Two such anonymizing proxies are

Anonymizer.com and Rewebber.de. These anonymizing proxies work by acting as the intermediary between you and the web site you wish to visit. For example, suppose you wish to anonymously view the web page with the URL *http://www.oreilly.com*. Instead of entering this address into the browser, you first visit the anonymizing proxy site (e.g., *http://www.anonymizer.com*). This site displays a form that asks you to enter the URL of the site you wish to visit. You enter *http://www.oreilly.com*, and the anonymizing proxy retrieves the web page corresponding to this URL and displays it in your browser. In addition, the anonymizing proxy rewrites all the hyperlinks on the retrieved page so that when you click on any of these hyperlinks the request is routed through the anonymizing proxy. Any logs being kept by the server *www.oreilly.com* will only record the anonymizing proxy's IP address, as this is the computer that actually made the request for the web page. The process is illustrated in Figure 15-2.

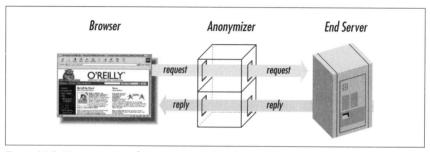

Figure 15-2. How requests and responses pass through an anonymizing proxy

The anonymizing proxy solves the problem of logging by the Publius servers but has introduced the problem of logging by the anonymizing proxy. In other words, if the people running the proxy are dishonest, they may try to use it to snare you.

In addition to concern over logging, one must also trust that the proxy properly transmits the request to the destination web server and that the correct document is being returned. For example, suppose you are using an anonymizing proxy and you decide to shop for a new computer. You enter the URL of your favorite computer company into the anonymizing proxy. The company running the anonymizing proxy examines the URL and notices that it is for a computer company. Instead of contacting the requested web site, the proxy contacts a competitor's web site and sends the content of the competitor's web page to your browser. If you are not very familiar with the company whose site you are visiting, you may not even realize this has happened. In general, if you use a proxy you must just resolve to trust it, so try to pick a proxy with a good reputation.

Censorship in Publius

Now that we have a possible solution to the logging problem, let's look at the censorship problem. Suppose that a Publius server administrator named Eve wishes to censor a particular Publius document. Eve happened to learn the Publius URL of the document and by coincidence her server is storing a copy of the encrypted document and a corresponding share. Eve can try a number of things to censor the document.

Upon inspecting the Publius URL for the document she wishes to censor, Eve learns that the encrypted document is stored on 20 servers and that 3 shares are needed to form the key that decrypts the document. After a bit of calculation Eve learns the names of the 19 other servers storing the encrypted document. Recall that Eve's server also holds a copy of the encrypted document and a corresponding share. If Eve simply deletes the encrypted document on her server she cannot censor the document, as it still exists on 19 other servers. Only one copy of the encrypted document and three shares are needed to read the document. If Eve can convince at least 17 other server administrators to delete the shares corresponding to the document then she can censor the document, as not enough shares will be available to form the key. (This possibility means that it is very difficult, but not impossible, to censor Publius documents. The small possibility of censorship can be viewed as a limitation of Publius. However, it can also be viewed as a "safety" feature that would allow a document to be censored if enough of the server operators agreed that it was objectionable.)

Using the Update mechanism to censor

Eve and her accomplices have not been able to censor the document by deleting it; however, they realize that they might have a chance to censor the document if they place an *update* file in the directory where the encrypted file and share once resided. The *update* file contains the Publius URL of a file published by Eve.

Using the Update file method described in Chapter 11, Eve and her accomplices have a chance, albeit a very slim one, of occasionally censoring the document. When the Publius client software is given a Publius URL it breaks up the URL to discover which servers are storing the encrypted document and shares. The client then randomly chooses three of these servers from which to retrieve the shares. The client also retrieves the encrypted document from one of these servers. If all three requests for the share return with the same *update* URL, instead of the share, the client follows the *update* URL and retrieves the corresponding document.

How successful can a spoofed update be? There are 1,140 ways to choose 3 servers from a set of 20. Only 1 of these 1,140 combinations leads to Eve's document. Therefore Eve and her cohorts have only a 1 in 1,140 chance of censoring the document each time someone tries to retrieve it. Of course, Eve's probability of success grows as she enlists more Publius server administrators to participate in her scheme. Furthermore, if large numbers of people are trying to retrieve a document of some social significance, and they discover any discrepancies by comparing documents, Eve could succeed in casting doubt on the whole process of retrieval.

A publisher worried about this sort of update attack has the option of specifying that the file is not updateable. This option sets a flag in the Publius URL that tells the Publius client software to ignore *update* URLs sent from any Publius server. Any time the Publius client receives an *update* URL, it simply treats it as an invalid response from the server and attempts to acquire the needed information from another server. In addition to the "do not update" option, a "do not delete" option is available to the publisher of a Publius document. While this cannot stop Eve or any other server administrator from deleting files, it does protect the publisher from someone trying to repeatedly guess the correct password to the delete the file. This is accomplished by not storing a password with the encrypted file. Because no password is stored on the server, the Publius server software program refuses to perform the Delete command.

As previously stated, the Publius URL also encodes the number of shares required to form the key. This is the same as the number of *update* URLs that must match before the Publius client retrieves an *update* URL. Therefore, another way to make the update attack more difficult is to raise the number of shares needed to reconstruct the key. The default is three, but it can be set to any number during the Publish operation. However, raising this value increases the amount of time it takes to retrieve a Publius document because more shares need to be retrieved in order to form the key.

On the other hand, requiring a large number of shares to reconstruct the document can make it easier for an adversary to censor it. Previously we discussed the possibility of Eve censoring the document if she and two friends delete the encrypted document and its associated shares. We mentioned that such an attack would be unsuccessful because 17 other shares and encrypted documents exist. If the document was published in such a way that 18 shares were required to form the key, Eve would have succeeded in censoring the document because only 17 of the required 18 shares would be available. Therefore, some care must be taken when choosing the required number of shares.

Alternatively, even if we do not increase the number of shares necessary to reconstruct a Publius document, we could develop software for retrieving Publius documents that retrieves more than the minimum number of required shares when an *update* file is discovered. While this slows down the process of retrieving updated documents, it can also provide additional assurance that a document has not been tampered with (or help the client find an unaltered version of a document that has been tampered with).

The attacks in this censorship section illustrate the problems that can occur when one blindly trusts a response from a server or peer. Responses can be carefully crafted to mislead the receiving party. In systems such as Publius, which lack any sort of trust or reputation mechanism, one of the few ways to try to overcome such problems is to utilize randomization and replication. By replication we mean that important information should be replicated widely so that the failure of one or a small number of components will not render the service inoperable (or, in the case of Publius, easy to censor). Randomization helps because it can make attacks on distributed systems more difficult. For example, if Publius always retrieved the first three shares from the first three servers in the Publius URL, then the previously described update attack would always succeed if Eve managed to add an *update* file to these three servers. By randomizing share retrieval the success of such an attack decreases from 100% to less than 1%.

Publius proxy volunteers

In order to perform any Publius operation one must use the Publius client software. The client software consists of an HTTP proxy that intercepts Publius commands and transparently handles non-Publius URLs as well. This HTTP proxy was designed so that many people could use it at once—just like a web server. This means that the proxy can be run on one computer on the Internet and others can connect to it. Individuals who run the proxy with the express purpose of allowing others to connect to it are called Publius proxy volunteers.

Why would someone elect to use a remote proxy rather than a local one? The current Publius proxy requires the computer language Perl and a cryptographic library package called Crypto++. Some individuals may have problems installing these software packages, and therefore the remote proxy provides an attractive alternative.

The problem with remote proxies is that the individual running the remote proxy must be trusted, as we stated in the "Anonymizing proxies" section earlier in this chapter. That individual has complete access to all data sent to the proxy. As a result, the remote proxy can log everything it is asked to publish, retrieve, update, or delete. Therefore, users may wish to use an anonymizing tool to access the Publius proxy.

The remote proxy, if altered by a malicious administrator, can also perform any sort of transformation on retrieved documents and can decide how to treat any

Publius commands it receives. The solutions to this problem are limited. Short of running your own proxy, probably the best thing you can do is use a second remote proxy to verify the actions of the first.

Third-party trust issues in Publius

Besides trusting the operators of the Publius servers and proxies, users of Publius may have to place trust in other parties. Fortunately some tools exist that reduce the amount of trust that must be placed in these parties.

Other anonymity tools

While not perfect, anonymizing proxies can hide your IP address from a Publius server or a particular web site. As previously stated, the anonymizing proxy itself could be keeping logs.

In addition, your Internet service provider (ISP) can monitor all messages you send over the Internet. An anonymizing proxy doesn't help us with this problem. Instead, we need some way of hiding all communication from the ISP. Cryptography helps us here. All traffic (messages) between you and another computer can be encrypted. Now the ISP sees only encrypted traffic, which looks like gibberish. The most popular method of encrypting web traffic is the Secure Sockets Layer (SSL) Protocol.

SSL

SSL allows two parties to create a private channel over the Internet. In our case this private channel can be between a Publius client and a server. All traffic to and from the Publius client and server can be encrypted. This hides everything from the ISP except the fact that you are talking to a Publius server. The ISP can see the encrypted channel setup messages between the Publius client and server. Is there a way to hide this piece of information too? It turns out there is.

Mix networks

Mix networks are systems for hiding both the content and destination of a particular message on the Internet.* One of the best-known mix networks is discussed in Chapter 7, *Mixmaster Remailers*.

---

* Mix networks were first introduced by David Chaum. See David Chaum (1981), "Untraceable Electronic Mail, Return Addresses, and Digital Pseudonyms," *Communications of the ACM*, vol. 24, no. 2, pp. 84–88.

A mix network consists of a collection of computers called routers that use a special layered encryption method to hide the content and true destination of a message. To send a message, the sender first decides on a path through a subset of the mixes. Each mix has an associated public and private key pair. All users of the mix network know all the public keys. The message is repeatedly encrypted using the public keys of the routers on the chosen path. First the message is encrypted with the public key of the last router in the chosen path. This encrypted message is then encrypted once again using the public key of the next-to-last router. This is repeated until the message is finally encrypted with the public key of the first router in the chosen path. As the encrypted message is received at each router, the outer layer of encryption is removed by decrypting it with the router's private key. This reveals only the next router in the mix network to receive the encrypted message. Each router can only decrypt the outer layer of encryption with its private key. Only the last router in the chosen path knows the ultimate destination of the message; however, it doesn't know where the message originated. The layers of encryption are represented in Figure 15-3.

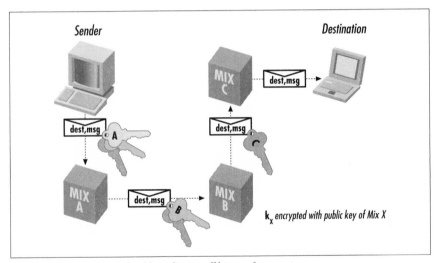

Figure 15-3. A mix network adds and strips off layers of encryption

Mix networks are also used to try to thwart traffic analysis. Traffic analysis is a method of correlating messages emanating from and arriving at various computers or routers. For instance, if a message leaves one node and is received by another shortly thereafter, and if the pattern is immediately repeated in the other direction, a monitor can guess that the two systems are engaged in a request and acknowledgment protocol. Even when a mix network is in use, this type of analysis is feasible if all or a large percentage of the mix network can be monitored by an adversary (perhaps a large government). In an effort to combat this type of analysis, mix networks usually pad messages to a fixed length, buffer messages for later transmission, and generate fake traffic on the network, called covering traffic. All of these help to complicate or defeat traffic analysis.

Researchers at the U.S. Department of Defense developed an implementation of mix networks called Onion Routing (*http://www.onion-router.net*) and deployed a prototype network. The network was taken offline in January 2000. Zero-Knowledge Systems developed a commercial implementation of mix networks in a product called Freedom—see *http://www.freedom.net* for more information.

Crowds

Crowds is a system whose goals are similar to that of mix networks but whose implementation is quite different. Crowds is based on the idea that people can be anonymous when they blend into a crowd. As with mix networks, Crowds users need not trust a single third party in order to maintain their anonymity. A crowd consists of a group of web surfers all running the Crowds software. When one crowd member makes a URL request, the Crowds software on the corresponding computer randomly chooses between retrieving the requested document or forwarding the request to a randomly selected member of the crowd. The receiving crowd member can also retrieve the requested document or forward the request to a randomly selected member of the crowd, and so on. Eventually, the web document corresponding to the URL is retrieved by some member of the crowd and sent back to the crowd member that initiated the request.

Suppose that computers A, B, C, D, E, and F are all members of a crowd. Computer B wants to anonymously retrieve the web page at the URL *http://www.oreilly.com*. The Crowds software on computer B sends this URL to a random member of the crowd, say computer F. Computer F decides to send it to computer C. Computer C decides to retrieve the URL. Computer C sends the web page back to computer F. Computer F then sends the web page back to computer B. Notice that the document is sent back over the path of forwarding computers and not directly from C to B. All communication between crowd members is encrypted using symmetric ciphers. Only the actual request from computer C to *http://www.oreilly.com* remains unencrypted (because the software has to assume that *http://www.oreilly.com* is uninterested in going along with the crowd). The structure of the system is shown in Figure 15-4.

Notice that each computer in the crowd is equally likely to make the request for the specific web page. Even though computer C's IP address will appear in the log of the server *http://www.oreilly.com*, the individual using computer C can plausibly deny visiting the server. Computer C is a member of the crowd and

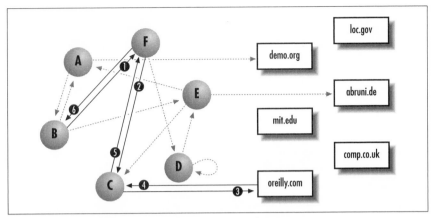

Figure 15-4. Crowds hides the origin of a request to a web server

therefore could have been retrieving the page for another member of the crowd. Notice that each crowd member cannot tell which other member of the crowd requested the particular URL. In the previous example, computer B sends the URL to computer F. Crowd member F cannot tell if the URL request originated with B or if B was simply an intermediary forwarding the request from another crowd member. This is the reason that the retrieved web page has to be passed back over the list of crowd members that forwarded the URL.

Crowds is itself an example of a peer-to-peer system.

Denial of service attacks

Publius relies on server volunteers to donate disk space so others can publish files in a censorship-resistant manner. Disk space, like all computer resources, is finite. Once all the disks on all the Publius servers are full, no more files can be published until others are deleted. Therefore an obvious attack on Publius is to fill up all the disks on the servers. Publius clients know the locations of all the servers, so identifying the servers to attack is a simple matter. Attacks with the intention of making resources unavailable are called denial of service attacks.

Systems that blindly trust users to conserve precious resources are extremely vulnerable to this kind of attack. Therefore, non–trust based mechanisms are needed to thwart such attacks.

Can systems be designed to prevent denial of service attacks? The initial version of Publius tried to do so by limiting the size of any file published with Publius to 100K. While this certainly won't prevent someone from trying to fill up the hard drives, it does make this kind of attack more time consuming. Other methods such as CPU payment schemes, anonymous e-cash payment schemes, or quota systems based on IP address may be incorporated into future versions of Publius. While these methods can help deter denial of service attacks, they cannot prevent them completely.

Quota systems

Quota systems based on IP address could work as follows. Each Publius server keeps track of the IP address of each computer that makes a Publish request. If a Publius client has made more than ten Publish requests to a particular server in the last 24 hours, subsequent Publish requests will be denied by that server. Only after a 24-hour time period has elapsed will the server once again honor Publish requests from that Publius client's IP address.

The problem with this scheme is that it is not foolproof. An attacker can easily fake IP addresses. In addition, the 10-file limit may unfairly limit individuals whose IP addresses are dynamically assigned. For example, suppose someone with an IP address from AOL publishes ten files on some server. If later in the day someone else is assigned that same IP address, the individual will be unfairly excluded from publishing on that particular server.

CPU-based payment schemes

CPU-based payment schemes are used to help prevent denial of service attacks by making it expensive, in terms of time, to carry out such an attack. In Publius, for example, before the server agrees to publish a file, it could ask the publishing client to solve some sort of puzzle. The client spends some time solving the puzzle and then sends the answer to the server. The server agrees to publish the file only if the answer is correct. Each time the particular client asks to publish a file the server can make the puzzle a bit harder—requiring the client to expend more CPU time to find the puzzle answer.

While this scheme makes denial of service attacks more expensive, it clearly does not prevent them. A small Publius system created by civic-minded individuals could be overwhelmed by a large company or government willing to expend the computing resources to do the necessary calculations.

By design, Publius and many other publishing systems have no way of authenticating individuals who wish to publish documents. This commitment to anonymous publishing makes it almost impossible to stop denial of service attacks of this sort.

Anonymous e-cash payment schemes

Another way of preventing denial of service attacks is to require publishers to pay money in order to publish their documents with Publius. An anonymous e-cash system could allow publishers to pay while still remaining anonymous. Even if a well-funded attacker could afford to pay to fill up all available Publius servers, the fees collected from that attacker could be used to buy more disks. This could, of course, result in an arms race if the attacker had enough money to spend on defeating Publius. Chapter 16 discusses CPU- and anonymous e-cash–based payment schemes in more detail.

Legal and physical attacks

All of the methods of censorship described so far involve using a computer. However, another method of trying to censor a document is to use the legal system. Attackers may try to use intellectual property law, obscenity laws, hate speech laws, or other laws to try to force server operators to remove Publius documents from their servers or to shut their servers down completely. However, as mentioned previously, in order for this attack to work, a document would have to be removed from a sufficient number of servers. If the Publius servers in question are all located in the same legal jurisdiction, a single court order could effectively shut down all of the servers. By placing Publius servers in many different jurisdictions, such attacks can be prevented to some extent.

Another way to censor Publius documents is to learn the identity of the publishers and force them to remove their documents from the Publius servers. By making threats of physical harm or job loss, attackers may "convince" publishers to remove their documents. For this reason, it may be especially important for some publishers to take precautions to hide their identities when publishing Publius documents. Furthermore, publishers can indicate at the time of publication that their documents should never be deleted. In this case, no password exists that will allow the publishers to delete their documents—only the server operators can delete the documents.

Trust in other systems

We now examine issues of trust in some popular file-sharing and anonymous publishing systems.

Mojo Nation and Free Haven

Many of the publishing systems described in this book rely on a collection of independently owned servers that volunteer disk space. As disk space is a limited resource, it is important to protect it from abuse. CPU-based payment schemes and quotas, both of which we mentioned previously, are possible deterrents to denial of service attacks, but other methods exist.

Mojo Nation uses a digital currency system called Mojo that must be paid before one can publish a file on a server. In order to publish or retrieve files in the Mojo Nation network, one must pay a certain amount of Mojo.

Mojo is obtained by performing a useful function in the Mojo Nation network. For example, you can earn Mojo by volunteering to host Mojo content on your server. Another way of earning Mojo is to run a search engine on your server that allows others to search for files on the Mojo Nation network.

The Free Haven project utilizes a trust network. Servers agree to store a document based on the trust relationship that exists between the publisher and the particular server. Trust relationships are developed over time and violations of trust are broadcast to other servers in the Free Haven network. Free Haven is described in Chapter 12.

The Eternity Service

Publius, Free Haven, and Mojo Nation all rely on volunteer disk space to store documents. All of these systems have their roots in a theoretical publishing system called the Eternity Service.* In 1996, Ross Anderson of Cambridge University first proposed the Eternity Service as a server-based storage medium that is resistant to denial of service attacks.

An individual wishing to anonymously publish a document simply submits it to the Eternity Service with an appropriate fee. The Eternity Service then copies the document onto a random subset of servers participating in the service. Once submitted, a document cannot be removed from the service. Therefore, an author cannot be forced, even under threat, to delete a document published on the Eternity Service.

Anderson envisioned a system in which servers were spread all over the world, making the system resistant to legal attacks as well as natural disasters. The

---

* See Ross Anderson (1996), "The Eternity Service," *PragoCrypt'96*.

distributed nature of the Eternity Service would allow it to withstand the loss of a majority of the servers and still function properly.

Anderson outlined the design of this ambitious system, but did not provide the crucial details of how one would construct such a service. Over the years, a few individuals have described in detail and actually implemented scaled-down versions of the Eternity Service. Publius, Free Haven, and the other distributed publishing systems described in this book fit into this category.

Eternity Usenet

An early implementation of a scaled-down version of the Eternity Service was proposed and implemented by Adam Back. Unlike the previously described publishing systems, this system didn't rely on volunteers to donate disk space. Instead, the publishing system was built on top of the Usenet news system. For this reason the system was called Eternity Usenet.

The Usenet news system propagates messages to servers all over the world and therefore qualifies as a distributed storage medium. However, Usenet is far from an ideal long-term storage mechanism. Messages posted to a Usenet newsgroup can take days to propagate to all Usenet servers. Not all Usenet news servers subscribe to all Usenet newsgroups. In fact, any system administrator can locally censor documents by not subscribing to a particular newsgroup. Usenet news posts can also become the victims of cancel or supercede messages. They are relatively easy to fake and therefore attractive to individuals who wish to censor a particular Usenet post.

The great volume of Usenet traffic necessitates the removal of old Usenet articles in favor of newer ones. This means that something posted to Usenet today may not be available two weeks from now, or even a few days from now. There are a few servers that archive Usenet articles for many years, but because there are not many of these servers, they present an easy target for those who wish to censor an archived document.

Finally, there is no way to tell if a Usenet message has been modified. Eternity Usenet addresses this by allowing an individual to digitally sign the message.

File-sharing systems

Up until now we have been discussing only systems that allow an individual to publish material on servers owned by others. However, Napster, a program that allows individuals to share files residing on their own hard drives, has been said to have started the whole peer-to-peer revolution. Napster allows individuals to share MP3 files over the Internet. The big debate concerning Napster is whether this file sharing is legal. Many of the shared MP3 files are actually copied from one computer to another without any sort of royalty being paid to the artist that created the file. We will not discuss this particular issue any further as it is beyond the scope of this chapter. We are interested in the file-sharing mechanism and the trust issues involved.

Napster

Let's say Alice has a collection of MP3 files on her computer's hard drive. Alice wishes to share these files with others. She downloads the Napster client software and installs it on her computer. She is now ready to share the MP3 files. The list of MP3 files and associated descriptions is sent to the Napster server by the client software. This server adds the list to its index of MP3 files. In addition to storing the name and description of the MP3 files, the server also stores Alice's IP address. Alice's IP address is necessary, as the Napster server does not actually store the MP3 files themselves, but rather just pointers to them.

Alice can also use the Napster client software to search for MP3 files. She submits a query to the Napster server and a list of matching MP3 files is returned. Using the information obtained from the Napster server, Alice's client can connect to any of the computers storing these MP3 files and initiate a file transfer. Once again the issue of logging becomes important. Not only does Alice have to worry about logging on the part of the Napster server, but she also has to worry about logging done by the computer that she is copying files from. It is this form of logging that allowed the band Metallica to identify individuals who downloaded their music.

The natural question to ask is whether one of our previously described anonymizing tools could be used to combat this form of logging. Unfortunately the current answer is no. The reason for this is that the Napster server and client software speak a protocol that is not recognized by any of our current anonymizing tools. A protocol is essentially a set of messages recognized by both programs involved in a conversation—in this case the Napster client and server. This does not mean that such an anonymizing tool is impossible to build, only that current tools won't fit the bill.

Gnutella

Gnutella, described in Chapter 8, is a pure peer-to-peer file-sharing system. Computers running the Gnutella software connect to some preexisting network and become part of this network. We call computers running the Gnutella software Gnutella clients. Once part of this network, the Gnutella client can respond to queries sent by other members of the network, generate queries itself, and participate in file sharing. Queries are passed from client to client and responses are passed back over the same set of clients that the requests originated from. This prevents meaningful logging of IP addresses and queries, because the client attempting to log the request has no way of knowing which client made the original request. Each client is essentially just forwarding the request made by another member of the network. Queries therefore remain for the most part anonymous. The individual that made the query is hidden among the other members of the peer-to-peer network, as with the Crowds system.

File transfer in Gnutella is done directly instead of via intermediaries. This is done for performance reasons; however, it also means that file transfer is not anonymous. The individual copying the file is no longer hidden among the other network members. The IP address of the client copying the file can now be logged.

Let's say that client A wishes to copy a file that resides on client B. Gnutella client A contacts client B and a file transfer is initiated. Client B can now log A's IP address and the fact that A copied a particular file. Although this sort of logging may seem trivial and harmless, it led to the creation of the web site called the Gnutella Wall of Shame. This web site lists the IP addresses and domain names of computers that allegedly downloaded a file that was advertised as containing child pornography. The file did not actually contain child pornography, but just the fact that a client downloaded the file was enough to get it placed on the list. Of course, any web site claiming to offer specific content could perform the same violation of privacy.

Freenet

Freenet, described in Chapter 9, is a pure peer-to-peer anonymous publishing system. Files are stored on a set of volunteer file servers. This set of file servers is dynamic—servers can join and leave the system at any time. A published file is copied to a subset of servers in a store-and-forward manner. Each time the file is forwarded to the next server, the origin address field associated with the file can be changed to some random value. This means that this field is essentially useless in trying to determine where the file originated. Therefore, files can be published anonymously.

Queries are handled in exactly the same way—the query is handed from one server to another and the resulting file (if any) is passed back through the same set of servers. As the file is passed back, each server can cache it locally and serve it in response to future requests for that file. It is from this local caching that Freenet derives its resistance to censorship. This method of file transfer also prevents meaningful logging, as each server doesn't know the ultimate destination of the file.

Content certification

Now that we have downloaded a file using one of the previously described systems, how do we know it is the genuine article? This is exactly the same question we asked at the beginning of this chapter. However, for certain files we may not really care that we have been duped into downloading the wrong file. A good example of this is MP3 files. While we may have wasted time downloading the file, no real harm was done to our computer. In fact, several artists have made bogus copies of their work available on such file-sharing programs as Napster. This is an attempt to prevent individuals from obtaining the legitimate version of the MP3 file.

The "problem" with many of the publishing systems described in this book is that we don't know who published the file. Indeed this is actually a feature required of anonymous publishing systems. Anonymously published files are not going to be accompanied by a digital certificate and signature (unless the signature is associated with a pseudonym). Some systems, such as Publius, provide a tamper-check mechanism. However, just because a file passes a tamper check does not mean that the file is virus-free and has actually been uploaded by the person believed by the recipient to have uploaded it.

Trust and search engines

File-sharing and anonymous publishing programs provide for distributed, and in some cases fault tolerant, file storage. But for most of these systems, the ability to store files is necessary but not sufficient to achieve their goals. Most of these systems have been built with the hope of enabling people to make their files available to others. For example, Publius was designed to allow people to publish documents so that they are resistant to censorship. But publishing a document that will never be read is of limited use. As with the proverbial tree falling in the forest that nobody was around to hear, an unread document makes no sound—it cannot inform, motivate, offend, or entertain. Therefore, indexes and search engines are important companions to file-sharing and anonymous publishing systems.

As previously stated, all of these file-sharing and anonymous publishing programs are still in their infancy. Continuing this analogy, we can say that searching technologies for these systems are in the embryonic stage. Unlike the Web, which now has mature search engines such as Google and Yahoo!, the world of peer-to-peer search engines consists of ad hoc methods, none of which work well in all situations. Web search engines such as Google catalogue millions of web pages by having web crawlers (special computer programs) read web pages and catalogue them. This method will not work with many of the systems described in this book. Publius, for example, encrypts its content and only someone possessing the URL can read the encrypted file. It makes no sense for a web crawler to visit each of the Publius servers and read all the files stored on them. The encrypted files will look like gibberish to the web crawler.

The obvious solution is to somehow send a list of known Publius URLs to a special web crawler that knows how to interpret them. Of course, submitting the Publius URL to the web crawler would be optional, as one may not wish to widely publicize a particular document.

Creating a Publius web crawler and search engine would be fairly straightforward. Unfortunately this introduces a new way to censor Publius documents. The company or individual operating the Publius web crawler can censor a document by simply removing its Publius URL from the crawler's list. The owners of the search engine can not only log your query but can also control exactly what results are returned from the search engine.

Let us illustrate this with a trivial example. You go to the Publius search engine and enter the phrase "Windows 95." The search engine examines the query and decides to send you pages that only mention Linux. Although this may seem like a silly example, one can easily see how this could lead to something much more serious. Of course, this is not a problem unique to Publius search engines—this problem can occur with the popular web search engines as well. Indeed, many of the popular search engines sell advertisements that are triggered by particular search queries, and reorder search results so that advertisers' pages are listed at the top.

Distributed search engines

The problem with a centralized search engine, even if it is completely honest, is that it has a single point of failure. It presents an enticing target to anyone who wishes to censor the system. This type of attack has already been used to temporarily shut down Napster. Because all searches for MP3 files are conducted via the Napster server, just shut down the server and the system becomes useless.

This dramatically illustrates the need for a distributed index, the type of index that we find in Freenet. Each Freenet server keeps an index of local files as well as an index of some files stored in some neighboring servers. When a Freenet server receives a query it first checks to see if the query can be satisfied locally. If it cannot, it uses the local index to decide which server to forward the request to. The index on each server is not static and changes as files move through the system.

One might characterize Gnutella as having a distributed index. However, each client in the network is concerned only with the files it has stored locally. If a query can be satisfied locally, the client sends a response. If not, it doesn't respond at all. In either case the previous client forwards its query to other members of the network. Therefore, one query can generate many responses. The query is essentially broadcast to all computers on the Gnutella network.

Each Gnutella client can interpret the query however it sees fit. Indeed, the Gnutella client can return a response that has nothing at all to do with the query. Therefore, the query results must be viewed with some suspicion. Again it boils down to the issue of trust.

In theory, an index of Publius documents generated by a web crawler that accepts submissions of Publius URLs could itself be published using Publius. This would prevent the index from being censored. Of course, the URL submission system and the forms for submitting queries to the index could be targeted for censorship.

Note that in many cases, indexes and search engines for the systems described in this book can be developed as companion systems without changing the underlying distributed system. It was not necessary for Tim Berners-Lee (the inventor of the World Wide Web) to build the many web search engines and indexes that have developed. The architecture of the Web was such that these services could be built on top of the underlying infrastructure.

Deniability

The ability to locate Publius documents can actually be a double-edged sword. On the one hand, being able to find a document is essential for that document to be read. On the other hand, the first step in censoring a document is locating it.

One of the features of Publius is that server administrators cannot read the content stored on their servers because the files are encrypted. A search engine could, in some sense, jeopardize this feature. Armed with a search engine, Publius administrators could conceivably learn that their servers are hosting something they find objectionable. They could then go ahead and delete the file from their servers. Therefore, a search engine could paradoxically lead to greater censorship in such anonymous publishing systems.

Furthermore, even if server administrators do not wish to censor documents, once presented with a Publius URL that indicates an objectionable document resides on their servers, they may have little choice under local laws. Once the server operators know what documents are on their servers, they lose the ability to deny knowledge of the kinds of content published with Publius.

Some Publius server operators may wish to help promote free speech but may not wish to specifically promote or endorse specific speech that they find objectionable. While they may be willing to host a server that may be used to publish content that they would find objectionable, they may draw the line at publicizing that content. In effect, they may be willing to provide a platform for free speech, but not to provide advertising for the speakers who use the platform.

Table 15-2 summarizes the problems with censorship-resistant and file sharing systems we have discussed in this chapter.

Table 15-2. Trust issues in censorship-resistant publishing systems

Risk	Solution	Trust principle
Servers, proxies, ISPs, or other "nodes" you interact with may log your requests (making it possible for your actions to be traced).	Use a secure channel and/or an anonymity tool so other parties do not get access to information that might link you to a particular action.	Reduce risk, and reduce the number of people that must be trusted.
Proxies and search engines may alter content they return to you in ways they don't disclose.	Try multiple proxies (and compare results before trusting any of them) or run your own proxy.	Reduce risk, and reduce the number of people that must be trusted.
Multiple parties may collaborate to censor your document.	Publish your document in a way that requires a large number of parties to collaborate before they can censor successfully. (Only a small subset of parties needs to be trusted not to collaborate, and any subset of that size will do.)	Reduce the number of people that must be trusted.
Parties may censor your document by making it appear as if you updated your document when you did not.	Publish your document in a way that it cannot be updated, or publish your document in a way that requires a large number of parties to collaborate before they can make it appear that you updated your document. (Only a small subset of parties needs to be trusted not to collaborate, and any subset of that size will do.)	Reduce the number of people that must be trusted.
Publishers may flood disks with bogus content as part of a denial of service attack.	Impose limits or quotas on publishers; require publishers to pay for space with money, computation, space donations; establish a reputation system for publishers.	Reduce risk; look for positive reputations.

Risk	Solution	Trust principle
Censors may use laws to try to force documents to be deleted.	Publish your document in a way that requires a large number of parties to collaborate before they can censor successfully. (Only a small subset of parties needs to be trusted not to collaborate, and any subset of that size will do.)	Reduce the number of people that must be trusted.
Censors may threaten publishers to get them to delete their own documents.	Publish your document in a way that even the publisher cannot delete it.	Reduce risk, and reduce the number of people that must be trusted.

Conclusions

In this chapter we have presented an overview of the areas where trust plays a role in distributed file-sharing systems, and we have described some of the methods that can be used to increase trust in these systems. By signing software they make available for download, authors can provide some assurance that their code hasn't been tampered with and facilitate the building of a reputation associated with their name and key. Anonymity tools and tools for establishing secure channels can reduce the need to trust ISPs and other intermediaries not to record or alter information sent over the Internet. Quota systems, CPU payment systems, and e-cash payment systems can reduce the risk of denial of service attacks. Search engines can help facilitate dissemination of files but can introduce additional trust issues.

There are several open issues. The first is the lack of existence of a global Public Key Infrastructure (PKI). Many people believe that such a PKI is not ever going to be possible. This has ramifications for trust, because it implies that people may never be able to trust signed code unless they have a direct relationship with the signer. While the problem of trusting strangers exists on the Net, strangely, it is also very difficult to truly be anonymous on the Internet. There are so many ways to trace people and correlate their online activity that the sense of anonymity that most people feel online is misplaced. Thus, there are two extremes of identity: both complete assurance of identity and total anonymity are very difficult to achieve. More research is needed to see how far from the middle we can push in both directions, because each extreme offers possibilities for increased trust in cyberspace.

chapter sixteen

Accountability

Roger Dingledine, Reputation Technologies, Inc., Michael J. Freedman, MIT, and David Molnar, Harvard University

One year after its meteoric rise to fame, Napster faces a host of problems. The best known of these problems is the lawsuit filed by the Recording Industry Association of America against Napster, Inc. Close behind is the decision by several major universities, including Yale, the University of Southern California, and Indiana University, to ban Napster traffic on their systems, thus depriving the Napster network of some of its highest-bandwidth music servers. The most popular perception is that universities are blocking Napster access out of fear of lawsuit. But there is another reason.

Napster users eat up large and unbounded amounts of bandwidth. By default, when a Napster client is installed, it configures the host computer to serve MP3s to as many other Napster clients as possible. University users, who tend to have faster connections than most others, are particularly effective servers. In the process, however, they can generate enough traffic to saturate a network. It was this reason that Harvard University cited when deciding to allow Napster, yet limit its bandwidth use.

Gnutella, the distributed replacement for Napster, is even worse: not only do downloads require large amounts of bandwidth, but searches require broadcasting to a set of neighboring Gnutella nodes, which in turn forward the request to other nodes. While the broadcast does not send the request to the entire Gnutella network, it still requires bandwidth for each of the many computers queried.

As universities limit Napster bandwidth or shut it off entirely due to bandwidth usage, the utility of the Napster network degrades. As the Gnutella network grows, searching and retrieving items becomes more cumbersome. Each service threatens to dig its own grave—and for reasons independent of the legality of trading MP3s. Instead, the problem is *resource allocation*.

Problems in resource allocation come up constantly in offering computer services. Traditionally they have been solved by making users *accountable* for their use of resources. Such accountability in distributed or peer-to-peer systems requires planning and discipline.

Traditional filesystems and communication mediums use accountability to maintain centralized control over their respective resources—in fact, the resources allocated to users are commonly managed by "user accounts." Filesystems use quotas to restrict the amount of data that users may store on the systems. ISPs measure the bandwidth their clients are using—such as the traffic generated from a hosted web site—and charge some monetary fee proportional to this amount.

Without these controls, each user has an incentive to squeeze all the value out of the resource in order to maximize personal gain. If one user has this incentive, so do all the users.

Biologist Garrett Hardin labeled this economic plight the "tragedy of the commons."[*] The "commons" (originally a grazing area in the middle of a village) is any resource shared by a group of people: it includes the air we breathe, the water we drink, land for farming and grazing, and fish from the sea. The tragedy of the commons is that a commonly owned resource will be overused until it is degraded, as all agents pursue self-interest first. Freedom in a commons brings ruin to all; in the end, the resource is exhausted.

We can describe the problem by further borrowing from economics and political science. Mancur Olson explained the problem of collective actions and public goods as follows:

> "[U]nless the number of individuals in a group is quite small, or unless there is coercion or some other special device to make individuals act in their common interest, rational, self-interested individuals will not act to achieve their common or group interests.[†]

The usual solution for commons problems is to assign ownership to the resource. This ownership allows a party to profit from the resource, thus providing the incentive to care for it. Most real-world systems take this approach with a fee-for-service business model.

---

[*] Garrett Hardin (1968), "The Tragedy of the Commons," *Science* 162, pp. 1243–1248.

[†] Mancur Olson (1982), "The Logic of Collective Action." In Brian Barry and Russell Hardin, eds., *Rational Man and Irrational Society*. Beverly Hills, CA: Sage, p. 44.

Decentralized peer-to-peer systems have similar resource allocation and protection requirements. The total storage or bandwidth provided by the sum of all peers is still finite. Systems need to protect against two main areas of attack:

Denial of service (DoS) attacks

Overload a system's bandwidth or processing ability, causing the loss of service of a particular network service or all network connectivity. For example, a web site accessed millions of times may show "503" unavailability messages or temporarily refuse connections.

Storage flooding attacks

Exploit a system by storing a disproportionally large amount of data so that no more space is available for other users.

As the Napster and Gnutella examples show, attacks need not be malicious. System administrators must be prepared for normal peaks in activity, accidental misuse, and the intentional exploitation of weaknesses by adversaries. Most computers that offer services on a network share these kinds of threats.

Without a way to protect against the tragedy of the commons, collaborative networking rests on shaky ground. Peers can abuse the protocol and rules of the system in any number of ways, such as the following:

- Providing corrupted or low-quality information
- Reneging on promises to store data
- Going down during periods when they are needed
- Claiming falsely that other peers have abused the system in these ways

These problems must be addressed before peer-to-peer systems can achieve lasting success. Through the use of various accountability measures, peer-to-peer systems—including systems that offer protection for anonymity—may continue to expand as overlay networks through the existing Internet.

This chapter focuses on types of accountability that collaborative systems can use to protect against resource allocation attacks. The problem of accountability is usually broken into two parts:

Restricting access

Each computer system tries to limit its users to a certain number of connections, a certain quantity of data that can be uploaded or downloaded, and so on. We will describe the technologies for doing this that are commonly called *micropayments*, a useful term even though at first it can be misleading. (They don't necessarily have to involve an exchange of money, or even of computer resources.)

Selecting favored users

This is normally done through maintaining a *reputation* for each user the system communicates with. Users with low reputations are allowed fewer resources, or they are mistrusted and find their transactions are rejected.

The two parts of the solution apply in different ways but work together to create accountability. In other words, a computer system that is capable of restricting access can then use a reputation system to grant favored access to users with good reputations.

The difficulty of accountability

In simple distributed systems, rudimentary accountability measures are often sufficient. If the list of peers is generally static and all are known to each other by hostname or address, misbehavior on anyone's part leads to a permanent bad reputation. Furthermore, if the operators of a system are known, preexisting mechanisms such as legal contracts help ensure that systems abide by protocol.

In the real world, these two social forces—reputation and law—have provided an impetus for fair trade for centuries. Since the earliest days of commerce, buyers and merchants have known each others' identities, at first through the immediacy of face-to-face contact, and later through postal mail and telephone conversations. This knowledge has allowed them to research the past histories of their trading partners and to seek legal reprisal when deals go bad. Much of today's e-commerce uses a similar authentication model: clients (both consumers and businesses) purchase items and services from known sources over the Internet and the World Wide Web. These sources are uniquely identified by digital certificates, registered trademarks, and other addressing mechanisms.

Peer-to-peer technology removes central control of such resources as communication, file storage and retrieval, and computation. Therefore, the traditional mechanisms for ensuring proper behavior can no longer provide the same level of protection.

Special problems posed by peer-to-peer systems

Peer-to-peer systems have to treat identity in special ways for several reasons:

- The technology makes it harder to uniquely and permanently identify peers and their operators. Connections and network maps might be transient. Peers might be able to join and leave the system. Participants in the system might wish to hide personal identifying information.

- Even if users have an identifying handle on the peer they're dealing with, they have no idea who the peer is and no good way to assess its history or predict its performance.

- Individuals running peer-to-peer services are rarely bound by contracts, and the cost and time delay of legal enforcement would generally outweigh their possible benefit.

We choose to deal with these problems—rather than give up and force everyone on to a centralized system with strong user identification—to pursue two valuable goals on the Internet: privacy and dynamic participation.

Privacy is a powerfully appealing goal in distributed systems, as discussed in Chapter 12, *Free Haven*. The design of many such systems features privacy protection for people offering and retrieving files.

Privacy for people offering files requires a mechanism for inserting and retrieving documents either anonymously or pseudonymously.* Privacy for people retrieving files requires a means to communicate—via email, Telnet, FTP, IRC, a web client, etc.—while not divulging any information that could link the user to his or her real-world persona.†

Dynamic participation has both philosophical and practical advantages. The Internet's loosely connected structure and explosive growth suggest that any peer-to-peer system must be similarly flexible and dynamic in order to be scalable and sustain long-term use. Similarly, the importance of ad hoc networks will probably increase in the near future as wireless connections get cheaper and more ubiquitous. A peer-to-peer system should therefore let peers join and leave smoothly, without impacting functionality. This design also decreases the risk of systemwide compromise as more peers join the system. (It helps if servers run a

---

* A pseudonymous identity allows other participants to link together some or all the activities a person does on the system, without being able to determine who the person is in real life. Pseudonymity is explored later in this chapter and in Chapter 12.

† In retrospect, the Internet appears not to be an ideal medium for anonymous communication and publishing. Internet services and protocols make both passive sniffing and active attack too easy. For instance, email headers include the routing paths of email messages, including DNS hostnames and IP addresses. Web browsers normally display user IP addresses; cookies on a client's browser may be used to store persistent user information. Commonly used online chat applications such as ICQ and Instant Messenger also divulge IP addresses. Network cards in promiscuous mode can read all data flowing through the local Ethernet. With all these possibilities, telephony or dedicated lines might be better suited for this goal of privacy protection. However, the ubiquitous nature of the Internet has made it the only practical consideration for digital transactions across a wide area, like the applications discussed in this book.

variety of operating systems and tools, so that a single exploit cannot compromise most of the servers at once.)

Peer-to-peer models and their impacts on accountability

There are many different models for peer-to-peer systems. As the systems become more dynamic and diverge from real-world notions of identity, it becomes more difficult to achieve accountability and protect against attacks on resources.

The simplest type of peer-to-peer system has two main characteristics. First, it contains a fairly static list of servers; additions and deletions are rare and may require manual intervention. Second, the identities of the servers (and to some extent their human operators) are known, generally by DNS hostname or static IP host address. Since the operators can be found, they may have a legal responsibility or economic incentive—leveraged by the power of reputation—to fulfill the protocols according to expectation.

An example of such a peer-to-peer system is the Mixmaster remailer. A summary of the system appears in Chapter 7, *Mixmaster Remailers*. The original Mixmaster client software was developed by Lance Cottrell and released in 1995.[*] Currently, the software runs on about 30 remailer nodes, whose locations are published to the newsgroup *alt.privacy.anon-server* and at web sites such as *http://efga.org*.[†] The software itself can be found at *http://mixmaster.anonymizer. com*.

Remailer nodes are known by hostname and remain generally fixed. While anybody can start running a remailer, the operator needs to spread information about her new node to web pages that publicize node statistics, using an out-of-band channel (meaning that something outside the Mixmaster system must be used—most of the time, manually sent email). The location of the new node is then manually added to each client's software configuration files. This process of manually adding new nodes leads to a system that remains generally static. Indeed, that's why there are so few Mixmaster nodes.

A slightly more complicated type of peer-to-peer system still has identified operators but is dynamic in terms of members. That is, the protocol itself has support for adding and removing participating servers. One example of such a system is

---

[*] Lance Cottrell (1995) "Mixmaster and Remailer Attacks," *http://www.obscura.com/~loki/ remailer/remailer-essay.html*.

[†] "Electronic Frontiers Georgia List of Public Mixmaster Remailers," *http://anon.efga.org/ Remailers*.

Gnutella. It has good support for new users (which are also servers) joining and leaving the system, but at the same time, the identity and location of each of these servers is generally known through the hosts list, which advertises existing hosts to new ones that wish to join the network. These sorts of systems can be very effective, because they're generally easy to deploy (there's no need to provide any real protection against people trying to learn the identity of other participants), while at the same time they allow many users to freely join the system and donate their resources.

Farther still along the scale of difficulty lie peer-to-peer systems that have dynamic participants and pseudonymous servers. In these systems, the actual servers that store files or proxy communication live within a digital fog that conceals their geographic locations and other identifying features. Thus, the mapping of pseudonym to real-world identity is not known. A given pseudonym may be pegged with negative attributes, but a user can just create a new pseudonym or manage several at once. Since a given server can simply disappear at any time and reappear as a completely new entity, these sorts of designs require a micropayment system or reputation system to provide accountability on the server end. An example of a system in this category is the Free Haven design: each server can be contacted via a remailer reply block and a public key, but no other identifying features are available.

The final peer-to-peer model on this scale is a dynamic system with fully anonymous operators. A server that is fully anonymous lacks even the level of temporary identity provided by a pseudonymous system like Free Haven. Since an anonymous peer's history is by definition unknown, all decisions in an anonymous system must be based only on the information made available during each protocol operation. In this case, peers cannot use a reputation system, since there is no real opportunity to establish a profile on any server. This leaves a micropayment system as the only reasonable way to establish accountability. On the other hand, because the servers themselves have no long-term identities, this may limit the number of services or operations such a system could provide. For instance, such a system would have difficulty offering long-term file storage and backup services.

Purposes of micropayments and reputation systems

The main goal of accountability is to maximize a server's *utility* to the overall system while minimizing its potential *threat*. There are two ways to minimize the threat.

- One approach is to limit our risk (in bandwidth used, disk space lost, or whatever) to an amount roughly equivalent to our benefit from the transaction. This suggests the fee-for-service or micropayment model mentioned at the beginning of the chapter.

- The other approach is to make our risk proportional to our trust in the other parties. This calls for a reputation system.

In the micropayment model, a server makes decisions based on fairly immediate information. Payments and the value of services are generally kept small, so that a server only gambles some small amount of lost resources for any single exchange. If both parties are satisfied with the result, they can continue with successive exchanges. Therefore, parties require little prior information about each other for this model, as the risk is small at any one time. As we will see later in this chapter, where we discuss real or existing micropayment systems, the notion of payment might not involve any actual currency or cash.

In the reputation model, for each exchange a server risks some amount of resources proportional to its trust that the result will be satisfactory. As a server's reputation grows, other nodes become more willing to make larger payments to it. The micropayment approach of small, successive exchanges is no longer necessary.

Reputation systems require careful development, however, if the system allows impermanent and pseudonymous identities. If an adversary can gain positive attributes too easily and establish a good reputation, she can damage the system. Worse, she may be able to "pseudospoof," or establish many seemingly distinct identities that all secretly collaborate with each other.

Conversely, if a well-intentioned server can incur negative points easily from short-lived operational problems, it can lose reputation too quickly. (This is the attitude feared by every system administrator: "Their web site happened to be down when I visited, so I'll never go there again.") The system would lose the utility offered by these "good" servers.

As we will see later in this chapter, complicated protocols and calculations are required for both micropayments and reputation systems. Several promising micropayment systems are in operation, while research on reputation systems is relatively young. These fields need to develop ways of checking the information being transferred, efficient tests for distributed computations, and, more broadly, some general algorithms to verify behavior of decentralized systems.

There is a third way to handle the accountability problem: ignore the issue and engineer the system simply to survive some faulty servers. Instead of spending time on ensuring that servers fulfill their function, leverage the vast resources of the Internet for redundancy and mirroring. We might not know, or have any way to find out, if a server is behaving according to protocol (i.e., whether that server is storing files and responding to file queries, forwarding email or other communications upon demand, and correctly computing values or analyzing data). Instead, if we replicate the file or functionality through the system, we can ensure that the system works correctly with high probability, despite misbehaving components. This is the model used by Napster, along with some of the systems discussed in this book, such as Freenet and Gnutella.

In general, the popular peer-to-peer systems take a wide variety of approaches to solving the accountability problem. For instance, consider the following examples:

- Freenet dumps unpopular data on the floor, so people flooding the system with unpopular data are ultimately ignored. Popular data is cached near the requester, so repeated requests won't traverse long sections of the network.

- Gnutella doesn't "publish" documents anywhere except on the publisher's computer, so there's no way to flood other systems. (This has a great impact on the level of anonymity actually offered.)

- Publius limits the submission size to 100K. (It remains to be seen how successful this will be; they recognize it as a problem.)

- Mojo Nation uses micropayments for all peer-to-peer exchanges.

- Free Haven requires publishers to provide reliable space of their own if they want to insert documents into the system. This economy of reputation tries to ensure that people donate to the system in proportion to how much space they use.

Junk mail as a resource allocation problem

The familiar problem of junk email (known more formally as *unsolicited commercial email*, and popularly as *spam*) yields some subtle insights into resource allocation and accountability. Junk mail abuses the unmetered nature of email and of Internet bandwidth in general. Even if junk email achieves only an extremely small success rate, the sender is still successful because the cost of sending each message is essentially zero.

Spam wastes both global and individual resources. On a broad scale, it congests the Internet, wasting bandwidth and server CPU cycles. On a more personal level, filtering and deleting spam can waste an individual's time (which, collectively, can represent significant person-hours). Users also may be faced with metered connection charges, although recent years have seen a trend toward unmetered service and always-on access.

Even though the motivations for junk email might be economic, not malicious, senders who engage in such behavior play a destructive role in "hogging" resources. This is a clear example of the tragedy of the commons.

Just as some environmental activists suggest curbing pollution by making consumers pay the "real costs" of the manufacturing processes that cause pollution, some Internet developers are considering ways of stopping junk email by placing a tiny burden on each email sent, thus forcing the sender to balance the costs of bulk email against the benefits of responses. The burden need not be a direct financial levy; it could simply require the originator of the email to use significant resources. The cost of an email message should be so small that it wouldn't bother any individual trying to reach another; it should be just high enough to make junk email unprofitable. We'll examine such micropayment schemes later in this chapter.

We don't have to change the infrastructure of the Internet to see a benefit from email micropayments. Individuals can adopt personal requirements as recipients. But realistically, individual, nonstandard practices will merely reduce the usability of email. Although individuals adopting a micropayment scheme may no longer be targeted, the scheme would make it hard for them to establish relationships with other Internet users, while junk emailers would continue to fight over the commons.

Pseudonymity and its consequences

Many, if not most, of the services on the Internet today do not deal directly with legal identities. Instead, web sites and chat rooms ask their users to create a *handle* or *pseudonym* by which they are known while using that system. These systems should be distinguished from those that are fully anonymous; in a fully anonymous system, there is no way to refer to the other members of the system.

Problems with pseudospoofing and possible defenses

The most important difficulty caused by pseudonymity is *pseudospoofing*. A term first coined by L. Detweiler on the Cypherpunks mailing list, pseudospoofing means that one person creates and controls many phony identities at once. This is a particularly bad loophole in reputation systems that blithely accept input from just any user, like current web auction sites. An untrustworthy person can pseudospoof to return to the system after earning a bad reputation, and he can even create an entire tribe of accounts that pat each other on the back. Pseudospoofing is a major problem inherent in pseudonymous systems.

Lots of systems fail in the presence of pseudospoofing. Web polls are one example; even if a web site requires registration, it's easy for someone to simply register and then vote 10, 15, or 1,500 times. Another example is a free web hosting site, such as GeoCities, which must take care to avoid someone registering under six or seven different names to obtain extra web space.

Pseudospoofing is hard in the real world, so most of us don't think about it. After all, in the real world, changing one's appearance and obtaining new identities is relatively rare, spy movies to the contrary. When we come online, we bring with us the assumptions built up over a lifetime of dealing with people who can be counted on to be the "same person" next time we meet them. Pseudospoofing works, and works so well, because these assumptions are *completely unjustified online*. As shown by the research of psychologist Sherry Turkle and others, multiple identities are common in online communities.

So what can we do about pseudospoofing? Several possibilities present themselves:

- Abandon pseudonymous systems entirely. Require participants in a peer-to-peer system to prove conclusively who they are. This is the direction taken by most work on Public Key Infrastructures (PKIs), which try to tie each online users to some legal identity. Indeed, VeriSign used to refer to its digital certificates as "driver's licenses for the information superhighway."

  This approach has a strong appeal. After all, why should people be allowed to "hide" behind a pseudonym? And how can we possibly have accountability without someone's real identity?

  Unfortunately, this approach is unnecessary, unworkable, and in some cases undesirable. It's unnecessary for at least three reasons:

  — Identity does not imply accountability. For example, if a misbehaving user is in a completely different jurisdiction, other users may know exactly who he or she is and yet be unable to do anything about it. Even if they are in the same jurisdiction, the behavior may be perfectly legal, just not very nice.

  — Accountability is possible even in pseudonymous systems. This point will be developed at length in the rest of this chapter.

  — The problem with pseudospoofing is not that someone acts under a "fake" name, but that someone acts under more than one name. If we could somehow build a system that ensured that every pseudonym was controlled by a distinct person, a reputation system could handle the problem.

Furthermore, absolute authentication is unworkable because it requires verifying the legal identities of all participants. On today's Internet, this is a daunting proposition. VeriSign and other PKI companies are making progress in issuing their "digital driver's licenses," but we are a far cry from that end. In addition, one then has to trust that the legal identities have not themselves been fabricated. Verification can be expensive and leaves a system that relies on it open to attack if it fails.

Finally, this proposed solution is undesirable because it excludes users who either cannot or will not participate. International users of a system may not have the same ways of verifying legal identity. Other users may have privacy concerns.

- Allow pseudonyms, but ensure that all participants are distinct entities. This is all that is strictly necessary to prevent pseudospoofing. Unfortunately, it tends to be not much easier than asking for everyone's legal identity.

- Monitor user behavior for evidence of pseudospoofing. Remove or "expose" accounts that seem to be controlled by the same person. The effectiveness of this approach varies widely with the application. It also raises privacy concerns for users.

- Make pseudospoofing unprofitable. Give new accounts in a system little or no resources until they can prove themselves by doing something for the system. Make it so expensive for an adversary to prove itself multiple times that it has no inclination to pseudospoof. This is the approach taken by the Free Haven project, which deals with new servers by asking them to donate resources to the good of the system as a whole.

All of these alternatives are just rules of thumb. Each of them might help us combat the problems of pseudospoofing, but it's hard to reach a conclusive solution. We'll return to possible technical solutions later in this chapter when we describe the Advogato system.

Reputation for sale—SOLD!

Pseudonymous systems are based on the assumption that each pseudonym is controlled by the same entity for the duration of the system. That is, the adversary's pseudonyms stay controlled by the adversary, and the good guys' pseudonyms stay controlled by the good guys.

What happens if the adversary takes control of someone who already has a huge amount of trust or resources in the system? Allowing accounts to change hands can lead to some surprising situations.

The most prevalent example of this phenomenon comes in online multiplayer games. One of the best-known such games is Ultima Online. Players gallivant around the world of Brittania, completing quests, fighting foes, and traipsing around dungeons, in the process accumulating massive quantities of loot. Over the course of many, many hours, a player can go from a nobody to the lord and master of his own castle. Then he can sell it all to someone else.

Simply by giving up his username and password, an Ultima Online player can transfer ownership of his account to someone else. The new owner obtains all the land and loot that belonged to the old player. More importantly, she obtains the reputation built up by the old player. The transfer can be carried out independently of the game; no one need ever know that it happened. As far as anyone else knows, the game personality is the same person. Until the new owner does something "out of character," or until the news spreads somehow, there is no way to tell that a transfer has occurred.

This has led to a sort of cottage industry in trading game identities for cash online. Ultima Online game identities, or "avatars," can be found on auction at eBay. Other multiplayer online games admit the occurrence of similar transactions. Game administrators can try to forbid selling avatars, but as long as it's just a matter of giving up a username and password, it will be an uphill battle.

The point of this example is that reputations and identities do not bind as tightly to people online as they do in the physical world. Reputations can be sold or stolen with a single password. While people can be coerced or "turned" in the physical world, it's much harder. Once again, the assumptions formed in the physical world turn out to be misleading online.

One way of dealing with this problem is to embed an important piece of information, such as a credit card number, into the password for an account. Then revealing the password reveals the original user's credit card number as well, creating a powerful incentive not to trade away the password. The problem is that if the password is ever accidentally compromised, the user now loses not just the use of his or her account, but the use of a credit card as well.

Another response is to make each password valid only for a certain number of logins; to get a new password, the user must prove that he is the same person who applied for the previous password. This does not stop trading passwords, however—it just means the "original" user must hang around to renew the password each time it expires.

Common methods for dealing with flooding and DoS attacks

We've seen some examples of resource allocation problems and denial of service attacks. These problems have been around for a long while in various forms, and there are several widespread strategies for dealing with them. We'll examine them in this section to show that even the most common strategies are subject to attack—and such attacks can be particularly devastating to peer-to-peer systems.

Caching and mirroring

One of the simplest ways to maintain data availability is to mirror it. Instead of hosting data on one machine, host it on several. When one machine becomes congested or goes down, the rest are still available. Popular software distributions like the Perl archive CPAN and the GNU system have a network of mirror sites, often spread across the globe to be convenient to several different nations at once.

Another common technique is caching: If certain data is requested very often, save it in a place that is closer to the requester. Web browsers themselves cache recently visited pages.

Simple to understand and straightforward to implement, caching and mirroring are often enough to withstand normal usage loads. Unfortunately, an adversary bent on a denial of service attack can target mirrors one by one until all are dead.

Active caching and mirroring

Simple mirroring is easy to do, but it also has drawbacks. Users must know where mirror sites are and decide for themselves which mirror to use. This is more hassle for users and inefficient to boot, as users do not generally know their networks well enough to pick the fastest web site. In addition, users have little idea of how loaded a particular mirror is; if many users suddenly decide to visit the same mirror, they may all receive worse connections than if they had been evenly distributed across mirror sites.

In 1999, Akamai Technologies became an overnight success with a service that could be called active mirroring. Web sites redirect their users to use special "Akamaized" URLs. These URLs contain information used by Akamai to dynamically direct the user to a farm of Akamai web servers that is close to the user on the network. As the network load and server loads change, Akamai can switch users to the best server farm of the moment.

For peer-to-peer systems, an example of active caching comes in the Freenet system for file retrieval. In Freenet, file requests are directed to a particular server, but this server is in touch with several other servers. If the initial server has the data, it simply returns the data. Otherwise, it forwards the request to a neighboring server which it believes more capable of answering the request, and keeps a record of the original requester's address. The neighboring server does the same thing, creating a chain of servers. Eventually the request reaches a server that has the data, or it times out. If the request reaches a server that has the data, the server sends the data back through the chain to the original requester. Every server in the chain, in addition, caches a copy of the requested data. This way, the next time the data is requested, the chance that the request will quickly hit a server with the data is increased.

Active caching and mirroring offer more protection than ordinary caching and mirroring against the "Slashdot effect" and flooding attacks. On the other hand, systems using these techniques then need to consider how an adversary could take advantage of them. For instance, is it possible for an adversary to fool Akamai into thinking a particular server farm is better- or worse-situated than it actually is? Can particular farms be targeted for denial of service attacks? In Freenet, what happens if the adversary spends all day long requesting copies of the complete movie *Lawrence of Arabia* and thus loads up all the local servers to the point where they have no room for data wanted by other people? These questions can be answered, but they require thought and attention.

For specific answers on a specific system, we might be able to answer these questions through a performance and security analysis. For instance, Chapter 14, *Performance*, uses Freenet and Gnutella as models for performance analysis. Here, we can note two general points about how active caching reacts to adversaries.

First, if the cache chooses to discard data according to which data was least recently used, the cache is vulnerable to an active attack. An adversary can simply start shoving material into the cache until it displaces anything already there. In particular, an adversary can simply request that random bits be cached. Active caching systems whose availability is important to their users should have some way of addressing this problem.

Next, guaranteeing service in an actively cached system with multiple users on the same cache is tricky. Different usage patterns fragment the cache and cause it to be less useful to any particular set of users. The situation becomes more difficult when adversaries enter the picture: by disrupting cache coherency on many different caches, an adversary may potentially wreak more havoc than by mounting a denial of service attack on a single server.

One method for addressing both these problems is to shunt users to caches based on their observed behavior. This is a radical step forward from a simple least-recently-used heuristic. By using past behavior to predict future results, a cache has the potential to work more efficiently. This past behavior can be considered a special kind of reputation, a topic we'll cover in general later in this chapter.

But systems can also handle resource allocation using simpler and relatively well tested methods involving micropayments. In the next section, we'll examine some of them closely.

Micropayment schemes

Accountability measures based on micropayments require that each party offer something of value in an exchange. Consider Alice and Bob, both servers in a peer-to-peer system that involves file sharing or publishing. Alice may be inserting a document into the system and want Bob to store it for her. Alternatively, Alice may want Bob to anonymously forward some email or real-time Internet protocol message for her. In either case, Alice seeks some resource commodity—storage and bandwidth, respectively—from Bob. In exchange, Bob asks for a micropayment from Alice to protect his resources from overuse.

There are two main flavors of micropayments schemes. Schemes of the first type do not offer Bob any real redeemable value; their goal is simply to slow Alice down when she requests resources from Bob. She pays with a *proof of work* (POW), showing that she performed some computationally difficult problem. These payments are called *nonfungible*, because Bob cannot turn around and use them to pay someone else. With the second type of scheme, *fungible* micropayments, Bob receives a payment that holds some intrinsic or redeemable value. The second type of payment is commonly known as digital cash. Both of these schemes may be used to protect against resource allocation attacks.

POWs can prevent communication denial of service attacks. Bob may require someone who wishes to connect to submit a POW before he allocates any nontrivial resources to communication. In a more sophisticated system, he may start charging only if he detects a possible DoS attack. Likewise, if Bob charges to store data, an attacker needs to pay some (prohibitively) large amount to flood Bob's disk space. Still, POWs are not a perfect defense against an attacker with a lot of CPU capacity; such an attacker could generate enough POWs to flood Bob with connection requests or data.

Varieties of micropayments or digital cash

The difference between micropayments and digital cash is a semantic one. The term "micropayment" has generally been used to describe schemes using small-value individual payments. Usually, Alice will send a micropayment for some small, incremental use of a resource instead of a single large digital cash "macro-payment" for, say, a month's worth of service. We'll continue to use the commonly accepted phrase "micropayment" in this chapter without formally differentiating between the two types, but we'll describe some common designs for each type.

Digital cash may be either anonymous or identified. Anonymous schemes do not reveal Alice's identity to Bob or the bank providing the cash, while identified spending schemes expose her information. Hybrid approaches can be taken: Alice might remain anonymous to Bob but not to the bank or anonymous to everybody yet traceable. The latter system is a kind of pseudonymity; the bank or recipient might be able to relate a sequence of purchases, but not link them to an identity.

No matter the flavor of payment—nonfungible, fungible, anonymous, identified, large, or small—we want to ensure that a malicious user can't commit forgery or spend the same coin more than once without getting caught. A system of small micropayments might not worry about forgeries of individual micropayments, but it would have to take steps to stop large-scale, multiple forgeries.

Schemes identifying the spender are the digital equivalent of debit or credit cards. Alice sends a "promise of payment" that will be honored by her bank or financial institution. Forgery is not much of a problem here because, as with a real debit card, the bank ensures that Alice has enough funds in her account to complete the payment and transfers the specified amount to Bob. Unfortunately, though, the bank has knowledge of all of Alice's transactions.

Anonymous schemes take a different approach and are the digital equivalent of real cash. The electronic coin itself is worth some dollar amount. If Alice loses the coin, she's lost the money. If Alice manages to pay both Bob and Charlie with the same coin and not get caught, she's successfully double-spent the coin.

In the real world, government mints use special paper, microprinting, holograms, and other technologies to prevent forgery. In a digital medium, duplication is easy: just copy the bits! We need to find alternative methods to prevent this type of fraud. Often, this involves looking up the coin in a database of spent coins. Bob might have a currency unique to him, so that the same coin couldn't be used to pay Charlie. Or coins might be payee-independent, and Bob would need to verify with the coin's issuing "mint" that it has not already been spent with Charlie.

With this description of micropayments and digital cash in mind, let's consider various schemes.

Nonfungible micropayments

Proofs of work were first advocated by Cynthia Dwork and Moni Naor[*] in 1992 as "pricing via processing" to handle resource allocation requests.

The premise is to make a user compute a moderately hard, but not intractable, computation problem before gaining access to some resource. It takes a long time to solve the problem but only a short time to verify that the user found the right solution. Therefore, Alice must perform a significantly greater amount of computational work to solve the problem than Bob has to perform to verify that she did it.

Dwork and Naor offer their system specifically as a way to combat electronic junk mail. As such, it can impose a kind of accountability within a distributed system.

To make this system work, a recipient refuses to receive email unless a POW is attached to each message. The POW is calculated using the address of the recipient and must therefore be generated specifically for the recipient by the sender. These POWs serve as a form of electronic postage stamp, and the way the recipient's address is included makes it trivial for the recipient to determine whether the POW is malformed. Also, a simple lookup in a local database can be used to check whether the POW has been spent before.

The computational problem takes some amount of time proportional to the time needed to write the email and small enough that its cost is negligible for an individual user or a mail distribution list. Only unsolicited bulk mailings would spend a large amount of computation cycles to generate the necessary POWs.

Recipients can also agree with individual users or mail distribution lists to use an access control list ("frequent correspondent list") so that some messages do not

---

[*] Cynthia Dwork and Moni Naor (1993), "Pricing via Processing or Combating Junk Mail," in Ernest F. Brickell, ed., *Advances in Cryptology— Crypto '92*, vol. 740 of *Lecture Notes in Computer Science*, pp. 139–147. Springer-Verlag, 16–20 August 1992.

require a POW. These techniques are useful for social efficiency: if private correspondence instead costs some actual usage fee, users may be less likely to send email that would otherwise be beneficial, and the high bandwidth of the electronic medium may be underutilized.

Dwork and Naor additionally introduced the idea of a POW with a trap door: A function that is moderately hard to compute without knowledge of some secret, but easy to compute given this secret. Therefore, central authorities could easily generate postage to sell for prespecified destinations.

Extended types of nonfungible micropayments

Hash cash, designed by Adam Back in late 1997,[*] is an alternative micropayment scheme that is also based on POWs. Here, Bob calculates a *hash* or *digest*, a number that can be generated easily from a secret input, but that cannot be used to guess the secret input. (See Chapter 15, *Trust*.) Bob then asks Alice to guess the input through a brute-force calculation; he can set how much time Alice has to "pay" by specifying how many bits she must guess. Typical hashes used for security are 128 bits or 160 bits in size. Finding another input that will produce the entire hash (which is called a "collision") requires a prohibitive amount of time.

Instead, Bob requires Alice to produce a number for which some of the low-order bits match those of the hash. If we call this number of bits k, Bob can set a very small k to require a small payment or a larger k to require a larger payment. Formally, this kind of problem is called a "k-bit partial hash collision."

For example, the probability of guessing a 17-bit collision is 2^{-17}; this problem takes approximately 65,000 tries on average. To give a benchmark for how efficient hash operations are, in one test, our Pentium-III 800 MHz machine performed approximately 312,000 hashes per second.

Hash cash protects against double-spending by using individual currencies. Bob generates his hash from an ID or name known to him alone. So the hash cash coins given to Bob must be specific to Bob, and he can immediately verify their validity against a local spent-coin database.

Another micropayment scheme based on partial hash collisions is *client puzzles*, suggested by researchers Ari Juels and John Brainard of RSA Labs.[†] Client

---

[*] Adam Back, "Hash Cash: A Partial Hash Collision Based Postage Scheme," *http://www. cypherspace.org/~adam/hashcash*.

[†] A. Juels and J. Brainard, "Client Puzzles: A Cryptographic Defense Against Connection Depletion Attacks," *NDSS '99*.

puzzles were introduced to provide a cryptographic countermeasure against connection depletion attacks, whereby an attacker exhausts a server's resources by making a large number of connection requests and leaving them unresolved.

When client puzzles are used, a server accepts connection requests as usual. However, when it suspects that it is under attack, marked by a significant rise in connection requests, it responds to requests by issuing each requestor a puzzle: A hard cryptographic problem based on the current time and on information specific to the server and client request.[*]

Like hash cash, client puzzles require that the client find some k-bit partial hash collisions. To decrease the chance that a client might just guess the puzzle, each puzzle could optionally be made up of multiple subpuzzles that the client must solve individually. Mathematically, a puzzle is a hash for which a client needs to find the corresponding input that would produce it.[†]

Nonparallelizable work functions

Both of the hash collision POW systems in the previous section can easily be solved in parallel. In other words, a group of n machines can solve each problem in $1/n$ the amount of time as a single machine. Historically, this situation is like the encryption challenges that were solved relatively quickly by dividing the work among thousands of users.

Parallel solutions may be acceptable from the point of view of accountability. After all, users still pay with the same expected amount of burnt CPU cycles, whether a single machine burns m cycles, or n machines burn m cycles collectively. But if the goal of nonfungible micropayments is to ensure public access to Bob's resources, parallelizable schemes are weak because they can be overwhelmed by distributed denial of service attacks.

Let's actually try to make Alice wait for a fixed period between two transactions, in order to better protect Bob's resources. Consider a "proof of time": we desire a client to spend some amount of time, as opposed to work, to solve a given problem. An example is MIT's LCS35 Time Capsule Crypto-Puzzle. The time cap-

---

[*] "RSA Laboratories Unveils Innovative Countermeasure to Recent 'Denial of Service' Hacker Attacks," press release, *http://www.rsasecurity.com/news/pr/000211.html*.

[†] For example, by breaking a puzzle into eight subpuzzles, you can increase the amount of average work required to solve the puzzle by the same amount as if you left the puzzle whole but increased the size by three bits. However, breaking up the puzzle is much better in terms of making it harder to guess. The chance of correctly guessing the subpuzzle version is 2^{-8k}, while the chance of guessing the larger single version is just $2^{-(k+3)}$, achieved by hashing randomly selected inputs to find a collision without performing a brute-force search.

sule, sealed in 1999, will be opened either after 35 years or when the supplied cryptographic problem is solved, whichever comes first. The problem is designed to foil any benefit of parallel or distributed computing. It can be solved only as quickly as the fastest single processor available.

Time-lock puzzles, such as the LCS35 time capsule, were first presented by Ron Rivest, Adi Shamir, and David Wagner.[*] These types of puzzles are designed to be "intrinsically" or "inherently" sequential in nature. The problem LCS35 used to compute is:

$$2^{2^t} \bmod n$$

where n is the product of two large primes p and q, and t can be arbitrarily chosen to set the difficulty of the puzzle. This puzzle can be solved only by performing t successive squares modulo n. There is no known way to speed up this calculation without knowing the factorization of n. The reason is the same reason conventional computer encryption is hard to break: there is no existing method for finding two primes when only their product is known.

It's worth noting in passing that the previous construction is not *proven* to be nonparallelizable. Besides the product-of-two-primes problem, its security rests on no one knowing how to perform the repeated modular squaring in parallel. This problem is tied up with the "P vs. NC" problem in computational complexity theory and is outside the scope of this chapter. Similar to the better known "P vs. NP" problem, which concerns the question, "Which problems are easy?" the P vs. NC problem asks, "Which problems are parallelizable?"[†]

Fungible micropayments

All of the micropayment schemes we have previously described are nonfungible. While Alice pays Bob for resource use with some coin that represents a proof of work, he cannot redeem this token for something of value to him. While this micropayment helps prevent DoS and flooding attacks, there's no measure of "wealth" in the system. Bob has no economic incentive to engage in this exchange.

---

[*] Ronald L. Rivest, Adi Shamir, and David A. Wagner (1996), "Time-Lock Puzzles and Timed-Release Crypto."

[†] Historical note: NC stands for Nick's Class, named after Nicholas Pippenger, one of the first researchers to investigate such problems. For more information, see Raymond Greenlaw, H. James Hoover, and Walter L. Ruzzo (1995), *Limits to Parallel Computation: P-Completeness Theory*. Oxford University Press.

Nonfungible micropayments are better suited for ephemeral resources, like TCP connections, than they are for long-term resources like data storage. Consider an attacker who wants to make a distributed datastore unusable. If an attacker is trying to fill up a system's storage capacity and is allowed to store data for a long time, the effects of DoS attacks can be cumulative. This is because the attacker can buy more and more space on the system as time goes on.

If micropayments just use up CPU cycles and cannot be redeemed for something of value, an attacker can slowly nibble at resources, requesting a megabyte now and then as it performs enough work to pay for the space. This can continue, bit by bit, until the attacker controls a large percentage of the total. Furthermore, the victim is unable to use these payments in exchange for other peers' resources, or alternatively to purchase more resources.

Enter redeemable payments. This compensation motivates users to donate resources and fixes the cost for resources in a more stable way.

Freeloading

The history of the Internet records a number of users who have freely donated resources. The hacker ethos and the free software movement can be relied on to provide resources to an extent. Johan Helsingius ran the initial "anonymous" remailer—*anon.penet.fi*—for its own sake. The Cypherpunks (Type I) and Mixmaster (Type II) remailers for anonymous email are run and maintained for free from around the globe. Processing for SETI@home and Distributed.net is also performed without compensation, other than the possibility of fame for finding an alien signature or cracking a key.

Unfortunately, not everybody donates equally. It is tempting for a user to "let somebody else pay for it" and just reap the rewards.

Peer-to-peer systems may combat this effect by incorporating coercive measures into their design or deployment, ensuring that users actually donate resources. This is not a trivial problem. Napster provides a good example: users need to connect to Napster only when actually searching for MP3 files; otherwise they can remain offline. Furthermore, users are not forced to publicly share files, although downloaded files are placed in a public directory by default.

A fairly recent analysis of Gnutella traffic showed a lot of freeloading. One well-known study[*] found that almost 70% of users share no files, and nearly 50% of all responses are returned by the top 1% of sharing hosts.

---

[*] Eytan Adar and Bernardo A. Huberman, "Free Riding on Gnutella." Xerox Palo Alto Research Center, *http://www.parc.xerox.com/istl/groups/iea/papers/gnutella*.

Free Haven tackles this problem by attempting to ensure that users donate resources in amounts proportional to the resources they use. The system relies on accountability via reputation, which we discuss later. Mojo Nation, on the other hand, pays users Mojo—the system's private digital currency—for donated resources. Mojo has no meaning outside the system yet, but it can be leveraged for other system resources.

Fungible payments for accountability

Fungible micropayments are not used solely, or even largely, for economic incentives. Instead, they act as an accountability measure. Peers can't freeload in the system, as they can earn wealth only by making their own resources available (or by purchasing resource tokens via some other means). This is a more natural and more effective way to protect a system from flooding than proofs of work. In order to tie up resources protected by fungible payments, an adversary needs to donate a proportional amount of resources. The attempted denial of service becomes self-defeating.

If payments can actually be redeemed for real-world currencies, they provide yet another defense against resource misuse. It may still be true that powerful organizations (as opposed to a script-kiddie downloading DoS scripts from *http://rootshell.com*) can afford to pay enough money to flood a system. But now the victim can purchase additional physical disk space or bandwidth with the money earned. Since the prices of these computer resources drop weekly, the cost of successfully attacking the system increases with time.

Business arrangements, not technology, link digital cash to real-world currencies. Transactions can be visualized as foreign currency exchanges, because users need to convert an amount of money to digital cash before spending it. The Mark Twain Bank "issued" DigiCash eCash in the U.S. in the mid-1990s, joined by other banks in Switzerland, Germany, Austria, Finland, Norway, Australia, and Japan.* eCash can as easily be used for private currencies lacking real-world counterparts; indeed, Mojo is based on eCash technology (although without, in default form, the blinding operations that provide anonymity). The digital cash schemes we describe, therefore, can be used for both private and real-world currencies.

---

* "DigiCash Loses U.S. Toehold," CNET news article, *http://www.canada.cnet.com/news/0-1003-200-332852.html*.

Micropayment digital cash schemes

Ronald Rivest and Adi Shamir introduced two simple micropayment schemes, PayWord and MicroMint, in 1996.* PayWord is a credit-based scheme based on chains of paywords (hash values), while MicroMint represents coins by k-way hash function collisions. Both of these schemes follow the lightweight philosophy of micropayments: nickels and dimes don't matter. If a user loses a payment or is able to forge a few payments, we can ignore such trivialities. The security mechanisms in these schemes are not as strong nor expensive as the full macropayment digital cash schemes we will discuss later. At a rough estimate, hashing is about 100 times faster than RSA signature verification and about 10,000 times faster than RSA signature generation.

PayWord is designed for applications in which users engage in many repetitive micropayment transactions. Some examples are pay-per-use web sites and pay-per-minute online games or movies. PayWord relies on a broker (better known as a "bank" in many digital cash schemes), mainly for online verification, but seeks to minimize communication with the broker in order to make the system as efficient as possible.

It works like this. Alice establishes an account with a broker and is issued a digital certificate. When she communicates with vendor Bob for the first time each day, she computes and commits to a new payword chain w_1, w_2, ..., w_n. This chain is created by choosing some random w_n and moving backward to calculate each hash w_i from the hash w_{i+1}.

Alice starts her relationship with Bob by offering w_0. With each micropayment she moves up the chain from w_0 toward w_n. Just knowing w_0, vendor Bob can't compute any paywords and therefore can't make false claims to the broker. But Bob can easily verify the ith payment if he knows only w_{i-1}. Bob reports to the broker only once at the end of the day, offering the last (highest-indexed) micropayment and the corresponding w_0 received that day. The broker adjusts accounts accordingly.

As payword chains are both user- and vendor-specific, the vendor can immediately determine if the user attempts to double-spend a payword. Unfortunately, however, PayWord does not provide any transaction anonymity. As this is a credit-based system, the broker knows that Alice paid Bob.

---

* R. Rivest and A. Shamir (1997), "PayWord and MicroMint: Two Simple Micropayment Schemes," Lecture Notes in Computer Science, vol. 1189, *Proc. Security Protocols Workshop*, Springer-Verlag, pp. 69–87.

MicroMint takes the different approach of providing less security, but doing so at a very low cost for unrelated, low-value payments. Earlier, we described k-bit collisions, in which Alice found a value that matched the lowest k bits in Bob's hash. MicroMint coins are represented instead by full collisions: all the bits of the hashes have to be identical. A k-way collision is a set of distinct inputs (x_1, x_2, ..., x_k) that all map to the same digests. In other words, hash(x_1) = hash(x_2) = ... = hash(x_k). These collisions are hard to find, as the hash functions are specifically designed to be collision-free!*

The security in MicroMint rests in an economy of scale: minting individual coins is difficult, yet once some threshold of calculations has been performed, coins can be minted with accelerated ease. Therefore, the broker can mint coins cost-effectively, while small-scale forgers can produce coins only at a cost exceeding their value.

As in PayWord, the MicroMint broker knows both Alice, to whom the coins are issued, and vendor Bob. This system is therefore not anonymous, allowing the broker to catch Alice if she attempts to double-spend a coin.

PayWord and MicroMint are just two representative examples of micropayment schemes. Many others exist. The point to notice in both schemes is the extreme ease of verification and the small space requirements for each coin. Not only are these schemes fast, but they remain fast even in environments with severe resource constraints or at larger amounts of money.

Micropayment schemes such as these make it possible to extend peer-to-peer applications beyond the desktop and into embedded and mobile environments. Routers can use micropayments to retard denial of service attacks with minimal extra computation and then store the proceeds. Music players can act as mobile Napster or Gnutella servers, creating ad hoc local networks to exchange music stored in their memories (and possibly make money in the process). These possibilities are just beginning to be explored.

Making money off others' work

Proofs of work can be exchanged for other resources in a system, even without a systemwide digital cash scheme. The key is to make a POW scheme in which Bob can take a POW submitted by Alice and pass it on to Charlie without expending any significant calculation of his own.

---

* Given a hash function with an n-bit output (e.g., for SHA-1, n=160), we must hash approximately $2^{n(k-1)/k}$ random strings in order to find a k-way collision. This follows from the "birthday paradox" as explained in Rivest and Shamir, *ibid*.

This scheme was introduced by Markus Jakobsson and Ari Juels in 1999 as a *bread pudding protocol*.* Bread pudding is a dish that originated with the purpose of reusing stale bread. In a similar spirit, this protocol defines a POW that may be reused for a separate, useful, and verifiably correct computation. This computation is not restricted to any specific problem, although the authors further specify a simple bread pudding protocol for minting MicroMint coins.

In this variant on MicroMint's original minting scheme, the broker no longer has to generate each individual payment made by each user. Instead, a single, valid coin can be redistributed by users in the system to satisfy each others' POWs. The fundamental idea is to make clients solve partial hash collisions, similar to the concept of hash cash. This computation is useful only to the mint, which holds some necessary secret. With enough of these POWs, the minter can offload the majority of computations necessary to minting a coin.

Effectively, Bob is asking Alice to compute part of a MicroMint coin, but this partial coin is useful only when combined with thousands or millions of other similar computations. Bob collects all of these computations and combines them into MicroMint coins. Without requiring systemwide fungible digital cash, Bob can reuse others' computation work for computations of value to him (and only to him). The scheme is extensible and can potentially be used with many different types of payment schemes, not just MicroMint.

Anonymous macropayment digital cash schemes

Up until now, we have described payments in which the value of each coin or token is fairly small. These make forgery difficult because it's useful only if it can be performed on a large scale. Now we will move to more complex schemes that allow large sums to be paid in a secure manner in a single transaction. These schemes also offer multiparty security and some protection for user privacy.

The macropayment digital cash schemes we are about to discuss offer stronger security and anonymity. However, these protections come at a cost. The computational and size requirements of such digital cash are much greater. In cryptographic literature, micropayments are usually considered extremely small (such as $0.01) and use very efficient primitives such as hash functions. In contrast, macropayment digital cash schemes use public key operations, such as exponentiation, which are much slower. The use of techniques from elliptic curve cryp-

---

* Markus Jakobsson and Ari Juels (1999), "Proofs and Work and Bread Pudding Protocols." In B. Preneel, ed., *Communications and Multimedia Security*. Kluwer Academic Publishers, pp. 258–272.

tography can alleviate this problem by making it possible to securely use much shorter keys.

Other clever tricks, such as "probabilistic" checking—checking selected payments on the grounds that large-scale forgery will be caught eventually—can help macropayment techniques compete with micropayment schemes. This is an active research area and a source of continual innovation. Macropayment schemes will prove useful when used with the reputation systems discussed later in this chapter in the section "Reputations," because reputation systems let us make large transactions without assuming incommensurate risk.

Pioneering work on the theoretical foundations of anonymous digital cash was carried out by David Chaum in the early 1980s.* Chaum held patents on his electronic cash system, and founded DigiCash in 1990 to implement his ideas, but he exclusively licensed his patents to Ecash Technologies in 1999.

The electronic cash system he developed is based on an extension of digital signatures, called blind signatures. A digital signature uses a PKI to authenticate that a particular message was sent by a particular person. (See Chapter 15 for a greater description of signatures and PKI.) A *blind* signature scheme allows a person to get a message signed by another party, while not revealing the message contents to that party or allowing the party to recognize the message later.

In digital cash, Alice creates some number called a *proto-coin* and "blinds" it by multiplying by a secret random number. She sends this blinded proto-coin to the bank, which cannot link it with the original proto-coin. The bank checks that she has a positive balance and signs the proto-coin with the assurance that "this is a valid coin," using a private key specific to the particular amount of money in the coin. The bank returns this to Alice and subtracts the corresponding amount from Alice's bank account. Alice then divides out the random number multiplier and finds herself with a properly minted coin, carrying a valid signature from the bank. This is just one way to do digital cash, but it will suffice for this discussion.

---

* D. Chaum (1983), "Blind Signatures for Untraceable Payments," *Advances in Cryptology—Crypto '82*, Springer-Verlag, pp. 199–203. D. Chaum (1985), "Security Without Identification: Transaction Systems to Make Big Brother Obsolete," *Communications of the ACM*, vol. 28, no. 10, pp. 1030–1044. D. Chaum, A. Fiat, and M. Naor (1988), "Untraceable Electronic Cash," *Advances in Cryptology—Crypto '88, Lecture Notes in Computer Science*, no. 403, Springer-Verlag, pp. 319–327. D. Chaum (August 1992), "Achieving Electronic Privacy" (invited), *Scientific American*, pp. 96–101, http://www.chaum.com/articles/Achieving_Electronic_Privacy.htm.

In real life, the digital cash transaction would be like Alice slipping a piece of paper into a carbon-lined envelope, representing the blinded proto-coin. The bank just writes its signature across the envelope, which imprints a carbon signature onto the inside paper. Alice removes the paper and is left with a valid coin.

Alice can then spend this coin with Bob. Before accepting it, Bob needs to check with the issuing bank that the coin hasn't already been spent, a process of online verification. Afterwards, Bob can deposit the coin with the bank, which has no record of to whom that coin was issued. It saw only the blinded proto-coin, not the underlying "serial" number.

This digital cash system is both anonymous and untraceable. Its disadvantage, however, is that coins need to be verified online during the transaction to prevent double-spending. This slows down each transaction.

Stefan Brands proposed an alternative digital cash scheme in 1993.* It forms the core of a system implemented and tested by CAFE, a European project with both academic and commercial members. His patents are currently held by the Montreal-based privacy company Zero-Knowledge Systems, Inc.

Brands's digital cash scheme allows offline checking of double-spending for fraud tracing, with obvious performance benefits compared to online verification. It is also well suited for incorporation into smart cards, and the underlying technology provides an entire framework for privacy-protecting credential systems.

Brands's scheme uses a restrictive blind signature protocol rather than a normal blind signature protocol as proposed by Chaum. In the digital cash context, this certificate is a valid coin, represented as three values—secret key, public key, and digital signature—certified by the bank. A key aspect of this protocol is that the bank knows—and encodes attributes into—*part* of Alice's secret key, but it has no idea what the corresponding public key and certificate look like (except that they are consistent with the known part of the secret key). At the end of the issuing protocol, Alice uses techniques somewhat similar to Chaum's protocol to generate a valid coin.

---

* Stefan Brands (1993), "Untraceable Off-Line Cash in Wallet with Observers," *Advances in Cryptology—Crypto '93, Lecture Notes in Computer Science,* no. 773, Springer-Verlag, pp. 302–318. Stefan Brands (2000), *Rethinking Public Key Infrastructures and Digital Certificates: Building in Privacy.* MIT Press. Stefan Brands, online book chapter from *Rethinking Public Key Infrastructures and Digital Certificates: Building in Privacy, http://www.xs4all.nl/~brands/cash. html.*

Payment is very different in Brands's system. Alice's coin contains her secret key, so she doesn't actually give her coin to the vendor Bob. Instead, she proves to Bob that she is the proper holder of that coin (that is, that she knows the secret key associated with the public key), without actually disclosing its contents. This type of payment, a signed proof of knowledge transcript, is a fundamental shift from Chaum's e-cash model, in which the coin is merely an "immutable" bit string.

Privacy is maintained together with honesty by Brands's system in a very clever manner. If Alice only spends the coin once, the bank can gain no information as to her identity. After all, during the issuing protocol, the bank saw only part of Alice's secret key, not the public key used to verify Alice's payment transcript signature. Nor did the bank see its own signature on that public key. Yet if Alice double-spends the coin, the bank can use it to extract her identity!

We won't provide the math necessary to understand the security in this system, but you can understand why it works by comparing it to a Cartesian x-y plane. The first random number challenge used during payment provides one point (x_0, y_0) on this plane. An infinite number of lines can pass through this one point. If Alice uses the same coin to pay Charlie, a different random number is used. Now we know a second (x_1, y_1) point, and two points uniquely define a line. In the same way, Alice's identity will be exposed if she spends the coin twice.

Brands's scheme—useful for both digital cash and credentials—can be used to encode other useful information, such as negotiable attributes exposed during payment or high-value secrets that can prevent lending. A "high-value secret" refers to the same strategy we discussed when trying to prevent people from sharing their accounts—if a certificate to do X includes the user's credit card number, the user will be less willing to loan the certificate to others.

The "negotiable attributes" are an extension of a powerful idea—that of "credentials without identity." If you have a credential without identity, you have a way of proving that you belong to a certain class of people without actually having to prove anything about who you are. For example, you may have a credential which certifies that you are over 21 but doesn't include your name. The entity that authorized your age wouldn't want you to be able to lend this certificate to someone else. Therefore, we utilize these high-value secrets: the user needs to know the secret in order to use the over-21 certificate. Brands's scheme takes this farther and allows you to selectively reveal or hide various certifications on the fly, thereby allowing you to negotiate your degree of privacy.

One final note: whether a peer-to-peer system uses micropayments or macro-payments, system designers must consider the possibility that these can be DoS targets in themselves. Perhaps an attacker can flood a system with cheaply minted counterfeit coins, eating up computational resources through verification-checking alone. The extent of this problem depends largely on the computational complexity of coin verification. Many of the systems we describe—hash cash, client puzzles, MicroMint, PayWord—can very quickly verify coins with only a single or a few hash operations. Public key operations, such as modular exponentiation, can be significantly more expensive. Again, digital cash schemes are an active area of cryptographic research; before specifying a scheme it is worth checking out the proceedings of the Financial Cryptography, CRYPTO, and EUROCRYPT conferences.

The use and effectiveness of micropayments in peer-to-peer systems

So far, we have spent quite a bit of time describing various micropayment and digital cash schemes. Our discussion is not meant as exhaustive, yet it provides some examples of various cryptographic primitives and technologies used for electronic cash: public key encryption, hash functions, digital signatures, certificates, blinding functions, proofs of knowledge, and different one-way and trap door problems based on complexity theory. The list reads like a cryptographic cookbook. Indeed, the theoretical foundations of digital cash—and the design of systems—have been actively researched and developed over the past two decades.

Only in the past few years, however, have we begun to see the real-world application of micropayments and digital cash, spurred by the growth of the Internet into a ubiquitous platform for connectivity, collaboration, and even commerce. Electronic cash surely has a place in future society. But its place is not yet secured. We are not going to try to predict either how fast or how widespread its adoption will be; that depends on too many economic, social, and institutional factors.

Instead, we'll focus on how micropayments might be useful for peer-to-peer systems: what issues the developers of peer-to-peer systems need to consider, when certain digital cash technologies are better than others, how to tell whether the micropayments are working, and how to achieve stronger or weaker protections as needed.

Identity-based payment policies

When designing a policy for accepting micropayments, a peer-to-peer system might wish to charge a varying amount to peers based on identity. For instance, a particular peer might charge less to local users, specified friends, users from academic or noncommercial subnets, or users within specified jurisdictional areas.

Such policies, of course, depend on being able to securely identify peers in the system. This can be hard to do both on the Internet as a whole (where domain names and IP addresses are routinely spoofed) and, in particular, on systems that allow anonymity or pseudonymity. Chapter 15 discusses this issue from several general angles, and Chapter 12 discusses how we try to solve the problem in one particular pseudonymous system, Free Haven. Many other systems, like ICQ and other instant messaging services, use their own naming schemes and ensure some security through passwords and central servers. Finally, systems with many far-flung peers need a reputation system to give some assurance that peers won't abuse their privileges.

General considerations in an economic analysis of micropayment design

Designers choosing a micropayment scheme for a peer-to-peer system should not consider merely the technical and implementation issues of different micropayment schemes, but also the overall economic impact of the entire system. Different micropayment schemes have different economic implications.

A classic economic analysis of bridge tolls serves as a good analogy for a peer-to-peer system. In 1842, the French engineer Jules Dupuit reached a major breakthrough in economic theory by arguing the following: the economically efficient toll on an uncongested bridge is zero, because the extra cost from one more person crossing the bridge is zero. Although bridge building and maintenance is not free—it costs some money to the owner—it is socially inefficient to extract this money through a toll. Society as a whole is worse off because some people choose not to cross due to this toll, even though their crossing would cost the owner nothing, and they would not interfere with anyone else's crossing (because the bridge is uncongested). Therefore, everyone should be allowed to cross the bridge for free, and the society should compensate the bridge builder through a lump-sum payment.[*]

---

[*] Arsene Jules Etienne Dupuit (1842), "On Tolls and Transport Charges," *Annales des Ponts et Chaussees*, trans. 1962, IEP.

This bridge example serves as a good analogy to a peer-to-peer system with micropayments. Tolls should be extracted only in order to limit congestion and to regulate access to people who value crossing the most. Given the same economic argument, resource allocation to limit congestion is the only justifiable reason for micropayments in a peer-to-peer system. Indeed, excessive micropayments can dissuade users from using the system, with negative consequences (known as "social inefficiencies") for the whole society. Users might not access certain content, engage in e-commerce, or anonymously publish information that exposes nefarious corporate behavior.

This analysis highlights the ability of micropayments to prevent attacks and adds the implied ability to manage congestion. Congestion management is a large research area in networking. Micropayments can play a useful role in peer-to-peer systems by helping peers prioritize their use of network bandwidth or access to storage space. Users who really want access will pay accordingly. Of course, such a system favors wealthy users, so it should be balanced against the goal of providing a system with the broadest social benefits. Reputation can also play a role in prioritizing resource allocation.

Most economic research relevant for micropayments has focused on owner-side strategies for maximizing profit. AT&T researchers compared flat-fee versus pay-per-use fee methods where the owner is a monopolist and concluded that more revenues are generated with a flat-fee model. Similar research at MIT and NYU independently concluded that content bundling and fixed fees can generate greater profits per good.*

We try to take a broader view. We have to consider the well-being of all economic agents participating in and affected by the system. Three general groups come to mind in the case of a peer-to-peer system: The owner of the system, the participants, and the rest of society.

How does a micropayment scheme impact these three agents? Participants face direct benefits and costs. The owner can collect fees or commissions to cover the fixed cost of designing the system and the variable costs of its operation. The rest of society can benefit indirectly by synergies made possible by the system, knowledge spillovers, alternative common resources that it frees up, and so on.

---

* P. C. Fishburn and A. M. Odlyzko (1999), "Competitive Pricing of Information Goods: Subscription Pricing Versus Pay-Per-Use," *Economic Theory*, vol. 13, pp. 447–470, *http://www.research.att.com/~amo/doc/competitive.pricing.ps*. Y. Bakos and E. Brynjolfsson (December 1999), "Bundling Information Goods: Pricing, Profits, and Efficiency," *Management Science*, *http://www.stern.nyu.edu/~bakos/big.pdf*.

To simplify our discussion, we assume that whatever benefits participants also benefits society. Furthermore, we can realistically assume a competitive market, so that the owner is probably best off serving the participants as well as possible. Therefore, we focus on the cost/benefit analysis for the participant.

We believe that a focus on costs and benefits to participants is more suited to the peer-to-peer market than the literature on information services, for several reasons. First, peer-to-peer system owners do not enjoy the luxury of dictating exchange terms, thanks to competition. Second, nonfungible micropayments do not generate revenues for the owner; it is not always worthwhile to even consider the benefit to the owner. Third, we expect that a large amount of resources in peer-to-peer systems will be donated by users: people donate otherwise unused CPU cycles to SETI@home calculations, unused bandwidth to forward Mixmaster anonymous email, and unused storage for Free Haven data shares. For these situations, the sole role of micropayments is to achieve optimal resource allocation among participants. In other words, micropayments in a peer-to-peer system should be used only to prevent congestion, where this concept covers both bandwidth and storage limitations.

Moderating security levels: An accountability slider

Poor protection of resources can hinder the use of a peer-to-peer system on one side; attempts to guard resources by imposing prohibitive costs can harm it on the other. Providing a widely used, highly available, stable peer-to-peer system requires a balance.

If a peer-to-peer system wishes only to prevent query-flooding (bandwidth) attacks, the congestion management approach taken by client puzzles—and usable with any form of micropayment—answers the problem. Query-flooding attacks are transient; once the adversary stops actively attacking the system, the bandwidth is readily available to others.

As we have suggested, other forms of congestion are cumulative, such as those related to storage space. Free Haven seeks "document permanence," whereby peers promise to store data for a given time period (although the Free Haven trading protocol seeks to keep this system dynamic, as discussed in Chapter 12). If we wait until the system is already full before charging micropayments, we've already lost our chance to adequately protect against congestion.

This is the freeloading problem: we wish to prevent parasitic users from congesting the system without offering something of value in return. Furthermore, an adversary can attempt to flood the system early to fill up all available space. Therefore, for systems in which resource pressures accrue cumulatively, micropayments should always be required. Free Haven's answer is to require that peers offer storage space proportional to that which they take up. (Even though cash-based micropayments are not used, the idea of payment by equivalent resources is similar.)

The alternative to this design is the caching approach taken by systems such as Freenet. Old data is dropped as newer and more "popular" data arrives. This approach does not remove the resource allocation problem, however; it only changes the issue. First, flooding the system can flush desirable data from nearby caches as well. System designers simply try to ensure that flooding will not congest the resources of more distant peers. Second, freeloading is not as much of a concern, because peers are not responsible for offering best-effort availability to documents. However, if many peers rely on a few peers to store data, only the most popular data remains. Social inefficiencies develop if the system loses data that could be desired in the long run because short-term storage is insufficient to handle the requirements of freeloading peers. Furthermore, disk space is only one of several resources to consider. Massive freeloading can also affect scalability through network congestion.

Always charging for resources can prevent both freeloading and attacks. On the other hand, excessive charges are disadvantageous in their own right. So it would be useful to find a balance.

Consider an *accountability slider*: Peers negotiate how much payment is required for a resource within a general model specified by the overall peer-to-peer system. Using only a micropayment model, systems like Free Haven or Publius may not have much leeway. Others, like Freenet, Gnutella, or Jabber, have notably more. When we later add the concept of reputation, this accounting process becomes even more flexible.

Each of the micropayment schemes described earlier in this chapter can be adapted to provide a sliding scale:

Hash cash
> Partial hashes can be made arbitrarily expensive to compute by choosing the desired number of bits of collision, denoted by k. No matter how big k gets, systems providing the resources can verify the requests almost instantly.

Client puzzles
> The work factor of these puzzles is also based on the number of bit collisions. The number of subpuzzles can also be increased to limit the possibility of random guessing being successful; this is especially important when k becomes smaller.

Time puzzles

The LCS35 time-lock includes a parameter t that sets the difficulty of the puzzle.

MicroMint

The "cost" of a coin is determined by its number of colliding hash values. The greater the k-way collision, the harder the coin is to generate.

PayWord

In the simplest adaptation, a commitment within PayWord can be a promise of varying amount. However, PayWord is designed for iterative payments. To be able to use the same PayWord chain for successive transactions, we want to always pay with coins of the same value. Therefore, to handle variable costs, we can just send several paywords for one transaction. The very lightweight cost of creating and verifying paywords (a single hash per payword) also makes this multiple-coin approach suitable for macropayment schemes.

Anonymous digital cash

Coins can have different denominations. In Chaum's design, the bank uses a different public key to sign the coin for different denominations. In Brands's model, the denomination of the coin is encoded within the coin's attributes; the bank's public key is unique to currency, not denomination. Brands's digital cash system also allows negotiable attributes to be revealed or kept secret during payment. This additional information can play a role in setting the accountability slider.

By negotiating these various values, we can change the level of accountability and security offered by a peer-to-peer system. Based on overall system requirements, this process can be fixed by the system designers, changed by the administrators of individual peer machines, or even fluctuate between acceptable levels at runtime!

While payment schemes can be used in a variety of peer-to-peer situations—ranging from systems in which peers are fully identified to systems in which peers are fully anonymous—they do involve some risk. Whenever Alice makes an electronic payment, she accepts some risk that Bob will not fulfill his bargain. When identities are known, we can rely on existing legal or social mechanisms. In fully anonymous systems, no such guarantee is made, so Alice attempts to minimize her risk at any given time by making small, incremental micropayments. However, there is another possibility for pseudonymous systems, or identified systems for which legal mechanisms should only be used as a last resort: reputation schemes. In this next section, we consider the problem of reputation in greater depth.

Reputations

While micropayments provide an excellent mechanism for anonymous exchange, a number of systems call for more long-term pseudonymous or even public relationships. For instance, in the case of transactions in which one party promises a service over a long period of time (such as storing a document for three years), a simple one-time payment generally makes one party in the transaction vulnerable to being cheated. A whistleblower or political dissident who publishes a document may not wish to monitor the availability of this document and make a number of incremental micropayments over the course of several years, since this requires periodic network access and since continued micropayments might compromise anonymity. (While third-party escrow monitoring services or third-party document sponsors might help to solve this issue, they introduce their own problems.) In addition, some systems might want to base decisions on the observed behavior of entities—how well they actually perform—rather than simply how many resources they can provide.

In the real world, we make use of information about users to help distribute resources and avoid poor results. Back before the days of ubiquitous communication and fast travel, doing business over long distances was a major problem. Massive amounts of risk were involved in, say, sending a ship from Europe to Asia for trade. Reputations helped make this risk bearable; large banks could issue letters of credit that could draw on the bank's good name both in Europe and Asia, and they could insure expeditions against loss. As the bank successfully helped expeditions finance their voyages, the bank's reputation grew, and its power along with it. Today's business relationships still follow the same path: two parties make a decision to trust each other based on the reputations involved.

While the online world is different from the brick-and-mortar world, it too has benefited from reputations—and can continue to benefit.

The main difference between reputation-based trust systems and micropayment-based trust systems is that, in reputation-based trust systems, parties base their decisions in part on information provided by third parties. Peers are motivated to remain honest by fear that news of misdealings will reach yet other third parties.

Reputation systems are not useful in all situations. For instance, if there were thousands of buyers and one or two vendors, being able to track vendor performance and reliability would not help buyers pick a good vendor. On the other hand, tracking performance might provide feedback to the vendor itself on areas in which it might need improvement. This in turn could result in better performance down the road, but only if the vendor acted on this feedback.

Similarly, in fields in which a given buyer generally doesn't perform transactions frequently, the benefits of a reputation system are more subtle. A buyer might benefit from a real estate reputation system, since she expects to rent from different people over time. Even for a domain in which she expects to do just one transaction over her whole lifetime (such as laser eye surgery), she would probably contribute to a reputation site—first out of altruism, and second in order to give the surgeon an incentive to do well.

This is the tragedy of the commons in reverse: when the cost of contributing to a system is low enough, people will contribute to it for reasons not *immediately* beneficial to themselves.

Chapter 17, *Reputation*, describes some of the practical uses for a reputation system and the difficulties of developing such a system. That chapter focuses on the solution found at Reputation Technologies, Inc. In this chapter we'll give some background on reputation and issues to consider when developing a reputation system.

Early reputation systems online

The online world carries over many kinds of reputation from the real world. The name "Dennis Ritchie" is still recognizable, whether listed in a phone book or in a posting to *comp.theory*. Of course, there is a problem online—how can you be sure that the person posting to *comp.theory* is *the* Dennis Ritchie? And what happens when "Night Avenger" turns out to be Brian Kernighan posting under a pseudonym? These problems of identity—covered earlier in this chapter—complicate the ways we think about reputations, because some of our old assumptions no longer hold.

In addition, new ways of developing reputations evolve online. In the bulletin board systems of the 1980s and early 1990s, one of the more important pieces of data about a particular user was her upload/download ratio. Users with particularly low ratios were derided as "leeches," because they consumed scarce system resources (remember, when one user was on via a phone line, no one else could log in) without giving anything in return. As we will see, making use of this data in an automated fashion is a promising strategy for providing accountability in peer-to-peer systems.

Codifying reputation on a wide scale: The PGP web of trust

Human beings reason about reputations all the time. A large-scale peer-to-peer application, however, cannot depend on human judgments for more than a negligible portion of its decisions if it has any hope of scalability. Therefore, the next step in using reputations is to make their development and consequences automatic.

We've already mentioned the value of knowing upload/download ratios in bulletin board systems. In many systems, gathering this data was automatic. In some cases, the consequences were automatic as well: drop below a certain level and your downloading privileges would be restricted or cut off entirely. Unfortunately, these statistics did not carry over from one BBS to another—certainly not in any organized way—so they provided for reputations only on a microscopic scale.

One of the first applications to handle reputations in an automated fashion on a genuinely large scale was the "web of trust" system introduced in Phil Zimmermann's Pretty Good Privacy (PGP). This was the first program to bring public key cryptography to the masses. In public key cryptography, there are two keys per user. One is public and can be used only to encrypt messages. The other key is private and can be used only to decrypt messages. A user publishes his public key and keeps the private key safe. Then others can use the public key to send him messages that only he can read.

With public key cryptography comes the key certification problem, a type of reputation issue. Reputations are necessary because there is no way to tell from the key alone which public key belongs to which person.

For example, suppose Alice would like people to be able to send encrypted messages to her. She creates a key and posts it with the name "Alice." Unbeknownst to her, Carol has also made up a key with the name "Alice" and posted it in the same place. When Bob wants to send a message to Alice, which key does he choose? This happens in real life; as an extreme example, the name "Bill Gates" is currently associated with dozens of different PGP keys available from popular PGP key servers.

So the key certification problem in PGP (and other public key services) consists of verifying that a particular public key really does belong to the entity to whom it "should" belong. PGP uses a system called a web of trust to combat this problem. Alice's key may have one or more certifications that say "Such and such person believes that this key belongs to Alice." These certifications exist because Alice knows these people personally; they have established to their satisfaction that Alice really does own this key. Carol's fake "Alice" key has no such certifications, because it was made up on the spot.

When Bob looks at the key, his copy of PGP will assign it a trust level based on how many of the certifications are made by people he knows. The higher the trust level, the more confidence Bob can have in using the key.

A perennial question about the web of trust, however, is whether or not it scales. Small groups of people can create a web of trust easily, especially if they can meet each other in person. What happens when we try to make the web of trust work for, say, a consumer and a merchant who have never met before? The conventional wisdom is that the web of trust does not scale. After all, there is a limit to how many people Alice and Bob can know.

The most frequently cited alternative to the web of trust is a so-called Public Key Infrastructure. Some trusted root party issues certificates for keys in the system, some of which go to parties that can issue certificates in turn. The result is to create a certification tree. An example is the certificate system used for SSL web browsers; here VeriSign is one of the trusted root certificate authorities responsible for ensuring that every public key belongs to the "right" entity. A hierarchical system has its own problems (not least the fact that compromise of the root key, as may recently have happened to Sun Microsystems,* is catastrophic), but at least it scales, right?

As it turns out, the web of trust may not be as unworkable as conventional wisdom suggests. A study of publicly available PGP keys in 1997 showed that on average, only six certificates linked one key to another.† This "six degrees of separation" or "small-world" effect (also discussed in Chapter 14) means that for a merchant and a user who are both good web of trust citizens—meaning that they certify others' keys and are in turn certified—the odds are good that they will have reason to trust each others' keys. In current practice, however, most commercial sites elect to go with VeriSign. The one major commercial exception is Thawte's Freemail Web of Trust system.‡

A more serious problem with PGP's implementation of the web of trust, however, comes with key revocation. How do you tell everyone that your key is no longer valid? How do you tell everyone that your certificate on a key should be changed? For that matter, what exactly did Bob mean when he certified Charlie's key, and does Charlie mean the same thing when he certifies David's key?

A more sophisticated—but still distributed—approach to trust management that tries to settle these questions is the Rivest and Lampson Simple Distributed

---

* Sun Security Bulletin 198, "Revocation of Sun Microsystems Browser Certificates," "How to Detect or Remove the Invalid Certificate," *http://sunsolve5.sun.com/secbull/certificate_howto.html*. Computer Emergency Response Team Bulletin CA-2000-19, *http://www.cert.org/advisories/CA-2000-19.html*.

† Neal McBurnett, "PGP Web of Trust Statistics," *http://bcn.boulder.co.us/~neal/pgpstat*.

‡ Thawte, "Personal Certificates for Web and Mail: The Web of Trust," *http://www.thawte.com/certs/personal/wot/about.html*.

Security Infrastructure/Simple Public Key Infrastructure (SDSI/SPKI). A thorough comparison of this with PGP's web of trust and PKI systems is given by Yang, Brown, and Newmarch.[*]

All of this brings up many issues of trust and public key semantics, about which we refer to Khare and Rifkin.[†] The point we're interested in here is the way in which the web of trust depends on reputation to extend trust to new parties.

Who will moderate the moderators: Slashdot

The news site Slashdot.org is a very popular news service that attracts a particular kind of "Slashdot reader"—lots of them. Each and every Slashdot reader is capable of posting comments on Slashdot news stories, and sometimes it seems like each and every one actually does. Reputations based on this interaction can help a user figure out which of the many comments are worth reading.

To help readers wade through the resulting mass of comments, Slashdot has a moderation system for postings. Certain users of the system are picked to become moderators. Moderators can assign scores to postings and posters. These scores are then aggregated and can be used to tweak a user's view of the posts depending on a user's preferences. For example, a user can request to see no posts rated lower than 2.

The Slashdot moderation system is one existing example of a partially automated reputation system. Ratings are entered by hand, using trusted human moderators, but then these ratings are collected, aggregated, and displayed in an automatic fashion.

Although moderation on Slashdot serves the needs of many of its readers, there are many complaints that a posting was rated too high or too low. It is probably the best that can be done without trying to maintain reputations for moderators themselves.

Reputations worth real money: eBay

The eBay feedback system is another example of a reputation service in practice. Because buyers and sellers on eBay usually have never met each other, neither has much reason to believe that the other will follow through on their part of the deal. They need to decide whether or not to trust each other.

---

[*] Yinan Yang, Lawrie Brown, and Jan Newmarch, "Issues of Trust in Digital Signature Certificates," *http://www.cs.adfa.oz.au/~yany97/auug98.html.*

[†] Rohit Khare and Adam Rifkin, "Weaving a Web of Trust," *http://www.cs.caltech.edu/~adam/papers/trust.html.*

To help them make the decision, eBay collects feedback about each eBay participant in the form of ratings and comments. After a trade, eBay users are encouraged to post feedback about the trade and rate their trading partner. Good
trades, in which the buyer and seller promptly exchange money for item, yield
good feedback for both parties. Bad trades, in which one party fails to come
through, yield bad feedback which goes into the eBay record. All this feedback
can be seen by someone considering a trade.

The idea is that such information will lead to more good trades and fewer bad
trades—which translates directly into more and better business for eBay. As we
will see, this isn't always the case in practice. It is the case often enough, however, to give eBay a reputation of its own as the preeminent web auction site.

A reputation system that resists pseudospoofing: Advogato

Another example of reputations at work is the "trust metric" implemented at
http://www.advogato.org, which is a portal for open source development work.
The reputation system is aimed at answering the fundamental question, "How
much can you trust code from person X?" This question is critical for people
working on open source projects, who may have limited time to audit contributed code. In addition, in an open source project, attempts by one contributor
to fix the perceived "mistakes" of another contributor may lead to flame wars
that destroy projects. As of this writing, the open source development site *http://
www.sourceforge.net* (host to Freenet) is considering using a similar reputation
system.

The stakes at Advogato are higher than they are at Slashdot. If the Slashdot moderation system fails, a user sees stupid posts or misses something important. If
the Advogato trust metric incorrectly certifies a potential volunteer as compe-
tent when he or she is not, a software project may fail. At least, this would be
the case if people depended on the trust metric to find and contact free software
volunteers. In practice, Advogato's trust metric is used mostly for the same
application as Slashdot's: screening out stupid posts.

The method of determining trust at Advogato also contains features that distinguish it from a simple rating system like Slashdot moderation. In particular, the
Advogato trust metric resists a scenario in which many people join the system
with the express purpose of boosting each others' reputation scores.[*]

Advogato considers trust relationships as a directed flow graph. That is, trust
relationships are represented by a collection of nodes, edges, and weights. The

---

[*] Raph Levien, "Advogato's Trust Metric," *http://www.advogato.org/trust-metric.html*.

system is illustrated in Figure 16-1 (we omit weights for simplicity). The nodes are the people involved. An edge exists between A and B if A trusts B. The weight is a measure of how much A trusts B.

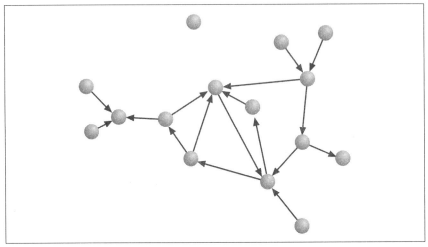

Figure 16-1. Users and trust relationships in Advogato

What we are interested in, however, is not just how much A trusts B, but how much B is trusted in general. So Advogato measures how much trust "flows to" B, by designating a few special trusted accounts as a source and by designating B as a sink. It then defines a flow of trust from the source to B as a path from the source to B. Advogato assigns numbers to edges on the path that are less than or equal to the edge weights. The edge weights act as constraints on how much trust can be "pushed" between two points on the flow path. Finally, the trust value of B is defined as the maximum amount of trust that can be pushed from the source to B—the maximum flow.

Calculating flows through networks is a classic problem in computer science. Advogato uses this history in two ways. First, the Ford-Fulkerson algorithm lets the system easily find the maximum flow, so B's trust value can always be computed.* Second, a result called the "maxflow-mincut theorem" shows that the Advogato system resists the pseudospoofing attacks described earlier, in the sec-

---

* Thomas H. Cormen, Charles E. Leiserson, and Ronald L. Rivest, *Introduction to Algorithms* (MIT Press and McGraw-Hill, Cambridge, MA, 1990).

tion "Problems with pseudospoofing and possible defenses." Even if one entity joins under many different assumed names, none of these names will gain very much more trust than if each had joined alone.

Pseudospoofing is resisted because each of the new names, at least at first, is connected only to itself in the graph. No one else has any reason whatsoever to trust it. Therefore, there is no trust flow from the source to any of the pseudospoofing nodes, and none of them are trusted at all. Even after the pseudospoofing nodes begin to form connections with the rest of the graph, there will still be "trust bottlenecks" that limit the amount of trust arriving at any of the pseudospoofing nodes.

This property is actually quite remarkable. No matter how many fake names an adversary uses, it is unable to boost its trust rating very much. The downside is that nodes "close" to the source must be careful to trust wisely. In addition, it may not be readily apparent what kinds of weights constitute high trust without knowing what the entire graph looks like.

System successes and failures

Reputation in the brick-and-mortar world seems to work quite well; spectacular failures, such as the destruction of Barings Bank by the actions of a rogue trader, are exceptions rather than the rule. Which reputation-based systems have worked online, and how well have they worked?

The Slashdot and Advogato moderation systems seem to work. While it is difficult to quantify what "working" means, there have been no spectacular failures so far. On the other hand, the eBay fraud of mid-2000* shows some of the problems with reputation systems used naively.

In the eBay case, a group of people engaged in auctions and behaved well. As a result, their trust ratings went up. Once their trust ratings were sufficiently high to engage in high-value deals, the group suddenly "turned evil and cashed out." That is, they used their reputations to start auctions for high-priced items, received payment for those items, and then disappeared, leaving dozens of eBay users holding the bag.

As for PGP's web of trust, it has been overtaken by hierarchical PKIs, like those offered by VeriSign, as a widespread means of certifying public keys. In this case, peer-to-peer did not automatically translate into success.

---

* "eBay, Authorities Probe Fraud Allegations," CNET news article, *http://www.canada.cnet.com/news/0-1007-200-1592233.html*.

Scoring systems

Reputation systems depend on *scores* to provide some meaning to the ratings as a whole. As shown in Chapter 17, scores can be very simple or involve multiple scales and complicated calculations.

In a reputation system for vendors, buyers might give ratings—that is, numbers that reflect their satisfaction with a given transaction—for a variety of different dimensions for each vendor. For instance, a given vendor might have good performance in terms of response time or customer service, but the vendor's geographic location might be inconvenient. Buyers provide feedback on a number of these rating dimensions at once, to provide a comprehensive view of the entity. The job of the reputation system is to aggregate these ratings into one or more published scores that are meaningful and useful to participants in the system. A good scoring system will possess many of the following qualities:

Accurate for long-term performance
> The system reflects the confidence (the likelihood of accuracy) of a given score. It can also distinguish between a new entity of unknown quality and an entity with bad long-term performance.

Weighted toward current behavior
> The system recognizes and reflects recent trends in entity performance. For instance, an entity that has behaved well for a long time but suddenly goes downhill is quickly recognized and no longer trusted.

Efficient
> It is convenient if the system can recalculate a score quickly. Calculations that can be performed incrementally are important.

Robust against attacks
> The system should resist attempts of any entity or entities to influence scores other than by being more honest or having higher quality.

Amenable to statistical evaluation
> It should be easy to find outliers and other factors that can make the system rate scores differently.

Private
> No one should be able to learn how a given rater rated an entity except the rater himself.

Smooth
> Adding any single rating or small number of ratings doesn't jar the score much.

Understandable

It should be easy to explain to people who use these scores what they mean—not only so they know how the system works, but so they can evaluate for themselves what each score implies.

Verifiable

A score under dispute can be supported with data.

Note that a number of these requirements seem to be contradictory. We will explore the benefits and trade-offs from each of them over the course of the rest of this section.

Attacks and adversaries

Two questions determine how we evaluate the security of reputation systems. First, what information needs to be protected? Second, who are the adversaries?

The capabilities of potential adversaries and the extent to which they can damage or influence the system dictate how much energy should be spent on security. For instance, in the case of Free Haven, if political dissidents actually began using the system to publish their reports and information, government intelligence organizations might be sufficiently motivated to spend millions of dollars to track the documents to their sources.

Similarly, if a corporation planning a $50 million transaction bases its decisions on a reputation score that Reputation Technologies, Inc., provides, it could be worth many millions of dollars to influence the system so that a particular company is chosen. Indeed, there are quite a few potential adversaries in the case of Reputation Technologies, Inc. A dishonest vendor might want to forge or use bribes to create good feedback to raise his resulting reputation. In addition to wanting good reputations, vendors might like their competitors' reputations to appear low. Exchanges—online marketplaces that try to bring together vendors to make transactions more convenient—would like their vendors' reputations to appear higher than those of vendors that do business on other exchanges. Vendors with low reputations—or those with an interest in people being kept in the dark—would like reputations to appear unusably random. Dishonest users might like the reputations of the vendors that they use to be inaccurate, so that their competitors will have inaccurate information.

Perhaps the simplest attack that can be made against a scoring system is called *shilling*. This term is often used to refer to submitting fake bids in an auction, but it can be considered in a broader context of submitting fake or misleading ratings. In particular, a person might submit positive ratings for one of her friends (positive shilling) or negative ratings for her competition (negative shilling). Either of these ideas introduces more subtle attacks, such as negatively rating a friend or positively rating a competitor to try to trick others into believing that competitors are trying to cheat.

Shilling is a very straightforward attack, but many systems are vulnerable to it. A very simple example is the AOL Instant Messenger system. You can click to claim that a given user is abusing the system. Since there is no support for detecting multiple comments from the same person, a series of repeated negative votes will exceed the threshold required to kick the user off the system for bad behavior, effectively denying him service. Even in a more sophisticated system that detects multiple comments by the same person, an attacker could mount the same attack by assuming a multitude of identities.

Vulnerabilities from overly simple scoring systems are not limited to "toy" systems like Instant Messenger. Indeed, eBay suffers from a similar problem. In eBay, the reputation score for an individual is a linear combination of good and bad ratings, one for each transaction. Thus, a vendor who has performed dozens of transactions and cheats on only 1 out of every 4 customers will have a steadily rising reputation, whereas a vendor who is completely honest but has only done 10 transactions will be displayed as less reputable. As we have seen, a vendor could make a good profit (and build a strong reputation!) by being honest for several small transactions and then being dishonest for a single large transaction.

Weighting ratings by size of transaction helps the issue but does not solve it. In this case, large transactions would have a large impact on the reputation score of a vendor, and small transactions would have only a small impact. Since small transactions don't have much weight, vendors have no real incentive to be honest for them—making the reputation services useless for small buyers. Breaking reputation into many different dimensions, each representing the behavior of the vendor on a given *category* of transaction (based on cost, volume, region, etc.), can solve a lot of these problems. See the section "Scoring algorithms", later in this chapter for more details and an analysis of this idea.

Aspects of a scoring system

The particular scoring system or algorithm used in a given domain should be based on the amount of information available, the extent to which information must be kept private, and the amount of accuracy required.

In some situations, such as verifying voting age, a fine-grained reputation measurement is not necessary—simply indicating who seems to be sufficient or insufficient is good enough.

In a lot of domains, it is very difficult to collect enough information to provide a comprehensive view of each entity's behavior. It might be difficult to collect information about entities because the volume of transactions is very low, as we see today in large online business markets.

But there's a deeper issue than just whether there are transactions, or whether these transactions are trackable. More generally: does there exist some sort of proof (a receipt or other evidence) that the rater and ratee have actually interacted?

Being able to prove the existence of transactions reduces problems on a wide variety of fronts. For instance, it makes it more difficult to forge large numbers of entities or transactions. Such verification would reduce the potential we described in the previous section for attacks on AOL Instant Messenger. Similarly, eBay users currently are able to directly purchase a high reputation by giving eBay a cut of a dozen false transactions which they claim to have performed with their friends. With transaction verification, they would be required to go through the extra step of actually shipping goods back and forth.

Proof of transaction provides the basis for Amazon.com's simple referral system, "Customers who bought this book also bought..." It is hard to imagine that someone would spend money on a book just to affect this system. It happens, however. For instance, a publishing company was able to identify the several dozen bookstores across America that are used as sample points for the New York Times bestseller list; they purchased thousands of copies of their author's book at these bookstores, skyrocketing the score of that book in the charts.*

In some domains, it is to most raters' perceived advantage that everyone agree with the rater. This is how chain letters, Amway, and Ponzi schemes get their shills: they establish a system in which customers are motivated to recruit other customers. Similarly, if a vendor offered to discount past purchases if enough future customers buy the same product, it would be hard to get honest ratings for that vendor. This applies to all kinds of investments; once you own an investment, it is not in your interest to rate it negatively so long as it holds any value at all.

---

* David D. Kirkpatrick, "Book Agent's Buying Fuels Concern on Influencing Best-Seller Lists," *New York Times Abstracts*, 08/23/2000, Section C, p. 1, col. 2, c. 2000, New York Times Company.

Collecting ratings

One of the first problems in developing reputation systems is how to collect ratings. The answer depends highly on the domain, of course, but there are a number of aspects that are common across many domains.

The first option is simply to observe as much activity as possible and draw conclusions based on this activity. This can be a very effective technique for automated reputation systems that have a lot of data available. If you can observe the transaction flow and notice that a particular vendor has very few repeat customers, he probably has a low reputation. On the other hand, lack of repeat customers may simply indicate a market in which any given buyer transacts infrequently. Similarly, finding a vendor with many repeat customers might indicate superior quality, or it might just indicate a market in which one or a few vendors hold a monopoly over a product. Knowledge of the domain in question is crucial to knowing how to correctly interpret data.

In many circumstances it may be difficult or impossible to observe the transaction flow, or it may be unreasonable to expect parties to take the initiative in providing feedback. In these cases, a reasonable option is to solicit feedback from parties involved in each transaction. This can be done either by publicizing interest in such feedback and providing incentives to respond, or even by actively going to each party after an observed transaction and requesting comments. Reputation Technologies, Inc., for instance, aggressively tries to obtain feedback after each transaction.

Tying feedback to transactions is a very powerful way of reducing vulnerabilities in the system. It's much more difficult for people to spam positive feedback, since each item of feedback has to be associated with a particular transaction, and presumably only the latest piece of feedback on a given transaction would actually count.

On the surface, it looks like this requires an exchange or other third-party transaction moderator, to make it difficult to simply fabricate a series of several thousand transactions and exploit the same vulnerability. However, vendors could provide blinded receipts for transactions—that is, the vendors would not be able to identify which buyer was providing the ratings. Without such a receipt, the reputation system would ignore feedback from a given buyer. Thus, buyers could not provide feedback about a vendor without that vendor's permission. There are a number of new problems introduced by this idea, such as how to respond if vendors fail to provide a receipt, but it seems to address many of the difficult issues about shilling in a decentralized environment.

A final issue to consider when collecting ratings is how fair the ratings will be—that is, how evenly distributed are the raters out of the set of people who have been doing transactions? If the only people who have incentive to provide ratings are those that are particularly unhappy with their transaction, or if only people with sufficient technical background can navigate the rating submission process, the resulting scores may be skewed to the point of being unusable. One solution to this could involve incentives that lead more people to respond; another approach is to simply collect so much data that the issue is no longer relevant. (The Slashdot moderation system, for instance, depends on the participation of huge numbers of independent moderators.) But systematic errors or biases in the ratings will generally defeat this second approach.

Bootstrapping

One of the tough questions for a reputation-based trust system is how to get started. If users make choices based on the scores that are available to them, but the system has not yet collected enough data to provide useful scores, what incentive do buyers have to use the system? More importantly, what incentive do they have to contribute ratings to the system?

Free Haven can avoid this problem through social means. Some participants will be generous and willing to try out new nodes just to test their stability and robustness. In effect, they will be performing a public service by risking some of their reputation and resources evaluating unknown nodes. However, businesses, particularly businesses just getting started in their fields and trying to make a name for themselves, won't necessarily be as eager to spend any of their already limited transaction volume on trying out unknown suppliers.

The way to present initial scores for entities depends on the domain. In some noncommercial domains, it might be perfectly fine to present a series of entities and declare no knowledge or preference; in others, it might be more reasonable to list only those entities for which a relatively certain score is known. Reputation Technologies needs to provide some initial value to the users; this can be done by asking vendors to provide references (that is, by obtaining out-of-band information) and then asking those references to fill out a survey describing overall performance of and happiness with that vendor. While this bootstrapping information may not be as useful as actual transaction-based feedback (and is more suspect because the vendors are choosing the references), it is a good starting point for a new system.

Bootstrapping is a much more pronounced issue in a centralized system than in a decentralized system. This is because in a decentralized system, each user develops his own picture of the universe: he builds his trust of each entity based on his own evidence of past performance and on referrals from other trusted parties. Thus, every new user effectively joins the system "at the beginning," and the process of building a profile for new users is an ongoing process throughout the entire lifetime of the system. In a centralized environment, on the other hand, ratings are accumulated across many different transactions and over long periods of time. New users trust the centralized repository to provide information about times and transactions that happened before the user joined the system.

In a newly developed system, or for a new entity in the system, the choice of the default reputation score is critical. If it's easy to create a new identity (that is, pseudonym), and new users start out with an average reputation, users who develop a bad reputation are encouraged to simply drop their old identities and start over with new ones. One way to deal with this problem is to start all new users with the lowest possible reputation score; even users with a bad track record will then have an incentive to keep their current identities.

Another approach to solving this problem is to make it difficult to create a new identity. For instance, this can be done by requiring some proof of identity or a monetary fee for registration. Tying the user to her real-world identity is the simplest, and probably the most effective, way to reduce abuse—but only if it's appropriate for that system.

Personalizing reputation searches

The user interface—that is, the way of presenting scores and asking questions—is a crucial element of a reputation system. Scores cannot simply be static universal values representing the overall quality of an individual. Since a score is an attempt to predict future performance, each score must be a prediction for a particular context. That is, the user interface must allow participants to query the system for the likelihood of a successful transaction for their particular situation. The more flexibility a client has, the more powerful and useful the system is (so long as users can still understand how to use it).

The user interface must also display a *confidence value* for each score—that is, how likely the score is to reflect the reality of the subject's behavior. The mechanism for generating this confidence value depends on the domain and the scoring algorithm. For instance, it might reflect the number of ratings used to generate the score, the standard deviation of the set of ratings, or the level of agreement between several different scoring algorithms that were all run against the ratings set. Confidence ratings are a major topic in Chapter 17.

Not only does a confidence value allow users to have a better feel for how firm a given score is, but it can also allow a more customized search. That is, a user might request that only scores with a certain minimum confidence value be displayed, which would weed out new users as well as users with unusual (widely varying) transaction patterns.

In some domains, qualitative statements (like verbal reviews) can enhance the value of a quantitative score. Simply providing a number may not feel as genuine or useful to users—indeed, allowing for qualitative statements can provide more flexibility in the system, because users providing feedback might discuss topics and dimensions which are difficult for survey authors to anticipate. On the other hand, it is very difficult to integrate these statements into numerical scores, particularly if they cover unanticipated dimensions. Also, as the number of statements increases, it becomes less useful to display all of them. Choosing which statements to display not only requires manual intervention and choice, but might also lead to legal liabilities. Another problem with providing verbal statements as part of the score is the issue of using this scoring system in different countries. Statements may need to be translated, but numbers are universal.

Scoring algorithms

As we've seen in the previous sections, there are many different aspects to scoring systems. While we believe that query flexibility is perhaps the most crucial aspect to the system, another important aspect is the actual algorithm used to aggregate ratings into scores. Such an algorithm needs to answer most of the requirements that we laid out in the section "Scoring systems." Broadly speaking, the scoring algorithm should provide accurate scores, while keeping dishonest users from affecting the system and also preventing privacy leaks (as detailed in the next section).

Keeping dishonest users from affecting the system can be done in several ways. One simple way is to run statistical tests independent of the actual aggregation algorithm, to attempt to detect outliers or other suspicious behavior such as a clique of conspiring users. Once this suspicious behavior has been identified, system operators can go back, manually examine the system, and try to prune the bad ratings. While this appears to be a very time-intensive approach that could not possibly be used in a deployed system, eBay has used exactly this method to try to clean up their system once dishonest users have been noticed.[*]

A more technically sound approach is to weight the ratings by the *credibility* of each rater. That is, certain people contribute more to the score of a given entity based on their past predictive ability. Google makes use of this idea in its Internet

---

[*] "eBay Feedback Removal Policy," *http://pages.ebay.com/help/community/fbremove.html.*

search engine algorithm. Its algorithm counts the number of references to a given page; the more pages that reference that page, the more popular it is. In addition, the pages that are referenced from popular pages are also given a lot of weight. This simple credibility metric produces much more accurate responses for web searches.

By introducing the notion of local credibility rather than simple global credibility for each entity, the system can provide a great deal of flexibility and thus stronger predictive value. Local credibility means that a rating is weighted more strongly if the situation in which that rating was given is similar to the current situation. For instance, a small farmer in Idaho looking into the reputation of chicken vendors cares more about the opinion of a small farmer in Arkansas than he does about the opinion of the Great Chinese Farming Association. Thus, the algorithm would generate a score that more accurately reflects the quality of the vendor according to other similar buyers. Similarly, if Google knew more about the person doing the web search, it could provide an even more accurate answer. Before being bought by Microsoft, firefly.net offered a service based on this idea.

One of the problems with incorporating credibility into the scoring algorithm is that, in some domains, an individual's ability to perform the protocol honestly is very separate from an individual's ability to predict performance of others.

In the Free Haven system, for instance, a server may be willing to store documents and supply them to readers, but keep no logs about transactions or trades (so it has no idea which other servers are behaving honestly). In the case of Reputation Technologies, one vendor might be excellent at providing high-quality products on time, leading to a high reputation score, but possess only average skill at assessing other vendors. Indeed, a consulting firm might specialize in predicting performance of vendors but not actually sell any products of its own.

One way to solve this problem is to have separate scores for performance and credibility. This makes it more complex to keep track of entities and their reputations, but it could provide tremendous increases in accuracy and flexibility for scoring systems.

Weighting by credibility is not the only way to improve the accuracy and robustness of the scoring algorithm. Another approach is to assert that previous transactions should carry more weight in relation to how similar they are to the current transaction. Thus, a vendor's ability to sell high-quality Granny Smith apples should have some bearing on his ability to sell high-quality Red Delicious apples. Of course, this could backfire if the vendor in question specializes only in Granny Smith apples and doesn't even sell Red Delicious apples. But in general, weighting by the so-called *category* of the transaction (and thus the vendor's reputation in related categories) is a very powerful idea. Separating reputations into categories can act as a defense against some of the subtle shilling attacks described above, such as when a vendor develops a good reputation at selling yo-yos and has a side business fraudulently selling used cars.

The category idea raises very difficult questions. How do we pick categories? How do we know which categories are related to which other categories, and how related they are? Can this be automated somehow, or do the correlation coefficients have to be estimated manually?

In the case of Free Haven, where there is only one real commodity—a document—and servers either behave or they don't, it might be feasible to develop a set of categories manually and allow each server to manually configure the numbers that specify how closely related the categories are. For instance, one category might be files of less than 100K that expire within a month. A strongly related category would be files between 100K and 200K that expire within a month; perhaps we would say that this category is 0.9-related to the first. A mostly unrelated category would be files more than 500MB in size that expire in 24 months. We might declare that this category is 0.05-related to the first two.

With some experience, an algorithm might be developed to tweak the correlation coefficients on the fly, based on how effective the current values have been at predicting the results of future transactions. Similarly, we might be able to reduce the discrete categories into a single continuous function that converts "distance" between file size and expiration date into a correlation coefficient.

Reputation Technologies is not so lucky. Within a given exchange, buyers and sellers might barter thousands of different types of goods, each with different qualities and prices; the correlation between any pair of categories might be entirely unclear. To make matters worse, each vendor might only have a few transactions on record, leaving data too sparse for any meaningful comparison.

While we've presented some techniques to provide more accuracy and flexibility in using ratings, we still haven't discussed actual algorithms that can be used to determine scores. The simplest such algorithm involves treating reputations as probabilities. Effectively, a reputation is an estimate of how likely a future transaction in that category is to be honest. In this case, scores are simply computed as the weighted sum of the ratings.

More complex systems can be built out of neural networks or data-clustering techniques, to try to come up with ways of applying nonlinear fitting and optimizing systems to the field of reputation. But as the complexity of the scoring algorithm increases, it becomes more and more difficult for actual users of these systems to understand the implications of a given score or understand what flaws might be present in the system.

Finally, we should mention the *adversarial approach* to scoring systems. That is, in many statistical or academic approaches, the goal is simply to combine the ratings into as accurate a score as possible. In the statistical analysis, no regard is given for whether participants in the system can conspire to provide ratings that break the particular algorithm used.

A concrete example might help to illustrate the gravity of this point. One of the often referenced pitfalls of applying neural networks to certain situations comes from the U.S. military. They wanted to teach their computers how to identify tanks in the battlefield. Thus they took a series of pictures that included tanks, and a series of pictures that did not include tanks. But it turns out that one of the sets was taken during the night, and the other set was taken during the day. This caused their high-tech neural network to learn not how to identify a tank but how to distinguish day from night. Artificial intelligence developers need to remember that there are a number of factors that might be different in a set of samples, and their neural network might not learn quite what they want it to learn.

But consider the situation from our perspective: what if the Russian military were in charge of providing the tank pictures? Is there a system that can be set up to resist bad data samples? Many would consider that learning how to identify a tank under those circumstances is impossible. How about if the Russians could provide only half of the pictures? Only a tenth? Clearly this is a much more complicated problem. When developing scoring systems, we need to keep in mind that simply applying evaluation techniques that are intended to be used in a "clean" environment may introduce serious vulnerabilities.

Privacy and information leaks

Yet another issue to consider when designing a good scoring system is whether the system will be vulnerable to attacks that attempt to learn about the tendencies or patterns of entities in the system. In a business-oriented domain, knowledge about transaction frequency, transaction volume, or even the existence of a particular transaction might be worth a lot of time and money to competitors. The use of a simple and accurate scoring algorithm implies that it should be easy to understand the implication of a vendor's score changing from 8.0 to 9.0 over the course of a day. Perhaps one or more ratings arrived regarding large transactions, and those ratings were very positive.

The objectives of providing timeliness and accuracy in the scoring algorithm and of maintaining privacy of transaction data seem to be at odds. Fortunately, there are a number of ways to help alleviate the leakage problems without affecting accuracy too significantly. We will describe some of the more straightforward of these techniques in this section.

The problem of hiding transaction data for individual transactions is very similar to the problem of hiding source and destination data for messages going through mix networks.* More specifically, figuring out what kind of rating influenced a published score by a certain amount is very similar to tracking a message across a middleman node in a mix network. In both cases, privacy becomes significantly easier as transaction volume increases. Also in both cases, adversaries observe external aspects of the system (in the case of the scoring system, the change in the score; in the case of the mix network, the messages on the links to and from the mix node) to try to determine the details of some particular message or group of messages (or the existence of any message at all).

One common attack against the privacy of a scoring system is a *timing attack*. For instance, the adversary might observe transactions and changes in the scores and then try to determine the rating values that certain individuals submitted. Alternatively, the adversary might observe changes in the scores and attempt to discover information about the timing or size of transactions. These attacks are like watching the timings of messages going through various nodes on a mix network, and trying to determine which incoming message corresponds to which outgoing message.

A number of solutions exist to protect privacy. First of all, introducing extra latency between the time that ratings are submitted and the time when the new score is published can make timing correlation more difficult. (On the other hand, this might reduce the quality of the system, because scores are not updated immediately.) Another good solution is to queue ratings and process them in bulk. This prevents the adversary from being able to determine which of the ratings in that bulk update had which effect on the score.

A variant of this approach is the *pooling* approach, in which some number of ratings are kept in a pool. When a new rating arrives, it is added to the pool and a rating from the pool is chosen at random and aggregated into the score. Obviously, in both cases, a higher transaction volume makes it easier to provide timely score updates.

---

* D. Chaum (1981), "Untraceable Electronic Mail, Return Addresses, and Digital Pseudonyms. " *Communications of the ACM*, vol. 24, no. 2, pp.84–88.

An active adversary can respond to bulk or pooled updates with what is known as an *identification flooding attack*. He submits ratings with known effect, and watches for changes in the score that are not due to those ratings. This approach works because he can "flush" the few anonymous ratings that remain by submitting enough known ratings to fill the queue. This attack requires the adversary to produce a significant fraction of the ratings during a given time period.

But all this concern over privacy may not be relevant at all. In some domains, such as Free Haven, the entire goal of the reputation system is to provide as much information about each pseudonymous server as possible. For instance, being able to figure out how Alice performed with Bob's transaction is always considered to be a good thing. In addition, even if privacy is a concern, the requirement of providing accurate, timely scores may be so important that no steps should be taken to increase user privacy.

Decentralizing the scoring system

Many of the issues we've presented apply to both centralized and decentralized reputation systems. In a decentralized system such as Free Haven, each server runs the entire reputation-gathering system independently. This requires each node to make do with only the information that it has gathered firsthand, and it generally requires a broadcast mechanism in order for all nodes to keep their information databases synchronized.

Another approach is to decentralize the scoring system itself, spreading it among the entire set of machines participating in the system. In this section, we present two ways of decentralizing a scoring system. The first exploits redundancy along with user flexibility to reduce the risk from cheating or compromised servers. The second is a more traditional approach to decentralizing a system, but it also brings along the more traditional problems associated with decentralization, such as high bandwidth requirements and difficult crypto problems.

Multiple trusted parties

Assume there is a set of scorers around the world, each independently run and operated. When a transaction happens, the vendor chooses a subset of the scorers and constructs a set of *tickets*. Each ticket is a receipt allowing the buyer to rate the vendor at a particular scorer. The receipts are blinded so that the vendor is not able to link a ticket with any given buyer.

At this point, the buyer can decide to which scorer or scorers he wishes to submit his ratings. Since each scorer could potentially use its own algorithm and have its own prices or publishing habits, each scorer might have its own set of trade-offs based on accuracy, privacy, and security. This technique allows the vendor to veto some of the scorers first. Then the rater chooses from among the remaining scorers. Thus, the ratings will only be submitted to mutually agreeable scorers.

We could extend this scenario to allow both parties in the transaction to provide tickets to each other, creating a more symmetric rating process. This approach introduces complications, because both parties in the transaction need to coordinate and agree on which tickets will be provided before the transaction is completed. There also needs to be some mechanism to enforce or publicize if one side of the transaction fails to provide the promised receipts.

The beauty of decentralizing the scoring system in this manner is that every individual in the system can choose which parts of the system they want to interact with. Participants in transactions can list scorers whom they trust to provide accurate scores, raters can choose scorers whom they trust not to leak rating information, and users looking for scores on various entities can choose scorers whom they trust to provide accurate scores.

Of course, this decentralization process introduces the issue of meta-reputation: how do we determine the reputations of the reputation servers? This sort of reputation issue is not new. Some Mixmaster nodes are more reliable than others,[*] and users and operators keep uptime and performance lists of various nodes as a public service. We expect that reputation scoring services would similarly gain (external) reputations based on their reliability or speed.

True decentralization

In this scenario, both sides of the transaction obtain blinded receipts as above. Apart from these *raters*, the system also consists of a set of *collectors* and a set of *scorers*. They are illustrated in Figure 16-2.

After the transaction, each rater splits up his rating using Shamir's secret sharing algorithm (described in Chapter 11, *Publius*) or some other k-of-n system. At this point, the rater submits one share of her rating to each collector. This means that the collectors together could combine the shares to determine her rating, but separately they can learn no information. It is the job of the scorers to provide useful information to clients: when a client does a reputation query for a specific category (situation), the scorer does the equivalent of an *encrypted database query* on the set of collectors.[†]

---

[*] "Electronic Frontiers Georgia Remailer Uptime List," *http://anon.efga.org*.

[†] Tal Malkin (1999), MIT Ph.D. thesis, "Private Information Retrieval and Oblivious Transfer."

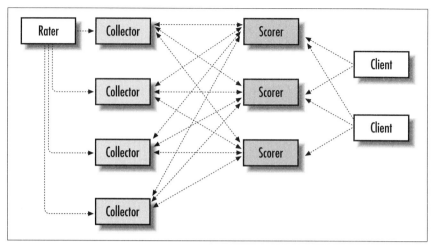

Figure 16-2. Truly decentralized scoring system

A number of technical challenges need to be solved in order to make this scheme work. First of all, the collectors need to have some mechanism for authenticating a rating without reading it. Similarly, they need to have some way to authorize a rater to put his share onto the system without their knowing the author of a given rating. Without this protection, malicious raters could simply flood the system with data until it overflowed.

Once these problems are solved, we need to come up with some sort of computationally feasible and bandwidth-feasible way of communication between the scorers and the collectors. We also need a set of rules that allow the scorers to get the information they need to answer a given query without allowing them to get too much information and learn more than they ought to learn about raters.

With this decentralization comes some subtle questions. Can scorers "accidentally forget" to include a specific rating when they're computing a score? Said another way, is there some way of allowing scorers to provide proof that they included a certain rating in the calculation of the score, without publishing the actual ratings that were used? This question is similar to the question of allowing mix nodes to prove that they forwarded a given message without yielding information that might help an adversary determine the source or destination of the message.*

---

* Masayuki Abe (1998), "Universally Verifiable MIX-Network with Verification Work Independent of the Number of MIX Servers," *EUROCRYPT '98*, Springer-Verlag LNCS.

A case study: Accountability in Free Haven

As described in Chapter 12, the Free Haven project is working toward creating a decentralized and dynamically changing storage service that simultaneously protects the anonymity of publishers, readers, and servers, while ensuring the availability of each document for a lifetime specified by the publisher. Our goals of strong anonymity and long-term persistent storage are at odds with each other. Providing as much anonymity as possible while still retaining sufficient accountability is a very difficult problem. Here we will describe the accountability requirements in greater detail than in Chapter 12 and discuss some approaches to solving them.

Our job is two-fold: We want to keep people from overfilling the bandwidth available from and between servers, and we want to keep people from overfilling the system with data. We will examine each of these goals separately.

Micropayments

In general, there are a number of overall problems with using micropayments in peer-to-peer systems. This general analysis will help motivate our discussion of using micropayments in the Free Haven context. We'll talk about them, then try to apply them to Free Haven.

The difficulty of distributed systems: How to exchange micropayments among peers

Consider the simple approach to micropayments introduced early in this chapter, in the section "Micropayment schemes." Alice wants resources operated by Bob. Alice pays Bob with some micropayments. Bob provides Alice with the access she purchased to his resources.

This sounds like a great model for economically-based distribution that provides both accountability and effective congestion-management of resources. However, the problem is rarely so simple in the case of peer-to-peer distributed systems on the Internet. The reason is that many intermediaries may be involved in a transaction—and one doesn't know who they are before the transaction starts, or perhaps even after the transaction is finished.

Consider an anonymous remailer like Mixmaster. Alice sends an email to Bob through a number of intermediate proxy remailers, which strip all identifying information from the message before transmitting it. This design is used to distribute trust across operational and often jurisdictional lines. Only a very powerful adversary—able to observe large sections of the network and use advanced traffic analysis techniques—should be able to link the sender and recipient of any given message. Hence, we achieve an essentially anonymous communications path for email.

Consider again the Gnutella routing protocol. Alice seeks some piece of information contained in the network. She sends out a query to all peers that she knows about (her "friends"); these peers in turn propagate the request along, branching it through the network. Hopefully, before the time-to-live (TTL) of the query expires, the request traverses enough intermediate hops to find Bob, who responds with the desired information. The Freenet routing protocol works similarly, covering some fraction of the surrounding network over the course of the search.

These examples highlight a design quite common in peer-to-peer systems, especially for systems focusing on anonymity (by distributing trust) or searching (by distributing content). That is, endpoint peers are not the only ones involved in an operation; Alice and Bob are joined by any number of intermediate peers. So how should we handle micropayments? What are the entities involved in a transaction? Four possible strategies are illustrated in Figure 16-3:

End-to-end model
> The simplest approach is to make Alice send Bob some form of payment and not worry about what happens to any intermediaries. This model works fine for operations that do not make use of intermediate nodes. But if intermediate peers are involved, they lack any protection from attack. Bob might even be fictitious. Alice can attack any number of intermediate peers by routing her queries through them, using up their bandwidth or wiping out the data in Freenet-style data caches. This problem is precisely our motivation for using micropayments!

Pairwise model
> Recognizing the problems of the end-to-end model, we can take a step upward in complexity and blindly throw micropayments into every transaction between every pair of peers. One long route can be modeled as a number of pairwise transactions. This model might appear to protect each recipient of payments, but it is also fundamentally flawed.

> Using fungible micropayments, each peer earns one unit from its predecessor and then spends one unit on its successor. Assuming equal costs throughout the network, Alice is the only net debtor and Bob the only net creditor. But if a single malicious operator is in charge of both Alice and Bob, these two peers have managed to extract work from the intermediate nodes without paying—a more subtle DoS or flooding attack!

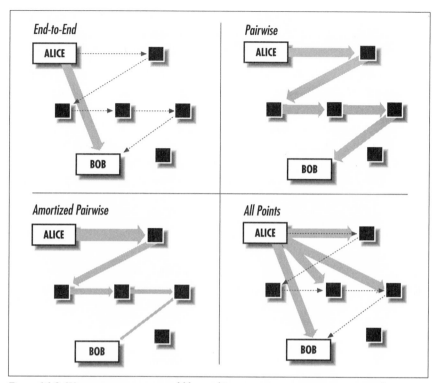

Figure 16-3. Ways micropayments could be used in a peer-to-peer communication path

Using nonfungible micropayments, Alice remains a net debtor, but so are all intermediate peers. Alice can make use of greater computational resources (centralized or distributed) to flood intermediate peers with POWs. Being properly-behaving nodes, these peers attempt to make good on the micropayment exchange, and start churning out POWs for the next hop in the protocol... and churning... and churning. Eventually Alice can exhaust the resources of a whole set of smaller, honest peers.

Amortized pairwise model

Taking what we learned about the risks of the pairwise model, we can design a more sophisticated one that amortizes Alice's cost throughout the network route by iteratively decreasing the cost of transactions as they move through the system. Say Alice pays X with four units of micropayment, X pays Y with three units, Y pays Z with two units, and Z finally pays Bob only one unit.

In the case of nonfungible POWs, we still lose. First of all, Alice can still make use of greater wealth, economies of scale, distributed computing, etc., in order to attack intermediate nodes. While the load decreases as it moves though the system, peers X, Y, and Z still need to devote some of their own resources; they may be unable to afford that load.

For fungible payments, this model appears more promising. Intermediate nodes end up as net creditors: their resources are paid for by the cut they take from Alice's initial lump-sum payment.

But this model has another weakness from a security point of view: we leak information regarding the route length. We mentioned the Mixmaster mix net at the beginning of this section; the system allows a sender to specify the number and identity of intermediate remailers. This number of hops and their corresponding identities are unknown to all other parties.[*] But if we use amortized payments, each peer in the chain has to know the amount it is given and the function used to decrease payments, so intermediate peers can extrapolate how many hops are in the route as well as their relative positions in the chain.

Furthermore, Alice may not know the route length. If a system uses Gnutella- or Freenet-type searching, Alice has no idea how many hops are necessary before the query reaches Bob.

As Alice's query branches out through the network, payments could become prohibitively expensive. For example, in Gnutella, we can estimate the number of nodes that a query traverses by treating the network as a binary tree rooted at the originating node, where the query traverses the first k levels (k is the query's time-to-live (TTL)). This gives a total of $2^{k+1}-1$ nodes visited by the query—and all of these nodes want to be paid. Thus the amount of nodes to pay is exponential in the TTL. Indeed, in reality the branching factor for the tree will be much greater than 2, leading to even more nodes that need payment. Freenet searching may be much more efficient; for more details, see Chapter 14.

All points model

These previous problems lead us to settle on an all points model. Alice pays each peer engaged in the protocol, intermediate and endpoint alike. Of course, we immediately run into the same problem we had in the previous model, where Alice may not know which peers are involved, especially during a search. But let's assume for this discussion that she knows which nodes she'll be using.

---

[*] We ignore the possibility of traffic analysis here and assume that the user chooses more than one hop.

This solution is ideal for such fully identified systems. The cost of resource use falls solely upon its instigating requestor.

Anonymous systems add a few difficulties to using this model. First of all, we lose some of our capacity to use interactive payment models. For the forward-only Mixmaster mix net, intermediate nodes cannot tell Alice what client puzzle she should solve for them because only the first hop knows Alice's identity. Therefore, payments must be of a noninteractive variety.

To stop double-spending, the scheme must use either a centralized bank server model (such as Chaumian e-cash) or have recipient-specific information encoded in the payment (such as hash cash). This recipient-specific information should further be hidden from view, so as to protect an eavesdropper from being able to piece together the route by looking at the micropayments. Recipient-hiding cryptosystems* help ensure that the act of encrypting the micropayment does not itself leak information about to whom the data is encrypted.

In short, the all points payment model—while offering advantages over the prior three models—presents its own difficulties.

Micropayment schemes can help ensure accountability and resource allocation in peer-to-peer systems. But the solution requires careful design and a consideration of all security problems: there are no simple, off-the-shelf solutions.

Micropayments in the Free Haven context

Most Free Haven communication is done by broadcast. Every document request or reputation referral is sent to every other Free Haven server. Even if we can solve the micropayments issue for mix nets as described above, we still need to ease the burden of multiple payments incurred by each server each time it sends even a single Free Haven broadcast.

The first step is to remember that our communications channel already has significant latency. Nobody will care if we introduce a little bit more. We can queue the broadcasts and send a batch of them out every so often—perhaps once an hour. This approach makes the problem of direct flooding less of a problem, because no matter how many broadcasts we do in the system, our overall use of the mix net by the n Free Haven servers is limited to n^2 messages per hour. We assume that the size of the message does not dramatically increase as we add more broadcasts to the batch; given that each Free Haven communication is very small, and given the padding already present in the mix net protocol, this seems like a reasonable assumption.

---

* David Hopwood, "Recipient-Hiding Blinded Public-Key Encryption," draft manuscript.

However, batching helps the situation only a little. For several reasons—the lack of a widely deployed electronic cash system, our desire to provide more friction-less access regardless of wealth, and the complex, central-server model used by most fungible payment systems to issue coins—nonfungible POW micropayments are better suited for Free Haven. Likewise, nonfungible payments work best with the expensive all-points payment scheme. We still have the problem, therefore, that every server must pay each intermediate node used to contact every other server each hour.

It is conceivable that spreading the waste of time for each message over the hour would produce a light enough load. Servers could simply do the computation with idle cycles and send out a batch of broadcasts whenever enough calculations have been performed.

We can solve this more directly by thinking of the server Alice as a mailing list that uses pay-per-send email as described earlier in this chapter, in the section "Nonfungible micropayments." In this case, users attach special tickets to messages sent to Alice, so they don't have to perform a timewasting computation. Similarly, we might be able to introduce into the mix net protocol a "one free message per hour" exception. But making this exception introduces a difficult new problem—our primary purpose is to maintain the anonymity of the senders and recipients through the mix net, but at the same time we want to limit each server to sending only one message per recipient in each hour. Thus, it seems that we need to track the endpoints of each message in order to keep count of who sent what.

Having Alice distribute blinded tickets as an end-to-end solution doesn't work easily either, as these tickets are used with the intermediate mix net nodes. The tickets would need to assure the nodes of both Alice's identity as a Free Haven server and her certification of the user's right to mail her, while still maintaining the pseudonymity of both parties.

The alternative is to have node-specific tickets for our all points model. More precisely, each mix net node issues a limited number of blinded tickets for each hour and user. This design also adds the functionality of a prepaid payment system, if we want one. Project Anon, an anonymous communications project, suggests such a technique.[*] It's important to note that most blind signature techniques use interactive protocols, which are less suitable for our type of application.

---

[*] Oliver Berthold, Hannes Federrath, and Marit Köhntopp (2000), "Anonymity and Unobserv-ability in the Internet," *Workshop on Freedom and Privacy by Design/Conference on Computers, Freedom and Privacy 2000,* Toronto, Canada, April 4–7.

Introducing a free message every hour to the mix net protocol also allows for smooth integration of another Free Haven feature: we want to allow anonymous users to proxy a document retrieve request through certain (public) Free Haven servers. Specifically, a user generates a one-time mix net reply block and a one-time key pair and passes these to a Free Haven node along with a handle to the document being requested. This Free Haven node broadcasts the query to all other servers, just as in a normal retrieve operation. Because bundling extra broadcasts into each hourly message is virtually free, we can allow these extra anonymous requests without much extra cost. Of course, a concerted flood of document requests onto a server could cause its hourly message to be very large; public Free Haven servers may have to drop document requests after a certain threshold or find some other mechanism for limiting this threat of flooding.

Overall, providing bandwidth accountability along with anonymity is a tough problem. What we describe above does not provide any clear solution for an environment in which we want to maintain strong anonymity. This discussion may help to explain why current mix net implementations don't use micropayments to address accountability. Further research is certainly necessary.

Reputation systems

The Free Haven reputation solution has two parts: first, we need to notice servers that drop data early, and second, we need to develop a process for "punishing" these servers.

It's very difficult to notice if a server drops data early, and we still haven't solved the problem completely. The buddy system laid out in Chapter 12 is our current approach, and it may well be good enough. After all, we simply have to provide a system that is difficult to *reliably* fool—it doesn't have to catch every single instance of misbehavior.

As for punishing misbehaving servers, that's where our reputation scheme comes in. The first step in developing a solution that uses reputation systems is to examine the situation more thoroughly and try to understand our goals and limitations. Every situation contains features that make it hard to develop a reputation solution and features that make it easier.

We expect the Free Haven domain to include a number of generous individuals who will take some risks with their reputations and resources. Since disk space is very cheap and getting cheaper, and there's no significant loss if a single trade goes bad, the Free Haven environment is relatively lenient.

Ratings in the reputation system are tied to transactions and include digitally signed receipts. So we can be pretty certain that either a given transaction actually did happen, or the two parties are conspiring. At regular intervals, each Free Haven server broadcasts a "reputation referral," a package of ratings of other servers. Nodes should broadcast reputation referrals in several circumstances:

- When they log the honest completion of a trade
- When they check to see if a buddy to a share they hold is still available and find that it is missing
- When there's a substantial change in the reputation or credibility of a given server, compared to the last reputation referral about that server

How often to broadcast a referral can be a choice made by each server. Sending referrals more often allows that server to more easily distribute its current information and opinions to other servers in the network. On the other hand, frequent broadcasts use more bandwidth, and other servers may ignore servers that talk too much.

Servers get most of their information from their own transactions and trades. After all, those are the data points that they are most certain they can trust. Each server keeps its own separate database of information that it knows, based on information it has observed locally and information that has come to it. Thus every server can have a different view of the universe and a different impression of which servers are reputable and which aren't. Indeed, these local decisions introduce a lot of flexibility into the design: Each server operator can choose her own thresholds for trust, broadcast frequency, which trades are accepted or offered, etc. These decisions can be made to suit her particular situation, based, for instance, on available bandwidth and storage or the expected amount of time that she'll be running a Free Haven server.

Since each server is collecting referrals from other servers (and some of those servers may be trying to discredit good servers or disrupt the system in other ways), we need a robust algorithm for combining the referrals. Each server operator can use an entirely separate algorithm, but realistically speaking, most of them will use a default configuration recommended by the Free Haven designers.

Some ways of choosing a good algorithm are described earlier in this chapter, in the section "Scoring systems." In Free Haven, we don't expect to have to focus on very many parameters in order to get a reasonable score. Our basic approach to developing a score for a given server is to iterate through each rating available on that server and weight each rating based on how important and relevant it appears to be. Parameters that we might want to examine while weighting a score include the following:

How recent is this rating?
Newer ratings should get more weight.

How similar (in terms of size and expiration date) is this rating to the transaction I'm currently considering?
Similar ratings should get more weight.

In my experience, has this server accurately predicted the behavior that I have observed?
This deals with the credibility of the rater.

How often does the server send referrals?
If a server is verbose, we might choose to assign a lower weight to each rating. On the other hand, if this is the first referral we've ever gotten from this server, we might regard it with skepticism.

How long has the rating server been a Free Haven server?
We will probably have greater confidence in servers that have been part of the system for a long time.

As explained in Chapter 12, each server needs to keep two values to describe each other server it knows about: reputation and credibility. Reputation signifies a belief that the server in question will obey the Free Haven Protocol. Credibility represents a belief that the referrals from that server are valuable information. For each of these two values, each server also needs to maintain a confidence rating. This indicates how firmly the server believes in these values, and indicates how much a value might move when a new rating comes in.

When new servers want to join the system, they must contact certain servers that are acting as *introducers*. These introducers are servers that are willing to advertise their existence in order to introduce new servers to the rest of the servnet. Introducing consists simply of broadcasting a reputation referral with some initial reputation values. Each introducer can of course choose her own initial values, but considering the discussion in the section "Problems with pseudospoofing and possible defenses," earlier in this chapter, it seems most reasonable to broadcast an initial referral value of zero for both reputation and credibility.

At first glance, it seems that we do not need to worry about information leaks from the compiled scores—after all, the entire goal of the system is to communicate as much information as possible about the behavior history of each pseudonym (server). But a closer examination indicates that a large group of ratings might reveal some interesting attributes about a given server. For instance, by looking at the frequency and quantity of transactions, we might be able to learn that a given server has a relatively large hard drive. We currently believe that leaking this type of information is acceptable.

Other considerations from the case study

Alice has paid for some resource. But did she get what she paid for? This question deals with the problem of trust, discussed more fully in Chapter 15. But given our discussion so far, we should note a few issues that apply to various distributed systems.

In the case of data storage, at a later date, Alice can query Bob for her document and verify its checksum in order to be sure Bob has properly stored her document. She cannot be sure Bob has answered all requests for that document, but she may be more convinced if Bob can't determine that she's the one doing the query.

A distributed computation system can check the accuracy of the results returned by each end user. As we saw earlier in this chapter, some problems take a lot longer to solve than a checker takes to verify the answer. In other situations, we can use special algorithms to check the validity of aggregate data much faster than performing each calculation individually. For example, there are special batch verification methods for verifying many digital signatures at once that run much faster than checking each signature individually.[*] On the other hand, sometimes these schemes leave themselves open to attack.[†]

The methods we've described take advantage of particular properties of the problem at hand. Not all problems are known to have these properties. For example, the SETI@home project would benefit from some quick method of checking correctness of its clients. This is because malicious clients have tried to disrupt the SETI@home project in the past. Unfortunately, no quick, practical methods for checking SETI@home computations are currently known.[‡]

Verifying bandwidth allocation can be a trickier issue. Bandwidth often goes hand-in-hand with data storage. For instance, Bob might host a web page for Alice, but is he always responding to requests? A starting point for verification is to sample anonymously at random and gain some statistical assurance that Bob's server is up. Still, the Mixmaster problem returns to haunt us. David Chaum, who proposed mix nets in 1981,[§] suggested that mix nodes publish the outgo-

---

[*] Mihir Bellare, Juan A. Garay, and Tal Rabin (1998), "Fast Batch Verification for Modular Exponentiation and Digital Signatures," *EUROCRYPT '98*, pp. 236–250.

[†] Colin Boyd and Chris Pavlovski (2000), "Attacking and Repairing Batch Verification Schemes," *ASIACRYPT 2000*.

[‡] David Molnar (September 2000), "The SETI@home Problem," *ACM Crossroads, http://www. acm.org/crossroads/columns/onpatrol/september2000.html*.

[§] D. Chaum, "Untraceable Electronic Mail, Return Addresses, and Digital Pseudonyms," *op. cit.*

ing batch of messages. Alternatively, they could publish some number per message, selected at random by Alice and known only to her. This suggestion works well for a theoretical mix net endowed with a public bulletin board, but in Internet systems, it is difficult to ensure that the mix node actually sends out these messages. Even a bulletin board could be tampered with.

Above, we have described some approaches to addressing accountability in Free Haven. We can protect against bandwidth flooding through the use of micropayments in the mix net that Free Haven uses for communication, and against data flooding through the use of a reputation system. While the exact details of these proposed solutions are not described here, hopefully the techniques described to choose each accountability solution will be useful in the development of similar peer-to-peer publication or storage systems.

Conclusion

Now we've seen a range of responses to the accountability problem. How can we tell which ones are best? We can certainly start making some judgments, but how does one know when one technique is better suited than another?

Peer-to-peer remains a fuzzy concept. A strict definition has yet to be accepted, and the term covers a wide array of systems that are only loosely related (such as the ones in this book). This makes hard and fast answers to these questions very difficult. When one describes operating systems or databases, there are accepted design criteria that all enterprise systems should fulfill, such as security and fault tolerance. In contrast, the criteria for peer-to-peer systems can differ widely for various distributed application architectures: file sharing, computation, instant messaging, intelligent searching, and so on.

Still, we *can* describe some general themes. This chapter has covered the theme of accountability. Our classification has largely focused on two key issues:

- Restricting access and protecting from attack
- Selecting favored users

Dealing with resource allocation and accountability problems is a fundamental part of designing any system that must serve many users. Systems that do not deal with these problems have found and will continue to find themselves in trouble, especially as adversaries find ways to make such problems glaringly apparent.

With all the peer-to-peer hype over the past year—which will probably be spurred on by the publication of this book—we want to note a simple fact: peer-to-peer won't save you from dealing with resource allocation problems.

Two examples of resource allocation problems are the Slashdot effect and distributed denial of service attacks. From these examples, it's tempting to think that somehow being peer-to-peer will save a system from thinking about such problems—after all, there's no longer any central point to attack or flood!

That's why we began the chapter talking about Napster and Gnutella. Unfortunately, as can be seen in Gnutella's scaling problems, the massive amounts of Napster traffic, and flooding attacks on file storage services, being peer-to-peer doesn't make the problems go away. It just makes the problems different. Indeed, it often makes the problems harder to solve, because with peer-to-peer there might be no central command or central store of data.

The history of cryptography provides a cautionary tale here. System designers have realized the limits of theoretical cryptography for providing practical security. Cryptography is not pixie dust to spread liberally and without regard over network protocols, hoping to magically achieve protection from adversaries. Buffer overflow attacks and unsalted dictionary passwords are only two examples of easy exploits. A system is only as secure as its weakest link.

The same assertion holds for decentralized peer-to-peer systems. A range of techniques exists for solving accountability and resource allocation problems. Particularly powerful are reputation and micropayment techniques, which allow a system to collect and leverage local information about its users. Which techniques should be used depends on the system being designed.

Acknowledgments

First and foremost, we'd like to thank our editor, Andy Oram, for helping us to make all of these sections fit together and make sense. Without him, this would still be just a jumble of really neat ideas. We would also like to thank a number of others for reviews and comments: Robert Zeithammer for economic discussion of micropayments, Jean-François Raymond and Stefan Brands for micropayments, Nick Mathewson and Blake Meike for the reputations section, and Daniel Freedman, Marc Waldman, Susan Born, and Theo Hong for overall edits and comments.

Reputation

Richard Lethin, Reputation Technologies, Inc.

Reputation is the memory and summary of behavior from past transactions. In real life, we use it to help us set our expectations when we consider future transactions. A buyer depends on the reputation of a seller when he considers buying. A student considers the reputation of a university when she considers applying for admission, and the university considers the student's reputation when it decides whether to admit her. In selecting a candidate, a voter considers the reputation of a politician for keeping his word.

The possible effect on one's reputation also influences how one behaves: an individual might behave properly or fairly to ensure that her reputation is preserved or enhanced. In situations without reputation, where there is no prospect of memory after the transaction, behavior in the negotiation of the transaction can be zero-sum. This is the classic used car salesman situation in which the customer is sold a lemon at an unreasonable price, because once the customer drives off the lot, the salesman is never going to see her again.

A trade with a prospective new partner is risky if we don't know how he behaved in the past. If we know something about how he's behaved in the past, and if our prospect puts his reputation on the line, we will be more willing to trade. So reputation makes exchange freer, smoother, and more liquid, removing barriers of risk aversion that interfere with trade's free flow.

Reputation does all this without a central authority. Naturally, therefore, reputation turns up frequently in any discussion about distributed entities interacting peer-to-peer—a situation that occurs at many levels over the Internet. Some of these levels are close to real life, such as trade in the emerging e-marketplaces and private exchanges. Others are more esoteric, such as the interaction of anonymous storage servers in the Free Haven system described in Chapter 12. Chapter 16, *Accountability*, includes a discussion of the value of reputation.

The use of reputation as a distributed means of control over fairness is a topic of much interest in the research literature. Economists and game theorists have analyzed the way reputation motivates fair play in repeated games, as opposed to a single interaction, which often results in selfish behavior as the most rational choice. Researchers in distributed artificial intelligence look to reputation as a system to control the behavior of distributed agents that are supposed to contribute collectively to intelligence. Researchers in computer security look at deeper meanings of trust, one of which is reputation.

In this chapter, I will present a commercial system called the Reputation Server™* that tries to bring everyday aspects of reputation and trust into online transactions. While not currently organized in a peer-to-peer fashion itself, the service has the potential to become more distributed and prove useful to peer-to-peer systems as well as traditional online businesses.

The Reputation Server is a computer system available to entities engaging in a prospective transaction—a third party to a trade that can be used by any two parties who want reputation to serve as motivation for fair dealing.

The server accepts feedback on the performance of the entities after each transaction is finished and stores the information for use by future entities. It also provides scores summarizing the history of transactions that an entity has engaged in. The Reputation Server, by holding onto the histories of transactions, acts as the memory that helps entities build reputations.

Examples of using the Reputation Server

A North American buyer of textiles might be considering purchasing from a new supplier in China. The buyer can check the Reputation Server for scores based on feedback from other buyers who have used that supplier. If the scores are good enough to go forward, the buyer will probably still insist that the trade be recorded in a transaction context on the Reputation Server—that the seller be willing to let others see feedback about its performance—in order to make it costly for the seller to perform poorly in the transaction. Without the Reputation Server, the buyer has to rely solely on other means of reducing risk, such as costly product inspections or insurance.†

---

* Reputation Server™ is a trademark of Reputation Technologies, Inc.

† These other risk reduction techniques can also be used with the Reputation Server.

But the motivation to use the Reputation Server is not exclusively on the buyer's side: A reliable seller may insist on using the Reputation Server so that the trade can reinforce his reputation.

In some cases, the Reputation Server may be the only way to reduce risk. For example, two entities might want to trade in a securely pseudonymous manner, with payment by a nonrepudiable anonymous digital cash protocol. Product inspection might be unwanted because it reveals the entity behind the pseudonym. Once the digital cash is spent, there's no chance of getting a refund. Reputation helps ease some of the buyer's concern about the risk of this transaction: she can check the reputation of the pseudonym, and she has the recourse of lowering that reputation should the transaction go bad. Thus, the inventors of anonymous digital cash have long recognized the interdependence of pseudonymous commerce systems and reputations. Also, the topic gets attention in the Cypherpunks *Cyphernomicon* as an enabling factor in the adoption of anonymous payment technologies.[*]

But more mundane risks can also make using the Reputation Server worthwhile. The example I started with in this section, of a buyer in North America purchasing textiles from China, has some aspects of functional anonymity: even though the buyer and seller aren't actively hiding from each other, they don't know each other because of the geographic, political, cultural, class, and language barriers that separate them. Reputation Servers can be the social network that is otherwise lacking and that enforces good behavior or allows the system to correct itself. As the Internet bridges the traditional barriers to create new relationships, the need for Reputation Servers grows.

At first, the implementation of this system seems trivial: just a database, some messaging, and some statistics. However, the following architecture discussion will reveal that the issues are quite complex. With keen competition and high-value transactions, the stakes are high. This makes it important to consider the design carefully and take a principled approach.

Reputation domains, entities, and multidimensional reputations

To understand how the Reputation Server accomplishes its task, you have to start with the abstraction of a *reputation domain*, which is a context in which a

---

[*] Tim May (1994). *The Cyphernomicon*, Sections 15.2–4, archived in various places on the Net, e.g., *http://swissnet.ai.mit.edu/6805/articles/crypto/cypherpunks/cyphernomicon/CP-FAQ* 1994.

sequence of trades will take place and in which reputations are formed and used. A domain is created, administered, and owned by one entity. For example, a consultant integrating the software components for a business-to-business, online e-marketplace might create a reputation domain for that e-marketplace on the Reputation Server. Thousands of businesses that will trade in the e-marketplace can use the same domain. Or someone might create a smaller domain consisting of auto mechanics in Cambridge and the car owners that purchase repairs. Or someone might create a domain for the anonymous servers forming Free Haven.

The domain owner can specify the domain's rules about which entities can join, the definition of reputation within that domain, which information is going to be collected, who can access the data, and what they can access. Reputations form within the domain according to the specified configuration. For the moment, we assume that there is no information transfer among domains: A reputation within one domain is meaningless in another domain.[*]

Entities in a Reputation Server correspond to the parties for whom reputations will be forming and the parties who will be providing feedback. Entities might correspond to people, companies, software agents, or Pretty Good Privacy (PGP) public keys. They exist outside the domains, so it is possible for an entity to be a participant in multiple domains.

The domain has a great degree of latitude in how it defines reputation. This definition might be a simple scalar quantity representing an overall reputation, or a multidimensional quantity representing different aspects of an entity's performance in transactions. For example, one of the dimensions of a seller's reputation might be a metric measuring the quality of goods a seller ships; another might be the ability to ship on time. The scoring algorithms do not depend on what the individual dimensions "mean"; the dimensions are measures within a range, and the domain configuration simply names them and hooks them up to sources and readers.

The notion of a domain is powerful, even for definitions that might be considered too small to be meaningful. For example, a domain with only one buyer seems solipsistic (self-absorbed) but can in fact be quite useful to an entity for privately monitoring its suppliers. The domain can provide a common area for the storage and processing of quality, docking, and exception information that might otherwise be used by only one small part of the buyer's organization or simply lost outright.

---

[*] This constraint is relaxed later in the chapter.

Reputation information about a supplier might be kept internal to the buyer if the buyer thinks this is of strategic importance (that is, if knowing which supplier is good or bad in particular areas conveys a competitive advantage to the buyer). On the other hand, if the buyer is willing to share the reputation information he has taken the trouble to accumulate, it could be useful so that a seller can attract other buyers. For example, ACME computer company might allow its ratings of suppliers to be shared outside to help its suppliers win other buyers; this benefits ACME by allowing its suppliers to amortize fixed costs, and it might even be able to negotiate preferred terms from the supplier to realize this benefit.

Identity as an element of reputation

Before gaining a reputation, an entity needs to have an identity that is made known to the Reputation Server. The domain defines how identities are determined.

Techniques for assuring an entity's identity are discussed in other areas of this book, notably Chapter 15, *Trust*, and Chapter 18, *Security*. An entity's identity, for instance, might be a certified public key or a simple username validated with password login on the Reputation Server.

Some properties of identities can influence the scoring system. One of the most critical questions is whether an entity can participate under multiple identities. Multiple participation might be difficult to prevent, because entities might be trivially able to adopt a new identity in a marketplace. In this situation, with weak identities, we have to be careful how we distinguish a bad reputation from a new reputation. This is because we may create a moral hazard: the gain from cheating may exceed the loss to reputation if the identity can be trivially discarded and a new identity trivially constructed. Weak identities also have implications for credibility, because it becomes hard to distinguish true feedback from feedback provided by the entity itself.

While it is possible to run a reputation domain for weak identities, it is easier to do so for strong identities. Reputation domains with weak identities require the system to obtain and process more data, while strong identities allow the system to "bootstrap" online reputations with some grounding in the real world.

Interface to the marketplace

We use the term marketplace loosely: generally it corresponds to an online e-marketplace, but a marketplace might also correspond to the distributed block trading that is taking place in Free Haven or the private purchasing activity of the single buyer who has set up a private reputation domain. While some marketplaces, such as eBay, include an embedded reputation system, our Reputation Server exists outside the marketplace so that it can serve many marketplaces of different types.

The separation of the Reputation Server from the marketplace creates relatively simple technical issues as well as more complex business issues. We discuss some of the business issues later in the section "Long-term vision." The main technical issue is that the marketplace and the Reputation Server need to communicate. This is easy to solve: The Internet supports many protocols for passing messages, such as email, HTTP, and MQ. The XML language is excellent for exchanging content-rich messages.

One of the simple messages that the marketplace can send to the Reputation Server indicates the completion of a transaction. This message identifies the buyer and seller entities and gives a description of the type of transaction and the monetary value of the transaction. The description is important: A reputation for selling textiles might not reflect on the ability to sell industrial solvents.

The transaction completion message permits the Reputation Server to accept feedback on the performance of entities in the transaction. For some domains, it also triggers the Reputation Server to send out a request for feedback on the transaction. In the most rudimentary case, the request for feedback and the results could be in electronic mail messages. Since a human being has to answer the email request for feedback, some messages may be discarded and only some transactions will get feedback. For this reason, obviously, it is preferable to automate the collection. So some businesses may interface the trader's Enterprise Resource Planning (ERP) systems into the Reputation Server. For automated peer-to-peer protocols like Free Haven, an automated exchange of feedback will be easier to generate.

The marketplace and the Reputation Server will also exchange other, more complex messages. For example, the marketplace might send a message indicating the start of a potential transaction. Some transactions take a long time from start to finish, perhaps several weeks. Providing the Reputation Server with an early indication of the prospective transaction allows the Reputation Server to provide supplementary services, such as messages indicating changes in reputation of a prospective supplier before the transaction is consummated.

Scoring system

One of the most interesting aspects of the Reputation Server is the scoring system, the manner in which it computes reputations from all of the feedback that is has gathered.

Why bother computing reputations at all? If, as asserted in the first sentence of this chapter, "Reputation is the memory and summary of behavior from past transactions," why not simply make the reputation be the complete summary of all feedback received, verbatim? Some online auctions do in fact implement this, so that a trader can view the entire chain of feedback for a prospective partner. This is okay when the trader has the facility to process the history as part of a decision whether to trade or not.

But more often, there is good reason for the Reputation Server to add value by processing the chain into a simple reputation score for the trader. First, the feedback chain may be sensitive information, because it includes a description of previous pricing and the good traded. Scoring algorithms can mask details and protect the privacy of previous raters. This trade-off between hiding and revealing data is more subtle than encryption. Encryption seeks to transform data so that, to the unauthorized reader, it looks as much like noise as possible. With reputation, there is a need to simultaneously mask private aspects of the transaction history—even to the authorized reader—while allowing some portion of the history through so it can influence the reputation. Some of this is accomplished simply by compressing the multiple dimensionality of the history into a single point, perhaps discretizing or adding another noise source to the point to constrain its dimensionality.

Furthermore, the Reputation Server has a more global view of the feedback data set than one can learn from viewing a simple history listing, and it can include other sources of information to give a better answer about reputation. Stated bluntly, the Reputation Server can process a whole bunch of data, including data outside the history. For example, the Reputation Server may have information about the credibility of feedback sources derived from the performance of those sources in other contexts.

Reputation metrics

The Reputation Server is a platform for multiple scoring functions, and each domain can choose the kinds of scoring used and the functions that compute the scores.

A number of reputation metrics have been proposed in the literature. Some simply provide ad hoc scales, dividing reputations into discrete steps or assigning boundaries and steps arbitrarily. While ad hoc definitions of reputation can seem reasonable at first, they can have undesirable properties.[*] For example, simply incrementing reputation by one for each good transaction and decrementing by one for each bad transaction allows a reputation to keep growing indefinitely if a seller cheats one buyer out of every four. If the seller does a lot of volume, she could have a higher reputation in this system than someone who trades perfectly but has less than three quarters the volume. Other reputation metrics can have high sensitivity to lies or losses of information.

Other approaches to reputation are principled.[†] One of the approaches to reputation that I like is working from statistical models of behavior, in which reputation is an unbound model parameter to be determined from the feedback data, using Maximum Likelihood Estimation (MLE). MLE is a standard statistical technique: it chooses model parameters that maximize the likelihood of getting the sample data.

The reputation calculation can also be performed with a Bayesian approach. In this approach, the Reputation Server makes explicit prior assumptions about a probability distribution for the reputation of entities, either the initial distribution that is assumed for every new entity or the distribution that has previously been calculated for entities. When new scores come in, this data is combined with the previous distribution to form a new posterior distribution that combines the new observations with the prior assumptions.

Our reputation scores are multidimensional vectors of continuous quantities. An entity's reputation is an ideal to be estimated from the samples as measured by the different entities providing feedback points. An entity's reputation is accompanied by an expression of the confidence or lack of confidence in the estimate.

Our reputation calculator is a platform that accepts different statistical models of how entities might behave during the transaction and in providing feedback. For example, one simple model might assume that an entity's performance rating follows a normal distribution (bell) curve with some average and standard deviation. To make things even simpler, one can assume that feedback is always given

---

[*] Raph Levien and Alexander Aiken (1998), "Attack-Resistant Trust Metrics for Public Key Certification," *Proceedings of the 7th USENIX Security Symposium*, UNIX Assoc., Berkeley, CA, pp. 229–241.

[†] Michael K. Reiter and Stuart G. Stubblebine, "Authentication Metric Analysis and Design," *ACM Transactions on Information Systems and Security*, vol. 2, no. 2, pp. 138–158.

honestly and with no bias. In this case, the MLE is a linear least squares fit of the feedback data.

This platform will accept more sophisticated reputation models as the amount of data grows. Some of the model enhancements our company is developing are described in the following list:

*   Allowing dynamic reputation. Without this, reputation is considered a static quantity with feedback data providing estimates. If an entity's reputation changes, the estimate of reputation changes only with the processing of more feedback data. When we incorporate drift explicitly, confidence in the reputation estimate diminishes without feedback data.

*   Incorporating source feedback models. With multiple ratings given by the same party, we can estimate statistically their bias in providing feedback. This might even permit the identification of sources that are not truthful.

*   Allowing performance in one context to project the entity's ability to perform in another context. For instance, the ability to sell shoes is some prediction of the ability to sell clothes.

The rate of reputation drift, the related weight assigned to more recent feedback, biases, the estimate of the credibility of sources, and contextual correlation become additional free parameters to be chosen by the MLE solver. Getting good estimates of these parameters requires more data, obviously.

A property of this approach is that reputation does not continue increasing arbitrarily as time advances; it stays within the bounds established when the reputation domain was configured. Additional data increase the data points on which the extracted parameters are based, so as a trader earns more feedback, we usually offer greater confidence in her reputation. Confidence is not being confused with the estimate of reputation.

It's interesting to think about how to incorporate the desire to punish poor performance quickly (making reputation "hard to build up, and easy to tear down") into the model-based approach. It seems reasonable to want to make the penalty for an entity's behaving in a dishonest way severe, to deter that dishonest behavior. With an ad hoc reputation-scoring function, positive interactions can be given fewer absolute reward points than absolute punishment points for negative behavior. But how is the ratio of positive to negative feedback chosen? There are a number of approaches that permit higher sensitivity to negative behavior.

One approach is to increase the amount of history transmitted with the reputation so the client's decision function can incorporate it. If recent negative behavior is of great concern, the reputation model can include a drift component that results in more weight toward recent feedback. Another approach is to weight positive and negative credibility differently, giving more credence to warnings.

The design choices (including ad hoc parameter choices) depend intimately on the goals of the client and the characteristics of the marketplace. Such changes could be addressed by adapting the model to each domain, by representing the assumptions as parameters that each domain can tune or that can be extracted mechanically, and perhaps even by customizing the reputation component in a particular client.

How is MLE calculated? For simple models, MLE can be calculated analytically, by solving the statistical equations algebraically. Doing MLE algebraically has advantages: The answer is exact, updates can be computed quickly, and it is easier to break up the calculation in a distributed version of a Reputation Server. But an exact analytical solution may be hard to find, nonexistent, or computationally expensive to solve, depending on the underlying models. In that case, it may be necessary to use an approximation algorithm. However, some of these algorithms may be difficult to compute in a distributed manner, so here a centralized Reputation Server may be better than a distributed one.

Credibility

One of the largest problems for the Reputation Server is the credibility of its sources. How can a source of feedback be trusted? Where possible, cryptographic techniques such as timestamps and digital signatures are used to gain confidence that a message originates from the right party. Even if we establish that the message is truly from the correct feedback source, how do we know that the source is telling the truth? This is the issue of source credibility, and it's a hairy, hairy problem.

We address this in our Reputation Server by maintaining credibility measures for sources. These credibility measures factor into the scoring algorithms that form reputations—both our estimated reputation and the confidence that our service has in the estimate. Credibility measures are initialized based on heuristic judgments, and then updated over time using the Bayesian/MLE framework previously described. Sources that prove reliable over time increase their credibility. Sources that do not prove reliable find their credibility diminished.

This process can be automated through the MLE solver and folded into the scoring algorithm. Patterns of noncredible feedback are identified by the algorithm and given lower weights. Doing this, though, requires something more than the accumulated feedback from transactions; we should have an external reference or benchmark source of credible data. One way that we solve this is by allowing the domain configuration to designate benchmark sources. The Reputation Server assigns high credibility to those sources because the designation indicates that there is something special backing them up, such as a contractual arrangement, bonding of the result, or their offline reputation. In a sense, credibility flows from these benchmark sources to bootstrap the credibility of other sources.

Interdomain sharing

Popular online marketplaces such as auctions have rudimentary reputation systems, providing transaction feedback for participants. These marketplaces strongly protect their control over the reputations that appear on their site, claiming they are proprietary to the marketplace company! The marketplaces fight cross-references from other auctions and complete copying of reputations with lawsuits, and they discourage users from referring to their reputations from other auctions.

These practices raise the question: Who owns your reputation? The popular auction sites claim that they own your reputation: It is their proprietary information. It is easy to understand why this is the case. Portable reputations would be a threat to the auction sites, because they reduce a barrier to buyers and suppliers trading on competitor auctions. Portable reputations make it more difficult for auctions to get a return from their investment in technology development and marketing that helped build the reputation.

The Reputation Server supports auction sites by isolating the reputation domains unless the owners of the domains permit sharing. In cases where the sharing can be economically beneficial, the scoring algorithms can permit joining the data of two domains to achieve higher confidence reputations. This is performed only with the permission of the domain owners.

Bootstrapping

One obstacle to the use of the Reputation Server is a bootstrapping or chicken-and-egg problem. While the server is of some use even when empty of transaction histories (because it serves as a place where entities can put their reputations on the line), it can be difficult to convince a marketplace to use it until some reputation information starts to appear.

Consequently, our server offers features to bootstrap reputations similar to the way reputations might be bootstrapped in a real-world domain: through the use of references. A supplier entering the system can supply the names of trade references and contact information for those references. The server uses that contact information to gather the initial ratings. While the reference gathering process is obviously open to abuse, credibility metrics are applied to those initial references. To limit the risk of trusting the references from outside the reputation system, those credibility metrics can signal that the consequent reputation is usable only for small transactions. As time passes and transactions occur within the reputation system, the feedback from transactions replaces the reference-based information in the computation of the reputation.

Long-term vision

Business theorists have observed that the ability to communicate broadly and deeply through the Internet at low cost is driving a process whereby large businesses break up into a more competitive system of smaller component companies. They call this process "deconstruction."[*] This process is an example of Coase's Law, which states that other things being equal, the cost of transacting—negotiating, paying, dealing with errors or fraud—between firms determines the optimal size of the firm.[†] When business transactions between firms are expensive, it's more economical to have larger firms, even though larger firms are considered less efficient because they are slower to make decisions. When transactions are cheaper, smaller firms can replace the larger integrated entity.

As an example, Evans and Wurster point to the financial industry. Where previously a bank provided all services like investments and mortgages, there are now many companies on the Internet filling small niches of the former service. Aggregation sites find the best mortgage rate out of hundreds of banks, investment news services are dedicated solely to investment news feeds, and so on. Even complex processes like the manufacturing of automobiles—already spread over chains of multiple companies for manufacturing parts, chassis, subsystems—could be further deconstructed into smaller companies.[‡]

---

[*] Philip Evans and Thomas Wurster (2000). *Blown to Bits: How the New Economics of Information Transforms Strategy.* Harvard Business School Press.

[†] Ronald Coase (1960). "The Problem of Social Cost," *Journal of Law and Economics*, vol. 3, pp. 1–44.

[‡] Clayton M. Christenson (1997) *The Innovator's Dilemma.* Harvard Business School Press.

With more entities, there is an increased need for tracking reputations at the interaction points between them. At the extreme, a firm might completely deconstruct: One vision is that the substations that currently make up a factory can become independent entities, all transacting in real time and automatically to accomplish the manufacturing task that previously occurred in the single firm. The Reputation Server, as one of the components reducing the cost of transacting between firms, serves as a factor to assist in this deconstruction, which results in lower manufacturing costs.

Central Reputation Server versus distributed Reputation Servers

The first version of the Reputation Server is a centralized web server with a narrow messaging interface. One could well argue that it should be decentralized so that the architecture conforms to our ultimate goal: to provide fairness in a non-centralized manner for peer-to-peer networks.

Can we design a network of distributed Reputation Servers? Yes, in some cases, such as when the reputation metric computation can be executed in a distributed fashion and can give meaningful results with partial information. Not all reputation metrics have these properties, however, so if the design goal of a distributed server is important, we should choose one that does.

Summary

Reputation is a subtle and important part of trade that motivates fair dealing. We have described technologies for translating the reputation concept into electronic trade, applicable to business transactions and peer-to-peer interaction. The Reputation Server provides these technologies. Scoring algorithms based on MLE and Bayesian techniques estimate reputations based on feedback received when trades occur. We describe enhancements for addressing the credibility of sources. Reputation domains, which are an abstraction mapped to the client marketplace, serve to store the configuration of rules about how reputations form for that marketplace, allowing the Reputation Server to be a platform for many different reputation systems.

chapter eighteen

Security

Jon Udell, BYTE.com, and Nimisha Asthagiri
and Walter Tuvell, Groove Networks

Security is hard enough in traditional networks that depend on central servers. It's harder still in peer-to-peer networks, particularly when you want to authenticate your communication partners and exchange data only with people you trust. Earlier chapters stressed protection for users' anonymity. The need to assert identity is actually more common than the need to hide it, though the two are not mutually exclusive. As shown in Chapter 16, *Accountability*, systems that assign pseudonyms to users need not absolve users of responsibility. This chapter touches on the interplay of identity and pseudonymity too, but will mainly focus on how to authenticate users and ensure they can communicate securely in a peer-to-peer system.

At Groove Networks Inc., we've developed a system that provides a type of strong security consistent with Groove's vision of a peer-to-peer system. The details are described in this chapter. We hope that our work can serve not only as proof that traditional conservative security principles can coexist with a novel distributed system, but also as a guide to developers in other projects. Groove is a peer-to-peer groupware system. Before we focus on its security architecture, we should first explain its goals and the environment in which it operates. Using Groove, teams of collaborators form spontaneous *shared spaces* in which they collect the documents, messages, applications, and application-specific data related to group projects. The software (which is available for Windows now and for Linux soon) works identically for users on a LAN, behind corporate firewalls, behind DSL or cable-modem Network Address Translation (NAT), on dial-up connections with dynamic IP addresses, or in any combination of such circumstances. The key benefits of Groove shared spaces are:

Spontaneity
> Groove needs no administrator. Nobody has to wait for IT to create the support system for a project. Users can do this for themselves, easily and right away.

Security
> Shared spaces are, in effect, instant virtual private networks (VPNs).

Context
> The shared space provides a context that helps users understand the nature, purpose, and history of all the messages and documents related to an activity.

Synchronization
> Shared spaces synchronize automatically among all members' devices and among all Groove devices owned by each member. Users can work offline; changes automatically synchronize when they reconnect.

Granularity
> Groove users don't typically exchange whole documents (though conventional file sharing is supported). Rather, they exchange incremental edits to documents. Groove-aware applications can even enable shared editing in real time.

Groove is really a new kind of Internet-based platform that delivers basic support for collaboration—in particular, security and synchronization. Users automatically enjoy these services with no special effort. Developers can build on them without needing to reinvent the wheel. In terms of data synchronization, Groove arguably breaks new technical ground with its distributed, transactional, serverless XML object store. But in terms of security—the focus of this chapter—Groove relies on tried-and-true techniques. What's novel isn't the algorithms and protocols, but rather the context in which they are used. Groove enables spontaneous peer-to-peer computing while at the same time abolishing the human factors problems that bedevil real-world security.

The environment in which Groove does all this is a hostile one. Firewall/NAT barriers often separate members of a group. Even within a group, people do not necessarily trust one another and do not typically share a common directory service or Public Key Infrastructure (PKI). People aren't always online, and when they are, they're not always using the same computer. People connect to the Net in different ways, using channels with very different bandwidths and latencies, so that, for example, an encrypted message may arrive before the message bearing its decryption key. Groups are dynamic; membership is fluid and constantly changing. The unit of secured data—that is, data that is authenticated, encrypted, and guaranteed not to have been tampered with—is not typically a whole document, but rather an incremental change (or *delta*), possibly an individual keystroke.

In the face of this hostile environment, Groove makes an impressive set of security guarantees to users. Here are some of them:

- Strong security is always in force. No user or administrator can accidentally or intentionally turn it off.

- All shared-space data is confidential. It's encrypted not only on the wire, where it's readable and writable by only group members, but also on disk, where it's readable and writable by only the owner of that copy of the data.

- No group member can impersonate another group member or tamper with the contents of any group message.

- A lost message can be recovered from any member, with assurance of the integrity of the recovered message and proof of its true originator.

- No nonmember or former member who has been uninvited from the group can eavesdrop on or tamper with group communication.

How Groove implements these security guarantees, thereby accomplishing its mission to deliver flexible and secure groupware in a hostile environment, is the subject of this chapter. We'll explore the implementation in detail, but first let's consider how and why Groove is like and unlike other groupware solutions.

Groove versus email

The world's dominant groupware application is email. Like Groove, email enables users to create primitive "shared spaces" that contain both messages and documents (i.e., attachments). Nobody needs to ask an administrator to create one of these shared spaces. We do it quite naturally by addressing messages to individuals and groups. Because firewalls are always permeable to email, we can easily form spaces that include people behind our own firewalls and people behind foreign firewalls. Email enables us to modify group membership on the fly by adjusting the *To:* and *Cc:* headers of our messages, adding or dropping members as needed. This is powerful stuff. It's no wonder we depend so heavily on it.

To the extent that we exchange sensitive information in email, though, we incur serious risks. People worry about the efficacy of the SSL encryption that guards against theft of a credit card number during an online shopping transaction. Yet they're oddly unconcerned about sending completely unencrypted personal and business secrets around in email. Secrets stored on disk typically enjoy no more protection than do secrets sent over the wire, a fact deeply regretted by the Qualcomm executive whose notebook computer was recently stolen.

Although it is convenient in many important ways, email is terribly inconvenient in others. The shared space of a group email exchange is a fragmentary construct. There is no definitive transcript that gathers all project-related messages and documents into a single container that's the same for all current (and future!) group members. Newsgroups, web forums, and web-accessible mail archives (such as Hypermail) or document archives (such as CVS) can make collaboration a more coherent and controlled exercise. But the IT support needed for these solutions is often missing within organizations, and especially across organizational boundaries.

There is, to be sure, an emerging breed of hosted collaborative solutions that make shared spaces a do-it-yourself proposition for end users. Anyone can go to eGroups (*http://www.eGroups.com*), for example, and create a project space for shared messages and documents. But eGroups provides only modest guarantees as to the privacy of such spaces, and none with respect to the integrity and authenticity of messages exchanged therein. What's more, services similar to eGroups fail the convenience test when users are connected poorly, or not at all. In these cases, users wind up manually replicating data to their local PCs—a procedure that is arduous, error-prone, and thus insecure.

Security, as cryptographer and security consultant Bruce Schneier likes to observe, is a process. When that process is too complex—which is to say, when it requires just about any effort or thought—people will opt out, with predictably disastrous results.

Collaboration places huge demands on any security architecture. It's a convenient fiction to believe that we are all safe behind our corporate firewalls, where we can form the groups in which we do our work, and create and exchange the documents that are the product of that work. But we never were safe behind the firewall, and the fiction grows less believable all the time as email worms burrow through firewalls and wreak havoc.

Furthermore, in a company of any substantial size, the firewall-protected realm cannot usefully be regarded as an undifferentiated zone of trust. Real people doing real work will want to form spontaneous workgroups; these workgroups ought to be isolated from one another. When we rely only on the firewall, we create the kind of security architecture that hackers call "crunchy on the outside, soft and chewy on the inside."

We need more granular security, distributed at the workgroup level rather than centralized in the firewall. Historically, people could form password-protected group spaces on departmental servers or even among their own peer-enabled PCs. But if the internal network is compromised, a sniffer anywhere on the LAN can scoop up all the unencrypted data that it can see. Likewise, if a server or desktop PC is compromised, the intruder (possibly a person with unauthorized physical access, possibly a virus) can scoop up all available unencrypted data.

The LAN, in any case, is a construct that few companies have successfully exported beyond the firewall to the homes, hotel rooms, public spaces, and foreign corporate zones in which employees are often doing their collaborative work. In theory, virtual private networks extend the LAN to these realms. In practice, for many companies that doesn't yet happen. When it does, there is typically only protection on the wire, not complementary protection on the disk.

So far, all these models assume that collaboration is an internal affair—that we work in groups under the umbrella of a single corporate security infrastructure. For many real-world collaborative projects, that assumption is plainly false. Consider the project that produced this chapter. Two of the authors (Nimisha Asthagiri and Walt Tuvell) are employees of Groove Networks, Inc. Another (Jon Udell) is an independent contractor. Beyond this core team, there was the editor (Andy Oram, an employee of O'Reilly & Associates, Inc.), and a group of reviewers with various corporate and academic affiliations. Projects like this aren't exceptions. They're becoming the norm.

To support our project, one of the authors created a Groove shared space. There, we used a suite of applications to collaborate on the writing of this chapter: persistent chat, a shared text editor, a discussion tool, and an archive of highly confidential Groove Networks security documents. As users of the shared space, we didn't have to make any conscious decisions or take any explicit actions to ensure the secure transmission and storage of our data. Under the covers, of course, were powerful security protocols that we'll explore in this chapter.

Why secure email is a failure

Before we dive into the details of Groove's security system, let's look again at the big picture. It's instructive to ask, "Why couldn't ordinary secure email support the kind of border-crossing collaboration we've been touting?" PGP, after all, has been widely available for years. Likewise S/MIME, which lies dormant within the popular mail clients. These are strong end-to-end solutions, delivering both on-the-wire and on-disk encryption. Why don't we routinely and easily use these tools to secure our shared email spaces? Because it's just too hard. In the case of PGP, users must acquire the software and integrate it with their email programs.

Then they confront a daunting user interface which, according to a study called *Why Johnny Can't Encrypt*,* few are able to master. S/MIME, though built into common email programs (Netscape Messenger and Microsoft Outlook Express), requires users to acquire client certificates (VeriSign calls them "digital IDs") that unleash signing and encryption.†

The next weakness of email shared spaces is that they aren't as coherent as we need, or as functional. Email is a good way to exchange interpersonal messages but a poor medium for group discussion and document archiving. When we ask it to serve these functions—as we often do, lacking other convenient tools—the result is a mess. Documents and pieces of conversations end up scattered across a bunch of computers. People get confused and waste time because they can't find everything related to the collaboration in one place; there's no single, consistent view of the project's data.

Finally, email can be a little too spontaneous for our own good. Information can leak out of an email shared space when anyone "ccs" someone else. That kind of spontaneity is a wonderful thing, and it's vital for effective collaboration. But it's not always a good idea to enable anybody in a shared space to include anybody else. People can leak information because of malice, poor judgment, or just operator error. The kinds of groups that form in email shared spaces are just too loosely defined. There's no way to balance the necessary freedom of spontaneous group formation with the equally necessary control of a centrally determined policy that governs modes of group formation.

The authors of this article could have used the S/MIME capabilities of our respective mail readers instead of Groove. And, in fact, we tried that experiment. But even for the three of us, all well versed in crypto software, S/MIME presented daunting configuration and use challenges. In any case, S/MIME only

---

* *http://www.cs.cmu.edu/~alma/johnny.pdf.*

† To the extent that we have any routine on-the-wire encryption at all on the Web, it's in the form of SSL-protected shopping carts. This works because although servers have certificates that authenticate them to clients (and that enable the SSL handshake to occur), almost no clients have certificates that reciprocally authenticate them to servers. It's unfortunate that this is so. E-commerce ought to have much more robust client authentication than it does. But the Public Key Infrastructure (PKI) gymnastics that server administrators are required to perform go way beyond what normal people are willing to put up with. So we settle for one-way, server-only authentication on the secure Web. And the only reason we have at least this much security is that it was possible to make it a no-brainer, an out-of-the-box default for a web shopper. You click the link, you see the golden key, it's "secure"—at least in a limited sense of that term, notwithstanding the risk of a hostile takeover of your PC, spoofing of the server's identity (since nobody actually checks the certificate sent from the server), or capture of your credit card number after decryption on the server.

governs the email domain. It doesn't empower users to form the coherent but replicated multiapplication workspace that makes Groove so effective. For us, the benefits of a secure shared space far outweighed the learning curve presented by Groove. The same will hold true for most typical Groove users.

The solution: A Groove shared space

Now we can start to put in place the foundations of a better data exchange system. A shared space is a copy of an XML object store. Incremental changes to objects are transmitted to all Groove devices participating in a shared space in the form of Groove delta messages. These messages may carry pieces of application data (a line of text in a chat, a stroke in a sketch) or pieces of administrative data (an invitation to join a shared space, a cryptographic key). The distributed communications engine ensures that delta messages are reliably delivered to and stored on each node. It adapts as needed (sometimes with the assistance of a central relay service) in order to reach nodes that are offline, that don't have fixed IP addresses, or that are behind firewalls and NATs.

Users see none of this plumbing.* They just interact with a viewer/editor called the transceiver. Figure 18-1 is a picture of a Groove transceiver displaying the shared space that we used to collaborate on this chapter.

The shared space is defined by a set of members, a set of tools, and the data created by members using those tools. In our case, the primary tools used for the collaboration included a persistent chat session, several threaded discussions, several notepads, a calendar, and a file archive. The tools are Groove-aware, which means that any change made in a notepad, discussion, or calendar propagates to all instances of the shared space. For an individual member, this synchronization may involve two or more devices (such as a desktop PC and a notebook PC).

Security characteristics of a shared space

In normal operation, a shared space has a fixed (steady state) population of members. Delta messages are being exchanged among the devices (one or more per user) that access the shared space. The kind of security that governs these messages may vary, for two different reasons. First, the Groove system can sup-

---

* In its base version, Groove does not require nor support the notion of a shared-space administrator. However, Groove Networks expects to offer an enterprise version of Groove that gives IT personnel more control over shared-space policy.

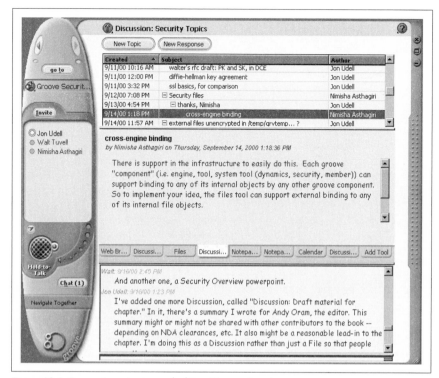

Figure 18-1. Transceiver viewing and editing Groove shared space

port different cryptographic algorithms (and key lengths) for each shared space. The default asymmetric algorithm for authentication and key exchange is ElGamal with a 1536-bit modulus. The default symmetric algorithm for bulk encryption on the wire is MARC4[*] with a 192-bit key.[†] But hooks exist to enable someone to use these algorithms in one shared space and other algorithms in a different shared space. These other algorithms might be stronger versions of ElGamal/MARC4 (though the Groove defaults are already massively strong) or different algorithms altogether, such as RSA/Blowfish. A Groove user

---

[*] Because the symbol RC4 is trademarked by RSA Data Security, Inc. (now RSA Security, Inc.), Groove uses the symbol MARC4, which stands for "Modified-Alleged-RC4." "Alleged" refers to a freely available algorithm that's plug-compatible with RSA Data Security, Inc.'s RC4. "Modified" means that the first 256 bytes of the keystream are discarded, to thwart a weak-key attack.

[†] In symmetric encryption, a single key is used for both encryption and decryption; in asymmetric encryption, the decryptor keeps a private key and the encryptor uses a public key. Symmetric encryption is more efficient, hence it's used wherever possible, subject to security considerations. For more information, see Chapter 15, *Trust*.

can choose different cryptographic algorithms to transact business with different organizations in parallel shared spaces. Imagine a consultant who works with the NSA on some projects and with a university on others.

Security for shared spaces can also vary in another way. The protocols that govern message encryption and authenticity/integrity can vary independently along these dimensions:

Encryption/confidentiality
> Who can read delta messages exchanged within the shared space? In theory, encryption can be turned off, just as SSL can use a null cipher. In practice, it's not interesting or useful to do this, and Groove doesn't.

Data-origin authenticity/integrity
> Is every delta message guaranteed to have come from its purported sender (and, perforce, not to have been tampered with)? Again, it's possible to turn off authenticity/integrity, although Groove doesn't. Messages are always authenticated and integrity-protected. There are, however, two flavors. A delta message may be guaranteed only to have come from some unspecified member of the group, or guaranteed to have come from a specific member. Each shared space, for its lifetime, uses one or another of these modes. The first, which we'll call "mutual trust," is the most common and least computationally expensive. The second, which we'll call "mutual suspicion," is less common and involves more overhead.

Mutually-trusting shared spaces

Let's assume a shared space in "mutual trust" mode—the most convenient and likely setup—and review the security model from that perspective. We'll also show why you might want to switch to "suspicious" mode.

Anatomy of a mutually-trusting shared space

Every Groove user maintains an account on one or more devices. An account is a container of identities. A user can project a single identity into all shared spaces but is not restricted to a single identity. Carol can be just "Carol" in spaces she shares with her friends, but "Carol Smith, Marketing Director" in spaces she shares with colleagues. Technically, a member of a shared space is an instantiation of an identity as a participant in that space; the same identity may be a member of many shared spaces.

Each identity is defined by two public/private key pairs—one for signing and verification, one for encryption and decryption. The private half of each of these key pairs is stored in the account. The public half is stored in the shared space, accessible to all members, and also (optionally) in each user's Groove Contacts (an address book), to protect and authenticate Groove instant messages. These Groove instant messages are exchanged among Groove identities, but outside the context of a shared space. So they're encrypted with one-time symmetric keys that are exchanged via the identity keys. By contrast, the delta messages that carry the user and administrative data are exchanged within a shared space, so they're encrypted using a symmetric key that's stored in the shared space and thus is available to the group, as we'll see later. (If you're confused already about the various keys, you can refer regularly to the final section of this chapter, "Taxonomy of Groove keys.")

Why each Groove identity requires two public and private keys

It's possible to combine the signature/verification and encryption/decryption functions into a single key pair. Beyond the obvious divide-and-conquer rationale, here are some subtler reasons why Groove doesn't combine these functions:

Plug-in cryptography
Groove's security subsystem is templatized (fully parameterized) and can work with virtually any public-key algorithms. Because some algorithms can only digitally sign while others can only encrypt, it's necessary to distinguish between the two purposes. Further, algorithms differ in the required length and properties of their keys.

External PKI policy
Groove plans (tentatively) to import key pairs from PKI sources. Such key pairs sometimes come with policy (as opposed to technical) constraints—for instance, signing might be allowed, but no encryption or key agreement. In order to comply with such policies, Groove must keep these key usages separate.

When members are joining or leaving a shared space, the identity's signing/verification key pair is used to authenticate the messages that invite (or uninvite) members. The encryption/decryption key pair is used to encrypt/decrypt the symmetric key, which is in turn used to encrypt/decrypt the invitation messages. We'll explore the invitation protocol later. But for now, let's complete the description of the security model when the shared space is in normal use.

When Bob types a line of text into his transceiver's chat window, the data flows in two directions—down to the disk, where it's written to the encrypted object store, and over the wire, in encrypted form, to the other members' transceivers and object stores. If Bob owns another Groove device, the data goes there too. The integrity of the message carrying Bob's chat line is protected by a Message Authentication Code (MAC).*

The encryption of each disk file is handled by a per-member, per-shared-space symmetric key. This key is in turn protected by a master symmetric key, stored in the account Bob created when he first installed Groove.† Why not just directly encrypt all on-disk shared spaces with the master key? The extra level of indirection isolates each shared-space file into its own security domain.

The encryption of Groove delta messages sent over the wire is handled by a symmetric key—which we'll call the group key—that's stored in the shared space and accessible to all members. In fact, there are two such keys—one MAC key, called L_G, for data integrity and authentication (the symmetric-key analogue of signing and verification), and one cipher key, called K_G, for encryption and decryption. Here, G denotes the set of group (shared space) members.

The default algorithm used for the MAC is HMAC-SHA1. SHA1 (FIPS 180–1) is used to produce a hash of the header and body of the message. HMAC (RFC 2104) provides authentication and integrity protection of the resulting hash.

The key to mutual trust

Our term "mutual trust" concerns how closely you can trace messages to senders. Upon receiving a message within a shared space, a member of the shared space can prove it was not tampered with by recomputing the MAC using the L_G key and comparing the resulting MAC with the transmitted MAC.

The message's sender is authenticated by the same means. Since the group key, L_G, was exchanged in an authenticated way (that is, via the invitation protocol or piggy-backed on a standard Groove delta message, as later described), only group members will have it. If the MACs match, the message must have been sent by a group member. But the exact member who sent the message cannot be verified,

---

* All Groove data that is encrypted is of course also integrity-protected. But to simplify the exposition, we sometimes abuse terminology and only explicitly mention the encryption aspect of data protection.

† The account itself is protected by a key derived from the passphrase chosen by the user when the account was created. Just as the master key is used to decrypt each shared-space-storage key, this passphrase-derived key is used to decrypt the account's storage key—and that's the only thing the passphrase is used for.

because L_G is common to all members of the shared space. That's why we call this a mutually-trusting shared space. Members are not prevented from spoofing each others' messages; they merely agree to trust one another not to do so.

To see why this mutual trust might not suffice, imagine a transcorporate shared space in which members engage in a high-stakes negotiation. It's not enough to know that a message came from an authenticated member of the group. It's crucial to know that a message came from an authenticated individual who's part of a particular negotiating team. In such cases, you'll need to form a mutually-suspicious shared space.

Why not always be suspicious? All things being equal, you'd rather bind message authenticity to individuals rather than just to the group. But all things aren't equal; it's more costly to authenticate individuals, as we'll see. And for many of the group activities that Groove can support, group-level authentication works just fine. When we were collaborating on this chapter, we cared about three things:

Confidentiality
    We didn't want anybody else reading our stuff.

Authenticity
    We didn't want anybody else impersonating a group member.

Integrity
    We didn't want any data corrupted in transit.

We got these assurances in a mutually-trusting shared space. And we got them just by installing and using Groove. When impersonation is a real risk, though, you'll want to create a mutually-suspicious shared space. Let's look at how that works.*

Mutually-suspicious shared spaces

It's time to introduce some more keys. Each member in each shared space has a Diffie-Hellman public/private key pair. These Diffie-Hellman keys (which are authenticated via the identity key pairs mentioned previously) are used to establish pairwise symmetric keys—that is, keys shared between each pair of members within a shared space. Through the magic of Diffie-Hellman, the pairwise keys aren't sent over the wire. Instead, they're independently computed by

---

* In the preview version of Groove available at the time this chapter was written, the ability to configure a shared space to run in trusting or suspicious mode was not exposed to the user. By default, shared spaces ran in trusting mode.

each pair of members. Bob computes a Bob/Carol pairwise key from his Diffie-Hellman private key and Carol's Diffie-Hellman public key. Carol computes the same pairwise key from her private key and Bob's public key.

There are two kinds of pairwise keys between members M_i and M_j. A cipher pairwise key, K_{ij}, encrypts the group keys (K_G, L_G) for distribution. A MAC pairwise key, L_{ij}, assures the data origin authenticity/integrity of messages in a suspicious shared space.

Recall that in the trusting case, a MAC is attached to each message. It's a MAC of the header and body of the message, protected in the group key: $\{X\}L_G$. Rather than a group-level MAC, suspicious mode uses a set of individual MACs denoted as $\{X\}L_{ij}$, one for each pair of members. Each of these uses HMAC-SHA1 to authenticate a message using the pairwise key shared between a pair of members. The resulting MACs are called authenticators (or multiauthenticators). These are symmetric-key analogues of public-key signatures.

Figure 18-2 shows what the authenticator looks like for a message in the trusting case. The size is the same for groups of any number. For each message, there's just a header, a body encrypted in the group key K_G, and an authenticator in the group key L_G. In a suspicious group, however, as shown in Figure 18-2, the multiauthenticator grows linearly with group number. For each message, there's a header, a body encrypted in the group key K_G, and one MAC per member in the pairwise keys L_{ij}.

Groove could have used public-key signatures instead of multiauthenticators. The advantage is that the size of such signatures and the time required to compute them remain constant. But public-key signatures are big, and they are very slow. For the small groups that are the focus of the initial release of Groove, multiauthenticators work best.

There are two different reasons to bundle authenticators into multiauthenticators: to support message fanout and to support the recovery of lost messages.

Message fanout

The Groove system supports pure peer-to-peer communication. In the simplest case, two Groove-equipped PCs connected by a null 10BaseT cable can communicate happily. But what if a member is firewalled, or offline, or connected by way of a very slow link? In these cases, the Groove software can use a relay server to enable or optimize peer communication.[*]

---

[*] Other companies may also offer relay services to support the Groove software.

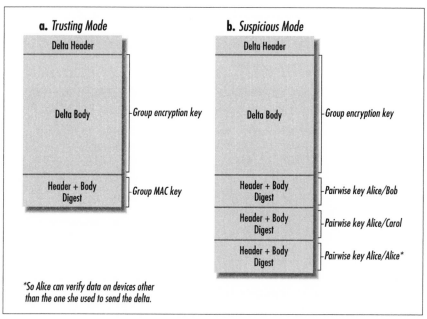

a. Trusting Mode

Delta Header

Delta Body — Group encryption key

Header + Body Digest — Group MAC key

*So Alice can verify data on devices other than the one she used to send the delta.

b. Suspicious Mode

Delta Header

Delta Body — Group encryption key

Header + Body Digest — Pairwise key Alice/Bob

Header + Body Digest — Pairwise key Alice/Carol

Header + Body Digest — Pairwise key Alice/Alice*

Figure 18-2. Authentication overhead: suspicious mode vs. trusting mode

A relay server is a system that understands Groove communication protocols and can route messages accordingly. The relay doesn't know anything about members, only about shared spaces and devices. Suppose Bob is on a modem link and sends a message to Carol and Alice. Rather than send two messages over that slow link, he'd like to send just one message to the relay and have the message fan out to everybody on its fast link. (The relay can also store and forward the message to someone who is offline.) The single multiauthenticator enables the sender to create a single delta message and push it to the relay server.

Consider the alternative: multiple deltas, each equipped with a single-authenticator. In that case, the sender would have to transmit n times the data through the pipe. Or the relay would have to interpret application layer data and then tag on the appropriate authenticator for the appropriate member, rather than just blindly relaying application data without parsing or interpreting it.

A complete description of Groove's communication protocols is beyond the scope of this chapter. Briefly, the Device Presence Protocol (DPP) solves the naming and awareness issues for devices. The Simple Symmetric Transport Protocol (SSTP) connects clients to clients, clients to relays, and relays to relays. It's SSTP that propagates information about a delta message, including its target endpoint.

For each target endpoint, there are three possible routes, listed here in order of preference:

1. Send directly (peer-to-peer) to the endpoint. This is impossible if target or sender is offline.

2. Send to the endpoint's preferred relay (currently hardcoded, but eventually user-customizable). This is impossible if either the relay or sender is offline.

3. Store it on the sender until it can be sent to the target or relay. This is always possible, as a last resort.

The preferred choice depends not only on who's online, but also on a heuristic calculation—by the sender—of the relative efficiency of the three choices. The sender considers line speed and message size to determine whether multicast (1) or fanout (2) would be better. The sender also needs to consider the firewall situation. Once the target's IP address is resolved through DPP, the source client will try to communicate directly to the target client. A direct peer-to-peer connection is always preferred over a relayed connection. However, sometimes it's necessary to use the relay as an intermediary even if both clients are online. Table 18-1 summarizes the possibilities.

Table 18-1. Relaying vs. direct connection

Source/client A	Target/client B	Connection
Public[a]	Public	Direct
Firewall/NAT/Proxy W/ 2492[b]	Public	Direct
Firewall/NAT/Proxy NO 2492[c]	Public	Via relay
Firewall/NAT/Proxy	Firewall/NAT/Proxy	Via relay
Public	Firewall/NAT/Proxy NO 2492	Via relay
Public	Firewall/NAT/Proxy W/ 2492	Initially via relay[d]

[a] Public: A device with a public IP address to which a direct connection is possible. This includes devices with DHCP-assigned public addresses.

[b] W/ 2492: A configuration where port 2492 (the network port used by Groove's proprietary SSTP protocol) is allowed inbound (if it appears in the "source" column) or outbound (if it appears in the "target" column).

[c] NO 2492: A configuration where Groove is forced (since other paths have failed) to use a path (such as an HTTP proxy) that blocks port 2492 inbound (if it appears in the "source" column) or outbound (if it appears in the "target" column). In this case, Groove must encapsulate all SSTP messages within HTTP messages and send them through port 80 (the HTTP port). This configuration also implies that the connection must go through the relay server since a Groove client cannot accept inbound connections on port 80 at this time. Groove does not want to conflict with other applications (such as a web server) that may be running on the client.

[d] The connection is initially established via the relay server. However, it is possible that the connection can transition into a direct connection if client B decides to change roles and become not only a listener from client A, but also a sender to client A. If so, client B creates a new connection to A that takes the properties of the second scenario (in the second row above), a direct connection. Since Groove favors direct connections over relayed connections, the original relayed connection from A to B terminates and is replaced by the direct connection from B to A.

Fetching lost messages

Suppose Alice never receives Bob's message. Because messages are sequenced, Alice's Groove software will discover that the message is missing and try to fetch it. Ideally, she'll fetch it from Bob. But what if Bob has, meanwhile, gone offline? In this case, Alice will try to fetch the lost message from Carol. Carol then encrypts the message in her Carol/Alice encryption key but attaches the Bob/Alice MAC (which Carol memorized earlier for this purpose) so Alice can correctly authenticate the message as one from Bob.

Shared space formation and trusted authentication

The person who sends an invitation to join a shared space is called the "chair"—in the sense of "chairperson of a meeting." If all of the members of a would-be shared space are already running Groove, the invitation protocol can begin with a Groove instant message from the chair to the invitees. Alternatively, this invitation can travel as email. The email alternative is especially important because it's a bootstrapping mechanism that brings non–Groove users into the Groove realm. In this case, the message's subject says "Please join our shared space." Its body describes the purpose of the shared space and offers a link to download and install the Groove software in case the recipient isn't already running it. Finally, the email message attaches the first in the sequence of Groove messages that comprise the Groove invitation protocol. Once the Groove software is installed, double-clicking that attachment "injects" the message into Groove and kicks off the invitation protocol.

Note that in this scenario, Groove uses email only as an unsecured carrier. This raises the specter of end-entity authentication: how do the chair and the invitee convince themselves that they're talking to the "right" person, i.e., that the invitation protocol hasn't been hijacked by an imposter? It's possible, though unlikely, that the sender and recipient will use S/MIME or PGP to authenticate and/or encrypt the invitation message.

In the case of S/MIME, trust resides in a PKI-based system. If an S/MIME signature were attached to the chair's invitation message, the invitee could examine the certificate bound to that message. The certificate would in turn be signed by a certification authority (CA). The CA assures the invitee that the chair's certificate—on the invitation—binds to a specified real-world identity.

In the case of PGP, trust resides in a more decentralized web of trust system. Rather than depending on a PKI hierarchy, PGP models trust in a more collegial way. Certificates are signed, not by specialized CAs, but by other people. PGP users sometimes expand their webs of trust by holding "signing parties" where people can meet face-to-face and cross-certify their keyrings.

It's plainly evident that neither the hierarchical nor the web of trust approach has taken the world by storm. For most people, PGP and S/MIME implementations are far too complex and hard to use. The result is that the percentage of signed and/or encrypted email on today's Internet is vanishingly small.

Groove aligns itself more closely with PGP than with S/MIME. And it's influenced by recent initiatives to simplify PKI: Simple Public Key Infrastructure (SPKI, RFC 2692), and Simple Distributed Security Infrastructure (SDSI, *http://theory.lcs.mit.edu/~rivest/sdsi1.html*). These initiatives, now merged, aim to make direct user-to-user cross-certification easy enough so that users can actually do it for themselves, in a natural way. Central to this approach is SDSI's notion that identities need not be represented by globally unique names, nor characterized by a fixed set of attributes. SDSI stresses that it is human judgment that must decide, given a set of attributes, whether to accept a claimed identity as valid. To that end, it should be easy to create and read certificates containing attributes that are meaningful to people: Phone numbers, photos, and free-form text. Groove, though not an implementation of SDSI, subscribes to these ideas.

In Groove, the public persona of an identity is called a contact. It contains a self-chosen free-form name,[*] and the public halves of the identity's two self-chosen key pairs.[†] In an enterprise version of Groove, it might also contain a student ID or an X.500 name (such as O="Big Corporation Ltd"/OU="Finance"/CN="John Doe").

When Bob creates his identity, he may decide to add more information to the contact—for example, his phone number. Here's how Alice can use that information to authenticate Bob's invitation message. The message is signed by Bob. It comes with the public key that is purportedly Bob's.[‡] Alice's Groove software first verifies the signature using the transported public key (thereby guaranteeing that the message was really signed by the private key corresponding to the

---

[*] The self-asserted name will typically be the user's real-world name, but it could also be an email name, or indeed any display name or alias the user chooses.

[†] The key pairs are currently "self-chosen" in the sense that Groove automatically generates them (locally, on the user's machine) and assigns them to the identity when it is created (there is a different set of generated key pairs for each identity). There is no central "identity authority." In the future, Groove will almost certainly allow users to import their key pairs from external sources, such as PKI certificates.

[‡] To simplify the narrative, we sometimes pretend the two Groove key pairs are just one key pair, used for signature/verification and encryption/decryption/key establishment.

transported public key) and then locally computes the fingerprint (hash of the public key, a string of hex digits). She can then phone Bob and ask Bob to report his genuine fingerprint to her. If the fingerprints match, the message could only have come from (i.e., been signed by) Bob—assuming that the private key for Bob's Groove identity, protected by Bob's passphrase, remains uncompromised under Bob's control.

Alice knows Bob, along with his phone number and his voice, through trusted, out-of-band, real-world channels. For example, Bob might have printed his fingerprint on his business card and given the card to Alice in a face-to-face meeting. Later, recalling that meeting, Alice matches the fingerprint on the business card to the fingerprint computed from a message claiming to come from Bob. Authentication doesn't depend on third-party certification of Bob's public key. Groove depends on relationships that are rooted in real-world collaboration, and it extends those relationships into the realm of shared spaces.

Admittedly, this scheme places the burden of establishing trust on the user. But the truth is that the burden always rests with the user. Technologies such as S/MIME and SSL purport to take matters out of users' hands. But they, too, ultimately rely on fingerprints that people should in theory check before investing trust, but in practice almost never do. From the user's perspective, what sets Groove apart from other systems is its all-crypto, all-the-time approach. You never have to worry about whether messages are confidential, because they always are. Messages are likewise always authentic—to precisely the degree that you care about authenticity. In a shared space that supports casual discussion, you may not care about the risk of impersonation. What's more, some spaces may be explicitly pseudonymous, with no use of real-world identities. In these cases, you may not bother to check fingerprints. In a shared space that supports highly confidential business activities, however, you should worry about impersonation, and you should check fingerprints.

Note that while Groove does not implement or require PKI, neither is it incompatible with PKI. Recall that Groove is flexible about the kinds of information stored in an identity's contact. If an enterprise has assigned X.500 names to employees, these names can be included in Groove identities. In this way Groove can ride on preexisting directory and naming structures. Further, its authentication protocols can be extended to handle PKI-style certificate validation. When an enterprise runs its own CA, for example, an enterprise version of Groove might be configured to trust that CA, just as browsers today accept SSL and S/MIME certificates signed by VeriSign, Entrust, and others. Look for PKI integration in post-preview editions of Groove.

Inviting people into shared spaces

When Bob invites Alice into a shared space that already includes Bob and Carol, the following things will have to happen:

- Bob and Alice must complete the invitation protocol.

- New pairwise keys (Alice/Bob, Alice/Carol) will need to be established.

- The group key will need to be given to Alice.

Note that the first step of the invitation may not be confidential. Alice isn't a member yet, and the key that will be used by the new group doesn't exist. What's more, Alice may not even be a Groove user yet, in which case she has no Groove account, identity, or public key that Bob can use to encrypt the first invitation message. In this case, the invitation is not confidential—unless Bob and Alice have established confidentiality in another way, for example, using S/MIME to encrypt an email version of the invitation message. But the invitation is always digitally signed by the Groove software with Bob's signature private key, regardless of the channel used to send it.

Alternatively, Bob and Alice may already be Groove users who have communicated before. In this case, the invitation—if sent as a Groove instant message—is confidential.

Either way, the invitation includes all the information needed to bring the new member into the shared space:

- A cryptographic context, which defines the algorithms to be used in that shared space. It includes, among other things, the Diffie-Hellman parameters used within the shared space. Alice's Groove software will use this information to generate her Diffie-Hellman key pair. Once Bob's Groove software has distributed Alice's Diffie-Hellman public key to everyone, she will be able to use the key to compute pairwise keys with other members.

- The public keys for Bob's identity.

On receiving the message, Alice can verify that it's intended for her (by checking the name on the invitation), authenticate Bob's contact (by calling the phone number listed there and checking the fingerprint), and consider what kind of shared space she's been asked to join. In practice, when the two parties have previously communicated in Groove, the authenticity of the message is not in question. It's only a question of whether to join for the stated purpose (for instance, to collaborate on a project), given the stated mode (for instance, trusting vs. suspicious).

To accept the invitation, Alice will have to install Groove if she hasn't already done so. If Alice then agrees to join the group, her Groove software sends Bob's software a message containing the following information:

- A one-time key encrypted in Bob's public key.

- Alice's Diffie-Hellman public key for the shared space, signed by the private half of the identity key in her account so that each member can verify its authenticity.

On receiving Alice's acceptance, Bob's Groove software decrypts the one-time key, decrypts Alice's reply with the one-time key, and verifies the validity of Alice's acceptance. Bob himself, after a fingerprint authentication of Alice, can then manually confirm (by clicking an OK button) that Alice should be added to the group. That confirmation triggers the following events:

- A New-Member-Added message is sent to the group.

- Alice receives a copy of the shared-space data, which includes the group keys, K_G and L_G. The shared-space data is encrypted in a one-time key which is, in turn, encrypted in Alice's public key.

The New-Member-Added delta message

The message that tells everybody a new member has joined is called, appropriately, the New-Member-Added delta. This message, sent from Bob to the preexisting members (in this case, only Carol), announces that Alice has joined the group. It includes Alice's Diffie-Hellman public key, which Carol stores in her member list and uses to establish her pairwise key with Alice.

Arguably, the New-Member-Added message should also trigger the establishment of a new group key. It doesn't. Only when a member is uninvited is a new group key established. When Alice is invited, she gets the same group key that Bob and Carol were already using. Therefore, she can read all previous messages stored in the shared space. The policy might instead be that Alice is not necessarily privy to the prior activities of the group. Resetting the group key on invitation would prevent her from reading messages (had she recorded them) that were exchanged among preexisting members before she joined. An early implementation of Groove in fact worked just this way. But this model conflicted with the way most people want to use Groove. When you join a shared space, you don't typically want to receive only future messages exchanged within it. You want to see the whole history of the shared space. Access to that prior transcript is, in many cases, the prime motivation to join. So when Alice joins the group, her shared space synchronizes fully with the group's.

Groove's security subsystem retains latent support for reestablishing the group key on invitation, and this feature may be reenabled, at least as an option, in post-preview editions of Groove. Of course, users can themselves achieve a similar effect. If Bob and Carol had been collaborating in a shared space and then wanted to invite Alice without giving away the contents of that shared space, they could simply create a new shared space and invite Alice into it.

If Carol uninvites someone, her Groove software sends a rekey delta message, which includes the changed group membership information plus "piggy-backed" rekey information. A rekey delta can include any combination of group rekeys. In the case of a simple member removal, it's used to establish a new group key. The new group key is transmitted by separately encrypting a copy of it, per member, in the pairwise key (K_{ij}) shared with that member. This applies in both modes: trusting and suspicious.

Groove adds rekey information onto the delta message for two reasons:

- So security metadata (including the rekey information and MACs) can be transparent to the higher-level application. It can MAC the delta without knowing that rekey information was added to it. On the receiving end, the security layer strips off the rekeys before handing the delta back to the application layer.

- So the new key sent in the piggy-back rekey information can be immediately used to encrypt the delta that it is being piggy-backed onto. If the rekey information were embedded inside the payload of the delta, then on the receiving side, the delta would first need to be decrypted in a previous key. Because the rekey information is piggy-backed outside the encrypted delta payload, that delta itself can be encrypted in the new key.

The uninvitation protocol cannot, as yet, be controlled administratively using credentials and permissions. Currently, any member can kick another member out of a shared space. An authorization architecture, for controlling access to this and other actions, is planned for a near-future release. In the meantime, tool writers can use the authentication machinery to implement tool-specific authorization rules, though we recommend waiting (if you can) for explicit authorization support in Groove.

Key versioning and key dependencies

Groove messages may arrive in any order. In particular, Carol might receive a message from Alice encrypted in the new group key, K_2, before she receives the message from Bob that bears that new key. This can happen, for example, if her link to Alice is faster than her link to Bob.

The solution is for Alice's message to state its dependence on a version of the group key. The message says, in effect, "I depend on a key-bearing message from Bob," and it includes the sequence number of that message. If Carol's Groove software hasn't yet seen the message bearing K_2, it will defer handling of Alice's K_2-encrypted message until the key arrives. Fortunately for Groove's security system, message sequencing is a fundamental property of the underlying communication layer.

In fact, things are a bit more complex. It's not just that Carol is waiting for a message from Bob in order to be able to decrypt a message from Alice. More accurately, Carol at her desktop PC is waiting for a message from Bob at his notebook PC in order to decrypt a message from Alice at her desktop PC. Sequence numbers are, in short, device-specific. Bob himself may have sent K_2 from his notebook PC but not yet received it at his desktop PC at work. Like all Groove messages, a rekey message has to propagate to all endpoints.

At some point, Carol's Groove software will want to delete the old group key, K_1. Can it do this once it knows that everyone has received K_2? No. It must also know that every message depending on K_1 has been received by all user/device pairs. To disseminate this knowledge, all Groove endpoints periodically broadcast their current state to the shared space members, and describe their latest dependency sequences.

The old and new keys, K_1 and K_2, represent major versions of the group key. There's also a need to further differentiate keys using minor versions. Here's why. Consider two companies, C1 and C2, participating in a shared space by way of their respective Internet connections, using group key K_3. Figure 18-3 shows the configuration of members in the shared space.

Now C1's T1 line goes down temporarily, isolating the C1 members from the C2 members. During this period of separation, M1 (in C2) uninvites M2, and M4 (in C1) uninvites M5. Figure 18-4 shows the result.

Each uninvitation independently produces a new group key, K_4. Now the T1 line comes back up. How does the system distinguish between the two K_4s? To handle this case, the major version of a key is qualified by a minor version, which is actually the sequence number of the message that transmitted the key.

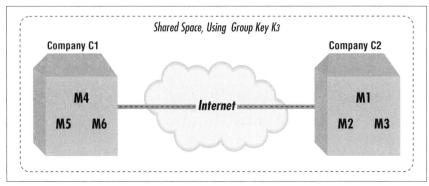

Figure 18-3. Shared space before disruption

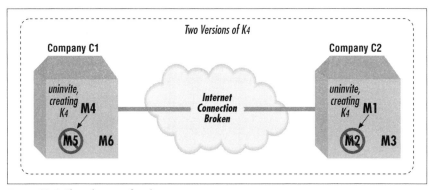

Figure 18-4. Shared space after disruption

Central control and local autonomy

Assuring that Groove would work in a fully decentralized, peer-to-peer mode was a major challenge. "It wasn't just for amusement that we undertook to do this," says Ray Ozzie, founder and CEO of Groove Networks, and before that the creator of Lotus Notes. He notes that the current trend toward hosting critical business software at ASP (application service provider) sites introduces worrisome points of failure. Groove de-emphasizes (but does not abolish) centralization. If a relay service provided by Groove Networks (or another provider) fails, Groove users can in general continue to communicate, and even execute such complex protocols as concurrent uninvitations involving disconnected subgroups.

At the same time, there are crucial aspects of security that should be at least logically centralized. For enterprise IT, a hybrid approach is better than a pure peer model. You want to centrally determine a policy for your network of peers and then distribute that policy to the individual desktops. Such a policy might control the following:

- The required length, complexity, and change frequency of the account passphrase
- Whether a user's PC can memorize the account passphrase
- Whether users are required to authenticate one another, and if so, how
- Whether everyone, or only designated shared-space administrators, can invite and uninvite members
- Who, outside of the enterprise, can join a group, and on what terms

The Groove product was designed to be as easy to use as a PalmPilot, because Ozzie's prior experience with Notes showed that the vast majority of security leaks were caused by human (that is, user and administrative) error. The goal was therefore to create a product that delivers high-grade security by default, requiring as little of the user (or administrator) as possible. Users, in particular, see no security-relevant configuration choices, and as a result their secure use of the system is as failsafe as possible. Administrators, likewise, will be constrained to a minimal set of security choices.

One such choice deserves special note. A user can ask the Groove software to memorize the account passphrase, so that it need not be retyped once per session. If the user must first authenticate to the operating system (Windows NT, 2000), this won't be a problem so long as there is a passphrase. (It's possible, but inadvisable, to create an account with no passphrase at all. In that case, nothing is securely protected on disk.) But if the user doesn't authenticate to the operating system (as Windows 95 and 98 allow), the machine boots up automatically into Groove and only physical security governs the Groove data. Because the goal is for the Groove software to become as ubiquitous as the browser, it was decided to allow this feature.* Clearly this is the kind of policy that you might want to reverse in an enterprise deployment of Groove, in order to ensure that users do the right thing.

There's another important sense in which Groove's central services help people do the right thing with respect to security—or, rather, discourage them from doing the wrong thing. The Groove relay server will proxy connections between

---

* There's more to the story. Memorized passphrases are, locally, the moral equivalent of null passphrases. But remotely they are superior. That's true because Groove accounts are mobile. A user can transfer an account from one device to an Internet-based service, and thence to another device. Memorized passphrases encourage long/strong passphrases, so are accounts stored on the Internet strongly protected.

peers when one or both are behind firewalls or NATs. Although Groove prefers direct connections between endpoints, it will always work out of the box for users who cannot establish such connections. That means people need not try to make complex, and thus error-prone, modifications to their perimeter security.

Practical security for real-world collaboration

At the end of the day, all software is rife with vulnerabilities. No one pretends that Groove is immune to this law. Although Groove encrypts to hard disk, it can't encrypt the virtual memory pages swapped out by the operating system. It can't save you from rogue software components that you trustingly install and use or Trojan horse programs that install themselves without your knowledge. It can't hide the data on your screen from a microcamera hovering over your shoulder or from a Van Eck device down the street.

Security is never wholly attainable, for a long and depressing list of reasons. But you should still take every reasonable precaution. Today, few people bother. And in truth, the popular decision to shun existing ways to secure our routine collaboration is not an irrational one. It's hard to take reasonable precautions. Doing so interferes with the spontaneity we require. The procedures are complex and therefore error-prone. Even when we try to secure our communications, we often fail to do so.

Groove aims to make reasonable precautions automatic and failsafe. It envisions a world in which peer-enabled groupware is as easy and spontaneous as email, yet as secure as anything transpiring on the Net today.

Taxonomy of Groove keys

The cryptographic keys used in Groove are described in the following list:

One passphrase per account
> Not shared with anybody else. Stored in the user's brain (unless the user requests Groove to memorize it on a machine, which is convenient but discouraged). The Unicode passphrase can have any length and take any form. It can be changed wherever you want, but if you have multiple copies of an account on multiple machines, you have to change the passphrase yourself on each machine.

One symmetric key per account

This key protects the account itself (actually, the storage key for the account file, described later in this list). By default, it is a MARC4 key generated from the user's passphrase using the PBKDF2 algorithm, with a salt and an iteration count. In this case, MARC4 uses 256-byte keys, rather than the Groove default 24-byte keys. The length of the salt is 20 bytes, and the iteration count is currently set at 256 (i.e., approximately one-tenth of a second on current typical CPUs). These unusual precautions ensure that the passphrase itself, not the cryptography surrounding it, is the weakest link— as it should be.

One asymmetric key pair per identity for signature/verification

The default algorithm is ElGamal. This key pair is used for several signature/verification purposes: to authenticate invitations, instant messages, and Diffie-Hellman public keys. It's stored in the account and cannot be changed (except by creating a new identity). The public half of the key pair is also stored in the identity's contact, which is shared with other users.

*Another asymmetric key pair per identity for encrypting/decrypting symmetric keys**

The default algorithm is ElGamal. This key pair is used to encrypt/decrypt the symmetric (by default, MARC4) keys that in turn protect the invitation protocol and instant messages. It's also stored in the account and cannot be changed (except by creating a new identity). The public half of the key pair is also stored in the identity's contact, which is shared with other users.

One digital fingerprint per identity

This is a hash of the public halves of the above two identity key pairs, as verifiably calculated by Groove on a per-use basis. It enables Groove users to authenticate one another.

One Diffie-Hellman key pair per member, per shared space

It's deterministically generated from the private halves of the previous two identity key pairs and the GUID (24-byte random globally unique ID) of the shared space. This key is constant for the duration of the member's participation in the shared space and is used to establish pairwise keys with other members of that shared space.

---

* As noted previously, this key pair and the preceding one are sometimes conflated in informal discussion. When we say "the key pair of the identity," we mean both the signature and the encryption key pairs.

One pairwise key (K_{ij}), per pair of members, per shared space, used for key distribution

The algorithm for this symmetric key is, by default, MARC4. The key is computed for each pair of members from the Diffie-Hellman key pairs, by means of the classical (authenticated) Diffie-Hellman key agreement algorithm. It's cached in each member's copy of the shared space and used to distribute the group key when it changes.

Another pairwise key (L_{ij}), per pair of members, per shared space, for message authentication

The associated algorithm is, by default, HMAC-SHA1. The key is again computed for each pair of members from the Diffie-Hellman key pairs, and it's used to assure message authenticity and integrity in mutually-suspicious mode.

One group key per shared space (K_G), for confidentiality

This key (by default, MARC4) is used for shared space confidentiality. It's stored in the shared space and is reestablished whenever a member leaves the shared space.

Another group key per shared space (L_G), for message integrity

This key (by default, HMAC-SHA1) is used for shared-space integrity in trusting mode. It's stored in the shared space, and is reestablished whenever a member leaves the shared space.

Master key

One per account, stored in the account (and hence protected by the passphrase). This key (MARC4 by default) is used to protect storage keys (next item).

Storage keys

One per shared-space file, including the account file. These keys encrypt/decrypt on-disk data. The storage keys for (non-account) shared spaces are protected by the master key and stored with the shared-space files. The storage key for the account is protected by the account's passphrase and stored with the account file.

chapter nineteen

Interoperability Through Gateways

Brandon Wiley, Freenet

In my travails as a Freenet developer, I often hear a vision of a file-sharing Utopia. They say, "Let's combine all of the best features of Freenet, Gnutella, Free Haven, Mojo Nation, Publius, Jabber, Blocks, Jungle Monkey, IRC, FTP, HTTP, and POP3. We can use XML and create an ÜberNetwork which will do everything. Then we can IPO and rule the world."

When I hear this vision, I shake my head sadly and walk slowly away. I have a different vision for solving the world's file-sharing problems. I envision a heterogeneous mish-mash of existing peer-to-peer applications creating one network with a thousand faces—what you might call an OmniNetwork.

Why unification?

Every network has its flaws. As a Freenet developer, I never miss an opportunity to give Gnutella's scalability and anonymity a good-natured ribbing. At the same time, Freenet is constantly criticized because (unlike with Gnutella) you have to donate your personal hard drive space to a bunch of strangers that may very well use it to host content that you disapprove of.

The obvious solution is to use only the network that best suits your needs. If you want anonymity, Freenet is a good choice. If you also want to be absolutely sure that you are not assisting the forces of evil (can you ever really be absolutely sure?) use Gnutella.

Ah, but what if you want Freenet's "smart routing" and yet you also want Gnutella's fast integration of new nodes into the network?

The answer is obvious: build an ÜberNetwork with anonymity and smart routing and fast node integration *and* a micropayment system *and* artist compensation *and* scalability to a large number of nodes *and* anti-spam safeguards *and* instant messaging capability, etc. It is ideas such as this that make me want to cast off the life of a peer-to-peer network developer in exchange for the gentle ways of a Shao-lin monk.

Why not an ÜberNetwork?

The problem with an ÜberNetwork is simple: it's impossible. The differences in file-sharing networks are not merely which combinations of features are included in each particular one. While many file-sharing networks differ only in choice of features, there are also distinct and mutually exclusive categories of systems. Several optimization decisions are made during the design of a network that cause it to fall into one of these categories. You can't optimize for everything simultaneously. An ÜberNetwork can't exist because there are always trade-offs.

Why not an ÜberClient?

The idea of an ÜberClient is similar to that of an ÜberNetwork: To create a single application that does everything. An example of such an application in the client/server world is the ubiquitous web browser. These days, web browsers can be used for much more than just browsing the Web. They are integrated web, news, email, and FTP clients. The majority of your client/server needs can be serviced by a single application. Unlike the ÜberNetwork, the ÜberClient need not force everyone to convert to a new system. An ÜberClient would be compatible with all of the current systems, allowing you to pick which networks you wanted to retrieve information from.

The problem with the ÜberClient is that it is a client, and clients belong in the client/server world, not the world of peer-to-peer. Furthermore, the ÜberClient that already exists—the web browser—can serve as a kind of gateway to peer-to-peer applications. Many file-sharing networks either act as miniature web servers or are developing browser plugins. Someday you will probably be able to access all of the file-sharing networks from your web browser.

However, there is a catch: you will have to be running a node on each file-sharing network that you want to access. To do otherwise would not be peer-to-peer, but client/server. Also, the advantages of files crossing over between networks are lost. Files on Free Haven will still take a long time to load and unpopular files on Freenet will still disappear.

Why not just use XML?

The next most popular solution after the creation of an ÜberClient is to link all of the existing networks together using an interoperable protocol, such as something based on XML, like XML-RPC or SOAP. The problem with this approach is that is doesn't solve the right problem. The beauty of XML is that it's a single syntax that can be used for many different purposes. It's a step in the right direction for cross-platform, language-independent object serialization and a universal syntax for configuration files. However, the problem of interoperability between file-sharing networks is not the lack of a shared syntax. The syntax parsers for all existing file-sharing networks are minor components of the code base. A message parser for any existing system could be written in a weekend if a clear specification was available.

The problem of interoperability is one of semantics. The protocols are not interoperable because they carry different information. You wouldn't expect Eliza to be a very good chess player or Deep Blue to be a good conversationalist even if they both used an XML-based protocol for communicating with you. Similarly, you should not expect a free system such as Gnutella to understand a micropayment transaction or an anonymous system such as Freenet to understand user trust ratings.

One network with a thousand faces

The solution to the problem, then, is not an ÜberNetwork, but the integration of all the different types of networks into a single, interoperable OmniNetwork. This has some advantages over the current state of many non-interoperable networks. Each person could use his or her network of choice and still get content from all of the other networks. This means that everyone gets to choose in what way they want to participate, but the data itself reflects the cumulative benefits of all systems.

To clarify this statement, I will describe how a gateway might work between Freenet and Free Haven. What are the advantages of a gateway? They pertain to the relative strengths and weaknesses of the systems. Data on Freenet can be retrieved quickly, whereas speed is recognized as a problem on Free Haven. However, data can disappear at unpredictable times on Freenet, whereas the person who publishes data on Free Haven specifies when it expires. Combine the two systems and you have readily available, potentially permanent data.

Suppose a user can insert information into either Free Haven or Freenet, depending on her preference. Then a second user can request the same information from either Free Haven or Freenet, depending on his preference. If the users are on the same network, the normal protocols are used for that network. What we're interested in here are the two possibilities left: either the information is on Free Haven and the requester is on Freenet, or the information is on Freenet and the requester is on Free Haven. In either case, the information should still be retrievable:

When Free Haven data is requested through Freenet
Requesting data through Freenet guarantees the anonymity of the requester even if he distrusts the Free Haven node. Additionally, every request of the file through Freenet causes the information to migrate to Freenet, lending the caching ability of Freenet to future requests. While the first request has to go all the way to Free Haven to fetch the information, subsequent requests need only traverse Freenet and will therefore be faster. If the information expires from Freenet, a copy still exists in Free Haven.

When Freenet data is requested through Free Haven
In this case, the information is retrieved from Freenet and cached in Free Haven. Since the information was fetched from a Freenet node, the anonymity of the requester is guaranteed even if he mistrusts the Freenet node. Additionally, requesting the data from Free Haven will cause it to be cached in Free Haven, so a copy with a guaranteed lifetime will now exist. If it should expire from Freenet, a copy still exists in Free Haven.

This is just one example of the ways that the synergy of systems with opposing designs can create a richer whole. Each of the major types of file-sharing systems adds its own benefits to the network and has its own deficiencies that are compensated for. We'll look at some details in the next section.

Well-known networks and their roles

In this section I'll list the characteristics that distinguish each of five popular networks—Freenet, Gnutella, Mojo Nation, Free Haven, and Publius—so we can evaluate the strengths each would offer to an all-encompassing OmniNetwork.

While the world of peer-to-peer is already large at quite a young age, I've chosen to focus here just on file storage and distribution systems. That's because they already have related goals, so comparisons are easy. There are also several such systems that have matured far enough to be good subjects for examination.

Freenet

Freenet adds several things to the OmniNetwork. Its niche is in the efficient and anonymous distribution of files. It is designed to find a file in the minimum number of node-to-node transactions. Additionally, it is designed to protect the privacy of the publisher of the information, the requester of the information, and all intervening nodes through which the information passes.

However, because of these design goals, Freenet is deficient in some other aspects. Since it is designed for file distribution and not fixed storage, it has no way to ensure the availability of a file. If the file is requested, it will stay in the network. If it is not requested, it will be eliminated to make room for other files. Freenet, then, is not an ideal place to store your important data for the rest of eternity.

Second, Freenet does not yet have a search system, because designing a search system which is sufficiently efficient and anonymous is very difficult. That particular part of the system just hasn't been implemented yet.

A final problem with Freenet is that in order to assure that the node operators cannot be held accountable for what is passing through their nodes, the system makes it very difficult for a node operator to determine what is being stored on his hard drive. For some this is fine, but some people want to know exactly what is being stored on their computers at all times.

Gnutella

Gnutella offers an interesting counterpoint to Freenet. It is also designed for file distribution. However, each node holds only what the node operator desires it to hold. Everything being served by a Gnutella node was either put there by the node operator or else has been requested from the network by the node operator. The node operator has complete control over what she serves to the network.

Additionally, this provides for a form of permanent storage. The Gnutella request propagation model allows that if a single node wants to act as a permanent storage facility for some data, it need do nothing more than keep the files it is serving. Requests with a high enough time-to-live (TTL) will eventually search the entire network, finding the information that they are looking for. Also, Gnutella provides searching and updating of files.

However, the Gnutella design, too, has some deficiencies. For instance, it does not provide support for any sort of verification of information to avoid tampering, spamming, squatting, or general maliciousness from evil nodes and users. It also does not have optimized routing or caching to correct load imbalances. In short, it does not scale as well as Freenet. Nor does it provide much anonymity or deniability for publishers, requesters, or node operators. By linking Freenet and Gnutella, those who wish to remain anonymous and those who wish to retain control over their computers can share information.

Mojo Nation

What Mojo Nation adds to the peer-to-peer file-sharing world is a micropayment system, and a rich and complex one at that. A micropayment system adds the following advantages to the OmniNetwork: Reciprocity of contribution of resources, compensation for the producer of content, and monetary commerce.

Reciprocity of contribution simply means that somebody has to give something in order to get something. Both Freenet and Gnutella must deal with a lack of reciprocity, an instance of the archetypal problem called the tragedy of the commons. Actually, this has been a problem for file-sharing systems throughout the ages, including BBSs, anonymous FTP sites, and Hotline servers. Now, in the peer-to-peer age, there is no centralized administrator to kick out the leeches. In an anonymous system, it's impossible even to tell who the leeches are (unless the providers of content want to voluntarily give up their anonymity, which they generally don't).

Micropayments solve the reciprocity of contribution problem by enforcing a general karmic balance. You might not give me a file for every file you get from me (after all, I might not want your files), but all in all you will have to upload a byte to someone for every byte you download. Otherwise, you will run out of electronic currency. This is indeed a boon for those who fear the network will be overrun by leeches and collapse under its own weight.[*]

Solving reciprocity is particularly important for controlling spam and denial of service attacks. For every piece of junk someone asks you to serve to the network, you receive some currency. If you are flooded with requests from a single host, you receive currency for each request. The attacker may be able to monopolize all of your time, effectively rendering your node inoperable to the rest of the network, but he will have to pay a high price in order to do so. With micropayments, you are, in effect, being paid to be attacked. Also, the attackers must have some way of generating the currency for the attack, which limits the attackers to those with enough motivation and resources.

There are other uses for micropayments besides reciprocity, particularly the ability to engage in actual commerce through a file-sharing network. If you want to trade other people's content for them in order to gain some currency, the handy tip button, a feature of the Mojo Nation interface, allows people to send some currency to the producers of content as well as the servers.

---

[*] See the Jargon File "Imminent Death of the Net Predicted!", *http://www.tuxedo.org/~esr/jargon/jargon.html*.

Also, the system could someday perhaps be used to exchange electronic currency for not just information, but things like food and rent. I can already see the kids dreaming of supporting themselves through savvy day trading of the latest underground indie tunes (the artists being supported by the tip button). Hipness can metamorphose from something that gets you ops on an IRC channel to a way to make mad cash.

However, not everyone wants to exchange currency for information. Even exchanges are certainly one mode of interaction, but it is very different from the Freenet/Gnutella philosophy of sharing information with everyone. Freenet and Gnutella serve a useful role in the Mojo Nation framework when a single node does not have the resources to make a transaction. If you don't have any resources (you have a slow machine, slow connection, and small hard drive) it is hard to get currency, since you get currency by contributing resources. Without currency you can't request anything. However, if a lot of low-resource nodes decided to get together and act as a single, pooled node, they would have significant resources. This is exactly how Freenet and Gnutella work. One node is the same as a whole network as far as your node is concerned. Thus, low-resource Mojo Nation nodes can form "syndicates" so that they will not be excluded from having a presence on the Mojo Nation network.

By combining the two types of networks, the free and communal networks of Freenet and Gnutella with the commercial network of Mojo Nation, people can choose whether to share freely or charge for resources as they see fit. Different people will choose differently on the matter, but they can still share content with each other.

Free Haven and Publius

Free Haven and Publius are in an entirely different category from other file-sharing networks. While the other networks concentrate on the distribution of content people want (reader-centric systems), these systems concentrate on anonymously preserving information (publisher-centric systems). The flaw people point out most often in Freenet is that data disappears if no one requests it for a long enough time. Luckily, Free Haven and Publius are optimized to provide for just that eventuality. They are conceptually derived from the mythical "Eternity Service" in which once you add a file it will be there forever. While it may be possible to delete a file from a Free Haven or Publius node, these networks are specifically designed to be resistant to the removal of content.

File storage networks have problems when viewed as file distribution networks. They are generally much slower to retrieve content from (because they are optimized for storage and not distribution). Additionally, they do not deal well with nodes fluttering on and off the network rapidly. To lose a node in a file storage network is problematic. To lose a node in a good file distribution network is unnoticeable.

There are great possibilities with the combination of reader-centric distribution networks with publisher-centric storage networks. It would be ideal to know that your information will always be available to everyone using a file-sharing network anywhere. People can choose to share, trade, buy, and sell your information, anonymously or non-anonymously, with all the benefits of distributed caching and a locationless namespace, and with no maintenance or popularity required to survive. Once the information is inserted in the network, it will live on without the publisher needing to provide a server to store it. Unfortunately, making gateways between networks actually work is somewhat problematic.

Problems creating gateways

The problem with creating gateways is finding a path. Each piece of information is inserted into a single network. From there it must either find its way into every connected network, or else a request originating in another network must find its way to the information. Both of these are very difficult. In short, the problem is that an insert or request must find its way to a node that serves as a gateway to the separate network where the information is stored.

Problems with inserts

The problem with finding a path to another network during an insert is that the paths of inserts are generally very short and directed. Each network routes its inserts using a different method:

- Freenet takes the "best" path to the "epicenter" for a given key. The length of the path is specified by the user. A longer path means that there is a greater chance for an insert to happen upon a gateway. However, longer paths also mean that you have to wait longer for the insert to complete.

- Gnutella doesn't have inserts.

- Mojo Nation splits a file into multiple parts and inserts each part into a node. The nodes are chosen by comparing the file part's hash to the range of hash values that a node advertises as serving.

- Free Haven splits up the file using k-of-n file splitting and inserts each part to a node. The nodes are chosen by asking trusted nodes if they want to trade their own data for that particular file part.

- Publius sends a file to a static lists of nodes and gives each node part of the key.

Some of these techniques could be extended to put material on a gateway node (for instance, Free Haven and Publius choose which nodes to use), but techniques that depend on randomizing the use of nodes are inimical to using gateways.

Problems with requests

The problem with finding a path on a request is that the networks do not take into account the presence of gateways when routing a request message. Therefore, it is unlikely that a request message will randomly happen upon a gateway. The easy solution, of course, is to have everyone running a node on any network also run a gateway to all of the other networks. It's an ideal solution, but probably infeasible.

The following sections describe the routing techniques used by each of the systems we're looking at.

Freenet

Freenet requests are routed just like inserts, using the "best" path to the "epicenter." The length of the path is set by the user if the information is in Freenet (and if it is, we don't need a gateway), but longer paths take longer to fail if the key is not in the network. You could, of course, find a gateway by searching *all* of Freenet, assuming that the number of nodes in the network is less than or equal to the maximum path length. That would almost certainly take longer than you would care to wait. Freenet is designed so that if the file is in the network, the path to the file is usually short. Consequently, Freenet is not optimized for long paths. Long paths are therefore very slow.

Gnutella

Gnutella messages are broadcast to all nodes within a certain time-to-live, so choosing a path is not an issue. You can't choose a path even if you want to. The issue with Gnutella is that a gateway has to be within the maximum path radius, which is usually seven hops away. Fortunately, Gnutella is generally a very shallow network in which your node knows of a whole lot of other nodes. Generally, a gateway out of Gnutella to another system would have a high probability of being reached, since every request will potentially search a large percentage of the network. If there is a gateway node anywhere in the reachable network, it will be found. This is good if you want to access the whole world through Gnutella. Of course, it doesn't help at all if you want to gateway into Gnutella from another system.

Mojo Nation

Mojo Nation requests are somewhat complicated. First, you must find the content you want on a content tracker that keeps a list of content and who has a copy of it. From the content tracker, you retrieve the address of a node that has a copy of the file part that you want. Then, you request the file part from the node. You do this until you have all of the parts needed to reconstruct the file.

This process actually lends itself quite well to gatewaying. As long as the gateways know what files are in Freenet, they can advertise for those keys. Unfortunately, gateways can't know what files are in Freenet. A gateway can only know what files have passed through it, which is only a fraction of the total content of the network.

However, if gateways also act as content trackers, they can translate requests for unknown keys into Freenet requests and place any keys found into the Mojo Nation content tracker index. In this way, you can access content from Freenet as long as you are willing to use a content tracker that is also a Freenet gateway. While it would be nice just to ask the network in general for a key and have it be found in Freenet (if appropriate), that is not how Mojo Nation works. In Mojo Nation, you ask a particular content tracker for content.

One way to integrate gatewayed and non-gatewayed content trackers in Mojo Nation would be to have a proxy node that acts as a Freenet gateway. Using that, any content tracker that functions as a gateway and a proxy could be used. The content tracker would be searched first, and if it failed, the gateway could be searched.

Publius

Gatewaying Publius is an interesting problem. Each file is split into a number of parts, each of which is sent to a different server. In order to reconstruct the file, you need a certain number of parts. It is therefore necessary for at least that number of parts to make it into gateways.

The length of the path for each part of the file is only 1 because the file goes directly to a single node and then stops. That means that if you need k parts of the file, k of the nodes contacted must be gateways in order for the file to be able to be reconstructed in the other network. The only solution, therefore, is to make most Publius nodes gateways.

Free Haven

Making a gateway out of Free Haven is not quite as difficult as making one out of Publius, because parts of files get routinely traded between nodes. Every time a trade is made, the file part could potentially find a gateway, thus reaching the other network. However, when and how often files are traded is unknown and unpredictable. Thus, file trading cannot be counted on to propagate files, although it certainly will increase the probability of propagation by a nontrivial amount.

Gateway implementation

There is much theoretical work to be done in the area of making actual, working gateways between the different networks. However, even once that has been worked out, there is still the issue of implementation specifics.

There are a couple of ways that this could be approached. The first is to make each gateway between networks X and Y a hybrid X-Y node, speaking the protocols of both networks. This is undesirable because it leads to a combinatorial explosion of customized nodes, each of which has to be updated if the protocol changes for one of the networks.

A preferable solution would be to define a simple and universal interface that one node can use to query another for a file. Then, a gateway would consist merely of a cluster of nodes running on different networks and speaking different protocols, but talking to each other via a common interface mechanism. Using a common interface mechanism, gateway nodes would not even have to know what foreign networks they were talking to.

There are different possible interface mechanisms: CORBA,[*] RMI,[†] XML-RPC,[‡] SOAP,[§] etc. The mechanism that I would recommend is HTTP. It is a standard protocol for requesting a file from a particular location (in this case a particular node, which represents a particular network). Also, some file-sharing networks already have support for HTTP. Freenet and Gnutella support interfacing through HTTP, for instance.

Modification of the code base for each system to make a normal node into a gateway would be minor. The node need merely keep a list of gateways and, upon the failure of the network to find a requested file, query the gateways. If a file is found on a gateway, it is transferred by HTTP to the local node and then treated exactly as if it was found in the node's local data storage.

---

[*] http://www.corba.org

[†] http://java.sun.com/docs/books/tutorial/rmi

[‡] http://www.xmlrpc.com

[§] http://www.w3.org/TR/SOAP

Existing projects

Despite the desire for interoperability among networks, little has been done to facilitate this. Network designers are largely consumed by the difficult implementation details of their individual networks.

The only gatewaying project currently underway, to my knowledge, is the World Free Web (WFW) project, which aims to combine Freenet and the World Wide Web. While the Web may not at first seem like a file-sharing network as much as a publication medium, now that we find web sites offering remote hosting of vacation photographs and business documents, the two uses are merging into one.

Freenet and the Web complement each other nicely. Freenet is adaptive, temporary, and locationless, whereas the Web is static, semipermanent, and location-based. The point of the WFW project is to ease the load of popular content on web servers by integrating Freenet into web browsers. A WFW-enabled web browser will first check Freenet for the requested file. If the browser can't find the file, it will fetch the file from the Web and insert it into Freenet. The net effect is that popular web sites will load faster and the web servers will not crash under the load. This project, like many open source projects existing today, really needs only developers. The concepts are sound and merely call for experts on the various browsers to integrate them.

Conclusion

The peer-to-peer file-sharing developer community is not large. While the peer-to-peer world is expected to explode in popularity, those who have code in the here and now are few. There has been much discussion of interoperability among the various projects, so it may well happen. The technical challenges of routing requests to gateways are difficult ones, but certainly no more difficult than the challenges involved in anonymity, scalability, performance, and security that network designers have already had to face.

Acknowledgments

I'd like to thank Christine and Steve for contributing greatly to my second draft, and Isolde for making me write when I'd rather go to the park.

Afterword

Andy Oram, O'Reilly & Associates, Inc.

Like many new ideas with substantial "disruptive" potential (that is, ideas whose impacts can fundamentally change the roles and relationships of people and institutions), peer-to-peer has been surrounded by a good amount of fear. In particular, it has been closely associated in the public mind with the legal difficulties faced by Napster over claims that the company engaged in copyright infringement. The association is ironic, because Napster depends heavily on a central server where users register information. It is precisely the existence of the central server that makes it technically possible for a court to shut down the service.

However, Napster does demonstrate important peer-to-peer aspects. Files are stored on users' individual systems, and each download creates a peer-to-peer Internet connection between the source and destination systems. Furthermore, each system must furnish metadata information about the title and artist of the song. The legal questions Napster raises naturally attach themselves to some of the other peer-to-peer technologies, notably Gnutella and Freenet.

Precedents and parries

The Napster case in itself may not be dangerous to other peer-to-peer technologies. Its particular business model, its dependence on the preexisting popularity of exchanging MP3 files that are unauthorized copies of copyrighted material, and the many precedents for the concepts invoked by both sides (fair use, vicarious and contributory copyright infringement, substantial non-infringing uses) make the case unique.

But there are several indications that large copyright holders wield their legal weapons too widely for the comfort of technological innovators. For instance, during the Napster case, the band Metallica conducted a search for Metallica

MP3s and created a list of 335,000 Napster users that it forced Napster to ban temporarily from the system. This raises the possibility that a determined plaintiff could try to prosecute all the individuals that form an entire community of peer-to-peer systems, such as Gnutella, Freenet, or Publius.

Users of those systems could then face the dilemma of being condemned for providing computer resources to a system that has social value, simply because one user of that system (perhaps a malicious user) provided material that raised the ire of a powerful commercial or political force. It would be interesting to see whether users would then try to invoke a kind of "ISP exemption," where they claim they are simply providing communications channels and have no control over content.

This legal status for ISPs is pretty well established in some countries. In the United States, numerous courts have refused to prosecute ISPs for Internet content. Still, a section of the enormous Digital Millennium Copyright Act, passed by the U.S. Congress in 1998, requires sites hosting content to take it down at the request of a copyright holder. Canada also protects ISPs from liability.

The status of ISPs and hosting sites is much shakier in other countries. In Britain, an ISP was successfully sued over defamatory content posted by an outsider to a newsgroup. The German parliament has shrouded the issue in ambiguity, stating that ISPs are responsible for blocking illegal content when it would be "technically feasible" to do so. Of course, some countries such as China and Saudi Arabia monitor all ISP traffic and severely restrict it.

France exempts ISPs from liability for content, but they have to remove access to illegal content when ordered to by a court, and maintain data that can be used to identify content providers in case of a court request. The latter clause would seem to make a system like Freenet, Publius, or Free Haven automatically illegal. The November 2000 French decision forcing Yahoo! to block the display of Nazi memorabilia auction sites sets a precedent that peer-to-peer users cannot ignore. It has already been echoed by a ruling in Germany's high court declaring that German laws apply to web sites outside the country. The trend will undoubtedly lead to a flood of specialized legal injunctions in other countries that try to control whether particular domain names and IP addresses can reach other domain names and IP addresses.

Further threats to technological development are represented by companies' invocation of copyrights and trade secrets to punish people who crack controls on software content filters or video playback devices. The latter happened in the much publicized DeCSS case, where the court went so far as to force web sites unrelated to the defendants to delete source code. In 1998, Congress acceded to the wishes of large content vendors and put clauses in the extensive Digital Millennium Copyright Act that criminalize technological development, like some types of encryption cracking and reverse engineering.

It would be irresponsible of me to suggest that copyright is obsolete (after all, this book is under copyright, as are most O'Reilly publications), but it is perfectly reasonable to suggest that new movements in society and technology should make governments reexamine previous guidelines and compromises. Copyright is just such a compromise, where government is trying to balance incentives to creative artists with benefits to the public.

Napster showed above all that there is now a new social context for music listening, as well as new technological possibilities. The courts, perhaps, cannot redefine fair use or other concepts invoked by both sides in the Napster case, but the U.S. Congress and the governing bodies of other countries can ask what balance is appropriate for this era.

Who gets to innovate?

Peer-to-peer, like all technologies, embodies certain assumptions about people and future directions for technology. It so happens that peer-to-peer is moving the compass of information use in a direction that directly contradicts the carefully mapped-out plans drawn by some large corporate and government players.

The question now posed is between two views of how to use technology and information. One common view gives consumers and users the maximum amount of control over the application of technology and information. One example will suffice to show how powerful this principle can be.

Despite Tim Berners-Lee's hope that the World Wide Web would be a two-way (or even multiperson to multiperson) medium, early browsers were pretty much glorified file transfer programs with some minimal GUI elements for displaying text and graphics together. The addition of CGI and forms allowed users to talk back, but did not in itself change the notion of the Web as an information transfer service. What caused the Web to take on new roles was the crazy idea invented by some visionary folks to use the available web tools for selling things. An innovative use of existing technology resulted in an economic and social upheaval.

Putting tools in the hands of users has an impact on business models, though. People might no longer buy a technical manual from O'Reilly & Associates; they might download it from a peer instead—or more creatively, extract and combine pieces of it along with other material from many peers. And peer-to-peer, of course, is just a recent option that joins many other trends currently weakening copyright.

When a revenue stream that information providers have counted on for over 2000 years threatens to dry up, powerful reactions emerge. Copyright holders have joined with a wide range of other companies to introduce legal changes that revolve around a single (often unstated) notion: that the entity providing information or technology should control all uses of it. The manufacturer of a disk decides what devices can display it. A compiler of information decides how much a person can use at any one time, and for how long. The owner of a famous name controls where that name can appear.

Trying to plug serious holes in the traditional web of information control—copyrights, trade secrets, patents, trademarks—information owners are extending that control into areas where they have previously been excluded. In their view, new ideas like selling over the Web would have to come from the company who provides the media or the service, not from people using the service.

So where do we look for the future uses of information and technology? The two answers to this question—users versus corporate owners—are likely to struggle for some time before either a winner or a workable compromise appears. But the thrust of peer-to-peer implicitly throws its weight behind the first answer: trust the users. The technological innovations of peer-to-peer assume that users have something to offer, and some peer-to-peer projects (notably Jabber in its community-building, and Gnutella in its search model) actually encourage or even provoke users to contribute something new and different.

A clean sweep?

Some people ask whether peer-to-peer will replace the client/server model entirely. Don't worry, it emphatically will not. Client/server remains extremely useful for many purposes, particularly where one site is recognized as the authoritative source for information and wants to maintain some control over that information.

Client/server is also a much simpler model than peer-to-peer, and we should never abandon simplicity for complexity without a clear benefit. Client/server rarely presents administrative problems except where the amount of traffic exceeds the server's capacity.

Peer-to-peer is useful where the goods you're trying to get at lie at many endpoints; in other words, where the value of the information lies in the contributions of many users rather than the authority of one. Peer-to-peer systems can also be a possible solution to bandwidth problems, when designed carefully. (Of course, they can also cause bandwidth problems, either because their design adds too much overhead or because people just want a lot of stuff without paying for the bandwidth that can accommodate it.)

In short, peer-to-peer and client/server will coexist. Many systems will partake of both models. In fact, I have avoided using the phrase "peer-to-peer model" in this book because such a variety of systems exist and so few can be considered pure peer-to-peer. The ones that are completely decentralized—Gnutella, Freenet, and Free Haven—are extremely valuable for research purposes in addition to the direct goals they were designed to meet. Whether or not other systems move in their direction, the viability of the most decentralized systems will help us judge the viability of peer-to-peer technology as a whole.

Directory of Peer-to-Peer Projects

This is a partial list of interesting projects, companies, and standards that could reasonably be considered examples of peer-to-peer technology. It is not meant to be exhaustive, and we apologize for any worthy projects that were not included. The field, of course, expands constantly.

Agents as Peers
    Infobot
    Sandia National Laboratories
    WebV2

Collaboration
    Engenia Software, Inc.
    eZ
    Interbind

Development Frameworks
    Mithral Communications & Design, Inc.
    WorldOS Corporation

Devices as Peers
    Bluetooth
    Brazil Project
    dHTTP (Distributed HTTP)
    Endeavors Technology, Inc.
    Jini

Distributed Computation
    2AM
    Applied MetaComputing
    Centrata
    Datasynapse

Distributed.net

DistributedScience

Entropia

Parabon Computation

Popular Power

Porivo Technologies, Inc.

SETI@home: The Search for Extraterrestrial Intelligence

Ubero

United Devices, Inc.: Individuals Accelerating Science

Distributed Search Engines

gonesilent.com (aka InfraSearch)

OpenCOLA

Plebio

WebV2

File Sharing

CuteMX.Com (GlobalScape, Inc.)

File Navigator

Free Haven

Freenet

Gnutella

Hotline Communications, Ltd.

Jungle Monkey

Mojo Nation

Napster

Ohaha

OnSystems, Inc.

OpenNap

Pointera

Publius

Spinfrenzy.com

Gaming

2AM

CenterSpan

Internet Operating System

Applied MetaComputing

Globus

ROKU

Static

Licensed Media Distribution
  eMikolo
  Flycode
  Kalepa Networks, Inc.

Messaging Frameworks
  AIMster
  BXXP
  CenterSpan
  IMXP
  Jabber

Metadata
  RDF
  RSS
  XNS (eXtensible Name Service)

Servers/Services as Peers
  .NET
  BXXP
  Meerkat: An Open Wire Service
  Simple Object Access Protocol (SOAP)
  Universal Description, Discovery and Integration (UDDI)
  XML-RPC

Superdistribution
  2AM
  3Path
  Freenet
  vTrails

The Writable Web
  Amaya Web Editor/Browser
  Blogger
  Brazil Project
  Endeavors Technology, Inc.
  Manila
  Radio Userland
  WebDAV
  Wiki Wiki Web

Contributors

NELSON MINAR, CTO and cofounder of distributed computing leader Popular Power, has an extensive history researching Internet systems. While at the MIT Media Lab, he built a mobile agent based peer-to-peer computing platform called Hive, and previously studied agent-based modeling at the Sante Fe Institute. Minar sees the Internet as a place, a world with its own rules and behaviors.

MARC HEDLUND is the chief executive officer and cofounder of Popular Power, the first distributed computing company to launch commercial software. He previously served as the founder and director of Lucasfilm Ltd.'s Internet division and director of engineering at Organic Online. His Internet experience dates to early 1994, when he worked on several IETF committees and built early e-commerce applications while CTO of a Web start-up.

CLAY SHIRKY is a Partner for Technology and Product Strategy at The Accelerator Group, which invests active strategic capital in digital businesses. Prior to joining the Accelerator Group, he was Professor of New Media at Hunter College, and CTO of Site Specific. Mr. Shirky writes extensively about the social and economic effects of the internet. His essays appear regularly in the O'Reilly Network, Business 2.0, and FEED, as well as the New York Times, the Wall Street Journal, and the Harvard Business Review. His writings are archived at *http://www.shirky.com*.

TIM O'REILLY is founder and president of O'Reilly & Associates, Inc. Tim's goal is to enable change by capturing and transmitting the knowledge of innovators and innovative communities via books, conferences, and web sites.

DANIEL BRICKLIN, a software designer, is best known as the cocreator of Visi-Calc, the first electronic spreadsheet. In addition to the spreadsheet, he helped develop one of the first word processing systems in the mid-1970's, programmed the most popular prototyping tool of the MSDOS world, and helped introduce the world to the capabilities of electronic ink on pen computers. Mr. Bricklin has served on the boards of the Software Publishers Association and the Boston Computer Society and has received many honors for his contributions to the computer industry, including the IEEE Computer Society's Computer Entrepreneur Award and Lifetime Achievement Award from the SPA. Most recently he is the founder and CTO of Trellix Corporation which creates web site building systems.

DAVID P. ANDERSON is the director of the SETI@home project. He co-founded Tunes.com and is currently CTO of United Devices. From 1985 to 1991 he was on the faculty of the U.C. Berkeley Computer Science Department.

JEREMIE MILLER has been developing Internet-related and Open Source projects since 1993, having been involved with the early Web standards and projects such as Apache and Linux. In 1997 he started following the DHTML and XML standards very closely, and in 1998 founded Jabber, an Open Source movement designed to create a new, standard, distributed XML-based platform for instant messaging and presence applications. Today he continues developing Jabber, helping to advance the new XML infrastructure available on the Internet.

ADAM LANGLEY is student in England and a free software programmer in his free time. Interests range from software to politics/freedom, typesetting, and theater. His current project is an implementation of Freenet in C++, with which he could really do with some help.

GENE KAN was among the first to produce an open source version (under the GNU General Public License) of Gnutella software after Gnutella was released by Justin Frankel and Tom Pepper of Gnullsoft. Soon, Mr. Kan became one of Gnutella's key spokesmen. Previously an SGML/XML consultant and kernel network engineer at Check Point Software, Mr. Kan is now CEO of InfraSearch. In his spare moments he enjoys racing his cars, LTLENDN and BIGENDN.

ALAN BROWN is currently the assistant director of a human rightsorganization. He has served on the executive committee of an ACLU state affiliate and taught mathematical logic at several midwest universities. He will launch a new cyber-rights organization in Russia this year and is engaged to the most beautiful woman in Russia.

MARC WALDMAN is a Ph.D. candidate in Computer Science at New York University. He is one of the co-developers of the Publius censorship-resistant publishing system. His research interests include privacy-enhancing technologies and computer security. Marc received a BA and MS in Computer Science from New York University.

DR. LORRIE FAITH CRANOR is a Senior Technical Staff Member in the Secure Systems Research Department at AT&T Labs-Research. She is also chair of the Platform for Privacy Preferences Project (P3P)Specification Working Group at the World Wide Web Consortium. Her research has focused on a variety of areas where technology and policy issues interact, including online privacy, electronic voting, and spam. She is frequently invited to speak about online privacy, and in1998 Internet Magazine named her an unsung hero of the Internet for her work on P3P.

DR. AVIEL RUBIN is a Principal Researcher at AT&T Labs-Research and a member of the board of directors of USENIX, the Advanced Computing Systems Association. He also has an appointment as an adjunct professor in the Computer Science department at NYU, and he serves as Associate Editor of the Electronic Commerce Research Journal.

ROGER DINGLEDINE graduated from MIT in May 2000 (B.Sc. computer science, B.Sc. mathematics, M.Eng. computer science and electrical engineering), where his Master's research in anonymous distributed publishing systems was supervised by Ronald Rivest. He is project leader for both the Simple End-User Linux project (seul.org) and the Free Haven project (freehaven.net). Currently he works as the Security Philosopher for Reputation Technologies, Inc. (reputation.com).

MICHAEL J. FREEDMAN is a graduate student in computer science at MIT. His research interests focus on cryptography and computer/network security, especially in the realm of distributed systems. He is a principal researcher of the Free Haven project, and has worked at Zero-Knowledge Systems implementing an electronic cash architecture.In his spare time, Michael enjoys climbing, mountaineering, and other outdoor pursuits, much to the concern of family and friends.

DAVID MOLNAR began using PGP in 1993. He became interested (obsessed?) with figuring out "why it worked" and has been studying cryptography ever since. Now an undergraduate at Harvard University, he keeps up with security issues by attending courses, reading newsgroups, mailing lists, and conference papers, and attending DEF CON in his home city of Las Vegas. David is an ACM Student Member and a member of the International Association for Cryptologic Research.

RAEL DORNFEST is a maven at the O'Reilly Network. He is the developer of Meerkat: An Open Wire Service and one of the architects of RSS 1.0.

DAN BRICKLEY is a longstanding RDF advocate and chair of the W3C RDF Interest Group.

THEODORE HONG, Freenet developer, is a graduate student in computer science at Imperial College, London. He holds an A.B. from Harvard University and is a 1995 Marshall scholar.

RICHARD LETHIN is a founder of Reputation.com, a provider of tools and services for the formation and use of online reputations in electronic commerce, president of Reservoir.com, a computer systems research and development firm, and Adjunct Professor in Electrical Engineering at Yale College. Richard is also one of the founders of the Digital Commerce Society of Boston. He received his Ph.D. from the MIT, wherein his research he developed analytical models of large scale message-passing systems.

JON UDELL was BYTE Magazine's executive editor for new media, the architect of the original *www.byte.com*, and author of BYTE's Web Project column. He's now an independent Web/Internet consultant. His first book, *Practical Internet Groupware*, was published by O'Reilly and Associates in 1999.

NIMISHA ASTHAGIRI, at Groove Networks, is a Senior Security Architect and the Security "Czar" (a title they give for someone who is "ultimately responsible for continuity and execution within certain specific technical areas that span across the product"). She has been with Groove since September 1998 (employee #17). Prior to Groove, she was at OSF Research Institute (later called The Open Group Research Institute) for one year, where she worked on security-related projects and proposals in the areas of intrusion detection systems and authorization. She graduated from MIT in 1997 with a Bachelors and Masters in Computer Science and Engineering. She did her Masters thesis on a history-based authorization framework for Java applets.

WALTER TUVELL has badge #11 at Groove Networks and is the senior security guru there. Before that he spent six years at Bell Labs, working on AT&T's Unix kernel and networking, and then became the security architect for DCE at the Open Software Foundation (now the Open Group). He went to MIT for his B.S., and to the University of Chicago for his M.S. and Ph.D., all in mathematics.

BRANDON WILEY cofounded the free software initiative to implement the Freenet architecture. When not coding for freedom, he is a freelance consultant, playwright, and filmmaker. He specializes in online communities and postmodern romantic comedies.

Index

A

Abe, Masayuki, 328
access control lists, POWs not needed, 288
account passphrase, 364
  cryptographic keys, 378
  security concerns and, 377
accountability, 11, 20, 271–340
  buddy system and, 173
  centralized control over resources, 272
  changing the level of, 305
  complicated by revoking documents, 170
  difficulty of, 274–283
  engineering polite behavior, 20
  Free Haven case study, 329–339
  fungible micropayments and, 293
  junk mail and, 279, 288
  micropayment schemes and, 286–305
  minimizing a server's threat, 277–279
  parallel solutions and, 290
  peer-to-peer and impact on, 276
  real world vs. Internet, 274
  vs. anonymity, 329
accountability slider, 303–305
active caching
  adversaries and, 285
  maintaining data availability with, 285
  protection against Slashdot effect, 285
active mirroring
  Akamai Technologies, 284
  maintaining data availability with, 284
  protection against Slashdot effect, 285
active-server document-anonymity, 164
ActiveState, 45
Adams, Rick, 50

Adar, Eytan, 206, 292
addresses, dynamic IP (see dynamic IP
    addresses)
addressing, protocol-centric, 30–32
ADSL (Asymmetric Digital Subscriber
    Line), 14, 36
adversarial approach to scoring
    systems, 324
Advogato, 311–313
  how trust is determined, 311
  resisting pseudospoofing, 312
  trust metric vs. Slashdot moderation
    system, 311
Aiken, Alexander, 348
AIM (AOL Instant Messenger)
  attacking by shilling, 316
  protocol-centric addressing, 30–32
AIMster, 52
Akamai Technologies, 284
Albert, Réka, 222, 225
all points payment model, 332
  node-specific tickets and, 334
"all you can eat" business models, 33
alt newsgroups, 6
America Online (AOL) and Gnutella, 95
amortized pairwise payment model, 331
Anderson, David, xv, 67–76, 404
Anderson, Ross, 170, 262
anonymity
  analysis of, 181–184
  attacks on, 180
  computational, 181–184
  Crowds software and, 258
  Freenet and, 125
  on the Internet, 251, 275

X
6l